ALT▲RITY

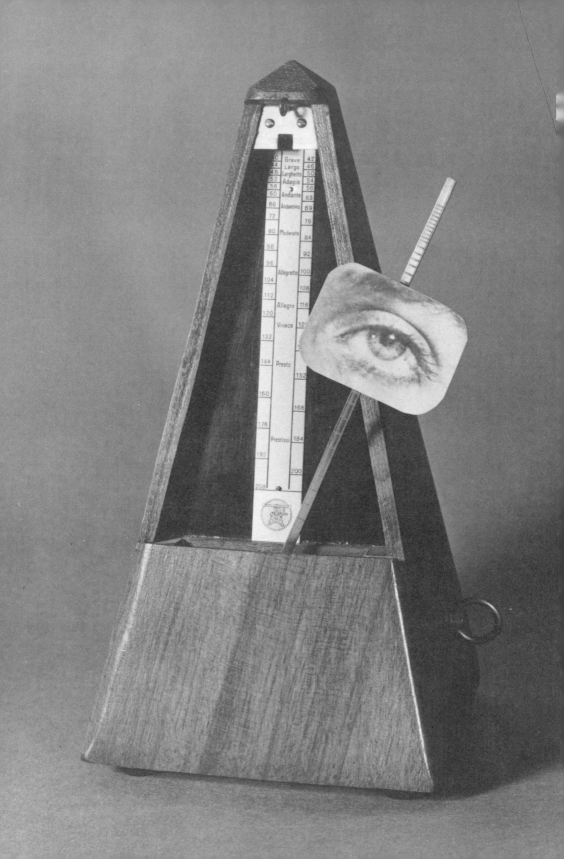

ALTRITY

Mark C. Taylor

THE UNIVERSITY OF CHICAGO PRESS

Chicago and London

Library of Congress Cataloging-in-Publication Data
Taylor, Mark C., 1945–
    Altarity.
    Bibliography: p.
    Includes index.
    1. Difference (Philosophy)—History.   2. Philosophy,
Modern—20th century.   3. Philosophy, Modern—19th
century.   I. Title.
B105.D5T39   1987   110   87-5880
ISBN 0-226-79137-8
ISBN 0-226-79138-6 (pbk.)

Frontispiece: Man Ray, *Indestructible Object*. © Juliet Man Ray, 1987.

MARK C. TAYLOR is the William R. Kenan, Jr., Professor of
Religion at Williams College. He is the author of
Erring: A Postmodern A/theology (1984) and editor of
Deconstruction in Context: Literature and Philosophy
(1986), both published by the University of Chicago Press.

FOR

H. GANSE LITTLE, JR.

Contents

CONTENTS

4
Real

5
Ecstasy

6
Woman

7
Infinity

8

Nots

9

Rewriting

10

Transgression

Acknowledgments

Writing is a solitary calling. Perhaps it is, as Maurice Blanchot suggests, "the essential solitude." And yet, paradoxically, the person who *must* write cannot write without the understanding and support of family, friends, and colleagues. I would like to express my sincere gratitude to certain others who, in one way or another, have made a difference: to my family—Dinny, Aaron, and Kirsten Taylor—for both their patience and impatience; to friends and colleagues— Thomas J. J. Altizer, Houston Baker, Joan Burns, William Doty, Ray Hart, Stephen Melville, Sara Suleri, David Tracy, Charles Winquist, and Edith Wyschogrod—for thoughtful comments and criticisms; to Leslie Boldt, Jacob Neusner, John Leavey, George Pistorius, Meredith Hoppin, and Margaret Wildrick for invaluable assistance in translating texts; to Thomas Krens, Joseph Marioni, and Elizabeth Morton for helping me find my way through the labyrinthine art world; to Stephen Crites, Gordon Kaufman, John Maguire, and Richard R. Niebuhr for raising questions that still obsess me; to Francis Oakley and John Reichert for continuing personal and institutional support; to Clifford Ruprecht for long hours of research; to Eileen Sahady, Peggy Bryant, Miriam Grabois, Dennis Aebersold, Lee Fallon, and Anthony Monsanto for helping to prepare the manuscript; to the students in my senior seminar in the spring of 1986 for wrestling with something other than they might have wished; to Jacques Derrida for reasons he understands; finally, to H. Ganse Little, Jr., a remarkable teacher-scholar and, more importantly, a genuine friend who often keeps solitude from becoming overwhelming, for his patience in sustaining what at times seems to be *l'entretien infini*.

M.C.T.

Williamstown
August 1986

Editions and Abbreviations Used

To facilitate reading this book, I have abbreviated references to the works cited most frequently. In many cases I have found it necessary to make changes in the published translations or to retranslate the German, French, and Danish sources. Where two citations appear, separated by a semicolon, the first is to the published translation and the second to the original edition. If a translation is based on more than one source, reference is made only to the English text. I have appended an alphabetical list of authors with the abbreviations of the works I have cited (see below, p. xvii).

A   Maurice Blanchot, *L'Amitié* (Paris: Gallimard, 1971).

BN   Georges Bataille, *The Blue of Noon,* trans. H. Mathews (New York: Urizen Books, 1978). *Le Bleu du ciel* (Paris: Jean-Jacques Pauvert, 1957).

CA   Søren Kierkegaard, *The Concept of Anxiety,* trans. R. Thomte (Princeton: Princeton University Press, 1980). For all of Kierkegaard's published works, I have used the following Danish edition: *Søren Kierkegaards Samlede Værker,* ed. A. B. Drachmann, J. L. Heiberg, and H. O. Lang (Copenhagen: Gyldendalske Boghandel, 1901–06).

D   Jacques Derrida, *Dissemination,* trans. B. Johnson (Chicago: University of Chicago Press, 1981). *La dissémination* (Paris: Editions de Seuil, 1972).

DL   Julia Kristeva, *Desire in Language: A Semiotic Approach to Literature and Art,* trans. L. S. Roudiez (New York: Columbia University Press, 1980). *Polylogue* (Paris: Editions du Seuil, 1977); *Semeiôtikê: Recherches pour une sémanalyse* (Paris: Editions du Seuil, 1979).

E   Jacques Lacan, *Ecrits,* trans. A. Sheridan (New York: Norton, 1977). *Ecrits* (Paris: Editions du Seuil, 1966).

EGT   Martin Heidegger, *Early Greek Thinking*, trans. D. F. Krell and F. A. Capuzzi (New York: Harper and Row, 1975). *Vorträge und Aufsätze* (Tübingen: Günter Neske, 1954).

EI   Maurice Blanchot, *L'Entretien infini* (Paris: Gallimard, 1969). Translations mine.

ETW   G. W. F. Hegel, *Early Theological Writings*, trans. T. M. Knox (Philadelphia: University of Pennsylvania Press, 1971). For all works other than *Phenomenology*, I have used the following German edition: G. W. F. Hegel, *Werke in zwanzig Bänden* (Frankfurt: Suhrkamp, 1969–71).

FFC   Jacques Lacan, *The Four Fundamental Concepts of Psycho-Analysis,* ed. Jacques–Alain Miller, trans. A. Sheridan (New York: Norton, 1981). *Le Séminaire, Livre XI, Les quatre concepts fondamentaux de la psychanalyse* (Paris: Editions du Seuil, 1973).

FS   Jacques Lacan, *Feminine Sexuality: Jacques Lacan and the école freudienne,* ed. J. Mitchell and J. Rose, trans. J. Rose (New York: Norton, 1982).

FT   Søren Kierkegaard, *Fear and Trembling,* trans. H. V. Hong and E. H. Hong (Princeton: Princeton University Press, 1983). For Danish, see *CA.*

G   Jacques Derrida, *Glas,* trans. J. P. Leavey and R. A. Rand (Lincoln: University of Nebraska Press, 1986). *Glas* (Paris: Editions Galilée, 1974). Since the translation of this work had not been published at the time of writing, page numbers refer to the original French. John Leavey was kind enough to make available to me the typescript of his translation, which I have, for the most part, followed.

HCE   Martin Heidegger, *Hegel's Concept of Experience,* trans. K. R. Dove (New York: Harper and Row, 1970). *Holzwege* (Frankfurt: Vittorio Klostermann, 1977).

ID   Martin Heidegger, *Identity and Difference,* trans. J. Stambaugh (New York: Harper and Row, 1969.) Bilingual edition.

IE   Georges Bataille, *L'expérience intérieure* (Paris: Gallimard, 1959). Translation forthcoming (see chap. 5, note 1).

JP   Søren Kierkegaard, *Journals and Papers,* trans. H. V. Hong and E. H. Hong (Bloomington: Indiana University Press, 1967–78). *Søren Kierkegaards Papirer,* ed. P. A. Heiberg and V. Kuhr (Copenhagen: Gyldendalske Boghandel, 1912).

L   G. W. F. Hegel, *Science of Logic,* trans. A. V. Miller (New York: Humanities Press, 1969). For German, see *ETW.*

LPR   G. W. F. Hegel, *Lectures on the Philosophy of Religion,* trans. E. B. Speirs and J. B. Sanderson, 3 vol. (New York: Humanities Press, 1968). For German, see *ETW.*

M   Jacques Derrida, *Margins of Philosophy,* trans. A. Bass (Chicago: University of Chicago Press, 1982). *Marges de la philosophie* (Paris: Editions de Minuit, 1972).

MM   Georges Bataille, *My Mother,* trans. A. Wainhouse (London: Jonathan Cape, 1972). *Ma Mère* (Paris: Jean-Jacques Pauvert, 1976).

OB   Emmanuel Levinas, *Otherwise than Being or Beyond Essence,* trans. A. Lingis (Boston: Martinus Nijhoff, 1981). *Autrement qu'être ou au-delà l'essence* (The Hague: Martinus Nijhoff, 1974).

OG   Jacques Derrida, *Of Grammatology,* trans. G. Spivak (Baltimore: Johns Hopkins University Press, 1976). *De la grammatologie* (Paris: Editions de Minuit, 1967).

PA   Maurice Blanchot, *Le Pas au-delà* (Paris: Gallimard, 1973). Translations mine.

PLT   Martin Heidegger, *Poetry, Language, Thought,* trans. A. Hofstadter (New York: Harper and Row, 1971). The German sources of these essays are *Holzwege* (see *HCE);* and *Vorträge und Aufsätze: Unterwegs zur Sprache* (Pfullingen: Günter Neske, 1959).

PP   Maurice Merleau-Ponty, *Phenomenology of Perception,* trans. C. Smith (London: Routledge and Kegan Paul, 1978). *La Phénoménologie de la perception* (Paris: Gallimard, 1945).

PH   Julia Kristeva, *Powers of Horror: An Essay on Abjection,* trans. L. S. Roudiez (New York: Columbia University Press, 1982). *Pouvoirs de l'horreur* (Paris: Editions du Seuil, 1980).

PM   G. W. F. Hegel, *Philosophy of Mind*, trans. W. Wallace (New York: Oxford University Press, 1971). For German, see *ETW.*

PS   G. W. F. Hegel, *Phenomenology of Spirit*, trans A. V. Miller (New York: Oxford University Press, 1977). *Phänomenologie des Geistes* (Hamburg: Felix Meiner, 1952).

QT   Martin Heidegger, *The Question Concerning Technology and Other Essays*, trans. W. Lovitt (New York: Harper and Row, 1977). The German sources of these essays are: *Holzwege* (see *HCE*); *Vorträge und Aufsätze* (see *PLT*); and *Die Technik und die Kehre* (Pfullingen: Günter Neske, 1962).

S   Jacques Derrida, *Spurs: Nietzsche's Styles / Eperons: Les Styles de Nietzsche*, trans. B. Harlow (Chicago: University of Chicago Press, 1979). Bilingual edition.

SL   Maurice Blanchot, *The Space of Literature*, trans. A. Smock (Lincoln: University of Nebraska Press, 1982). *L'Espace littéraire* (Paris: Gallimard, 1955).

SLW   Søren Kierkegaard, *Stages on Life's Way*, trans. W. Lowrie (New York: Schocken Books, 1967). For Danish, see *CA.*

TA   Emmanuel Levinas, "The Trace of the Other," in *Deconstruction in Context: Literature and Philosophy*, ed. M. C. Taylor (Chicago: University of Chicago Press, 1986). *Tijdschrift voor Philosophie*, September 1963, 605–23.

TB   Martin Heidegger, *On Time and Being*, trans. J. Stambaugh (New York: Harper and Row, 1972). *Zur Sache des Denkens* (Tübingen: Max Niemeyer, 1969).

TO   Maurice Blanchot, *Thomas the Obscure*, trans. R. Lamberton (New York: David Lewis, 1973). *Thomas L'Obscur* (Paris: Gallimard, 1950).

VE   Georges Bataille, *Visions of Excess: Selected Writings, 1927– 39*, trans. A. Stoekl with C. R. Lovitt and D. M. Leslie (Minneapolis: University of Minnesota Press, 1985). For the French original, I have referred to *Oeuvres completes*, 9 vols. (Paris: Gallimard, 1970–79).

VI   Maurice Merleau-Ponty, *The Visible and the Invisible*, trans. A. Lingis (Evanston: Northwestern University Press, 1968). *Le Visible et l'invisible* (Paris: Gallimard, 1964).

VP   Jacques Derrida, *La Vérité en peinture* (Paris: Flammarion, 1978). Translated by Geoff Bennington and Ian McLeod as *The Truth in Painting* (Chicago: University of Chicago Press, 1987). Since this translation was unavailable to me at the time of writing, page numbers refer to the original French.

WD   Jacques Derrida, *Writing and Difference*, trans. A. Bass (Chicago: University of Chicago Press, 1978). *L'Ecriture et la différence* (Paris: Editions du Seuil, 1967).

Bataille, Georges. See *BN, IE, MM*.
Blanchot, Maurice. See A, EI, PA, SL, TO.
Derrida, Jacques. See D, G, M, OG, S, VP, WD.
Hegel, G. W. F. See *ETW, L, LPR, PM, PS*.
Heidegger, Martin. See *EGT, HCE, ID, PLT, QT, TB*.
Kierkegaard, Søren. See *CA, FT, JP, SLW*.
Kristeva, Julia. See *DL, PH*.
Lacan, Jacques. See *E, FFC, FS*.
Levinas, Emmanuel. See *OB, TA*.
Merleau-Ponty, Maurice. See *PP, VI*.

The presence and absence of the gods, their withdrawal and
immanence, defined the central and empty space for European culture
where there appeared, bound in a single interrogation,
the finitude of man and the return of time. The nineteenth century is
commonly thought to have discovered the historical dimension;
it was able to pen history on the basis of the circle,
the spatial form that negates time, the form in which the gods
manifest their arrival and flight and men manifest their return to
their native ground of finitude. More than simply an event that
affected our emotions, the death of God profoundly influenced our
language; the silence that replaced its source remains
impenetrable. . . . Language thus assumes a sovereign position;
it rises as coming from elsewhere, from a place of
which no one can speak, but it is a work
only if, in ascending to its proper
discourse, it speaks in the
direction of this absence.
MICHEL FOUCAULT

. . . everything is profoundly cracked.

GEORGES BATAILLE

What is it that rings false in the system? What makes it limp?
The question itself is lame and does not amount to a question.
What exceeds the system is the impossibility of its failure,
and likewise the impossibility of its success. Finally nothing can be
said of it, and there is a way of keeping still
(the lacunary silence of writing) that arrests the system,
leaving it idle, unemployed, delivered to the
seriousness of irony.

MAURICE BLANCHOT

It is necessary to save the tear and for that
to play seam against seam.

JACQUES DERRIDA

Overleaf: Shiva. Photograph by Alphonso Lingis.

Encore

The history of society and culture is, in large measure, a history of the struggle with the endlessly complex problems of difference and otherness. Never have the questions posed by difference and otherness been more pressing than they are today. For an era dominated by the struggle between, among, and against various "isms"—communism, fascism, totalitarianism, capitalism, racism, sexism, etc.—the issue of difference is undeniably political. Is difference tolerable? Are others to be encouraged to express and cultivate their differences? Or is difference intolerable? Are others who are different to be converted, integrated, dominated, excluded, or repressed? The ghettos of Europe, America, and South Africa, the walls in Germany, China, and Korea, and battlefields throughout the world testify to the urgency of the issue of difference. A century that opened with the publication of *The Interpretation of Dreams* should have learned by now that the repressed never goes away but always returns—sometimes violently. As we approach the close of the millennium, the fires ingited in the ovens of Europe threaten to encompass the entire globe. Holocaust is one response to difference.

The problem of the other, however, is not only political; it is also an issue of considerable artistic, philosophical, psychological, and theological importance. The search for irreducible difference and radical otherness obsesses many of our most imaginative and creative artists, writers, philosophers, psychologists, and theologians. Although it recurs throughout the century, concern with difference and otherness is a distinguishing trait of thinkers who can be described as "postmodern." "Postmodern" is a notoriously vague term. The obscurity of postmodernism reflects, in part, the continuing confusion surrounding the notion of the modern. The precise meaning of modernity varies from context to context and from time to time. Indeed, such ceaseless change seems to be inherent in the very idea of the modern. While it is impossible to define and delimit modernity with any degree of precision, there seems to be a consensus that modern philoso-

phy begins with Descartes's inward turn to the subject. Plagued by
uncertainty and doubt, Descartes seeks certainty through doubt. He
doubts everything until he reaches what he regards as indubitable—
his own doubting self. Descartes labels this self-certain subject *res
cogitans,* which he distinguishes from all else, described as *res extensa.*
Having radically differentiated *res cogitans* from *res extensa,* Descartes
faces the problem of establishing the relationship between subjectivity and objectivity. In a move that becomes decisive for many later
thinkers, Descartes insists that the subject's relation to otherness is
mediated by and reducible to its relationship to itself.

In the wake of Descartes's meditations, modern philosophy becomes a *philosophy of the subject.* As the locus of certainty and truth,
subjectivity is the first principle from which everything arises and to
which all must be returned. With the movement from Descartes,
through the Enlightenment to idealism and romanticism, attributes
traditionally predicated of the divine subject are gradually displaced
onto the human subject. Through a dialectical reversal, the creator
God dies and is resurrected in the creative subject. As God created the
world through the Logos, so man creates a "world" through conscious
and unconscious projection. In different terms, the modern subject
defines itself by its *constructive* activity. Like God, this sovereign subject relates only to what it constructs and therefore is unaffected by
anything other than itself. What appears to be a relationship to
otherness—be that other God, nature, objects, subjects, culture,
or history—always turns out to be an aspect of mediate self-relation
that is necessary for complete self-realization in transparent self-
consciousness. Absolute knowledge actualized in the full self-
consciousness of the subject seems to realize Western philosophy's
dream of enjoying a total presence that is neither disturbed by irreducible difference nor interrupted by the return of an absolute other.

As these remarks suggest, the modern philosophical project that
begins with Descartes achieves closure in Hegel's systematic philosophy. Hegel's construction of an all-inclusive System is the result of his
lifelong wrestling with the problem of difference and the question of
the other. His systematic treatment of difference and otherness remains decisive for subsequent philosophy, theology, and literary criticism. From Hegel's perspective, "the source of *the need of philosophy*" is
Entzweiung. Derived from *entzwei,* which means "in two, asunder,
torn," and *entzweien,* "to separate, estrange, alienate," *Entzweiung*
designates "dissension, estrangement, and hostility," as well as "dichotomy and division." *Entzweiung* always carries the hint of duplicity
implied by *zwei* and the shadow of doubt cast by *Zweifel.* To sublate

Entzweiung is to overcome doubt—Cartesian and otherwise.

In an early essay bearing the suggestive title *Differenzschrift*, Hegel maintains that "the sole interest of reason is to sublate . . . rigid opposites [*Gegensätze*]. But this does not mean that reason is altogether opposed to opposition and limitation. For the necessary dichotomy [*Entzweiung*] is *one* factor in life. Life eternally forms itself by setting up oppositions, and totality at the highest pitch of living energy is only possible through its [i.e., totality's] own restoration out of the deepest separation. What reason opposes, rather, is just the absolute fixity that the understanding gives to the dichotomy; and it does so all the more if the absolute opposites themselves originated in reason. When the might of union vanishes from the life of men and the opposites lose their living relation and reciprocity and gain independence, the need of philosophy arises."[1] Hegel is convinced that the major philosophical options of his day—for example, Kant's critical philosophy, Fichte's practical idealism, Jacobi's intuitionism, and Schelling's aestheticism—fail to address this need adequately. While Kant does not reestablish the union that rejoins opposites, the contrasting efforts of Fichte, Jacobi, and Schelling to regain lost unity lead to a dissolution of difference in identity. Though obviously divergent in many ways, the paths charted by these post-Kantians all end up in what Hegel describes as "the night in which all cows are black." To emerge from this darkness into the full light of reason, it is necessary to establish the mean between extremes. This mean both joins and distinguishes opposites like identity/difference and same/other. In his search for a reconciling middle ground, Hegel, in keeping with the tendency of Western thought, privileges identity and unity. Hegelian philosophy can be understood as a systematic attempt to secure the *identity* of identity and nonidentity and the *union* of union and nonunion. Be revealing the Logos of everything to be the logical *structure* of identity-in-difference, speculative philosophy is supposed to reconcile opposites without destroying difference(s). The reestablishment of the integrity of the Logos marks the end, i.e., both the goal and the completion, of modern philosophy.

Hegel's final solution has met with the suspicion of many of his most sensitive and insightful interpreters. The sensualism of Feuerbach, the materialism of Marx, and the individualism of Kierkegaard already ask what the System leaves out. This question can be posed in

1. G. W. F. Hegel, *The Difference between Fichte's and Schelling's System of Philosophy*, trans. H. S. Harris and W. Cerf (Albany NY: State University of New York Press, 1977) pp. 90–91; 2:21–22 (for original, see above, Abbreviations and Editions used, under *ETW*).

other ways: Is Hegel's *Mitte* an irreducible *limen* that maintains difference, or does this mean finally fall on the side of identity? Does
Hegel's reconciliation of opposites actually represent identity's mastery of difference? What does Hegel "include" by way of repression?
Does the repressed return to subvert the System?

Nowhere have such questions been probed with greater rigor than
in French literature and philosophy. The works of many of France's
most important twentieth-century writers can be understood as extended responses to and critiques of Hegelian philosophy. The impact
of Hegel on French philosophy and art can be traced to the extraordinary influence of lectures that Alexandre Kojève delivered between
1933 and 1939 at L'Ecole Pratique des Hautes Etudes.[2] Subsequently
published under the title *Introduction à la lecture de Hegel*,[3] Kojève's
reading of Hegel effectively sets the intellectual agenda for several
generations of French intellectuals. Among those who, at one time or
another, attended Kojève's lectures were Raymond Aron, Raymond
Queneau, Georges Bataille, Maurice Merleau-Ponty, Jacques Lacan,
and Jean-Paul Sartre. The center of the *Phenomenology* is, for Kojève,
the master-slave relation in which individuals engage in a seemingly
irrational contest for recognition. History, which grows out of violent
struggle, is a dialectical process in which irrational aspects of experience are overcome and opposites reconciled in all-encompassing reason. According to Kojève, this reconciliation marks the end of both
history and its subject—man.

Less often acknowledged but no less important than Kojève's lectures on Hegel is the work of Jean Hyppolite. Hyppolite's brilliant
commentary on the *Phenomenology*, *Genèse et structure de la Phénoménologie de l'esprit de Hegel*,[4] concentrates on the different forms of
"unhappy consciousness" that Hegel identifies. Developing insights
initially advanced by Jean Wahl in *Le Malheur de la conscience dans la*

2. In his very useful study, Vincent Descombes stresses the importance of Kojève's
reading of Hegel for twentieth-century French thought. See *Modern French Philosophy*,
trans. L. Scott-Fox and J. M. Harding (New York: Cambridge University Press,
1982), especially chapter 2. The title of the French edition, *Le Même et L'Autre*,
suggests points of intersection between Descombes's work and this study. Descombes,
however, is chiefly concerned to present a historical survey that traces the continuity
of several themes (e.g., nothingness, humanism, truth, semiology, history, time, and
difference) through this period. As will become evident, I have significant reserva-
tions about this approach to these materials.

3. A portion of this work of Kojève's is translated into English by J. Nicholas as
Introduction to the Reading of Hegel, ed. A. Bloom (New York: Basic Books, 1969).

4. *Genesis and Structure of Hegel's Phenomenology of Spirit*, trans. S. Cherniak and
J. Heckman (Evanston: Northwestern University Press, 1974). In my judgment, this
book remains the best commentary on the *Phenomenology*.

philosophie de Hegel (1929) and *Etudes kierkegaardiennes* (1938), Hyppolite maintains that Hegel's entire philosophical enterprise is motivated by the desire to reunite the opposites sundering self and society. Unlike Wahl, Hyppolite does not limit his reassessment of Hegel to questions raised by Kierkegaardian existentialism. As his important work, *Etudes sur Marx et Hegel* (1955), makes clear, Hyppolite also subjects Hegel to a Marxist analysis and criticism. It is, however, a work that is virtually unknown outside France, *Logique et existence: Essai sur la logique de Hegel* (1953), that is most significant for later thinkers. In this study, Hyppolite contends that Hegel's speculative logic forms the *structural* foundation of his whole System. More important, Hyppolite's account of Hegelian logic uncovers an unexpectedly close relationship between speculative philosophy and both phenomenology and structuralism. When read in the context of Hyppolite's Hegel, Husserlian phenomenology and the varieties of structuralism seem to be extensions of the logocentrism characteristic of Western philosophy. From this point of view, Hegel appears to be a structuralist *avant la lettre* and structuralism little more than latter-day idealism. In light of this understanding of the complex interplay of Hegelianism and structuralism, it is not surprising that many leading postmodern writers are drawn to poststructuralism. To think after the end of modern philosophy is to think poststructurally.

Taken as a whole, Hyppolite's work establishes the undeniable significance of Hegel's philosophy for most of the intellectual movements that dominate twentieth-century French thought: existentialism, Marxism, phenomenology, structuralism, and psychoanalysis.[5] Until his death in 1968, students who attended Hyppolite's seminars at the Ecole Normale Supérieure and the Collège de France were introduced to contemporary intellectual debate by way of a critical reading of the intricacies of Hegel's thought. Returning to Hyppolite's texts nearly twenty years after his death, one is startled to rediscover themes and problems that have become commonplace in the aftermath of May 1968.[6]

5. Although Hyppolite does not devote a book-length study to the relation between Hegel and psychoanalysis, he stresses the importance of this connection. See, for example, "Hegel's Phenomenology and Psychoanalysis," *Studies in Hegel's Philosophy,* ed. W. E. Steinkraus (New York: Holt, Rinehart and Winston, 1971), pp. 57–70.

6. Jacques Derrida reflects: "The death of Jean Hyppolite in 1968 was not only for me, as for others, a moment of great sadness. By a strange coincidence, it marked at that date—the autumn of 1968 and it was indeed the autumn—the end of a certain type of membership of the university." "The time of a thesis: punctuations," in *Philosophy in France Today,* ed. A. Montefiore (New York: Cambridge University Press,

The French encounter with modern philosophy has not been unaffected by influential currents circulating beyond the Left Bank.
Neither Kojève's nor Hyppolite's reading of Hegel would have been
possible without the work of Martin Heidegger. For Heidegger, modern philosophy comes to an end in Hegel's System, thereby bringing
to a close the Western "ontotheological tradition" that began centuries
ago in Greece. Within this tradition, thinking tends to be either
overtly or covertly metaphysical. "What characterizes metaphysical
thinking, which grounds the ground for beings, is the fact that
metaphysical thinking departs from what is present in its presence,
and thus represents it in terms of its ground as something grounded"
(TB, 56; 62). During the modern epoch, the presence that grounds
everything is interpreted in terms of subjectivity. Commenting on
what he regards as the common foundation of Hegelian and Husserlian phenomenology, Heidegger writes: " 'The principle of principles' requires reduction to absolute subjectivity as the matter of
philosophy. The transcendental reduction to absolute subjectivity
gives and secures the possibility of grounding the objectivity of all
objects (the Being of this being) in its valid structure and consistency,
that is, in its constitution, in and through subjectivity. Thus transcendental subjectivity proves to be 'the sole absolute being'" (TB,
63; 70).

From Heidegger's perspective, ontotheology rests on an important
mistake. This error takes the form of a subtle forgetfulness, exclusion,
or repression. The recognition of the oblivion with which ontotheology begins announces the end of the metaphysical tradition. On
what Derrida describes as "the eve and aftermath of philosophy," Heidegger asks "what has always remained unasked throughout this
history of thinking" (ID, 50). The unasked intervenes in what seem
to be the most complete philosophical works in the tradition. "The
talk about the 'truth of Being' has a justified meaning in Hegel's *Science
of Logic,* because here truth means the certainty of absolute knowledge. But Hegel also, as little as Husserl, as little as all metaphysics,
does not ask about Being as Being, that is, does not raise the question

1983), p. 44. Some of Derrida's most important early work was done under
Hyppolite. For example, "The Pit and the Pyramid: Introduction to Hegel's Semi-
ology" (M, 69–108; 79–127), was originally presented in Hyppolite's seminar at the
Collège de France (16 January 1968). *Edmund Husserl's "Origin of Geometry": An
Introduction,* trans. J. P. Leavey (New York: Nicholas Hays, 1978), was occasioned by
Hyppolite's appointment of Derrida to teach Husserl's phenomenology. For reasons
that will become clear in what follows, it is not insignificant that Derrida was
studying Hegel's *Phenomenology* at the time he was writing on Husserl.

how there can be presence as such" (*TB*, 70; 75). To "ask about Being as Being" or to "raise the question how there can be presence as such" is to direct "thinking to the region that the key words of metaphysics—Being and beings, the ground and what is grounded—are no longer adequate to utter" (*ID*, 71). What ontotheology cannot think—*cannot* think because metaphysics constitutes itself by the very act of excluding this unthinkable—is "Being as difference," "Being thought in terms of the difference" (*ID*, 64, 65). In other words, what Western philosophy leaves unthought is "difference as such." "In contrast to Hegel," Heidegger explains, "this is not a traditional problem, already posed, but what has always remained unasked throughout this history of thinking. We speak of the *difference* between Being and beings. The step back goes from what is unthought, from the difference as such, into what gives us thought. That is the *oblivion* of the difference. The oblivion here to be thought is the veiling of the difference as such, thought in terms of *Lēthē* (concealment); this veiling has in turn withdrawn itself from the beginning. The oblivion belongs to the difference because the difference belongs to oblivion. The oblivion does not happen to the difference only afterward, in consequence of the forgetfulness of thinking" (*ID*, 50–51). To think after the end of philosophy is to struggle to think the unthinkable, say the unsayable, name the unnameable. This task is, of course, *impossible.*

And yet precisely this impossible undertaking preoccupies many of the most important thinkers and writers of our epoch. Together they ask: What remains to be thought, said, written after Hegel?

> As for what "begins" then—"beyond" absolute knowledge—
> *unheard-of* thoughts are required, sought for across the memory of
> old signs. . . . In the openness of this question *we no longer know.*
> This does not mean that we know nothing but that we are beyond
> absolute knowledge (and its ethical, aesthetic, or religious system), approaching that on the basis of which its closure is announced and decided. Such a question will legitimately be understood as *meaning* nothing, as no longer belonging to the system of
> meaning [*vouloir-dire*].[7]

In the following pages, I examine some of the most important efforts to rethink the difference and otherness that lie "beyond absolute knowledge." The "unheard-of" thought of *altarity* provides the

---

7. Jacques Derrida, *Speech and Phenomena and Other Essays on Husserl's Theory of Signs,* trans. D. B. Allison (Evanston: Northwestern University Press, 1973), pp. 102–3.

framework within which I cast my analysis. "Altarity" is a slippery word whose meaning can be neither stated clearly nor fixed firmly. Though never completely decidable, the field of the word "altarity" can be approached through the network of its associations: altar, alter, alternate, alternative, alternation, alterity.

"Altar," which derives from the Latin *altus*, high, and *altare*, material for burning sacrificial offerings, designates "a block, pile, stand, or other raised structure, with a plane top, on which to place or sacrifice offerings to a deity."[8] In Christian churches, the altar is the raised structure where the eucharist or communion service commemorating the Son's sacrifice is performed. Familial traces of the word extend to the "family altar" that marks "the scene of family devotions." When a daughter is offered in the marriage ceremony, the altar is known as "the hymenal altar" or "the altar of pleasure." These sexual connotations carry over in certain slang expressions. "Altar" can mean "the female pudendum," i.e., the external genital organs of a woman. "Pudendum," in turn, points toward *pudere*, to cause shame (cf. the use of the slang term "pud" to refer to the *male* genitalia), as well as *pudeur*, modesty, bashfulness, and reserve. In yet another slang usage, "altar" refers to a toilet or more specifically the porcelain bowl of the toilet. The semantic range of "altar" extends from high to low, sacred to sexual, eschatological to scatological: a toilet, the sex that modestly withdraws, a platform for offerings, or the communion table. So understood, the altar might mark and remark the site where one almost encounters the deity through the release of sacrifice, the sacrifice of a substitute victim—a ram, a daughter, a son, perhaps the word itself.

"Altar" can easily be associated with "alter." "To alter" (*alterare*, from *alter*, other) means both "to make otherwise or different in some respect" and "to become otherwise, to undergo some change in character or appearance." "Alter" also means "to affect mentally, to disturb," as when one speaks of "altered states of consciousness." "Alter," like "altar," is sexually suggestive. "To alter" is "to castrate or spay." The negative connotations of "alter" are more evident in the French *altérer*. *Altérer* means, among other things, "to change (for the worse); spoil, taint, corrupt (meat, wine, character); impair (health); tamper with; adulterate; debase; falsify; garble (a text); misstate, give a garbled version of (the facts); twist the truth."[9]

"Alter" is closely related to "alternate," which can function as a

8. Unless otherwise indicated, definitions and etymologies throughout this work are taken from the *Oxford English Dictionary*.

9. *Harrap's New Standard French and English Dictionary* (London: Harrap, 1981).

verb, noun, and adjective. "Alternate" (from the Latin *alternare,* to do one thing after another, *alternus,* every other, every second, and *alter,* the other of two, the second) "is said of things of *two* kinds, so arranged that one of one kind always succeeds, and is in turn succeeded by, one of the other kind." "To alternate" is "to interchange, to succeed and be succeeded by another continuously; to succeed each other by turns, in time or space." "Alternation" is, then, "the action of two things succeeding each other by turns." The turning and returning of alternation disclose contrasting and often conflicting alternatives. The alternative current generated by an alternator, however, never forms a closed circuit.

"Altarity" most closely approximates "alterity;" the difference between them is nothing more and nothing less than the difference between an *e* and an *a.* A strange, nearly foreign word in English, "alterity" (Latin, alteritatem—being outside) means "the state of being other or different; diversity, otherness." The more common French term *altérité,* is the contrary of *identité* and specifies otherness or that which is other. "Altarity" folds into "alterity," even as "alterity" is implicated in "altarity." Though recalling the Derridean gesture of substituting an *a* for an *e,* the writing of *Altarity* is *not* a simple repetition of the translation of *différence* into *différance. Altarity* evokes dimensions of difference and aspects of otherness overlooked, excluded, or repressed by the notion of *différance.*

Even the tangled web of associations I have sketched does not exhaust "altarity." There is always more to this puzzling term. In this case, "more" is, paradoxically, a certain less that hollows out semantic plenitude. The absence of "more" is the excessive lack that resounds in the "Again, Again, Again" of *Encore.*[10] The repetition of altarity precipitates a crisis of the word that signals the impossibility of language. The word suffers crisis when a difference that is not the opposite of identity and an other that is not reducible to same draw near. The ceaseless oscillation of "altarity" implies the proximity of a difference and an other that call into question every word and all language.

In exploring the uncertain territory opened by writers who attempt to think after Hegel, I do not propose a straightforward history of recent philosophy and nonphilosophy, nor do I elaborate a thematic genealogy or genealogy of a theme. In the "beyond" of absolute

10. I have borrowed this word from one of Jacques Lacan's most important seminars: *Encore: Le séminaire XX, 1972–73* (Paris: Editions du Seuil, 1975).

knowledge—amid the debris of Western philosophy—history, thematics, and genealogy are impossible. Confronted with this impossibility, I attempt to graph a complex network of alternating associations and changing relations, tracing lines that are neither strictly logical nor chronological. Connections arise and pass away through an association of ideas that approximates the play of metaphor and metonymy. Images return repeatedly, intersecting and transecting various texts. In order to think these unthinkable thoughts and glimpse these unimaginable images, it is necessary to think and imagine differently. Analysis must constantly oscillate to and fro in an endless series of detours and displacements: Conception . . . Cleaving . . . Carnality . . . Real . . . Ecstasy . . . Woman . . . Infinity . . . Nots . . . Rewriting . . . Transgression. . . . The list is admittedly limited and could be extended . . . ad infinitum.

For nearly two decades I have been alternating between Kierkegaard and Hegel—oscillating from one to the other and back again. This oscillation repeats the rhythm of much modern and postmodern thought. The longer I waver, the less satisfactory the extremes become. Neither Hegel's both-and nor Kierkegaard's either-or any longer seems persuasive. In my oscillation I have begun to suspect that the neither-nor between both-and and either-or involves a different difference and an other other. This difference is neither simply identical nor different; this other is neither merely the same nor other. The margin of difference and the threshold of otherness return eternally to disrupt the "transparent and simple repose" of Hegel's "bacchanalian revel." After all, the Latin word for swing, *oscillum*, originally designated a mask of Bacchus, hung from a tree in a vineyard, that swung in the wind. Suspended between Hegel and Kierkegaard, *Altarity* probes the postmodern crisis of the word by retracing the oscillation of the masks of Bacchus. Bacchus is also known as Dionysus, whose other name is "the Anti-Christ."

As I have suggested, the marginal space of postmodernism is opened by Heidegger's effort to think what philosophy leaves unthought by rethinking the time of difference and the difference of time. From *Being and Time* to *Time and Being,* Heidegger questions the entire Western philosophical tradition by recasting the Hegelian problematic of identity and difference in terms of the difference between Being and beings. Either directly or indirectly, Heidegger's interrogation continues in the writings of those who follow him. Each, in his or her own way, undertakes the impossible task of thinking that which exceeds, escapes, and eludes philosophical reflection. While the course is neither direct nor continuous, the way from

Heidegger to Derrida can be understood in terms of the repeated return of difference.

Though not usually considered in relation to the writers here assembled, Maurice Merleau-Ponty anticipates some of the most important insights advanced in poststructuralist thinking. Through the critique of the constructive subject developed in his phenomenology of perception, Merleau-Ponty formulates a "dialectics without synthesis" in which he both draws upon and renders suspect Hegel's synthetic dialectic. The far-reaching implications of Merleau-Ponty's position become clear in his late and incomplete writings—most notably, *Philosophy and Non-Philosophy since Hegel* and *The Visible and the Invisible.* An imaginative examination of sensual experience in terms of the chiasmic structure of the body points to important psychological insights that emerge in surprising ways in the work of Lacan.

The attempt to extend structural interpretation to the domain of psychological experience by bringing together Freudian analysis and Saussurean linguistics should not obscure Lacan's abiding debt to philosophers like Hegel, Heidegger, and Merleau-Ponty. Lacan turns Hegel's philosophical speculation against itself by approaching the struggle for recognition in terms of the oedipal conflict. Building on Hegel's account of desire in the *Phenomenology,* Lacan insists that the impossibility of total satisfaction subverts the possibility of complete self-consciousness. Since there is always an Other "within," the subject can never coincide with itself and thus is forever split. What Lacan describes as the incomprehensible *reel* keeps the wound of subjectivity open. The frustrating styles and strategies of Lacanian discourse reflect a ceaseless effort to draw near that which is unnameable without making the Other present.

Even the most superficial perusal of Lacan's texts discloses their extraordinary "literary" quality. Neither simply psychology nor philosophy, Lacan's writings fall between genres as traditionally defined. This aspect of Lacan's work is, in part, the result of his lifelong preoccupation with surrealism. Deeply impressed by surrealism and seriously interested in psychology, sociology, and anthropology, Georges Bataille mediated developments in avant-garde literature and art to psychologists and philosophers. His critique of Hegelianism has proved to be extremely influential. Rather than attacking the System from "without," Bataille approaches it from "within" by arguing that Hegel "did not know to what extent he was right." After recognizing the importance of negation for knowledge and life, Hegel proceeds to undercut his own insight by claiming that negation is finally negated. To think beyond absolute knowledge, Bataille argues, one must imagine a "Hegelianism without reserve" in which negation cannot be negated. Such radical negativity involves an "expenditure without return," which forms "the blind spot of Hegelianism."

The efforts of writers like Lacan and Bataille to solicit a difference that cannot be reduced to identity raises complex questions about long-standing assumptions concerning sexual difference. Throughout much of the Western tradition, the voice of the other has been the voice of woman. Among the many writers who recently have re-examined issues bearing on customary views of woman, the work of Julia Kristeva is distinguished by an unusual conjunction of philosophy, literature, psychology, and theology. Her most important book, *Powers of Horror: An Essay on Abjection,* can best be understood as a reinterpretation of the experience of woman in terms of Lacan's and Bataille's psychosocial investigations. By developing Lacan's brief remarks about the relationship of the goddess to the unconscious and Bataille's treatment of heterogeneity, Kristeva effectively describes the important interplay between the abjection of women and the ambiguity of the sacred.

Emmanuel Levinas, approaching the problem of the other from a very different perspective, also recognizes the religious, theological, and ethical import of altarity. Firmly rooted in the Jewish theological tradition, Levinas tries to think "otherwise than Being" by reformulating the ancient notion of the infinite. Never comprehensible by or in finitude, the infinite is the "trace of the other" that disrupts and dislocates human subjectivity. The interruption of the other sends the subject into an exile from which there is no return.

The errancy of nomadic reflection is inscribed in the uncanny writings of Maurice Blanchot. Having established a reputation for sophisticated literary criticism, Blanchot pursues, in effect, an "infinite conversation" with major twentieth-century artists and philosophers. In strange *récits* and baffling fragments, Blanchot searches for a textual enactment of an other that cannot be named and a difference that cannot be described. Blanchot's extensive writings create a non-philosophical dialogue that sets the stage for the emergence of what has been labeled or mislabeled "deconstruction."

When read against this backdrop, the thoroughgoing intertextuality of Derrida's undertaking becomes clear. Derrida has long acknowledged that his ongoing struggle to think beyond absolute knowledge in and through an endless series of substitutions and supplements is actually an extended effort to think "what is most irreducible in our 'era.'" Derrida's richest and most demanding attempt to carry out what Heidegger describes as "the task of thinking at the end of philosophy" is his provocative rereading of Hegel advanced in *Glas*. Having "begun" with a certain conception of Hegel, I "end"—or almost end—with a text that demonstrates the impossibility of any return to or of Hegel.

There is, I admit, a certain contradiction involved in the effort to examine the *similarities* and *differences* among various ways in which difference has been thought, imagined, and imaged. It is always possible to err in the direction of clarity by proposing continuity where there is discontinuity and reducing differences to identity. In an effort to avoid the philosophical temptation to draw conclusions, I resist writing a conclusion. In place of a final summation, I offer an unconcluding postscript in which I suggest, albeit indirectly, that the thinking and rethinking to which Heidegger calls us have already begun in Kierkegaard's writings. After all that has happened between Hegel and Derrida, to return to Kierkegaard is to insist that *Altarity* can, indeed must, be read differently. Postmodern critiques of modern philosophy might be reinterpreted as a lengthly p.s. to Kierkegaard's *Postscript* to Hegel's System. If the other that obsesses Kierkegaard is, in Blanchot's terms, "the dreadfully ancient," then one might ask: What is the relation of the unthought difference inscribed *in* and *between* the texts of Heidegger, Merleau-Ponty, Lacan, Bataille, Kristeva, Levinas, Blanchot, and Derrida to the sacred? While the question of the religious, which might be neither theological nor ontotheological, is silent in the *a* of différance, it tolls endlessly in the *a* of altarity.

A p.s. is, of course, something like an encore—a supplement to what appeared closed, a remainder left after everything seemed finished. The encore delays and defers: No . . . Not yet . . . Not here . . . Not now . . . Again, Again, Again . . . More, More, More . . . Almost . . . Not quite . . . The Beginning (of) The End. . . . The End (of) The Beginning. To "begin" with an encore is not to bring the argument full circle but is to call into question all forms of circularity by confessing (at the outset) the uncertainty of conclusions and the impossibility of concluding.

> "I must explain things clearly to you," I said. "Up to the last moment, I'm going to be tempted to add one word to what has been said. But why would one word be the last? The last word is

no longer a word, and yet it is not the beginning of anything else. I ask you to remember this, so you'll understand what you're seeing: the last word cannot be a word, nor the absence of words, nor anything else but a word." [11]

The impossibility yet inevitability of the last word marks the double-bind that haunts *Altarity*. The question that remains after all is said is whether this double-bind has anything to do with the re-binding of *religio*.

11. Maurice Blanchot, *Vicious Circles*, trans. P. Auster (Barrytown, NY: Station Hill Press, 1985), pp. 52–53.

1

Conception

G. W. F. HEGEL

—

Absence of Unhappy Consciousness

what, after all, of the remain(s), for us, here, now of a Hegel?	*"what remained of a Rembrandt torn into small, very regular squares*
For us, here, now: from now on that is what cannot be thought without him.	*and rammed down the shithole"* is divided in two.
	As the remain(s) (*G*, 7).

Glas opens with the juxtaposition of Hegel and Rembrandt. While many of Hegel's books are quoted and discussed at length in the pages that follow, the identity of Rembrandt's work remains obscure. In the absence of any direct reference, we are left to speculate. Perhaps Derrida is recalling Rembrandt's drawing *Abraham's Sacrifice*. If this is the work of art, why "tear it to pieces" (*déchirer*) and ram it down the shithole? Is Abraham, father of the Jewish faith, a shit, perhaps *the* shit that the System proper must flush away? Why would a father (Father) wound his son (Son)? Who or what is behind Abraham whispering in his ear?[1] What does the murmur coming toward Abraham from behind have to do with dividing or cutting in two? What does Rembrandt have to do with Hegel? What does philosophy have to do with graphics, etchings, or drawings? What does it mean to draw? Does drawing join or separate? Is the drawing that fascinates the philosopher *Abraham's Sacrifice,* or is it the drawing (and quartering) of another Son? Perhaps, as Kierkegaard suggests, these two drawings

---

1. Compare Rembrandt's drawing of Abraham to the drawing of Plato and Socrates that is reproduced on the cover of Derrida's *La Carte postale: De Socrate à Freud et au-delà* (Paris: Aubier-Flammarion, 1980), translated by A. Bass as *The Post Card* (Chicago: University of Chicago Press, 1987).

In developing this account of Hegel's System, I have stressed aspects of his work that play a significant role in the texts of writers considered in this study. I have tried (not always with success) to resist the temptation to comment on Hegel's position and to anticipate the arguments of his critics. My purpose in this chapter is to identify issues, concepts, and images that return repeatedly in post-Hegelian thinking.

are not as different as they seem to Hegel. Is it difference—this difference or another difference—that leads Hegel to call Jews "shit": "The Jewish multitude was bound to wreck his [Jesus'] attempt to give the consciousness of something divine, for faith in something divine, something great, cannot make its home in feces [*im Kote; Kot:* filth, mire, dung, excrement]" (*ETW*, 265; 1:381). Does Hegel try to ram Abraham down the shithole by repressing the wound he inflicts or almost inflicts? Is this repression the negation of negation through which the philosopher seeks to heal everything that is "divided in two"? Can philosophy silence the incessant murmur that "wounds from behind,"[2] or does *Abraham's Sacrifice* return eternally to toll "Fear and Trembling"?

Derrida ends an important essay on Levinas by asking:

> Are we Greeks? Are we Jews? But who, we? Are we (not a chrono-logical, but a pre-logical question) *first* Jews or *first* Greeks? And does the strange dialogue between the Jew and the Greek, peace itself, have the form of the absolute speculative logic of Hegel, the living logic that *reconciles* formal tautology and empirical heterology after having *thought* prophetic discourse in the preface to the *Phenomenology of Spirit?* Or, on the contrary, does this peace have the form of an infinite separation and of the unthinkable, unsayable transcendence of the other? To what horizon of peace does the language that asks this question belong? From whence does it draw the energy of its question? Can it account for the historical *coupling* of Judaism and Hellenism? And what is the legitimacy, what is the meaning of the *copula* in this proposition from perhaps the most Hegelian of modern novelists: *"Jewgreek is greekjew. Extremes meet"* (*WD*, 153; 227–28).

Jew . . . Greek; Greek . . . Jew. Do extremes meet or only seem to meet in the "is"? The question of the unity of opposites involves the copula. Is copulation legitimate or illegitimate? The problem of copulation is inseparable from the problem of conception. The question of the copula can, therefore, be translated: Is conception legitimate or illegitimate? If "the mean" (*die Mitte*) between extremes is "the living logic that *reconciles* formal tautology and empirical heterology," copulation and conception are legitimate. If, however, the difference between extremes takes "the form of infinite separation and of the unthinkable, unsayable transcendence of the other," copulation and conception are illegitimate. Hegel's systematic philosophy is, among other things, an extended effort to secure the legitimacy of

---

2. Kierkegaard frequently describes his own unsettling thoughts in these terms.

copulation and conception. For Hegel, the extremes of Greek and Jew meet in the Christian. Jesus Christ, the legitimate Son of God, is "the mediator" (*der Mittler*) in whom all extremes are reconciled. The concept of speculative philosophy renders explicit what is implicit in the copula.

Neither philosophy nor anything else, however, *begins* with conception. Conception is always secondary—something of an afterthought. Copulation presupposes the separation of the opposites it seeks to join. For Hegel, philosophical conceptions issuing from the copulation of contraries are different responses to the experience of *need*. "When the might of union vanishes from the life of men and the oppositions lose their living relation and reciprocity and gain independence, the need of philosophy arises."[3] Need, Hegel implies, is no more original than conception. Behind or beneath both need and conception lies a more primal union which, though once enjoyed, now has vanished. Conception, born of the copulation of opposites, is less a union than a reunion satisfying need. By unfolding the implications of the origin of conception, it is possible to discern three stages in the deployment of Hegel's dialectic: primal union (identity), loss or separation (difference), and reunion or reconciliation (identity of identity and difference, or union of union and nonunion). One of the ways in which Hegel represents these three moments is as Greek, Jew, and Christian. In Hegel's speculative dialectic, we are first (logically and chronologically, for, as we shall see, history is logical and logic is historical) Greek, then Jew, and finally Christian. As the mean that reconciles extremes, Christianity takes up into itself both Hellenic unity and Hebraic separation. What the Greek enjoyed and the Jew lost, the Christian regains. The speculative philosopher knows all this *absolutely*.

The basic structure of what eventually becomes Hegel's mature dialectic can be discerned in a series of interpretations of the figure of Abraham, written in 1799. The story Hegel narrates in these early fragments begins with the traumatic separation of man from mother nature. This rending is the result of the duplicity of femininity. "The impression made on men's hearts by the flood in the time of Noah must have been a deep rending [*ein tiefes Zerreissen*] and it must have caused the most monstrous disbelief in nature. Formerly friendly or tranquil, nature now abandoned the balance of her elements, now requited the faith the human race had in her and with the most destructive, invincible, irresistible hostility; in her fury she spared nothing; she

3. Hegel, *The Difference between Fichte's and Schelling's System*, p. 91; 2:22.

made none of the distinctions that love might have made but poured savage destruction over everything" (*ETW* 182; 1:274–75). In "The Spirit of Christianity and Its Fate," Hegel structures his argument around three typical responses to this tear: Greek, Jewish, and Christian.

The beautiful Greek "couple" Deucalion and Pyrrha provides one of the few "dim traces" (*dunkle Spuren*) of the "unity" lost in the flood (*ETW,* 182; 1:274). "After the flood in their time," Hegel explains, Deucalion and Pyrrha "invited men once again to friendship with the world, to nature, made them forget their need and their hostility in satisfaction and pleasure, made a peace of love, were the progenitors of more beautiful people, and made their age the mother of a newborn natural life that maintained its bloom of youth" (*ETW* 184–85; 1:276–77). Some of the details of the story of Deucalion and Pyrrha that Hegel omits further illuminate the significance of this Greek couple.[4] Deucalion, son of Prometheus and Pronoea, and Pyrrha, daughter of Epimetheus and Pandora, were advised by Prometheus to build a boat to protect themselves from the deluge with which Zeus planned to destroy the human race. After floating on the vast seas created by the flood for nine days and nights, the couple landed at Mount Parnassus. Though grateful to have survived, they were terribly lonely. In their isolation, they appealed to the earth-goddess Themis, who, at this time, presided over the Delphic oracle. Themis's oracle instructed them to throw the bones of their mother over their shoulders. Deciphering this enigmatic message, Deucalion realized that the bones of their mother (i.e., earth) were, in fact, stones. When they fulfilled the request of the oracle, the stones Deucalion threw became men and the stones Pyrrha threw became women. These couples, known as the Lelegians, proceeded to "mother" Hegel's "beautiful people." Taken together, Deucalion and Pyrrha represent an inverse image of Medusa. Rather than turning people to stone, they transform dead stones into living people. By overcoming the trauma of separation, the pleasure of Greek coupling satisfies human need.

"The spirit of Judaism," embodied in the patriarch Abraham, is more akin to the petrifying Medusa than to the healing, mothering couple Deucalion/Phyrrha.

> Abraham, born in Chaldaea, had in youth already left a fatherland in his father's company. Now, in the plains of Mesopotamia, he also tore himself [*riss er sich*] completely from his family, in order to be

4. My chief source for this information is: Edward Tripp, *Crowell's Handbook of Classical Mythology* (New York: Thomas Y. Crowell, 1970), p. 199.

a wholly self-subsistent, independent man, to be an overlord of himself. He did this without having been offended or violated, without grief which, after a wrong or an outrage, signifies the enduring need of love, when love, wounded indeed but not lost, goes in quest of a new fatherland in order there to flower and enjoy itself. The first act that made Abraham the progenitor of a nation is a severing [*eine Trennung*] that tears to pieces [*zerreist*] the bonds of communal life and love. The whole [*das Ganze*] of the relationships in which he had previously lived with men and nature, these beautiful relationships of his youth he spurned. (*ETW* 185; 1:278)

Derived from Abraham, the spirit of Judaism is "the spirit of self-preservation in strict opposition to everything." Hegel insists that "this principle involves the rending [*die Zerreissung*] of life" (*ETW,* 186, 259; 1:278, 375).

In contrast to the "harmony" (*Einklang*) resounding in the Hellenic principles of unification and identification, "dissonance" (*Missklang*) echoes in Hebraic *separation* and *difference*. The sources of this dissonance are theological. The divisions rending Jewish life reflect the "insurmountable cleavage [*Kluft:* fissure, gap, chasm, abyss] between the being of God and the being of men" (*ETW,* 265; 1:381). For Jews, God is radically other, totally transcendent, and completely exterior. The Holy is "always outside them, unseen and unfelt" (*ETW,* 193; 1:285). Devotion to the wholly Other sets the Jews apart. Always different from others, "the antitheses are the Jewish nation, on the one hand, and, on the other, the world and all the rest of the human race" (*ETW,* 191; 1:283). In order the express this difference, the Jew must persist in "cutting himself off from others" (*ETW,* 186; 1:278). The rending difference, demanded by the Other, is what Abraham seeks to express in his willingness to sacrifice Isaac. Abraham's *coeur de pierre* is "quieted only through the certainty of the feeling that this love [is] not so strong as to render him unable to immolate his beloved son with his own hand" (*ETW,* 187; 1:279).

In a supplementary note concerning the Phrygian goddess of nature, appended to an account of "the principle of the entire [Jewish] legislation," Hegel suggests, but does not develop, further implications of Abraham's sacrifice of Isaac. "The priests of Cybele, the sublime godhead which is all that is, was, and is to be, and their veils [*ihre Schleier*] no mortal has unveiled—her priests were castrated, emasculated in body and spirit" (*ETW,* 191; 1:283). A person who is wounded as deeply as the devotees of the sublime godhead cannot participate in the blissful pleasures and satisfactions enjoyed by

7

couples like Deucalion and Pyrrha. For Abraham, the Messiah has not yet come and hence human fulfillment is deferred and delayed. In the absence of the Messiah's presence, there is no *parousia* here and now. Never allowing himself to be domesticated, the Jew remains a nomad who constantly wanders, roams, and errs. "Abraham wandered [*irrte; irren:* to go astray, lose one's way, be mistaken, err] with his herds hither and thither over a boundless territory without bringing parts of it any nearer to him by cultivating and improving them . . . He was a stranger on earth, a stranger to the soil and to men alike. Among men, he was and remained a foreigner" (*ETW,* 186; 1:278). In this life of exile, completion is never possible, for satisfaction always lies elsewhere. The words of Edmond Jabès's Yukel capture this "nomadic thought":

> *"What are you dreaming of?"*
> *"The earth."*
> *"But you are on the earth."*
> *"I am thinking of the earth in which I will be."*
> *"We are facing each other and have our feet on the earth."*
> *"I only know the stones on the road which, they say, leads to the earth."* [5]

According to Hegel, the wandering Jew is the most extreme example of a form of experience he later describes as "unhappy consciousness." In the life of Jews, "mournful, melancholy, unfelt unity is what is highest" (*ETW,* 194; 1:286). By the time he writes the *Phenomenology of Spirit,* Hegel is persuaded that such "mourning and melancholy" arise from the Jewish experience of having been divided or cut in two. Unhappy consciousness is *"inwardly divided in two, disunited* consciousness [*in sich ent-zwei-tes Bewusstsein*]" (*PS,* 126; 158). Unaware of its implicit unity, unhappy consciousness takes the contraries that constitute it "to be, not the same, but opposites, one of them, viz. the simple unchangeable, it takes to be the *essence;* but the other, the multiply changeable, it takes to be the *inessential.* The two are for unhappy consciousness estranged from one another; and because it is itself the consciousness of this contradiction, it identifies itself with the changeable consciousness, and takes itself to be the inessential" (*PS,* 127; 159). Hegel uses a particularly suggestive image to describe the unbridgeabale gap between the essential and the inessential in Jewish experience. He writes of Moses:

5. Edmond Jabès, *The Book of Yukel, Return to the Book,* trans. R. Waldrop (Middletown, CT: Wesleyan University Press, 1977), p. 27.

In the survey of his political life,[6] he compares the way in which his God had led the Jews, through his instrumentality, with the behavior of the eagle [*des Adlers*] that wishes to train its young to fly—it continually flutters its wings over the nest, takes the young on its wings, and there bears them forth. Only the Israelites did not complete this fine image; these young never became eagles. In relation to their God they rather afford the image of an eagle which by mistake warmed stones, showed them how to fly and took them on its wings into the clouds, but never raised their weight into flight or fanned their borrowed warmth into the flame of life. (*ETW,* 199; 1:291)[7]

Never attaining the lofty status of the eagle, the Jew is not simply immature but is actually abject. Nowhere is this abjection more evident than in slavish obedience to the "heteronomous" Law. Unhappy consciousness's realization of its infinite *difference* from everything other than itself exposes outer and inner wounds that never heal. Plagued by division within and without, the Jew is impotent to recognize salvation when it truly arrives. "How were *they* to recognize divinity in a man, poor things that they were, possessing only a consciousness of their misery, of the depth of their slavery, of their opposition to the divine, of an unsurmountable cleavage between the being of God and the being of men? Spirit alone recognizes spirit. They saw in Jesus only the man, the Nazarene, the carpenter's son whose brothers and kinsfolk lived among them; so much he was, and more he could not be, for he was only one like themselves, and they felt themselves to be nothing. The Jewish multitude was bound to wreck his attempt to give the consciousness of something divine, for faith in something divine, something great, cannot make its home in feces" (*ETW,* 265; 1:381).

As the implicit truth of every philosophical conception, Jesus

6. The passage to which Hegel refers is Deuteronomy 32:11. "As an eagle stirreth up her nest, fluttereth over her young, spreadeth abroad her wings, taketh them, beareth them on her wings, so the Lord alone did lead him."

7. The figure of the eagle appears in many of the works I will be analyzing. Writers from Merleau-Ponty to Derrida frequently represent the philosopher with the image of an eagle whose all-encompassing vision sees everything. On the first page of *Glas,* Derrida writes: "His [Hegel's] name is so strange. From the eagle it draws its imperial or historic power. Those who still pronounce his name like the French (there are some) are ludicrous only up to a certain point: the restitution (semantically infallible for those who have read him a little—but only a little) of magisterial coldness and imperturbable seriousness, the eagle caught in ice and frost, glass and gel" (*G,* 7).

embodies the "copula" that reconciles the opposites faulting unhappy Jewish consciousness. Legitimate copulation leads to *proper* conception, which elevates humankind above "the filth, mire, dung, and excrement" of Jewish experience. "The Sermon [on the Mount] does not teach reverence for the laws; on the contrary, it exhibits that which fulfills the law but sublates it as law and so is something higher than obedience to law and makes law superfluous. Since the commands of duty presuppose a severing [*eine Trennung*] and since the mastery of the concept declares itself in a 'thou shalt,' that which is raised above this severing is, by contrast, an *is* [Sein], a modification of life" (*ETW;* 212; 1:324.)[8] For the young Hegel, the essence of the Christian conception of copulation is revealed in love. Unlike the law, which presupposes lingering fault, love heals every wound opened by divisive opposites. In contrast to the Jew, who sees himself as a servile subject standing over against an omnipotent "infinite Object" (*ETW,* 191; 1:283), Jesus declares: "between man and God, between spirit and spirit, there is no such cleavage of objectivity and subjectivity; one is to the other an other only in that one recognizes the other; both are one" (*ETW,* 265; 1:381). Christian love brings a reunion of opposites in which inclination and obligation correspond perfectly. "This correspondence with inclination is the *plerōma* [fulfillment] of the law; i.e., an is [*ein Sein*], which, to use an old expression, is the 'complement of possibility,' since possibility is the object as something thought, as a universal, while 'is' [is] the synthesis of subject and object in which subject and object have lost their opposition" (*ETW,* 214; 1:326).

Like the petrifying gaze of father Abraham, the law discloses "the gap in life" (*ETW,* 230; 1:343). The total presence of the incarnate God actualized in the coming of the Messiah fills all emptiness and hence overcomes the absence haunting unhappy consciousness. "To love God is to feel oneself in the all of life, with no restrictions, in the infinite" (*ETW,* 247; 1:363). When one is at home in the All, wandering, roaming, and errancy cease. By restoring the harmony once enjoyed by the Greeks, Christian love brings the satisfaction the Jew

---

8. It is impossible to tell from the context whether Hegel intends to stress the verb *sein* or the noun *Sein*. To appreciate the different dimensions of Hegel's argument in this passage, it is important to note that he is commenting on both Jewish law and the Kantian moral law. Kant's practical philosophy, Hegel insists, perpetuates the oppositions sundering unhappy consciousness. From this perspective, Kantianism appears to be a latter-day form of Judaism. For an elaboration of Hegel's view of Kant, see Mark C. Taylor, *Journeys to Selfhood: Hegel and Kierkegaard* (Berkeley: University of California Press, 1980), pp. 41–49.

yearns for but never enjoys. This wedding of opposites is celebrated in the "love feast."

The love feast raises its participants to heights where only eagles dare soar. In this ritual reenactment of the unification of spirit with spirit, bread and wine give objective expression to the harmonious bond enjoyed by those who are in love. As the external elements are incorporated, the spirit of Jesus "penetrates" individuals and becomes incarnate in the spirit of the group.

> The spirit of Jesus, in which his disciples are one, has become a present object, a reality, for external feeling. Yet the love made objective, this subjective element become a thing, reverts once more to its nature, becomes subjective again in the eating. This return may perhaps in this respect be compared with the thought, which in the written word becomes a thing and which recaptures its subjectivity out of an object, out of something lifeless, when we read. The simile would be more striking if the written word were read away, if by being understood it vanished as a thing, just as in the enjoyment of bread and wine not only is a feeling for these mystical objects aroused, not only is the spirit made alive, but the objects vanish as objects. (*ETW,* 251; 1:367)

The elevation of the material to the spiritual and the return of objectivity to subjectivity take place through a process of incorporation or "inwardization" (*Erinnerung*) akin to eating and reading. To read the living word truly is to be nourished by the spirit that translates from death to life. "Inspired" (*be-geist-ertes*) reading releases the "spirit" (*Geist*) imprisoned in the petrified rigidities of Jewish law. For life to be complete, consumption must be total. If spiritual reading is to erase every trace of the written word, there must be nothing left over—no crumbs or fragments, surely no philosophical crumbs or fragments.

Identity Working-Through Difference

Within the strictures of Hegel's System, conception is not legitimate unless it is *properly* conceptual and knows itself as such. Between the copulation of love and the conception of the concept lies the intermediate domain of representation. *Vorstellung* is the marginal site (or non-site) of religion *sensu strictissimo*. Religion is *no longer* love but is *not yet* true knowledge or knowledge of the truth. Preoccupied with healing the wounds that rend self and other, love remains insufficiently sensitive to difference and otherness. Love, therefore, falls short of Hegel's ideal of unifying union and *nonunion* and identifying identity and *difference*. The transition from the sensuous experience of love to reflective thought inevitably passes through representation.

Representation is the mean that mediates the extremes of sense experience and conceptual thought. This mean is, in effect, the incarnation of the Logos in which reason descends into space and time (i.e., nature and history) and space and time ascend to reason. If the Mediator remains a *Vorstellung* that is not translated into a *Begriff* (concept), opposites coincide but are not truly reconciled. The complete reunification of opposites becomes actual only in the total transparency of the concept. Absolute knowledge presupposes perfect self-consciousness. One arrives at such self-knowledge by re-cognizing the way in which the subject re-presents itself to itself in representation. In *Vorstellung,* the subject "places" (*stellt*) itself "before" (*vor*) itself. Hegel unfolds his analysis of *Vorstellung* in three parts (the last two of which are further divided into three subsections): recollection (*Erinnerung*); imagination (*Einbildungskraft*): reproductive, associative, and productive imagination (*Phantasie*); and memory (*Gedächtnis*): memory retentive of names (*namenbehaltendes*), reproductive, and mechanical (*mechanisches*) memory.[9] Recollection, Hegel agrues, is "the germ" (*der Keim:* spore, nucleus, origin) of all thought. Though sense images are transient, they are "unconsciously preserved" (*PM,* 204; 10:260). This unconscious is actually a preconscious that Hegel describes as "the night-like pit" (*nächtlichen Schacht; Schacht:* mine, shaft, hollow, gorge) in which images and representations are stored. When triggered by a similar intuition, these sense images involuntarily emerge from the unconscious and enter consciousness. In this recollection, the "mine" (i.e., pit) of unconscious mind becomes the "mine" (i.e., possession) of the conscious ego.

> Thus intelligence recognizes the determinate sensation and intuition of it [i.e., recollection] as what is already its own—in them it is still within itself; at the same time it is aware that what at first is only its inner image is, as the immediacy of intuition, also known as *verified.* The image, which in the pit of intelligence was only its property [*Eigentum*], now, with the determination of ex-

9. It is important to recognize the different nuances of the terms Hegel uses. *Erinnerung* includes the word *inner* and thus connotes inwardness. To recollect is to make inward or interiorize. *Einbildungskraft* suggests the activity of "building" (*bilden*) into "one" (*ein*). The noun *Bild* also means image, picture, figure, and portrait. Finally, the close relationship that Hegel stresses between memory and thought is suggested by the similarity between *das Gedächtnis* and *das Denken.*

ternality, actually comes into its possession. Therewith the image is at once differentiated from intuition and separated from the simple night in which it was originally submerged. (*PM*, 205; 10:261)

Through the activity of the reproductive imagination, involuntary recollection becomes voluntary recall. In this way, the ego assumes power over the images that issue from "its own inwardness." Having recalled representations stored deep within itself, the subject is able to associate images freely. The associative imagination establishes connections among the images stored within the deep well of the mind. The links that "fashion" (*bilden*) different representations into a single object of the "imagination" (*Ein-bildungs-kraft*) are *constituted* by the cognitive activity of the subject. In the object, the subject re-presents itself to itself or places itself before itself. When the imagination is productive, "intelligence makes itself *be* as a *thing* [*Sache*]" (*PM*, 211; 10:268). Conversely, the object posited by the imagination is a "sign" (*Zeichen*) that "points" (*zeigt*) beyond itself to the mental activity of the *constructive* subject. Since the association of images is free, the sign, unlike the symbol, is arbitrary. The arbitrariness of the sign testifies to the freedom of mind or spirit. Since it is always haunted by something foreign to its sensuous materiality, Hegel suggests that the cryptic sign resembles a "pyramid." "The sign," he explains, "is some immediate intuition, representing a totally different content from what naturally belongs to it; it is the *pyramid,* into which a foreign soul has been transferred and where it is preserved" (*PM*, 213; 10:270). Elsewhere, Hegel elaborates the implications of this pyramid through several associated images, the most important of which is a tombstone.

> The sign must be regarded as a great advance over the symbol. Intelligence, in indicating something by a sign, has finished with the content of intuition, and the sensuous material receives for its soul a meaning [*Bedeutung*] *foreign* to it. Thus, for example, a cockade [*eine Kokarde:* from the Latin *coccus,* by way of the French *coquard,* strutting, and *coq,* cock], a flag or a *tombstone* [Grabstein], means something totally different from what it immediately indicates. The arbitrary connection between the sensuous material and the general representation occurring here, has the necessary consequence that the meaning of the sign first has to be learned" (*PM,* 212; 10:269).[10]

10. Hegel concludes this *Zusatz* with the following statement: "This is especially true of linguistic signs" (*Sprachzeichen*). In the two following paragraphs, he develops

As a marker of the boundary that simultaneously joins and separates the material and spiritual, the tombstone not only commemorates the fall of life into death, but also inscribes the site of the resurrection and re-erection of life. Like Deucalion and Pyrrha tossing the "bones" of mother earth over their shoulders, one who possesses true memory can *begin* the miracle of breathing life into stone. To escape the grave, sensuous material must be thoughtfully conceived.

Convinced that "we think [*denken*] in names," Hegel argues that "memory" (*Gedächtnis*) is primarily concerned with names. In its most rudimentary form, memory recognizes the name etched on the tombstone of the sign. Hegel labels this form of mnemic activity *namenbehaltend*—memory retentive of names. Retentive memory supplies the "stuff" with which reproductive memory works. Having recognized the *difference* between the thing and its name, reproductive memory is able to reproduce meaning without explicitly evoking a real or imagined referent. "Given the name lion, we need neither the actual vision of the animal, nor even its image: the name alone, if we *understand* it, is the simple imageless representation" (*PM* 220; 10:278). In a more contemporary idiom, reproductive memory discerns "meaning" (*Bedeutung*) in "sense" (*Sinn*) by differentiating signified and signifier. Mechanical memory extends reproductive memory by assembling the meanings of signs through a process of inwardizing "senseless words" in the "universal space of names as such" (*PM* 222; 10:281). This universal space is the locus of abstract subjectivity. The abstract "I" or ego possesses "power over different names—the empty band [*das leere Band*] which, having nothing in itself, fixes in itself a series of [names] and keeps them in a stable order. Insofar as they merely *are,* and intelligence is here itself this *being* of theirs, it is this power as *entirely abstract subjectivity*—memory, which because of the complete externality in which the members of such series stand to one another, and because it is itself this externality (subjective though it be), is called *mechanical*" (*PM,* 222; 10:281).

As the final moment in Hegel's account of *Vorstellung,* mechanical memory discloses the remaining inadequacy of representation. While the feeling of love privileges identity at the expense of difference, representation is governed by the principle of difference and thus fails to do justice to the identity of identity and difference. Hegel argues

---

an analysis of the linguistic sign and presents an account of writing or of "written language" (*Schriftsprache*; 212–18; 10:270–77). Derrida devotes considerable attention to these pages in "The Pit and the Pyramid: Introduction to Hegel's Semiology" (*M,* 69–108; 79–127).

that inasmuch as "representation begins from intuition and the *ready-found* material of intuition, this activity is still burdened with this difference [*Differenz*], and makes its concrete products still *syntheses* that do not become the concrete immanence of the concept that they first become in thought" (*PM*, 202; 10:257). The priority of differentiation over unification is evident in the "externality" (*Äusserlichkeit*) that characterizes the three aspects of representation: objectivity, subjectivity, and the relationship between the object of representation and the subjective activity of representing. The represented object is a "collection" (*Zusammenhang*) of attributes. The rose, for example, is red, and "also" fragrant, and "also" prickly, etc. The representing subject makes no effort to discern or establish the internal relationship among the attributes through which the object becomes an integrated totality. Traits that remain external to each other are merely accidentally or arbitrarily related. The vestiges of disunity in the constituted object represent the persistent arbitrariness of the constituting subject. In the activity of representation, the subject does not yet comprehend its own internal unity and coherence. Like the attributes of its object, the different aspects of the subject's mental activity remain externally related to each other. This makes it impossible to grasp the internal relationship between subject and object. In representation, subject and object continue to stand over against each other as constituting and constituted.

To complete the transition from the pyramidal sign to the living concept, it is necessary to transform moribund exteriority into vital inwardness. The proper conception of the Hegelian concept is possible only if the complex interrelation of identity and difference is reconceived. Hegel undertakes this task in the second book of his *Science of Logic*. Through an extraordinarily complex consideration of the "determinations of reflection," he attempts to establish the conversion of identity and difference into each other and their dialectical unity in contradiction. Identity, Hegel argues, is simple selfsameness, which usually is regarded as exclusive of difference. When such exclusive self-relation is examined more carefully, it appears that abstract self-identity is actually inseparable from absolute difference. "Identity is the reflection-into-self that is identity only as internal repulsion, and is this repulsion as reflection-into-itself, repulsion that immediately takes itself back into itself. Thus it is identity as difference that is identical with itself. But difference is only identical with itself insofar as it is not identity, but absolute non-identity. But non-identity is absolute insofar as it contains nothing of its other but only itself, that is, insofar as it is absolute identity. Identity, therefore, is *in its own self* absolute non-identity" (*L,* 413; 6:40–41). The self-relation that forms identity is necessarily mediated by opposition to otherness. In the act of affirming itself, identity negates itself and becomes *its* opposite, difference. "*Identity is difference,*" for "*identity is different from difference*" (*L,* 413; 6:41). In this dialectical interplay, difference, the other of identity, is identity's *own* other. Such ownership of difference is essential to identity.

Conversely, difference *as* difference, pure or absolute difference, is indistinguishable from identity. Difference constitutes itself by opposition to *its* opposite, identity. Having established that identity is inherently difference, Hegel proceeds to argue that in relating itself to its apparent other, difference really relates to itself. Relation to "other" turns out to be self-relation. In the act of affirming itself, difference likewise negates itself and becomes its *own* opposite, identity. "Difference in itself is self-related difference; as such, it is the negativity of itself, the difference not of an other, but *of itself from itself;* it is not itself but its other. But that which is different from difference is identity. Difference, therefore, is itself and identity. Both together constitute difference; it is the whole, and its moment" (*L,* 417; 6:46–47).

Identity, in itself difference, and difference, in itself identity, join in contradiction, which Hegel defines as the *identity* of identity and difference. Inasmuch as identity and difference necessarily include their opposites within themselves, they are inherently self-contradictory. "Each has an indifferent self-subsistence of its own through the fact that it has within itself the relation to its other moment; it is thus the whole, self-contained opposition. As this whole, each is mediated with itself *by its other* and *contains* it. But further, it is mediated with itself by the *non-being of its other;* hence it is a unity existing on its own account and it *excludes* the other from itself. . . . It is thus contradiction" (*L,* 431; 6:65). In Hegel's System, such contradiction is the root of all movement and vitality; it is the pulse of life universal.

A product of love, life is generated by the complete copulation of opposites. From his *Early Theological Writings* to his mature *Science of Logic,* Hegel insists that the task of the philosopher, lover of wisdom, is "to conceive pure [*reines:* clean, clear, neat, tidy, chaste] life" (*ETW,* 254; 1:371). Life is a complex process of self-differentiation and reintegration comprised of three moments: undifferentiated identity (abstract universality), the differentiation of identity and difference (abstract particularity), and the reunification of identity and difference (concrete universality, which is the full realization of individuality). In the *Phenomenology,* Hegel describes life as *process:* "The simple universal fluid medium is the *in-itself* [*Ansich*], and the difference of the forms [of life] is the *other* [*das Andere*]. But this fluid medium itself becomes the *other* through this difference; for now it is *for the difference* [*für den Unterschied*] that exists in and for itself, and consequently is the unending movement by which this tranquil medium is consumed: Life as something living" (*PS,* 107; 137). Since every living being is a concrete embodiment of universal life force, nothing can be fully comprehended until it is conceived as an integral member of an intricate totality. Inasmuch as life is all-encompassing, its divisions are *internal* differentiations, which, in the final analysis, must be taken up within the whole of which they are necessary parts.

> The independent members are *for themselves;* but this *being-for-self* is really no less immediately their reflection into the unity than this unity is the dividing-in-two [*Entzweiung*] in independent forms. The unity is divided within itself because it is an absolutely negative or infinite unity; and because it is what *subsists,* the difference also has independence only in *it.* This independence of the form appears as something *determinate, for an other,* for the form is divided-in-two within itself; and the *sublation* [*Aufheben*] of this division-in-two takes place, accordingly, through an other. But this sublation is just as much within the form itself, for it is just that flux that is the substance of the independent shapes. This substance, however, is infinite, and hence the shape in its very subsistence is a division-in-two within itself, or the sublation of its being-for-self (*PS,* 107; 136).

The absolute negativity that is generative of life constitutes the structure of the Hegelian concept. To understand the complex notion of absolute negativity, it is necessary to return to the problem of the relation between identity and difference.

The law of identity upon which traditional, i.e., Aristotelian, logic is based asserts that everything is identical with itself. What usually goes unnoticed, Hegel points out, is that the principle of identity is inherently self-contradictory. Those who attempt to affirm abstract self-identity "do not see that in this very assertion, they are saying that *identity is different;* for they are saying that *identity* is different from difference; while this must at the same time be admitted to the nature of identity, their assertion implies that identity, not externally, but in its own self, in its very nature, is this: to be different" (*L,* 413; 6:41). Determinate identity posits itself in and through the negation of *its own* other. But the other, i.e., difference, constitutes itself in and through the negation of the determinate identity it opposes. Each member of this reciprocal relationship becomes itself through the negation of *its own* negation. "Each, therefore, *is* only insofar as its *not-being is*, and is in an identical relationship with it" (*L*, 425; 6:57). The structure of double negativity sustains identity-in-difference by simultaneously distinguishing and reconciling opposites.

Infinite, absolute, or double negation is the structure of the concept that grounds everything that *is*. Hegel defines *den Begriff des Begriffes* in the following terms:

> Because being that is in-and-for-itself is immediately a *positedness* [*Gesetztsein*], the conception in its simple self-relation is an absolute *determinateness*, which, however, as purely self-related is no less immediately a simple identity. But this self-relation of the determinateness as the union of itself with itself is equally the negation of the determinateness, and the concept as this equality with itself is the *universal*. But this identity has equally the determination of negativity; it is the negation or determinateness that is self-related; thus the concept is the *individual*. Each of them, the universal and individual, is the totality, each contains within itself the determination of the other and therefore these totalities are *one* and one only, just as this unity is the differentiation of itself into the free *illusion* [*Schein*] of this duality [*Zweiheit*]—of a duality which, in the difference of the individual and universal, appears as a complete opposition, yet an opposition that is so entirely *illusory* that in grasping and expressing the one, the other also is immediately grasped and expressed. (*L*, 582; 6:251–52)

In the eternal life of the concept, all negation is finally negated. By reuniting opposites, the negation of negation returns difference to identity and rejoins other to same. Within Hegel's dialectical economy, identity *works* through difference; identity *is* the working-through of difference. Difference and otherness are, therefore, penultimate moments that silmultaneously pass away and are resurrected in the concept. For Hegel, this concept "is the sole object and content of philosophy. Since it contains *all determinateness* within it, and its essence is to return to itself through its self-determination or particularization, it has different shapes, and the business of philosophy is to cognize it [i.e., the concept] in these. Nature and spirit are in general different modes of presenting *its existence* [*ihr Dasein*], art and religion its different modes of apprehending itself and giving itself an adequate existence. Philosophy has the same content and the same goal as

18

art and religion; but it is the highest mode of apprehending [*erfassen*] [11] the absolute idea because its mode is the highest mode—the concept. (*L,* 824; 6:549).

Eagle Eye /I: Panoptics of Speculation

As the ground of all reality, Hegel's speculative concept reveals the foundational structure of self-conscious subjectivity. When fully developed, the self-conscious subject realizes the total incarnation of spirit. For Hegel, "the living substance is being that is in truth *subject* or, what is the same, is in truth actual only insofar as it is the movement of positing itself, or is the mediation of its self-othering [*Sichanderswerden*] with itself. This substance is, as subject, pure, *simple negativity,* and is for this very reason the division-in-two [*Entzweiung*] of the simple; it is the doubling that sets up opposition and then again the negation of this indifferent diversity and of its opposition. Only this self-*restoring* identity, or this reflection into otherness [*Anderssein*] within itself—not an *original* or *immediate* unity as such—is the True. It is the process of becoming itself, the circle that presupposes its end as its goal, having its end also as its beginning; and only by being worked through to its end is it actual" (*PS,* 10; 20). Subjectivity, like everything else, is composed of three moments: undifferentiated identity, self-positing in difference, and self-reconciliation in which identity is reestablished by working through difference. Authentic subjectivity emerges through the activity of self-relation in which the subject externalizes or expresses itself in determinate thoughts and deeds, and then reconciles itself with otherness by reappropriating difference as its own self-objectification. The long and arduous process of externalization and reappropriation ends when spirit returns to itself from the condition of exteriority in philosophical reflection. Philosophy, Hegel argues, comes to completion in absolute knowledge, which for the first time is fully unfolded in his own System. In the "preface" to this System, i.e., the *Phenomenology,* Hegel charts the "experience of consciousness" as it proceeds from its "natural" attitude through the necessary stages that

11. *Begriff, begreifen,* and *erfassen* all carry connotations of grasping and seizing. *Fassen* is to grasp, seize, hold, lay hold of, contain, include, apprehend, comprehend, conceive. The noun *Griff* means grip, grasp, hold, catch, or hand-hold. By extension, *Griff* is used to designate claws and talons—like those of an *eagle.* It is, however, necessary to beware of this slippery word, for it can also mean art, trick, or artifice.

lead to absolute knowledge."[12] The direction and implications of Hegel's dialectical analysis are clearly discernible in his account of the first moments of self-consciousness, i.e., desire and the struggle for recognition, and last moments of spirit, i.e., conscience and the beautiful soul.

Hegel's consideration of self-consciousness in the *Phenomenology* falls between his interpretation of consciousness and reason. While consciousness begins with a belief in the essentiality of the object and the inessentiality of the subject, self-consciousness initially assumes the essentiality of the subject and the inessentiality of the object. Throughout the circuitous course of its education, self-consciousness attempts to achieve satisfaction by giving objective expression to its subjective certainty. The most primitive form of self-consciousness is desire.[13] The desiring subject seeks to assert its own substantiality and independence, and to establish the insubstantiality and dependence of that which opposes it by negating its object. Desire, however, is always frustrated and inevitably fails to achieve complete satisfaction. Perpetually requiring another object through whose negation it can assert itself, desire is insatiable. Moreover, intended self-affirmation unexpectedly turns into self-negation. In quest of fulfillment, the desiring subject annuls its self-sufficiency and demonstrates its reliance on the object of desire. The once seemingly dependent object now appears to be independent of the subject. In light of this independence, Hegel concludes that self-consciousness "can achieve satisfaction only when the object itself effects the negation within itself." The *self*-negation of the other upon which the truth of self-consciousness depends can be brought about solely by a self-conscious being. In Hegel's own terms: *"Self-consciousness achieves its satisfaction only in another self-consciousness"* (*PS*, 110; 139).

"Self-consciousness," Hegel argues, "exists in and for itself when,

12. Although Hegel wrestles with the question of whether it is possible for a system of philosophy to have a preface and yet remain systematic throughout his entire career, he never resolves this difficulty. Critics of Hegel frequently concentrate on the place of phenomenology and of the *Phenomenology* within his System. There seems to be an inherent contradiction in the notion of an introduction to a system of philosophy. Either the introduction is already philosophical, and hence within the system, in which case it is not really an introduction, or the introduction is not philosophical, in which case the system is not all-inclusive and thus cannot be totally systematic. I will consider different aspects of this problem in the chapters on Blanchot, Derrida, and Kierkegaard.

13. As I have noted, Kojève's analysis of desire has been especially influential for twentieth-century French thought. See his *Introduction to the Reading of Hegel*, chapter 1.

and by the fact that, it so exists for another; that is, it exists only in being recognized" (*PS*, 111; 141). In order to establish the objective truth of its subjective certainty, a self-conscious subject must confront another self-conscious agent and win from that other the acknowledgment of the subject's own substantiality and independence. The recognition granted by the other presupposes the other's own self-negation as an autonomous individual. Since the other is also a self-conscious being, however, he is an equal partner in the struggle for recognition and seeks the same acknowledgment from the subject confronting him. Consequently, the endeavor of each self-conscious subject to affirm itself by exacting the self-negation of its other involves the effort to accomplish the negation of its own negation. In the language of speculative logic, the self-identity of the participants in the struggle-for recognition is mediated by the negation of negation. Determinate subjects are bound together in an internal relation of double negativity. Each subject becomes itself through relation to the other, and thus includes the other *within* it as constitutive of *its own* being. This relationship of double negativity re-presents the identity-in-difference that forms the essential structure of the concept. The struggle for recognition is properly comprehended only when it is conceived conceptually.

It is obvious that if carried to completion, the struggle for recognition is self-destructive. Realizing that self-consciousness presupposes life, one contestant concedes the recognition sought by the other. By so doing, the vanquished "subject" (*sub-jectum*) becomes a slave, and the victor lord and master. Apparently the master has established the truth of his own independence, or his being for self. Correlatively, the slave seems to be completely dependent upon the master, or merely to possess being for another. But as always in Hegel's all-encompassing dialectic, everything contains its opposite *within* itself. Since one can be a master only in relation to a slave, the master is dependent upon the slave for his mastery, and the slave is, in effect, master of the master. The lord *needs* the obedient acknowledgment and servile labor of his own slave. At first the bondsman is unaware of his implicit mastery. In the face of the terrifying lord, the servant believes himself absolutely dependent upon the fortuitous grace of the other. For Hegel, such fear and trembling is but a passing moment. As the seemingly independent master is inherently for another, so the ostensibly dependent slave is essentially for self.

The bondsman becomes aware of his independence through the discipline of work. Unlike desire, work does not entail the thoroughgoing negation of objectivity, but involves the subject's *construction* of the object in its own self-image. In the labor process, the subject alienates itself from itself by positing itself as an object, and returns to itself by reappropriating this object as its own self-objectification. By sublating the *difference* between subject and object, self-consciousness overcomes its bondage to everything other than itself. When truly comprehended, relation to other is a relation to self that is necessary for total self-realization.

Self-consciousness, for Hegel, is not merely a theoretical matter. To the contrary, theoretical self-consciousness comes to completion in the practical activity of a conscientious subject. In "conscience" (*Gewissen*), the subject, in its particularity, is "certain" (*gewiss*) of its identity with the universal moral law, which appears to be absolutely essential. As in the case of desire, the truth of the subject's certainty presupposes recognition by other subjects. Such acknowledgment is again the product of prolonged struggle. The initial phase of this struggle is marked by the individual's failure to win the recognition of opposing moral agents. Though inwardly certain of the universal validity of its actions, the subject's self-objectification in particular acts always retains "the stain of determinacy" and hence is not acknowledged by other conscientious individuals. Instead of recognizing the moral actor's deeds as concrete expressions of a universal ethical law, others tend to view them as inexpungeably contingent, arbitrary, and idiosyncratic. From the perspective of the person who follows his conscience, the response of others is what seems to be tainted by partiality.

Increasingly aware of "the opposition between what it is for itself and what it is for others," the conscientious subject retreats from active engagement to the contemplation of its own inner purity. Hegel labels the form of experience issuing from this inward turn of consciousness "the beautiful soul." Having forsaken resolute participation in the outer world, the beautiful soul is reduced to judging himself and others. Such a person attempts to reassure himself of his own purity by regarding others as impure. The beautiful soul steadfastly maintains that the rejection he suffers results from selfish motives that arise from the unwillingness of others to renounce their private interests. From the viewpoint of the judged subject, the judging beautiful soul appears inexcusably corrupt. Professing "duty without deeds," the beautiful soul represents "the hypocrisy that wants its judging to be taken for an *actual* deed, and instead of proving its rectitude by actions, does so by uttering fine sentiments" (*PS,* 403; 466). The judgment by which the beautiful soul tries to confirm its purity really affirms the "evil" that attaches to its character and actions. Through "hardhearted judgment" (*Urteil: Ur,* origin, source; *teilen,* to divide, separate, sever), the subject separates itself from, and opposes itself to, an other subject. Rather than establishing the beautiful soul's universal validity and the inadequacy of all other subjects, unacknowledged judgment reveals the persistent division of the judging self that grows out of lingering opposition to, and separation from, otherness. The cleft between self and other can be overcome only through a reciprocal act in which each opposing subject recognizes *itself* in the other. The judging self admits the insufficiency of words without deeds, and the judged self accepts the inevitable partiality of its thoughts and actions. The reconciliation that arises from the twofold deed of confession and forgiveness is the fulfillment of the life of spirit. "The word of reconciliation is *concretely existing* spirit [*daseiender Geist*], which beholds the pure, clean, neat, tidy knowledge of itself as *universal* essence, in its opposite, in the pure knowledge of itself as *individuality* absolutely existing in itself—a reciprocal recognition that is *absolute* spirit (*PS*, 408; 471). The word of forgiveness is the Word of love in which "the wounds of spirit heal and leave no scars" (*PS*, 407; 470).

For Hegel, spirit is *"pure* self-recognition in absolute otherness" (*absolutem Anderssein*). More precisely, spirit "is that which *relates itself to itself* and is *determinate* in its *other-being* and *being-for-self,* and in this determinateness, or in its self-externality [*Aussersichsein*], abides within itself; in other words, it is *in and for itself"* (*PS*, 14; 24). Seeing *itself* mirrored in every other, the "speculative" (*speculum:* mirror) philosopher penetrates every difference. Within Hegel's panoptical system, difference *always* returns to identity. The eagle eye of the philosopher who possesses absolute knowledge reveals the sovereign "I" of the constructive subject, which relates only to itself. "[This] is the *actual* 'I,' the universal knowledge *of itself* in its *absolute opposite,* in the knowledge that remains *internal,* and which, on account of the purity of its separated *being-within-itself,* is itself completely universal. The reconciling *Yea,* in which the two 'I's' let go of their oppositional *existence,* is the *determinate existence* of the 'I' that has distended into two-ness [*Zweiheit*], and therein remains identical with itself, and, in its complete externalization and opposite, possesses the certainty of itself in the form of pure knowledge" (*PS*, 409; 472).

Domestic Bliss: Conception in the Family Circle

The reconciling Word of forgiveness heals the wounds left open by the Jewish faith. Unlike the divisive God of the Jews, the Christian God of love, "as living spirit, differentiates Himself from Himself,

23

posits an other [*ein Anderes*], and in this other remains identical with Himself, and in this other has his own identity with Himself" (*LPR*, 3:69; 17:271). In contrast to the "opposition" between father and son disclosed in Abraham's willingness to sacrifice Isaac, the Christian trinity reveals a perfect "harmony" (*Einklang*) between Father and Son. In the Christian vision, "Father is the other of son, and son the other of father and each is only as this other of the other; and at the same time, the one determination is only in relation to the other; their being is *one* subsistence" (*L*, 441; 6:77). Prefiguring the speculative concept of identity-in-difference, the notion of the trinity is the end product of the progressive development of humankind's religious consciousness, which is plotted in the penultimate chapter of the *Phenomenology*. The phenomenology of religion retraces the steps of the *Phenomenology* as a whole. Passage through the different forms of religious experience results in the evermore adequate self-representation of spirit and, correspondingly, the incremental reconciliation of the human subject and the divine object. There are three stages in this dialectic: natural, artistic, and revealed religion.

Natural religion assumes three forms: "the essence of light" (*das Lichtwesen*), "plant and animal" religion, and religion of "the artificer" (*der Werkmeister*). These moments reproduce at a spiritual level the earlier stages of sense-certainty, perception, and understanding. As with the immediacy of sense-certainty, the religious subject initially regards its object as essential and its own subjectivity as inessential. The devotee first represents absolute spirit as omnipotent substance. "In virture of this determination, the 'shape' is the pure, all-embracing and all pervading *essential light* of sunrise, which preserves itself in formless substantiality" (*PS*, 419; 484). In the presence of this light, individual subjects "have no will of their own" and thus become "merely superfluous messengers" of divine substance's "power, visions of its majesty [*Herrlichkeit*], and voices of its praise" (*PS*, 419–20; 484).

The utter indeterminacy of the religious object is negated when undifferentiated substance is scattered in pantheistic worship of different plants and animals in the natural world. "In this [manifoldness], it [i.e., formless essence] falls apart or disintegrates into the numberless multiplicity of weaker and stronger, richer and poorer spirits. This pantheism which, to begin with, is the passive subsistence of these spiritual atoms [*Geisteratome*] develops into a *hostile* movement within itself. The innocence of the *flower religion*, which is merely the selfless representation of the self, gives way to the earnestness of warring life, to the guilt of *animal religion*" (*PS*, 420;

485).[14] The hostility among believers in different totems reflects the unreconciled opposition characteristic of particular plants and animals when they are not comprehended as determinate manifestations of an all-embracing organic totality. The movement out of dispersion and back to unity *begins* with the transition from plant and animal religion to the religion of the *Werkmeister*.[15]

In the religion of the artificer, the object of devotion is artificial rather than natural. The religious object is not simply *found* in the world of nature but is *made* by a human subject. The activity of the artisan, however, is instinctive rather than self-conscious and as such remains animal-like. The product of such an artificial construction "is not yet in its own self filled with spirit." The images Hegel uses to illustrate the fabrication of the artisan suggest a close parallel between the artificial object and the arbitrary sign.

> The crystals of pyramids and obelisks, simple bindings of straight lines with plane surfaces and equal proportions of parts, in which the incommensurability of the round is destroyed, these are the works of this artificer of rigid or stiff form. Because of the merely *abstract* intelligibility [*Verständigkeit*][16] of form, the significance of the work is not in the work itself, is not the spiritual self. Thus either the works receive spirit into them only as an alien, departed spirit that has forsaken its living penetration of reality and, being itself dead, takes up its abode in this lifeless crystal; or they have an external relation to spirit as something that is itself there externally and not as spirit. (*PS*, 421; 486)

In themselves lifeless, the pyramid and the obelisk are haunted by an alien spirit that is the breath of life. The movement from the rigid, stiff, petrified object of the artificer to the vital object of the artist is marked by a progression from the straight to the circular, the mechanical and crystalline to the organic, and exteriority to interiority. The first *sign* of the vitality of the imagination can be discerned when

14. This is the only sentence in the entire *Phenomenology* in which Hegel mentions flower religion (*Blumenreligion*).

15. *Werkmeister* (composed of *Werk*, work or labor, and *Meister*, master, chief, or leader) carries the connotation of control and mastery. The *Werkmeister* is the master builder whose works are controlled and controlling constructions. *Werkmeister* is often used interchangeably with *Werkführer*.

16. Throughout this passage, Hegel identifies the work of the *Werkmeister* with the activity of "understanding" (*Verstand*). Elsewhere, he explains that understanding "refuse[s] to move beyond absolute separation" (*absolute Trennung; ETW*, 264; 1:380). Understanding, therefore, does not reach the integration of opposites achieved in "reason" (*Vernunft*).

the artificer produces "a more animated, inspired form." "For this purpose [the artificer] employs plant life, which is no longer sacred as it was to the earlier, impotent pantheism; on the contrary, the artificer who grasps *himself* as the being that is for itself, takes that plant life as something to be used and reduces it to an outer aspect, a mere ornament [*Zierde*]. But it is not used unaltered; for the artificer of the self-conscious form at the same time destroys the transitoriness inherent in the immediate existence of this life and brings its organic forms nearer to the more rigid and more universal forms of thought. The organic form which, left to itself, proliferates unchecked in particularity, being itself subjugated by the form of thought, in turn animates these rectilinear flat shapes with a roundness more typical of organic form" (*PS*, 422; 487).

The artificer who is in the process of becoming an artist must demonstrate his mastery of both plant and animal forms by moving beyond the art of ornamental decoration. As animal eclipses plant religion, so hieroglyphic inscription surpasses flowery ornamentation. "The artificer lays hold first of all of the form of *being-for-self* in general in the animal form. He proves that he is no longer conscious of himself immediately in animal life by constituting himself the productive power in relation to it, and knows himself in it as *his* work, whereby the animal shape is at the same time sublated and becomes the hieroglyph of another meaning [*Bedeutung*], of a thought. Consequently, the form, too, is no longer solely and entirely used by the artificer, but is mixed with the form of thought, with the human form. But the work still lacks the form and outer reality in which the self [or subject] exists as self; it still does not in its own self proclaim that it includes within it an inner meaning, it lacks speech [*Sprache*], the element in which the sense [*Sinn*] filling [*erfüllende:* fulfilling, accomplishing, impregnating] it is present" (*PS*, 423; 488).[17] The

17. Hegel presents his most extended discussion of hieroglyphics in paragraph 459 of the *Encyclopedia*. The following remark indicates further implications of his analysis: "It is only a stationary civilization, like the Chinese, that admits of the hieroglyphic written language of that people; and its method of writing, moreover, can only be the lot of that small part of a people which is in exclusive possession of spiritual culture. The progress of the vocal language [*Tonsprache*] depends most closely on the habit of alphabetical writing; by means of which only the vocal language acquires the precision and purity of its articulation. The imperfection of the Chinese vocal language is notorious: numbers of its words possess several utterly different meanings, as many as ten and twenty, so that, in speaking, the distinction is made perceptible merely by accent and intensity, by speaking low and soft or crying out. The European, learning to speak Chinese, falls into the most ridiculous blunders before he has mastered these absurd refinements of accentuation. Perfection here

artificer juxtaposes but does not integrate opposites like inner and outer, and spiritual and material. Anyone who tries to decipher such hieroglyphs is in the position of Oedipus attempting to solve the riddle of the sphinx. "The artificer," Hegel explains, "unites the two [interiority and exteriority] by mixing the natural and the self-conscious form, and this ambiguous [*zwei-deutige:* equivocal, unseemly, improper, ribald] being that is a riddle to itself [i.e., the sphinx], the conscious wrestling with the unconscious, the simple inner with the multiform outer, the darkness of thought coupling with the clarity of utterance [*Äusserung*], these break out into language of a profound, but scarcely intelligible wisdom" (*PS*, 424; 489). Within Hegel's speculative dialectic, it remains impossible to solve the riddle of the sphinx until the analyzed/analysand *speaks* for itself, himself, or herself.

In artistic religion, dead stone gradually is animated through the in-spiration of the living word. In contrast to the instinctive artisan, the artist creates self-consciously. The different forms of artistic religiosity illustrate an ever closer correlation between the active subject and the object of belief. The conclusion of this movement is an identification of subject and object in which divine substance is taken up into the creative activity of the human subject. The original object of devotion in artistic religion is a stone statue of a human being. Unlike the hieroglyph in which spirit "empties" itself into an animal form, the statue joins the subjectivity of the artist to a material embodiment of the human figure. "The human form strips off the animal shape with which it was mixed; the animal is for the god merely an accidental disguise; it steps alongside its true shape and no longer has any worth on its own account, but is reduced to signifying something else and has sunk to the level of a mere sign" (*PS*, 428; 492). [18] Although this concrete object represents "nature transfigured by thought," it nonetheless remains abstract in two important senses. In the first place, the petrified figure is unable to express the animation of spirit. The repose of stone cannot capture the movement and unrest vital to spiritual life. Second, statuesque stasis fails to embody artistic activity. The work of art does not satisfactorily represent the work of the artist. Though the artist objectifies himself in the object of his labor, he finds it difficult to rediscover his subjectivity in the

---

consists in the opposite of that *parler sans accent* that in Europe is justly required of an educated speaker. The hieroglyphic mode of writing keeps the Chinese vocal language from reaching that objective precision that is gained in articulation by alphabetic writing" (*PM*, 216; 10:274).

18. It is important to underscore Hegel's association of the sign with animality.

substance of his work. When creation confronts its creator as alien, "the artist learns that in his work, he did not produce a being *like himself*" (*PS*, 429; 495).

The movement from the abstract to the living work of art involves the interrelated vitalization of the object of belief, and the identification of believing subject and believed substance. In the cultic activity of a community that unknowingly worships its own spirit in the form of a living person, divine substance and the human subject are directly identified. In this way, "man puts himself in the place of the statue as the form that has been raised and fashioned for completely free *movement*, just as the statue is perfectly free *rest*. . . . [The man who is worshiped] is an inspired and living work of art that matches strength with its beauty; and on him is bestowed, as a reward for his strength, the decoration with which the statue was honored, and the honor of being, in place of the god in stone, the highest bodily representation among his people of their essence" (*PS*, 438; 505). In a manner reminiscent of Deucalion and Pyrrha, cultic activity seems to transform inanimate stones into living beings. But even the "living corporeality" of the cult remains an incomplete representation of spirit. Whether in the form of frenzied cultic animation or mere bodily presence of a human deemed divine, the living work of art lacks the inwardness of genuine spirituality. Spirit remains dumb, inarticulate—speechless, wordless.

When spirit is manifest as word, the work of art is spiritualized. The spiritual work of art is the culmination of artistic and the prefiguration of revealed religion. "Language or speech [*Sprache*] is the perfect or complete element in which inwardness is just as external as externality is inward" (*PS*, 439; 505). The moments constituting the final stage of artistic religion repeat, on a higher level, the antecedent forms of religious life. Through the words of the epic poet, the classical tragedian, and the ancient comedian, creative subjectivity becomes transparent to itself. In the movement from epic poetry to comedy, there is a gradual return of substance to subject, which culminates in the identification of the universal divine object with the particular human subject. At the beginning of this progression, the creative artist is completely absorbed in his work; poet is lost in poem, singer in song. Recalling the essence of light with which the dialectic of religion begins, the minstrel effaces himself in order to sing the praises of the gods he believes essential and the heroes he seeks to immortalize. This "singer or bard" "is the individual and actual spirit from whom, as subject of this world, it [the world] is produced and by whom it is borne. His pathos is not the deafening power of nature, but

28

is Mnemosyne, recollection [*Erinnerung*] and a gradually developed inwardness [*Innerlichkeit*], the remembrance of essence that formerly was directly present. He is the organ vanishing [*verschwindendes Organ:* disappearing organ] in its content; what counts is not his own self, but his Muse, his universal song" (*PS,* 440–41; 507).

The human subject's increasing appreciation of its own powers of production is inversely proportional to its recognition of the divine object's creative power. As the opposite of epic poetry, comedy is the form of experience in which creative subjectivity becomes self-certain. The comedian insists that "the self is absolute being" (*PS,* 435; 521). The gods, by contrast, are mere "clouds, an evanescent mist"—nothing more than "imaginary representations."[19] Through a dialectical reversal, the wordless body of the living work of art becomes the bodiless word of the spiritual work of art. In the religion of art, the "incarnation [*Menschwerdung*] of divine being starts from the statue that wears only the *outer* shape of the self; *inwardness,* the self's activity, falls outside of it. But in the cult the two sides have become one; and in the outcome of artistic religion, this oneness, in its consummation, has, at the same time, gone right over into the extreme of the self. In spirit that is totally certain of itself in the individuality of consciousness, all essentiality is absorbed" (*PS,* 453; 521). As self-consciousness sublates consciousness, so comedy inverts the most primal form of natural religion. While the subjectivity of the worshiper of light is overshadowed by the divine object, the comic subject regards every sacred object as merely a projection of its own creativity.

Revealed religion "overcomes the one-sidedness" of natural and artistic religion by uniting the consciousness and self-consciousness of spirit. Spirit becomes totally real when absolute spirit achieves self-consciousness and self-conscious spirit recognizes its absoluteness. In the eyes of the Christian believer, "God is immediately and sensuously intuited as a self, as an actual individual man; only so *is* this God self-consciousness" (*PS,* 459; 528). Neither a souless body nor a bodiless soul, the object of this form of belief is the Word incarnate—Logos made flesh and flesh made logical. In the consummate moment of religious awareness, the cleft between the divine and the human is completely closed, the tear perfectly mended, the wound totally healed. Divine substance and human subject are reconciled in the self-conscious identity-in-difference of God and man. Subject and substance, self and other, humanity and divinity are internally related in

19. Hegel is alluding to Aristophanes' *Clouds.*

such a way that each becomes *itself* in and through the other, and therefore each *includes* difference within itself as formative of *its own* identity. This dialectical mediation of opposites constitutes spirit— true spirit that "is the knowledge of oneself in the externalization of oneself; the being that is the movement of retaining its self-identity in its otherness [*in seinem Anderssein*]" (*PS*, 459; 528). This union of union and nonunion involves the inseparable, though distinguishable, moments of subjectifying substantiality and substantializing subjectivity.

In the original form of revealed religion, however, the true nature of spirit is disclosed only in its sensuous immediacy. While apparently concrete, this revelation is actually abstract. The object of devotion, the Mediator in whom the most extreme opposites are reunited, is regarded as separate from and other than the devoted subject. "Spirit, in the immediacy of self-consciousness, is this *particular* self-consciousness, the opposite of *universal* self-consciousness. It is an exclusive one that has the still unresolved form of a *sensuous other* for the consciousness for which it is immediately present" (*PS*, 461; 530). Like all immediacy, this abstraction can be overcome only through the sublation of the isolated particularity of the sensuous "here and now" in the concrete universality of the concept. Conception reintegrates fissured subjectivity and objectivity to form a thoroughly *reciprocal* relation. In other words, the immediate truth embodied in the Mediator must be mediated conceptually. This mediation arises through the universalization of the particular self-consciousness of the sensuous object effected by the believing subject's recognition of *itself* in *its* other—i.e., in the object of its belief. Consciousness of other is, in truth, self-consciousness. This "inversion" (*Umkehrung*) of consciousness into self-consciousness is the "conversion" (*Umkehrung*) of consciousness that creates the awareness of "absolute reconciliation." The unity of opposites embodied in the Mediator reveals the implicit nature of all individuals. When the believer recognizes the identity-in-difference of *his own self* and the divine, the truth of the *historical* divine man is appropriated as the *eternal* truth of every subject. In this act of re-cognition, the *particular* human subject grasps itself as a finite, spatial, and temporal moment in the *universal,* infinite, and eternal life of the divine. God, by implication, no longer is regarded as wholly other or radically transcendent, but now is apprehended as the all-inclusive subjectivity that comes to completion in and through the drama of incarnation, crucifixion, and resurrection, which is concretely enacted in the processes of nature and history.

Within the totality of Hegel's System, nature and history appear as the externalization of spirit. Through the speculative concept, the philosoper struggles to reunite every form of opposition. Such conception is impossible apart from the perfect copulation of contraries incarnate in the Christian Mediator. The rational comprehension of the reconciliation revealed in the Logos brings the natural and historical process to a close. While nature and history represent the incarnation of spirit in space and time, speculative philosophy realizes the resurrection of spatial and temporal experience in the eternal life of the concept. Philosophy overcomes all forms of fragmentation through the re-inwardization or re-collection of the exteriority plaguing nature and history.

> The self-knowing spirit knows not only itself but also the negative of itself, or its limit: to know one's limit is to know how to sacrifice oneself. This sacrifice [*Aufopferung*] is the externalization in which spirit presents the process of its becoming spirit in the form of *free contingent happening,* intuiting its pure self as *time* outside of it, and equally its *being* as space. This last becoming of spirit, *nature,* is its living immediate becoming; nature, externalized spirit, is in its existence [*Dasein*] nothing but this eternal externalization and its *continuing existence* and the movement that restores the *subject.*
>
> But the other side of its becoming, *history,* is a *conscious,* self-mediating becoming—spirit externalized in time; yet this externalization is equally an externalization of itself. This becoming presents a slow-moving succession of spirits, a gallery of images, each of which, endowed with the riches of spirit, moves thus slowly just because the self has to penetrate and digest [*zu durchdringen und zu verdauen*] this entire wealth of its substance. Inasmuch as its fulfillment consists in perfectly *knowing* what *it is,* in knowing its substance, this knowing is its *withdrawal into itself* in which it abandons its outer existence and gives its concretely existing form over to recollection [*Erinnerung*]. (*PS,* 492; 563)

In a well-known image, Hegel describes the movement of his thought as "the circle that returns into itself, the circle that presupposes its beginning and reaches it only at the end" (*PS,* 488; 559). Though rarely recognized, this closed circle, whose roundness smoothes rough edges and softens rigid angularity, is actually an extension of Hegel's family circle. The philosopher is not a nomadic wanderer who, never settling down, has no place to lay his head. To the contrary, the philosopher is the prodigal son who faithfully returns to the home of the father. Within this father's house, the son who saves rather than the son who spends is rewarded. The father of speculative philosophy runs a profitable domestic economy in which there must be a return on every investment. Within the System, profitless expenditure, senseless prodigality, and excessive loss cannot be tolerated and therefore must be excluded or repressed. Each negation is, in the final analysis, negated. The negation of negation domesticates any difference that is not an identity and every other that is not the same.[20] This double negativity, which is the logical structure of the concept, is, in effect, a process of amortization intended to negate the most disturbing difference and overcome the most unsettling other—death itself. When everything is conceived within the living concept, loss loses and death dies. In the most powerful formulation of the goal of his entire philosophical enterprise, Hegel insists: "the life of spirit is not the life that shrinks from death and keeps itself untouched by devastation, but rather the life that endures it and maintains itself in it. It wins its truth only when, in absolute dismemberment [*absoluter Zerrissenheit*], it finds itself. It is this power, not as something positive, which closes its eyes to the negative, as when we say of something that it is nothing or is false, and then, having finished with it, turn away and pass on to something else; on the contrary, spirit is this power only by looking the negative in the face, and lingering with it. This lingering with the negative is magical power that converts it into being. This power is identical with what we earlier called the subject,

20. The etymology of "domesticate" suggests further dimensions of the circularity of this familial economy. "Domesticate" derives from the Latin word *domus,* which means house or home. In Italian, *duomo* refers to the house of God. A dome is "a rounded vault forming the roof of a building or chief part of it, and having a circular, elliptical, or polygonal base." Furthermore, "dome" can be used to designate a cathedral church. Economy and domesticity or domestication are closely related. "Economy," which derives from the Greek *oikonomos: oikos* house + *nomos,* to manage, control, means "management of a house; the art or science of managing a household." Such management is, of course, primarily concerned with expenses or, more precisely, with controlling expenditure. When considering the various implications of "domestic" and "economy," it is also important to note that Christian theology develops an economic doctrine of the trinity. In contrast to the "immanent trinity," which describes the internal life of the godhead, the "economic trinity" refers to the way in which God deals with the world and His people. Within this context, the economic trinity depicts different phases in the process of salvation. The economic relationship of the Father and Son in and through the Spirit is all-encompassing. Nothing is left out. When Son returns to Father in Spirit, the fall is overcome and no remains are left in the tomb. The resurrection of the Son is the ultimate return on the Father's investment. This return finally closes the family circle.

which by giving determinateness a concrete existence in its own element, sublates abstract immediacy, i.e., the immediacy that *is* only generally, and thereby is true substance: that being or immediacy whose mediation is not outside of it but that is this mediation itself" (*PS*, 19; 29–30).

As magical power that transforms water to wine, stones to flesh, lines to circles, pyramids to spheres, letter to spirit, sign to concept, nonsense to sense, negative to positive, sacrifice to profit, loss to gain . . . death to life, the absolute knowledge born of legitimate philosophical conception is salvific. Hegel believes—*truly believes*—that "thinking is the loosening of hardness; the meeting of oneself with *oneself* in the other. This is a *release* [*Befreiung*][21] that is not the flight of abstraction, but consists in what is actual having itself not as something else, but as its own being and place [*sein eigenes Sein und Setzen*] in the other actuality with which it is bound together by the force of necessity. As existing for self, this release is called *ego* or *I;* as unfolded to its totality, it is *free spirit;* as feeling it is *love;* as enjoyment, pleasure, delight, gratification, or profit [*Genuss*], it is bliss [*Seligkeit*]" (*PM*, 285; 8:305–6). The cleavage left gaping on the sacrificial altar of Moriah is finally closed atop Golgotha.

---

21. *Befreiung* can also mean liberation, deliverance, exemption, immunity, and riddance. The closely related verb *befrieden* means to pacify and the noun *Befriedung* means pacification. *Befriedigen* is to satisfy, gratify, content, please, and *Befriedigung* is satisfaction or gratification.

Overleaf: Ed Epping, *Soundings*. Courtesy of the artist.

2

Cleaving

MARTIN HEIDEGGER

▬

Construction: Modern Nihilism

Standing at the threshold of the twentieth century, Nietzsche, one of the most prescient prophets of our time, records the words of a "madman":

> "Whither is God?" he cried: "I will tell you. *We have killed him—* you and I. All of us are his murderers. But how did we do this? How could we drink up the sea? Who gave us the sponge to wipe away the entire horizon? What were we doing when we unchained this earth from its sun? Whither is it moving now? Whither are we moving? Away from all suns? Is there still any up or down? Are we not wandering [*Irren wir nicht*] as through an infinite nothing? Do we not feel the breath of empty space? Has it not become colder? Is not night continually closing in on us? Do we hear nothing as yet of the noise of the gravediggers who are burying God? Do we smell nothing as yet of the divine decomposition? Gods, too, decompose. God is dead, God remains dead. And we have killed him." [1]

With the death of God, there is a loss of the center that for centuries had grounded thought, guided judgment, and organized experience. As the sun/son that had been the light of the world gradually is eclipsed, darkness falls and coldness spreads. No longer certain of either origin or destination, we are left to err through an endless middle that seems to lead nowhere. Nietzsche's madman anticipates the cold words of Wallace Stevens's "Snow Man."

> For the listener, who listens in the snow,
> And, nothing himself, beholds
> Nothing that is not there and the nothing that is. [2]

---

1. Friedrich Nietzsche, *The Gay Science,* trans. W. Kaufmann (New York: Random House, 1974), p. 181.
2. *The Collected Poems of Wallace Stevens* (New York: Knopf, 1981), p. 10.

If nothing remains but nothing, "Nihilism stands at the door." In the first line of his posthumously published collection of aphorisms, *The Will to Power*, Nietzsche asks: "Whence comes this uncanniest [*unheimlichste*] of all guests?"[3]

Heidegger is obsessed with Nietzsche's question. For Heidegger, modernity is *essentially* nihilistic. Throughout his philosophical career, Heidegger struggles to identify various sources and suggest possible remedies for the nihilism he believes threatens to engulf the world. The most poignant expression of this nihilism, according to Heidegger, is "the will to power," which Nietzsche correctly identifies as characteristic of modern man's thinking and acting. "When God and the gods are dead . . . and when the will to power is deliberately willed as the principle of all positing of the conditions governing whatever is, i.e., as the principle of value-positing, then dominion over the earth passes to the new willing of man determined by the will to power" (*QT*, 99).[4] As is evident in Hegel's speculative philosophy, the death of God is, in effect, the apotheosis of man.[5] In Heidegger's view, Hegel's System constitutes the closure of the modern epoch of philosophy that begins with Descartes. The subject of modern philosophy, Heidegger argues, is the *constructive* subject for whom "to will is to will-to-be-master" (*QT*, 77). The thoughts and deeds of this constructive subject make explicit certain implications of Western philosophy that have remained hidden for centuries.

3. Friedrich Nietzsche, *The Will to Power*, trans. W. Kaufmann (New York: Random House, 1968), p. 5.

4. Heidegger insists that Nietzsche's philosophy is symptomatic of the ills of modernity. While correctly recognizing "the will to power" as the culmination of "the ontotheological tradition," Nietzsche, Heidegger argues, fails to provide a way out of this philosophical, social, and cultural impasse. Heidegger goes so far as to insist that the nihilism inherent in Western philosophy in general and modern philosophy in particular comes to its fullest expression in Nietzsche's "will to power." This understanding of Nietzsche's relation to nihilism stands in marked contrast to recent French interpretations of Nietzsche as a precursor of the postmodern critique of modernity. For a useful collection of alternative readings of Nietzsche, see *The New Nietzsche: Contemporary Styles of Interpretation*, ed. D. Allison (New York: Delta, 1979).

5. Heidegger and most of those who follow him do not recognize the subtle ways in which Hegel anticipates their critiques of modernity. In a section of the *Phenomenology* entitled "Absolute Freedom and Terror," Hegel explains the way in which the principle of utility upon which Enlightenment thinking and acting are grounded leads to a thoroughly negative notion of freedom. "Universal freedom, therefore, can produce neither a positive work nor a deed; there is left for it only *negative* action; it is merely the *fury* of destruction" (*PS*, 359; 418). Hegel's "fury of destruction" closely resembles what Heidegger describes as "the fury of self-assertion that is resolutely self-reliant" (*PLT*, 116).

Exploring the task of thinking after the end of philosophy, Heidegger claims that "philosophy is metaphysics," and "metaphysics is Platonism" (*TB*, 55, 57). Ever since its beginnings in ancient Greece, Western philosophy has been preoccupied with the question of Being. Within the ontotheological tradition, which grows out of Platonic thought, the philosopher seeks to comprehend the *totality* of all that *is* by grasping the *whole* uniting every part. "The matter of thinking has been handed down to Western thinking under the name 'Being.' If we think of this matter just a bit more rigorously, if we take more heed of what is in contest in this matter, we see that *Being* means always and everywhere: the Being of *beings* [*Sein des Seienden*]" (*ID*, 61). The philosophical search for the Being of beings is the quest for the origin or primal "ground [*arche, aition*]" of all reality. "What characterizes metaphysical thinking which grounds the ground for beings is the fact that metaphysical thinking departs from what is present in its presence, and thus represents it in terms of its ground as something grounded" (*TB*, 56). Metaphysics, in other words, thinks the origin and ground of beings as Being, and thinks Being as presence. As original source, Being is *hypokeimenon*—the absolute *sub-iectum* that stands behind or underlies all that *is*.[6] From Plato's *eidos* and *idea* to Spinoza's substance, Being has been presented and re-presented in many different ways. By gathering the ontotheological tradition "into the most extreme possibilities," modern philosophy signals the end of Western metaphysics.

The distinguishing characteristic of modern philosophy is its tendency to think Being in terms of subjectivity. "The metaphysics of the modern age," Heidegger argues, "begins with and has its essence in the fact that it seeks the unconditionally indubitable, the certain and assured [*das Gewisse*], certainty. It is a matter, according to the words of Descartes, of *firmum et mansurum quid stabilire*, of bringing to a stand something that is firmly fixed and that remains. This standing established as object is adequate to the essence, ruling from of old, of what is as the constantly presencing, which everywhere already lies before (*hypokeimenon, subiectum*). Descartes also asks, as does Aristotle, concerning the *hypokeimenon*. Inasmuch as Descartes seeks this *subiectum* along the path previously marked out by metaphysics, he, thinking truth as certainty, finds the *ego cogito* to be that which presences as fixed and constant. In this way, the *ego sum* is transformed into the *subiectum*, i.e., the subject becomes self-consciousness. The subject-

---

6. Within this framework, to understand is to grasp that which stands under or lurks behind the immediate data of experience.

ness of the subject is determined out of this sureness, the certainty, of that consciousness" (*QT,* 82–83). With an inward turn of consciousness, Descartes constitutes the subject of modern philosophy. As I have suggested, this subject is essentially *creative* or *constructive.* When Being is interpreted in terms of subjectivity, "man becomes that being upon whom all that is, is grounded as regards the manner of its Being and its truth. Man becomes the relational center of that which is as such" (*QT,* 128). Heidegger is convinced that what Descartes initiates Hegel brings to completion. By totally transforming "substance into subject," Hegel expresses his conviction that the truth of Being is "absolute reflection" in which "Being is the absolute self-thinking of thinking" (*ID,* 43).

> Inasmuch as within modern metaphysics the Being of whatever is has determined itself as will and therewith as self-willing, and, moreover, self-willing is already inherently self-knowing-itself, therefore that which is, the *hypokeimenon,* the *subiectum,* comes to presence in the mode of self-knowing-itself. That which is (*subiectum*) presents itself [*präsentiert sich*], and indeed presents itself to itself, in the mode of the *ego cogito.* This self-presenting, this re-presenting, [*Re-präsentation*] (placing-before [*Vor-stellung*]), is the Being of that which is in being *qua subiectum.* Self-knowing-itself is transformed into subject purely and simply. In self-knowing-itself, all knowing and what is knowable for it gathers itself together. . . . The subjectivity of the subject is, as such, a gathering together, *co-agitatio (cogitatio), coscientia,* a gathering of knowing [*Ge-wissen*], consciousness (*conscience*). (*QT,* 88)[7]

Hegel's speculative System demonstrates that the modern philosophy of the subject is a philosophy of self-consciousness. In absolute knowledge, the substance present in all reality becomes conscious of itself through the act of representation in which the knowing subject

7. Heidegger interprets the work of his teacher, Husserl, as an extension of the modern philosophy of the subject. Commenting on Husserl's *Formal and Transcendental Logic,* Heidegger remarks: "'The principle of all principles' requires reduction to absolute subjectivity as the matter of philosophy. The transcendental reduction to absolute subjectivity gives and secures the possibility of grounding the objectivity of all objects (the Being of this being) in its valid structure and consistency, that is, in its constitution, in and through subjectivity. Thus transcendental subjectivity proves to be 'the sole absolute being'" (*TB,* 63). The recognition of the close relationship between Hegelian and Husserlian phenomenology has been especially important for the development of recent French thought. The two books most responsible for establishing this reading of phenomenology are Jean Hyppolite, *Logique et existence: Essai sur la logique de Hegel* (Paris: Presses Universitaires de France, 1953) and Jean-François Lyotard, *La Phénoménologie* (Paris: Presses Universitaires de France, 1976).

re-presents itself to itself by "placing" (*stellend*) itself "before" (*vor*) itself in the form of a known object. The representing subject sees *itself* reflected in the "object" (*Gegenstand*) that seems to stand over against (*gegen*) it. When the self (i.e., subject) discovers itself in an other (i.e., object), subjectivity appears to be the "essence" (*ousia*) of all reality. The self-consciousness of constructive subjectivity is the transparent appearance of essence (*parousia*) to itself. Commenting on the Introduction to the *Phenomenology of Spirit*, Heidegger explains the way in which Hegel's dialectic of self-consciousness extends and completes the Cartesian turn to the subject.

> The *essentia* of the *ens* in its *esse* is the presence. But presence has being in the mode of presentation. However, since the *ens*, the *subiectum*, has in the meantime become the *res cogitans*, the presentation [*Präsentation*] in itself is at the same time representing [*vorstellend*]—it is a representation [*Repräsentation*]. What Hegel has in mind with the word "experience" first makes clear what the *res cogitans*, as the *subiectum co-agitans*, is. Experience is the presentation of the absolute subject that has its being in the representation, and so absolves itself. Experience is the subjectivity of the absolute subject. Experience, the presentation of the absolute representation, is the *parousia* of the Absolute. Experience is the absoluteness of the Absolute, its appearance, in absolving experience, to itself. Everything depends on our thinking of experience . . . as the Being of consciousness. But Being means being present. Being present manifests itself as appearance. Appearance now is appearance of knowledge. Being, as that which experience *is*, implies representation (in the sense of making present) as the characteristic of experience. (*HCE*, 120–21; 185–86)

The subject makes itself present to itself by first positing itself in the form of a determinate object, and then reappropriating this object as its (i.e., the subject's) own self-objectification. "Objectifying, in representing, in setting before, delivers up the object to the *ego cogito*. In that delivering up, the *ego* proves to be that which underlies its own activity (the delivering up that sets before), i.e., proves to be the *subiectum*. The subject is subject for itself. The essence of consciousness is self-consciousness" (*QT*, 100). Through the subjection of the object, the subject exercises its mastery over everything other than itself. Nothing can be present to self-consciousness unless it is represented by the subject's *own* representative activity. "That which is, is no longer that which presences; it is rather that which, in representing, is first set over against, that which stands fixedly over against, which has the character of object. Representing is making-stand-over-against, an objectifying that goes forward and masters. In this way representing drives everything together into the unity of that which is thus given the character of object. Representing is *coagitatio*" (*QT,* 150).

In the activity of representation, the subject transforms the world into its own image. The world, therefore, is the picture of the creative subject. This "picture" is "the structured image that is the creature of man's producing, which represents and stands before" (*QT,* 134). When taken as a totality, the world picture constitutes an all-inclusive system. "Where the world becomes picture," Heidegger maintains, "the system, and not only in thinking, comes to dominance" (*QT,* 141). The smooth functioning of this system presupposes the integral relation of all its parts. That which does not fit or function properly must be controlled or excluded. In the course of the modern era, this all-powerful system becomes actual through the development of science and technology. Scientific calculation prepares the way for instrumental technology, which is designed to secure *human* existence by controlling or dominating nature. Within the "framework" (*Gestell*) of science and technology, natural and human resources appear to be nothing more than a "standing reserve" open to the manipulation of powerful agents. Nietzsche's "overman" is the precursor of modern scientific-technological man who, in his "will to power" or "struggle for mastery," sets for himself "the task of taking over dominion of the earth" (*QT,* 92, 96–97). In the absence of the creator God, "man exalts himself to the posture of lord of the earth. In this way the impression comes to prevail that everything man encounters exists only insofar as it is his *construct.* This illusion, in turn, gives rise to one final delusion: It seems as though man everywhere and always encounters only himself" (*QT,* 27; emphasis added). If man meets only himself, he never encounters otherness or difference.

With the full realization of the mastery of self-consciousness, "man has risen up into the I-ness of the *ego cogito.* Through this uprising, all that is, is transformed into object. That which is, as the objective, is swallowed up into the immanence of subjectivity. The horizon no longer emits light of itself" (*QT,* 107). When subjectivity "swallows up" objectivity, man drinks up the entire sea. The sponge that wipes away the horizon is nothing other than the self-conscious subject of modern philosophy. In his struggle to domesticate all forms of otherness by negating or repressing everything different from himself, modern man seeks the self-certainty and security for which Descartes longed and that Hegel believed had been clearly revealed in the absolute knowledge of his speculative System. Heidegger summarizes his assessment of "the modern epoch of the subject" by returning to the words of Nietzsche's madman.

> By means of the three key images (sun, horizon, and sea), which are for thinking presumably something other than images, the three questions elucidate what is meant by the event of the killing of God. The killing means the act of doing away with the supra-sensory world that *is* in itself—an act accomplished through man. It speaks of the event wherein that which is as such does not simply come to nothing, but does indeed become different in its Being. But above all, in this event man also becomes different. He becomes the one who does away with that which is, in the sense of that which *is* in itself. The uprising of man into subjectivity transforms that which is into an object. But that which is objective is that which is brought to a stand through representing. The doing away with that which *is* in itself, i.e., the killing of God, is accomplished in the making secure of the constant reserve by means of which man makes secure for himself material, bodily, psychic, and spiritual resources, and this for the sake of his own security, which wills dominion over whatever is—as the potentially objective—in order to correspond to the Being of whatever is, to the will to power. (*QT*, 107)

The quest for certainty and security, however, yields unexpected results. By attempting to domesticate (*heimisch machen*) the uncanny (*unheimlich*) guest that Nietzsche names "nihilism," modern man falls prey to an even more terrifying nihilism. Midday is also midnight. "The great noon" of self-consciousness harbors unheard-of darkness (*QT*, 107). The *parousia* of the absolute subject points toward an all-encompassing holocaust—nuclear and otherwise. How, asks Heidegger, can this apocalyptic end be avoided, averted . . . delayed, deferred?

Reveilation: Delivery of Difference

Is it possible to fathom the darkness exposed in the midst of the high noon of modernity? "Everyday opinion," Heidegger avers, "sees in the shadow only the lack of light, if not light's complete denial. In truth, however, the shadow is a manifest, though impenetrable, testimony to the concealed emitting of light. In keeping with this concept of shadow, we experience the incalculable as that which, withdrawn from representation, is nevertheless manifest in whatever is, pointing to Being, which remains concealed" (*QT*, 154). In order to think the obscurity of the shadow as such, it is necessary to "step back" from the Western ontotheological tradition and ask "what has always remained unasked throughout this history of thinking" (*ID*, 50). This "unthought" is, for Heidegger, "what is most worthy of thinking."

The unthought that Heidegger attempts to think "conceals itself precisely where philosophy has brought its matter to absolute knowledge and to ultimate evidence." After arguing that Western philosophy culminates in Hegel's System and its extension in Husserl's phenomenology, Heidegger proceeds to maintain that "Hegel, as little as Husserl, as little as all metaphysics, does not ask about Being as Being, that is, does not raise the question how there can be presence as such" (*TB*, 64, 70). As I have stressed, different forms of metaphysics are united in the effort to think the *ground* (*arche*) of what *is* in terms of *presence*. From Heidegger's point of view, such reflection does not go far enough. The metaphysician does not attempt to uncover the origin of presence. To think what philosophy leaves unthought,[8] it is necessary to think in a more "*originary*" way. Truly original thinking "strives to reach back into the essential ground from which thought concerning the truth of Being emerges. By initiating another inquiry, this thinking is already removed from the 'ontology' of metaphysics. . . . 'Ontology' itself, however, whether transcendental or precritical, is subject to criticism, not because it thinks the Being of beings and thereby reduces Being to a concept, but because it does not think the truth of Being and so fails to recognize that there is a thinking more rigorous than the conceptual."[9] This more rigorous form of thinking cannot be described in terms of the traditional binary opposites that define conceptual reflection. It is neither theoretical nor practical, metaphysical nor scientific, rational nor irrational. In contrast to the utilitarian calculations of scientific-technological man, "such thinking has no result. It has no effect."[10] Its "value" is (the) incalculable. The "nonrepresentational thinking" that seeks to recover what metaphysics excludes and philosophy represses "directs our thinking to the region that the key words of metaphysics—Being and beings, the ground and what is grounded—are no longer adequate to utter" (*ID*, 71). While philosophy's other always slips through the structure imposed by conceptual reflection, the unthought can only be evoked

8. It is important to recall that Heidegger is convinced that all Western philosophy is metaphysical: "Philosophy is metaphysics" (*TB*, 55).

9. Martin Heidegger, "Letter on Humanism," *Basic Writings*, trans. and ed. D. Krell (New York: Harper and Row, 1977), p. 235.

10. Ibid., p. 236.

through the language of philosophy itself. The postphilosophical thinker must strategically use language *against* language. "In order to make the attempt of thinking recognizable and at the same time understandable for existing philosophy, it could at first be expressed only within the horizon of that existing philosophy and its use of current terms." [11]

Thinking, *sensu strictissimo,* has no object; nor is it merely subjective. "The matter of thinking," Heidegger insists, "is difference *as* difference" (*Differenz* als *Differenz; ID,* 47). Neither subject nor object, difference is the condition of the possibility of all subjectivity and objectivity. To think "difference *as* difference" is, in the final analysis, to think "Being as difference" (*ID,* 64). By attempting to think the Being of beings in terms of the grounding presence of Being itself, traditional metaphysics leaves unthought the intermediate *difference* in and through which both Being and beings originate. Difference is "the between" (*das Zwischen*) that is "the essential origin" (*Wesensherkunft; ID,* 63, 65) of all identity and every difference. [12] In other words, difference *delivers* the differences that constitute identity. Irreducible to the opposites it sustains, "the deliverance [*Austrag*] [13] of that which grounds and that which is grounded, as such, not only holds the two apart, it holds them together" (*ID,* 68). The differential "between" that simultaneously joins and separates ground and grounded is the irreducible mean that founds the world and everything in it. In this way, difference originates by differentiating. "*Differenz*" is, therefore, "*Unter-schied.*" In one of his richest explorations of the notion of difference, Heidegger writes:

> For world and things do not subsist alongside one another. They penetrate each other. Hence the two traverse a mean [*Mitte*]. In it, they are at one. Thus at one, they are intimate [*innig*]. The mean of the two is inwardness [*Innigkeit*]. In our language, the mean of the two is called the between [*das Zwischen*]. The Latin language used *inter.* The corresponding German term is *unter.* The intimacy or inwardness of world and thing is not a fusion. Intimacy

11. Ibid., p. 235.

12. Heidegger uses *Herkunft* rather than *Ursprung* in this context. In addition to origin or descent, *Herkunft* also means coming and arrival. The reasons for Heidegger's choice of this word will become clearer after we have examined his notion of "nearness" or "proximity." By way of anticipation, it is important to realize that while the differential origin approaches, it never totally or finally arrives.

13. Heidegger's use of *Austrag* is both rich and bewildering. *Austrag* can mean issue, decision, arbitration, product, or end. In the English translation, *Austrag* is misleadingly rendered "perdurance." The verbal form *austragen* (deliver, carry [letters], or distribute) provides a more reliable clue to the nuances of the term.

obtains only where the intimate—world and thing—divides itself cleanly and remains separated [*rein sich scheidet und geschieden bleibt*]. In the midst [*Mitte*] of the two, in the between of world and thing, in the *inter,* division prevails: *dif-ference* [*Unter-Schied*]. The intimacy of world and thing is present in the boundary [*Schied:* border, limit, divide; sheath, vagina] of the between; it is present in the dif-ference. The word difference is now removed from its usual and customary usage. What it now names is not a species concept for various kinds of differences. It exists only as this single difference. It is unique. Of itself, it holds apart the mean in and through which the world and things are at one with each other. The intimacy of the difference is the unifying element of the *diaphora,* the carrying out that carries through. The dif-ference carries out world in its worlding, carries out things in their thinging. Thus carrying them out, it carries them toward one another. The dif-ference does not mediate after the fact by binding together world and things through a mean added on to them. Being the mean, it first determines world and things in their presence, i.e., in their being toward one another, whose unity it carries out. (*PLT,* 202)

Heidegger's *Mitte* is not the Hegelian mean [*Mitte*] that mediates identity and difference by securing the *identity* of identity and difference. The delivery *of* difference is also the delivery *from* every form of all-inclusive identity that negates, reduces, absorbs, or swallows up otherness. As "the threshold" of identity and difference, *dif-ference* is neither identical nor different. This distinctive *Unter-Schied* is what Heidegger labels "the same [*das Selbe*]." "The identical always moves toward the absence of difference, so that everything may be reduced to a common denominator. The same, by contrast, is the belonging together of what differs, through a gathering by way of the difference. We can say 'the same' only if we think difference" (*PLT,* 218).[14] The "sameness" (*Selbigkeit*) with which Heidegger tries to pass beyond Western philosophy "approaches [*herkommt*] from further back than the kind of identity defined by metaphysics in terms of Being as a characteristic of Being" (*ID,* 28). By taking a "step back" (*Schritt zurück*) from the ontotheological tradition, Heidegger attempts "to return to" (*zurückgehen*) that which is "prior to thought."[15]

14. Elsewhere Heidegger writes: "But the same [*das Selbe*] is not merely the identical [*das Gleiche*]. In the merely identical, the difference [*Verschiedenheit*] disappears. In the same, difference appears, and appears all the more pressingly, the more resolutely thinking is concerned with the same matter in the same way" (*ID,* 45).

15. Martin Heidegger, *Discourse on Thinking,* trans. J. M. Anderson and E. H. Freund (New York: Harper and Row, 1966), p. 83.

This irreducible "before," which is never present as such, marks the elusive time-space where "the event of appropriation [*das Ereignis*]" occurs. "Appropriation neither *is*, nor *is* appropriation *there*" (*TB*, 24). To ask what appropriation *is*, is to attempt to define appropriation in terms of Being, whereas for Heidegger, Being must be understood in terms of the event of appropriation. Since it "is" not, or "is not there," appropriation "is, so to speak, a '*neutrale tantum*'" (*TB*, 43). Neither masculine nor feminine, the event of appropriation is the "neuter" *it* that lies *between* all differences—sexual and otherwise.[16] By "oscillating within itself" (*in sich schwingend*), this neutral *Es* gives or sends Being as well as beings. "To think Being itself explicitly requires us to relinquish Being as the ground of beings in favor of the giving that prevails concealed in unconcealment, that is, in favor of the It gives [*Es gibt*]. As the gift [*Gabe*] of this It gives, Being belongs to giving. As a gift, Being is not expelled from giving [*Geben*]. Being, presencing is transmuted. As allowing-to-presence, it belongs to unconcealing; as the gift of unconcealing it is retained in the giving. Being *is* not. There is, It gives Being as the unconcealing; as the gift of unconcealing it is retained in the giving. Being *is* not. There is, It gives Being as the unconcealing of presencing" (*TB*, 6; 5–6).

That which sends Being and beings is not completely *revealed* in the missionary act. The "It" that gives "holds back" or "withdraws" in its very donation. Though never properly present, the presencing of *Es gibt,* which establishes all presence and constitutes every present, is not precisely absent. The event of "sending" or "giving" Being and beings escapes the simple alternative of presence and absence. The interplay of presence and absence issues in the inseparability of concealment and unconcealment. In different terms, the dis-closure of the origin of presence inevitably entails a certain "dissemblance" (*Verstellung*).[17] As a result of this dissemblance, the origin of presence harbors a "reservoir of the not-yet-uncovered, the un-uncovered in the sense of concealment" (*PLT*, 60). Always withdrawing in its very approach, "It" (*Es*) *remains* "unfathomable." The region of this remainder is the "abyss" (*Abgrund*) opened by oblivion.

16. In the following chapters, the importance of the notion of neutrality will become evident.

17. *Verstellung,* which recalls *Vorstellung,* carries a broad range of associations. *Verstellen* is to put one thing in the place of another, shift, remove, misplace, bar, obstruct; feign, sham, counterfeit. Accordingly, *Verstellung* can also mean disguise, dissimulation, or hypocrisy. *Verstellen* and *Verstellung* play a central role in Freud's interpretation of dreamwork. In what follows, it will become apparent that in Heidegger's analysis there is an important relationship between *Verstellung* and the inevitable oblivion that forever faults consciousness.

Since presence and absence, as well as concealment and unconcealment are inseparable, the revelation of difference is always at the same time its reveilation. In the delivery of Being and beings, difference as such withdraws, thereby reveiling itself. Stressing his differences with Hegel, Heidegger writes:

> In contrast to Hegel, this is not a traditional problem, already posed, but what has always remained unasked throughout the history of thinking. We speak of it, tentatively and unavoidably, in the language of tradition. We speak of the *difference* between Being and beings. The step back goes from what is unthought, from the difference as such, into what gives us thought [*das Zu-Denkende*]. That is the *oblivion* [*Vergessenheit*] of the difference. The oblivion here to be thought is the veiling [*Verhüllung*] of the difference as such, thought in terms of *lēthē* (concealment); this veiling has in turn withdrawn itself from the beginning. The oblivion belongs to the difference because the difference belongs to the oblivion. The oblivion does not happen to the difference only afterward, in consequence of the forgetfulness of human thinking.(*ID*, 50–51)

Since difference itself is never present, it cannot be re-presented. This non-representable origin gives rise to conceptual and representational thought only insofar as it is forgotten, excluded, or repressed. As the non-representable "before," which is always already "prior to thought," difference constitutes an "essential past" that can never be present-ed. "The criterion of what has not been thought does not lead to the inclusion of previous thought within a still higher development and systematization that surpass it. Rather, the criterion demands that traditional thinking be set free into its essential past that is still preserved [*sein noch aufgespartes Gewesenes*]. This essential past prevails throughout the tradition in an originary way, is always in being in advance of it, and yet is never expressly thought in its own right and as the originary" (*ID*, 48–49). The essential past that is repressed by conceptual reflection repeatedly returns to dislocate self-consciousness by disrupting all presence and every present. In this way, difference functions as something like an irreducible unconscious that simultaneously gives rise to and escapes consciousness. Ever reveiling itself, difference is an "excess" (*Übermass*) that can never be contained, controlled, or mastered. Consciousness, therefore, is always incomplete, and transparent self-consciousness forever impossible. Since forgetfulness is not accidental, the knowing subject can never totally "swallow up" the "reservoir" of forgetfulness [*lēthē*].

Neither absent nor present, the repressed is, in Heidegger's terms, "proximate" or "near" (*nahe*). "The proximate" (*die Nähe*) is what is nearest yet farthest. Closer than anything present and farther than anything absent, the near cannot be re-presented. "We are too quick to believe that the mystery of what is to be thought always lies distant and deeply hidden under a hardly penetrable layer of strangeness. On the contrary, it has its essential abode in what is nearby, which approaches what is coming into presence and preserves what has drawn near. The presencing of the near is too close for our customary mode of representational thought—which exhausts itself in securing what is present—to experience the governance of the near, and without preparation to think it adequately. Presumably, the mystery that beckons in what is to be thought is nothing other than essentially what we have attempted to suggest in the name the 'lighting'" (*EGT*, 121). This "lighting" displays the shadow that "is a manifest, though impenetrable, testimony to the concealed emitting of light. In keeping with the concept of shadow, we experience the incalculable as that which, withdrawn from representation, is nevertheless manifest in whatever is, pointing to Being, which remains concealed." To walk in the shadow of this light, to enter this "obscurity," one "must first learn to exist in the nameless." [18] The neuter "It" of *Es gibt* remains anonymous. "The area of the meaning meant by the It extends from the irrelevant to the demonic." And beyond—to the holy. The mystery of the holy, however, "cannot be mediated cognitively, not even in terms of questions, but must be experienced" (*TB*, 18, 26). The possibility of this experience opens with the work of art.

Opening: Art Works

Art opens or reopens the cleavage that philosophy struggles to close. "Cleavage" is a polyvalent term that carries contrasting, even contradictory, meanings. "To cleave" (from the Greek *glyph*, to cut with a knife or carve, and the Latin, *glubere*, to peel [which will return unexpectedly in a certain pealing]) means to part or divide by a cutting blow, to split, to intersect, to fissure, to separate. "Cleavage" is "the action of cleaving or splitting crystals and certain rocks along their lines of natural fissure; or the state of being so cleft." A "cleavage" is "the fissile structure in certain rocks," or "the direction in which a

18. "Letter on Humanism," p. 199.

crystal or rock may be split." "Cleavage" can also refer to "the separation between a woman's breasts." In French, breast is *sein,* which, of course, is spelled the same as the German word for being. Cleavage thus suggests a separation of *sein* or a split in *S-ein.* The cutting edge of "cleave" is carried over in the expression "cleave a path in the forest." Heidegger calls paths cut in woodland *Holzwege*—"woodpaths' or "timber tracks" (*Spuren*). *Spur* designates a trace, track, mark, sign, vestige, clue, gutter, groove, wake, bit, scrap. If one follows this "bit or scrap" (Danish: *Smule,* as in *Philosophiske Smuler*) from German to Danish, *Spur* becomes *spor.* In addition to train track, *spor* means mark and trail. With a supplementary *e,* the Danish *spor* becomes the English "spore," "an asexual [i.e., neither masculine nor feminine], usually single-celled reproductive organ characteristic of nonflowering plants such as fungi, mosses, or ferns." It is not clear where the different traces of *Holzwege* lead. After all, "to be 'on a woodpath' is a popular German expression meaning to be on the wrong track or in a *cul-de-sac:* to be confused and lost. Hence the French translators of Heidegger's *Holzwege* [which includes "The Origin of the Work of Art"] call it *Chemins qui mènent à nulle part,* 'ways that lead nowhere.' This is not quite right: woodpaths always lead somewhere—but where they lead cannot be predicted or controlled. They force us to plunge into unknown territory and often to retrace our steps." [19] To realize the multiple directions charted in Heidegger's *Holzwege,* it is necessary to note a different rhythm of "cleave." "Cleave" means not only divide, separate, split, and fissure, but also adhere, stick, and cling. Cleaving, therefore, simultaneously divides and joins. This joint is the hinge upon which "The Origin of the Work of Art" swings.

The site of the origin of the work of art is the temple. But what is a "temple"? "Temple" derives from the Latin *templum,* which, like *tempus* (time), comes from the Greek *temnos.* While *temnō* means "cut," *temenos* designates that which is "cut off". Accordingly, *templum* is a section, a part cut off. [20] By extension, *templum* is "a space in the sky or on the earth marked out by the augur for the purpose of taking auspices; a consecrated piece of ground, especially a sanctuary or asylum; a place dedicated to a particular deity, a shrine." [21] While

19. David F. Krell, "General Introduction: 'The Question of Being,'" *Basic Writings,* p. 34.

20. In a similar way, *tempus* means a division, section. In relation to time, *tempus* is a portion of time or a period of time.

21. *Cassell's Latin Dictionary* (New York: Macmillan, 1968).

the site of the origin of the work of art is the temple, the site of the temple is a cleavage—"a tear" (*Riss;* cf. *zerrissen* and *Zerrissenheit*) that fissures what seemed to be the most solid foundation by faulting the rock of ages.

Exploring the origin of the work of art in *Holzwege,* Heidegger explains: "A construction [*Bauwerk*], a Greek temple, images nothing. It simply stands in the midst of a rock-cleft valley [*zer-klüft-eten Felsentales*]" (*PLT,* 41). The temple images nothing by holding open the differential *interval* of the between.

> Standing there, the construction rests on rocky ground. This resting of the work draws up out of the rock the obscurity of the rock's monstrous yet spontaneous support. Standing there, the construction holds its ground against the storm raging above it and so makes the storm itself manifest in its violence. The luster and gleam of the stone, though itself apparently glowing by grace of the sun, yet first bring to light the light of the day, the breadth of the sky, the darkness of the night. The secure tower makes visible the invisible space of air. The steadfastness [*das Unerschütterte; unerschütterlich:* firm as a rock] of the work contrasts with the surge of the surf, and its own repose brings out the raging of the sea. Tree and grass, eagle and bull, snake and cricket first enter into their distinctive forms and thus come to appear as what they are (*PLT,* 42).[22]

Neither eagle nor bull, tree nor grass, snake nor cricket is original, for each arises in and through the work of art. The origin *of* art is an "original" cleavage that makes possible all such paired opposites. The work of art works by opening this opening.[23] The cleavage of artwork is traced by the altar in the midst of the temple.

Heidegger opens his essay, "The Origin of the Work of Art," by asking: "Where and how does art occur?" "Art," he proceeds to argue,

22. Heidegger's temple recalls the erection of Nietzsche's bull that Derrida examines in *Spurs.* "Here I stand in the mist of the surging of the breakers [this is an untranslatable play on words: *Hier stehe ich inmitten des Brandes der Brandung. Brandung* is related to the conflagration expressed in *Brand,* which itself also signifies the mark left by a burning branding iron. It is the seething surf, the waves rolling back over themselves as they crash against the rocky shoreline or break on the reefs, the cliffs, the *éperons,*] whose white flames fork up to my feet [so I too am an *éperon*];—from all sides there is howling, threatening, crying, and screaming at me, while in the lowest depths, the old earth shaker sings his aria [*seine Arie singt,* beware, Ariane is not far away] hollow like a roaring bull; he beats such an earth shaker's measure to it, that even the hearts of these demons of the rocks tremble at the sound" (*S,* 43, 45).

23. As these remarks indicate, the "work" (*Werk*) in "The Origin of the Work of Art" (*Kunstwerkes*) must be understood as both a noun and a verb.

"breaks open an open place" (*PLT,* 17, 72). In the space and time of this opening, revelation and reveilation repeatedly intersect in a play of differences that constitutes "the essential strife" of "world," i.e., "the self-disclosing openness" (*sich öffende Offenheit*) and "earth," i.e., "the essentially self-secluding" (*wesenhaft Sichverschliessende*) (*PLT,* 47–48). The artwork works by setting up the world as the region within which Being and beings emerge, and setting forth the earth as the sheltering domain where they withdraw. The alternating strife of world and earth forms the "tear" (*Riss*) that lies in the midst of Being and beings.

> But as a world opens itself, the earth comes to rise up [*zum Ragen:* to tower]. It stands forth as that which bears all, as that which is sheltered in its own law and always self-secluding. World demands its decisiveness [*Entschiedenheit*][24] and its measure and lets beings extend into the open of their paths. Earth, bearing and jutting strives to keep itself closed and to entrust everything to its law. The strife is not a tear [*Riss*] as the gaping crack [*Aufreissen*] of a pure cleft [*Kluft*], but the strife is the intimacy [*Innigkeit*] with which combatants belong to each other. This tear pulls the opponents together in the origin [*Herkunft*] of their unity by virtue of their common ground. It is a basic design [*Grundriss*], an outline sketch [*Aufriss*], that draws the basic features of the rise of the lighting of beings. This tear does not let the opponents burst apart; it brings the opposition of measure and boundary [*Grenze*] into their common outline [*Umriss*]. (*PLT,* 63)

The strife of the tear captures the duplicity of cleaving. To cleave, I have stressed, is both to separate, divide, or split, and to adhere, cling, or stick. Tearing alternates between two rhythms—one centrifugal, the other centripetal. By holding open this alternating difference, the origin of the work of art simultaneously joins and separates. This separation that joins and joining that separates transforms the tear of cleaving into the tear of pain.

> But what is pain? Pain tears or rends [*reisst*]. It is the tear or rift [*Riss*]. But it does not tear apart into dispersive fragments. Pain indeed tears asunder, it separates [*scheidet*], yet in such a way that it at the same time draws everything together to itself. Its rending, as a separating that gathers, is at the same time that drawing [*Ziehen*], which, like the pre-drawing [*Vorriss*] and sketch [*Aufriss*], draws and joins together what is held apart in separation.

24. Compare *Entscheid,* which includes *Scheide:* boundary, border, limit, divide, sheath, vagina; and *scheiden:* to separate, part, depart. See also, *schneiden:* to cut, carve, engrave; *Schneide:* edge, cutting edge.

Pain is the jointing [*Fügende*] in the tearing/rending that divides and gathers [*schneidend-sammelnden Reissen*]. Pain is the joining or articulation of the rift. The joining is the threshold. It delivers the between [*Zwischen*], the mean [*Mitte*] of the two that are separated in it. Pain articulates the rift of the difference. Pain is dif-ference [*Unter-schied*] itself.

Pain has turned the threshold to stone.   (*PLT,* 204)

While Hegel maintains that when love is truly conceived, "the wounds of spirit heal and leave no scars," Heidegger insists that the rending of difference can never be totally healed. The stone that Hegel tries to bring to life remains—always remains for Heidegger.[25] What Hegel struggles to close, Heidegger tries to open and reopen. This opening is the work of art. So understood, the work of art is a drawing that recalls Rembrandt's "sketch" (*Auf-riss*) of Abraham who, listening to the strange voice of an Other, stands at the sacrificial altar with knife drawn, ready to tear asunder his only beloved son. For Heidegger, truth occurs in such (a) drawing.

Truth, according to Heidegger, is not *certitudo* or *adequatio;* nor is it *mimesis.* Truth is *aletheia. A-letheia* is the un-concealment that arises through un-forgetting. The history of Western metaphysics, I have noted, is inseparably bound up with oblivion. Representational and conceptual thought originate by forgetting their origin. To think what philosophy represses, it is necessary to return to this origin through an act of un-forgetting. *A-letheia,* however, is not simply identical with recollection or remembering. The oblivion that obsesses Heidegger is not an accident that can be avoided. To the contrary, the inevitability of oblivion reflects the necessity of concealment in all disclosure. To un-forget the origin is to remember *that* one has forgotten and to recognize that such forgetting is inescapable. Since the origin remains an inaccessible "abyss," remembering does not issue in the total recollection necessary for transparent self-consciousness. Remembering, therefore, can no more re-member than recollection can re-collect. The *Riss* forever remains to rend the remembering subject. The truth "known" in the un-forgetting of *a-letheia* is a truth that always carries a shadow in the midst of its lighting. "Truth occurs precisely as itself insofar as the concealing denial, as refusal, provides the constant source of all clearing or lighting, and yet, as dissem-

25. In the discussion of *Glas* in chapter 9, I will consider the relationship between the stone threshold and the tombstone. The remaining stone marks the site of remains that cannot be taken up into life. The recognition of this remainder and these remains involves a "being toward death" in which one does not attempt to escape mortality through the expectation of eternal life.

bling, it metes out to all clearing, the unavoidable edge of diversion and confusion [*Beirrung*].[26] Concealing denial is intended to denote that opposition in the essence of truth which persists between clearing or lighting and concealing. It is the opposition of the original or primal strife [*ursprünglichen Streites*]. The essence of truth is, in itself, the original or primal strife in which that open mean [*Mitte*] is sought within which what is [*das Seiende*], stands, and from which it sets itself back into itself" (*PLT,* 55). As the original strife of unconcealment and concealment, or light and darkness, truth is inseparable from error.

> Being sets [beings] adrift in errancy [*Irre*]. Beings come to pass in that errancy by which they circumvent Being and establish the realm of error [*Irrtum*] (in the sense of a prince's realm or the realm of poetry). Error is the space in which history unfolds. In error, what happens in history bypasses what is like Being. Therefore, whatever unfolds historically is necessarily misinterpreted. During the course of this misinterpretation, destiny awaits what will become of its seed. It brings those whom it concerns to the possibilities of the fateful and fatal. Man's destiny gropes toward its fate. Man's inability to see himself corresponds to the self-concealing of the lighting of Being. Without errancy there would be no connection from destiny to destiny: there would be no history. (*EGT,* 26; 337)

Having (partly) awakened from the dream of Western ontotheology, Heidegger realizes that erring is endless. The prodigal son does not come home again—the seed once sown does not return to the father. Since the wound never heals and the tear never mends, the "kindgom of ends" never arrives; it is forever delayed.

The ceaseless deferral of the end reflects the infinite inaccessibility of the beginning (and vice versa). In attempting to think what philosophy leaves unthought, Heidegger discovers a difference that cannot be reduced to identity. This difference is an *other* that can never be named properly.

> And yet—beyond what is, not away from it but before it, there is an other [*ein Anderes*] that occurs. In the midst of beings as a whole, there is an open place. There is a clearing, a lighting. Thought of in relation to what is, to beings, this clearing is in a greater degree than are beings. This open center, therefore, is not surrounded by what is; rather, the lighting middle itself encircles all that is, like the nothing [*Nichts*] we hardly know. (*PLT,* 53)

26. While *beirren* can be translated mislead, confuse, or lead astray, the adjective *irre* means in error, wrong, astray, wandering, oscillating, doubtful, and insane.

This unnameable other is not only "obscure" and "mysterious;" "It" (*Es*) is "monstrous" (*ungeheuer:* huge, colossal atrocious, frightful, shocking; *geheuer:* uncanny, haunting; *PLT,* 68).

Poetry: Tolling Traces:

How can the unnameable be named—the unspeakable spoken? What "eye" "sees" difference as difference? What "ear" "hears" the other? What thought thinks *das Ungeheuer* that philosophy does not, indeed, cannot think? The response Heidegger ventures to such questions is: "*poetry.*" *Poiesis* discloses "how there can be presence as such." For Heidegger, "there is presence only when opening is dominant. Opening is named with *aletheia,* unconcealment, but not thought as such" (*TB,* 70). To think unconcealment, *aletheia* must be thought as *poiesis.* Instead of a specific artistic form, the poetry that allows opening to occur designates art itself.[27] "*All art,* as the letting happen of the advent of the truth of what is, is, as such, *in essence poetry* [*Dichtung*]. The essence of art, on which both the art work and the artist depend, is the setting-itself-into-work of truth. It is due to the poetic essence of art that, in the midst of what is, art breaks open an open place, in whose openness everything is other [*anders*] than usual" (*PLT,* 72; 59). So understood, poetry is the act of articulation that holds open the mean differentiating everything that is. The expression that renders existence articulate is "saying" (*Sagen*). "Poetry," Heidegger explains, "is the saying of the unconcealedness of what is. Actual language at any given moment is the happening of this saying, in which a people's world arises historically and the earth is preserved as that which remains closed. Saying sketchily [*das entwerfende Sagen*][28] is saying which, in the preparation of the sayable, simultaneously brings the unsayable as such into the world" (*PLT,* 74). Saying

27. This exceedingly broad definition of poetry does not prevent Heidegger from giving priority to poetry in the strict sense of the word. He writes: "Nevertheless, the linguistic work [*Sprachwerk*], the poem in the narrower sense, has a privileged position in the domain of the arts" (*PLT,* 73).

28. It is very difficult to know how to translate *das entwerfende Sagen* in this context. *Entwerfen* can mean sketch, trace out, draft, project, frame, outline, or plan. *Werfen* means to throw, toss, or fling. In *Being and Time,* Heidegger presents detailed analyses of the "throwness" of *Dasein.* When the English translator renders *das entwerfende Sagen* as "Projective saying," the passivity essential to Heidegger's notion of throwness is lost. By translating this phrase "saying sketchily," I have attempted to stress the way in which saying implies that which withdraws and conceals itself. "Sketchily" also has the virtue of suggesting an association with the various forms of *Riss* (e.g., *Aufriss, Vorriss, Umriss*) that I have already noted.

can no more be reduced to specific speech acts than poetry can be exhausted by particular poems. By analyzing poetry in terms of saying, Heidegger attempts to establish the linguisticality of Being itself.

While poetry is intrinsically linguistic, language is fundamentally poetic. Heidegger goes so far as to insist that "Language [*Sprache*] itself is essentially poetry" (*PLT,* 74). *Poiesis* means to make or create. Like Yahweh whose creative word brings form to formlessness by separating the primal waters, language is poetic insofar as it creates through an act of separation. Unlike the Old Testament narrative, however, the division of opposites that bestows determinate identity is not, according to Heidegger, secondary to a more original unity, but is an "*original* or *primal* strife." The creative origin of language is the "*temple*" of Being.

> Being, as itself, spans its own precinct, which is cut off (*temnein, tempus*) by Being being in the word. Language is the precinct (*templum*), that is, the house of Being. The essence of language does not exhaust itself in meaning or signifying [*Bedeuten*], nor is it merely something that has the character of sign or cipher. It is because language is the house of Being, that we reach what is by constantly going through this house. When we go to the well, when we go through the woods, we are always already going through the word "well," through the word "woods," even if we do not speak the words and do not think of anything relating to language. (*PLT,* 132)

Language, in this context, is not a means of communication by which decipherable messages are sent and received. Rather, language articulates the opening—the between—that makes possible all "comm-*uni*-cation" (*communicare:* to make common). In this way, language is always antecedent to and escapes from the communicative acts it enables to transpire. As the temple of Being, language exhibits the contrasting rhythms characteristic of all cleaving. The *poiesis* of language both joins and separates.

> The *Hen Panta* lets lie together before us in one presencing things that are usually separated from, and opposed to, one another, such as day and night, winter and summer, peace and war, waking and sleeping, Dionysos and Hades. Such opposites, borne along the farthest distance between presence and absence, *diapheromenon,* let the Laying that gathers lie before us in its full bearing. Its laying is itself that which carries things along by bearing them out. The *Logos* is itself a carrying out. (*EGT,* 71; 221)

The mean that joins extremes is the Logos. The Logos, in turn, designates language in its capacity to gather, assemble, and unify. Heidegger points out that "here our reflections reach a provocative juncture. Being becomes present as Logos in the sense of ground, of allowing to let lie before us. The same Logos, as the gathering of what unifies, is the *Hen*. This *Hen,* however, is twofold [*zweifältig*]" (*ID,* 69).

The irreducible duplicity[29] of language implies a rhythm that counters the unifying force of the Logos. While language holds together opposites usually set apart, it also holds apart the opposites it brings together. In this way, language eternally returns to difference—the difference that is the origin of the work of art and the temple of everything that is.

> Language speaks [*Die Sprache spricht*]. It speaks by bidding the bidden, thing-world and world-thing, to come to the between of dif-ference [*Zwischen des Unter-Schiedes*]. What is so bidden is commanded to arrive from out of the dif-ference into the dif-ference. Here we are thinking of the old sense of command, which we recognize still in the phrase, "Commit thy way unto the Lord." In this way, the bidding of language commits the bidden thus to the bidding of the dif-ference. The dif-ference lets the thinging of the thing rest in the world. The dif-ference expropriates the repose of the fourfold.[30] Such expropriation does not diminish the thing. Only so is the thing exalted into its own, so that it stays [*verweilt*] world. To keep in repose is to still. The dif-ference stills the thing, as thing, into the world. (*PLT,* 206)[31]

I have already observed that the threshold between world ("self-disclosing openness") and earth ("the essentially self-secluding") is

29. The doubleness of language makes doubt inescapable and Cartesian certainty impossible. This close relationship between duplicity and doubt is suggested by the word *Zwei-fel:* doubt, uncertainty, hesitation, misgiving, suspicion. As a result of unavoidable inward division, the knowing subject is always of at least *two* minds about everything.

30. Throughout this essay, Heidegger probes the interplay of differences in and through which everything arises and passes away in terms of the fourfold relationship of "sky, earth, mortals, and divinities."

31. The two rhythms of language that Heidegger describes recall the dialectic of identity and difference in Hegel's concept. There is, however, a significant *difference.* Whereas Hegel always attempts to return difference to identity, Heidegger regards the relation of opposites as a ceaseless oscillation of differences. Nonetheless, there are points at which Heidegger's language privileges gathering and joining over dispersing and separating, thereby extending the ontotheological tradition whose end he nevertheless proclaims.

the site at which Being and beings, i.e., determinate things, both emerge and withdraw. Heidegger maintains that this productive mean must be understood in terms of language. As the elusive margin of unconcealment and concealment, the poetic language of dif-ference speaks the unspeakable that allows all saying to occur. In speaking the unspeakable, "Language speaks as the tolling of stillness" (*Die Sprache spricht als das Geläut der Stille; PLT,* 207).

The endless alter-nation of language enacts a play of differences that cannot be stilled. This oscillation is, nonetheless, a stillness that promises rest without end. "As the stilling of stillness, rest [*Ruhe:* silence], thought strictly, is always more in motion and agitated than any agitation" (*PLT,* 207). At the threshold of language, movement and rest, saying and silence meet. To hear the stillness of this silence, one must do nothing. But how can one *do* nothing? How can nothing *be*—or *be done?* To do nothing, Heidegger responds, one must wait. More precisely, for nothing to be done, waiting must occur. When one waits *purposefully,* waiting does not take place. If waiting is not to be awaiting, it must be purposeless. Those who *wander* along "a country path" reflect:

> *Teacher:* Waiting, all right; but never awaiting, for awaiting already links itself with re-presenting and what is re-presented.
> *Scholar:* Waiting, however, lets go of that; or rather I should say that waiting lets re-presenting entirely alone. It really has no object.
> *Scientist:* Yet if we wait we always wait for something.
> *Scholar:* Why?
> *Teacher:* Because waiting releases into openness . . .
> *Scholar:* . . . into the expanse of distance . . .
> *Teacher:* . . . in whose nearness it finds the abiding in which it remains.
> *Scientist:* But remaining is a returning.
> *Scholar:* Openness itself would be that for which we could do nothing but wait.
> *Scientist:* But openness itself is that-which-regions . . .
> *Teacher:* . . . into which we are released by way of waiting, when we think.
> *Scientist:* Then thinking would be coming-into-the-nearness of distance.[32]

Purposeless waiting, which, Heidegger insists, is "beyond the distinction between activity and passivity,"[33] displaces the purposeful

32. Heidegger, *Discourse on Thinking,* p. 68.
33. Ibid., p. 61.

striving of the constructive subject. The release [34] from masterful self-assertion is, in effect, a conversion that borders on the religious. "Recollection or re-inwardization [Er-innerung] converts that nature of ours that merely wills to impose, together with its objects, into the innermost invisible region of the heart's space. Here everything is inward [inwendig]: not only does it remain turned toward this proper inner [eigentlichen Innen] of consciousness, but inside this inner, one thing turns, free of all bounds, into the other. The interiority of the inner-world-space [Das Inwendige des Weltinnenraumes] unbars the open for us" (PLT, 130). Heidegger's "Er-innerung" recalls Hegel's use of the same word in the final paragraph of the Phenomenology. [35] Unlike Hegelian Er-Innerung, Heideggerian re-collection does not overcome Zerrissenheit by closing every wound that rends and every tear that lacerates. To the contrary, waiting releases one into a Riss that forever remains open. Instead of the security and certainty of the self-possession that is supposed to be produced by the mastery of otherness and the domination of difference, the converted subject discovers that "the more venturesome risk produces no shelter. But it creates a safety or secureness [Sichersein] for us. Secure, securus, sine cure means: without care [Sorge]. Here care has the character of purposeful self-assertion [vorsätzlichen Sichdurchsetzens] by the ways and means of unconditional production. We are without such care only when we do not establish our nature exclusively within the precinct of production and constitution—the useful and the defensible. We are secure only where we neither reckon with the defenseless nor count on a defense erected within willing. A security or certainty exists only outside the objectifying turn away from the open, 'outside all shelter or defense' [Schutz], outside the parting against the pure relation [Bezug]. That relation is the exorbitant middle [unerhörte Mitte] of all drawing [Anziehens] that draws everything into the boundless [Schrankenlose], and covers [bezieht] them for the mean [Mitte]. [36] This mean is the

34. The word Heidegger uses here is Gelassenheit, which usually is translated "releasement." For reasons that will become apparent in chapter 8, Blanchot's term "patience" suggests further dimensions of the experience Heidegger describes.

35. This association of terms is underscored by Heidegger's repetition of Hegel's hyphenation of "Er-innerung." In both cases, the division of the word calls attention to the notion inwardness or interiority. The difference between Hegel and Heidegger concerns the way in which this Innerung is understood.

36. This extremely important sentence defies translation. To appreciate the range of issues it raises, it is necessary to note the multiple nuances of the words Heidegger uses. Though unerhört can be translated "unheard of," it also means disallowed, unprecedented, shocking, and scandalous. As if to echo some of the implications of unerhört, Schrankenlosigkeit means not only boundlessness but also licentiousness. Furthermore, Heidegger plays on various aspects of the verb ziehen, which can mean

"'yonder' [*dort*] where the gravity of pure forces rules, weaves, operates [*wirkt*]. Being secure or certain is the safe repose in the draw [*Gezüge*] of the whole relation" (*PLT,* 120). Heidegger's "exorbitant middle" subverts every domestic economy founded upon the principle of profitable return. *Poiesis* simultaneously draws one away from purposeful striving and useful willing, and toward purposeless waiting and useless contemplation. To hear the silent tolling of the exorbitant middle, the careful subject, who avoids everything excessive, must undergo a conversion to care-less excess.

For those with ears to hear, the tolling of poetry is the "coming-into-the-nearness-of-distance." The "mysterious proximity" into which the words of the poet *draw* the waiting listener "is nothing human" (*PLT,* 207). By holding open the exorbitant middle, the word of the poet tolls "the trace of the holy" (*Spur des Heiligen; PLT,* 141). This trace of difference can never be expressed directly, revealed totally, or known completely. It is ever elusive, evasive, excessive. Irreducibly ex-orbitant, the holy eternally returns to interrupt the circulation of knowledge and to disrupt every form of reciprocal exchange. To hear the "inhuman," "anonymous," "uncanny" murmur of the holy is to become open to that which cannot be conceived, grasped, mastered, or controlled. To be "released" or "drawn" into the un-dis-closable openness of this rending difference is to overcome nihilism by no longer "giving a negative reading to that which is" (*PLT,* 125). Released from the need to assert self by negating other and incorporating difference, one is free "to read the word 'death' *without* negation" (*PLT,* 125).[37] By "tolling" (*laüten*) the "trace" (*Spur*) of the holy, poetry sounds the "death knell" (*Toten-geläut*)"[38] of the all-knowing, constructive subject of modern philosophy. The death of this subject is the sacrifice forever occurring at the altar of the temple that always remains suspended above the cleavage opened by the work of art.

---

draw, pull, drag, or tug. *Anziehen* is to draw, pull (on, in, etc.); draw tight, haul home, stretch, screw, absorb, attract, quote, breed, raise, cultivate, and train. *Einziehen* means to draw in, retract, collect, call up, absorb, remove, and withdraw. *Beziehen* is to cover, draw or stretch over. *Bezug* derives from *beziehen* and means covering, and case, as well as relation, reference, and context. In all these terms, Heidegger stresses the gathering dimension of the mean he is exploring. The play of these words suggests a movement that can be neither stopped nor clearly defined.

37. Heidegger borrows this line from Rilke.
38. The French translation of *Totengeläute* is *Glas.*

Overleaf: Stanley Tigerman, *View Looking toward the Unresolved Dialectic.*
Courtesy of the artist.

3

Carnality

MAURICE MERLEAU-PONTY

━━

Philosophy and Nonphilosophy

It—*Es*—is a question—a question of interruption—a question of the interruption *of* texts: the interruption that subverts texts and the interruption through which texts subvert. In February 1964, Jacques Lacan was preparing a text on the question of *interrumpere* (to break in the middle, to sever), which eventually was entitled "The Split between the Eye and the Gaze," when his work was interrupted by the delivery of a mail message: "It is not mere chance—belonging to the order of the pure *tychic*—if this very week I have received a copy of the newly published, posthumous work of my friend Maurice Merleau-Ponty, *Le Visible et l'invisible*" (FFC, 71; 68). *The Visible and the Invisible* is itself a *textus interruptus*—a work abruptly broken off by the "untimely" death of the author. Lacan explains some of the important implications of the nonphilosophical fragments collected under this title:[1]

> This work, *Le Visible et l'invisible,* may indicate for us the moment of arrival of the philosophical tradition—the tradition that begins with Plato with the promulgation of the idea, of which one may say that, setting out from an aesthetic world, it is determined by an end given to being as sovereign good, thus attaining a beauty that is also its limit. And it is not by chance that Maurice Merleau-Ponty recognizes its guide in the eye.
>
> In this work, which is both an end and a beginning, you will find a reminder and a step [*pas*] forward in the path of what had first been formulated in Merleau-Ponty's *La Phénoménologie de la perception*. . . . [He] now makes the next step by forcing the limits of this very phenomenology. You will see that the ways through which he will lead you are not only of the order of visual phenomenology, since they set out to rediscover—this is the

1. Among other titles that Merleau-Ponty entertained for this work were *Being and Meaning, Genealogy of the True,* and *The Origin of Truth.*

essential point—the dependence of the visible on that which places us under the eye of the seer. But this is going too far, for that eye is only the metaphor of something that I would prefer to call the *pousse* of the seer [*la pousse du voyant*]—something prior to his eye.[2] What we have to circumscribe [*cerner:* to cut or hem in] by means of the track [*chemin*] he indicates for us, is the pre-existence of a gaze—I see only from one point, but in my existence I am looked at from all sides. (*FFC,* 71–72; 68–69)

The way that leads to the *pousse* before or behind the eye of the seer cuts through the Elysian Fields. To discover the "before" that blinds the philosopher by obscuring philosophical vision, Merleau-Ponty proposes that one simply saunter from the Etoile to the waiting arms of a "woman" named "Our Lady," and return to the Etoile. The way from the Etoile to Notre-Dame passes along the Avenue des Champs Elysées (Avenue of the Elysian Fields), past the obelisk erected in the midst of the Place de la Concorde and the pyramid rising in the bosom of the "temple" of art, across a "bridge" (*pont*) to the isle that lies in the middle of the Sein-e, which both joins and separates right (bank) and left (bank). If one follows the steps of Merleau-Pont-y on this journey and return, the Elysian Fields are transformed into a field of illusion and the Etoile becomes less an Arc de Triomphe than a monument to an unmendable "crack in glass."[3] This "profound" crack is "the blind spot" of philosophy.

Merleau-Ponty's philosophical and/or "nonphilosophical" venture is inseparably bound up with his reading and rereading of Hegel. In an early essay, "Hegel's Existentialism," occasioned by Hyppolite's lecture bearing the same title, Merleau-Ponty explains the continuing significance of Hegel's writings. "All of the great philosophical ideas of the past century—the philosophies of Marx and Nietzsche, phenomenology, German existentialism, and psychoanalysis—had their beginnings in Hegel; it was he who started the attempt to explore the irrational and integrate it into an expanded reason, which

2. I leave *la pousse,* which Lacan underscores, untranslated to suggest its multiple meanings. *La pousse* means shoot, sprout; heaves, broken wind (in horses); and overfermentation (in wines). The verb *pousser* means to push, thrust, impel, grow, urge, provoke, and to deal (a blow). The English translator, Alan Sheridan, renders *pousse* as "shoot."

3. While *étoile* means star as well as fate and destiny, it also designates a "star (crack) in glass." *Etoiler* means not only to star but also to crack, and *étoilement* can be translated either as starring or cracking. I will consider the implications of the Etoile–Place de la Concorde–Louvre–Notre-Dame axis later in this chapter. The images Merleau-Ponty introduces in this context return repeatedly in the texts of the authors discussed in subsequent chapters.

remains the task of our century."[4] Merleau-Ponty insists that there are at least two Hegels. In his early writings, which culminate in the *Phenomenology,* Hegel emerges as an "existential" thinker who never loses sight of the tensions and contradictions of concrete experience. After 1807, Hegel's systematic preoccupations lead him to insist that since antithetical difference and unreconciled otherness are epiphenomenal, every opposition can, in the final analysis, be overcome through all-encompassing reason. While Merleau-Ponty remains drawn to and influenced by the early Hegel, he is increasingly critical of later developments in Hegel's thought. The critique of Hegel and Hegelianism that begins in *Phenomenology of Perception*[5] comes to full expression in Merleau-Ponty's last lecture course, *Philosophy and Non-Philosophy since Hegel* (concluded less than a month before his death) and his unfinished work, *The Visible and the Invisible.*

In *Philosophy and Non-Philosophy since Hegel,* Merleau-Ponty develops a critique of modern philosophy through an analysis of the Introduction to Hegel's *Phenomenology.* Drawing extensively on Heidegger's *Holzwege,* Merleau-Ponty argues that Descartes's effort to reconcile *res extensa* and *res cogito* results in the collapse of objectivity into subjectivity. Kant's critical philosophy extends Descartes's reduction by developing the notion of a transcendental subject that constitutes objects of perception and knowledge. Through the creative intervention of forms of intuition and categories of understanding, the subject synthesizes data of sensation into coherent objects that can be first perceived and then known. For Merleau-Ponty, as for Heidegger, the modern philosophy of the constructive subject is fully articulated in Hegel's mature System. Hegel attempts to "decode" experience by interpreting the world of space and time, i.e., nature and history, as the objective manifestation of absolute subjectivity. In contrast to Hegel's early philosophy, such a reduction of objectivity to subjectivity dissolves the tensions and contradictions characteristic of real life and actual experience. Summarizing what he regards as Hegel's final position, Merleau-Ponty writes: "'Identity of identity and non-identity' eventually subordinates *difference.* This is inevitable as soon

4. Maurice Merleau-Ponty, "Hegel's Existentialism," *Sense and Non-Sense,* trans. H. L. and P. A. Dreyfus (Evanston, IL: Northwestern University Press, 1964), p. 63.
5. Merleau-Ponty devotes this entire book to forms of experience that Hegel considers in the first part of the *Phenomenology* (especially the sections entitled "Sense-Certainty: or The 'This' and 'Meaning,'" and 'Perception: or The Thing and Deception'"). Whereas Hegel moves methodically from perception to absolute knowledge, Merleau-Ponty maintains that perception makes absolute knowledge impossible and thus undercuts the idealism Hegel attempts to establish.

as [difference] ceases being experience and becomes *signification,*
. . . that is, as soon as it ceases reconsidering itself, thinking itself
encompassed by an englobing: the present vertical world. At this
point it is presumed to have totalized, included *everything,* surpassed
everything."[6] As Merleau-Ponty implies, such totalizing consciousness
is presumptuous. The goal of his "nonphilosophical" critique of modern philosophy is to subvert the constructive subject by exposing the
errors and dangers of its presumptuousness.

In *The Visible and the Invisible,* Merleau-Ponty elaborates the implications of his criticism of the modern interpretation of subjectivity
in an account of what he describes as "the philosophy of reflection."[7]
By interpreting the subject as "thetic," i.e., the constitutive source or
origin of the world of experience, "the philosophy of reflection metamorphoses the effective world into a transcendental field; in doing
so it only puts me back at the origin of a spectacle that I could never
have had unless, unbeknown to myself, I organized it. It only makes
me consciously what I have always been distractedly; it only makes me
give its name to a dimension behind myself, a depth whence, in fact,
already my vision was formed. Through the reflection, the 'I,' lost in
its perceptions, rediscovers itself by rediscovering them as thoughts.
It [the 'I'] thought it had quit itself for them, deployed in them; it
comes to realize that if it had quit itself, they would not be and that
the very deployment [*déploiement*][8] of the distances and the things was
only the 'outside' [*dehors*] of its own inward intimacy with itself, that
the unfolding [*déroulement*] of the world was the enfolding [*enroulement*] on itself of a thought that thinks anything whatever only because it thinks itself first" (*VI,* 44; 68). If the subject thinks only by
first thinking itself, then all knowledge is actually self-knowledge.

6. "Philosophy and Non-Philosophy Since Hegel," trans. by H. J. Silverman,
Telos, 29 (1976): 79.
7. Again in keeping with Heidegger, Merleau-Ponty views Husserl's phenomenology as an extension of Hegelian idealism. There are, however, two points at
which Merleau-Ponty believes Husserl advances beyond Hegel: in his analysis of
time in *The Phenomenology of Internal Time Consciousness,* and in his examination of the
Lebenswelt in *The Crisis of European Sciences and Transcendental Phenomenology.* From
Merleau-Ponty's perspective, Husserl fails to realize the far-reaching significance of
his own insights and therefore never overcomes the solipsism that plagues his interpretation of subjectivity. In the course of reconsidering the relationship of the closely
connected notions of temporality and the *Lebenswelt* to the experience of perception,
Merleau-Ponty subjects the conclusions of both Hegelian and Husserlian phenomenology to a rigorous reassessment.
8. *Déployer* and *déploiement* can be translated "unfold" and "unfolding." Merleau-
Ponty is convinced that subjectivity and objectivity, as well as self and other are
enfolded in a way that resists every effort to unfold them.

When the knower becomes fully aware of what and how he knows, consciousness is necessarily transformed into self-consciousness. Transparent self-consciousness dispels the obscurity of consciousness by effecting a perfect coincidence of subjectivity and objectivity. Within the philosophy of reflection, ambiguity is a penultimate moment that inevitably gives way to the univocity of certain knowledge.

> A logically consistent transcendental idealism strips the world of its opacity and its transcendence. The world is the same [*même*] that we represent to ourselves, not as men or as empirical subjects, but insofar as we are all one light and participate in the One without dividing it. Reflexive analysis ignores the problem of others [*autrui*], as well as of the world, because it insists that with the first glimmer of consciousness, there appears in me the power of reaching a universal truth, and that the other [*autre*], being equally without thisness [*eccéité*], location and body, the Alter and the Ego are one and the same in the true world that is the bond of spirits. (*PP*, xi–xii; vi)[9]

The perfect light of this "true world" is the light of eternity that frees the subject from bondage to time. As Hegel insists, absolute knowledge is the apotheosis of self-consciousness.

Merleau-Ponty outlines the genesis of this eternal subject: "'The Cartesian doctrine of the *cogito* was, therefore, bound to lead logically to the assertion of the timelessness of spirit [*intemporalité de l'esprit*], and to the admission of a consciousness of the eternal: *experimur nos aeternos esse.*' Eternity, understood as the power to embrace and anticipate temporal developments in a single intention, becomes the very definition of subjectivity" (*PP*, 372; 426). If the subject constitutes *its* world, then the subject appears to be liberated from the uncertainties and vicissitudes of temporal experience. Recalling Kierkegaard's image of the "Archimedean point" toward which the philosopher aspires, Merleau-Ponty describes the eternal vision of the reflective subject as "high-altitude thought" (*pensée en survol*), which issues from the sovereign gaze of "the eagle."

> For a philosophy that installs itself in pure vision, in the high-altitude view of the panorama, there can be no encounter with another [*autrui*]: for the gaze dominates; it can dominate only

9. While Merleau-Ponty makes this remark in the context of a consideration of Husserl's solipsistic impasse, his later analysis makes it clear that Husserl's position provides an illustration of problems generally encountered in the philosophy of reflection. It is also important to note that the issue of otherness or difference does not merely concern the relationship between subjectivity and objectivity. The reflective subject sees *itself* reflected *everywhere*—in other subjects and in all objects.

things, and if it falls upon men, it transforms them into puppets that move only by springs or elastics [*ressorts*]. From the heights of the towers of Notre-Dame, I cannot, when I like, feel myself to be on equal footing with those who, enclosed within those walls, there minutely pursue incomprehensible tasks. High places attract those [like Hegel] who wish to cast over the world the gaze of the eagle [*le regard de l'aigle*]. (*VI*, 77–78; 109)

The "eagle eye" of the philosopher reflects the longing to realize the dream of the ontotheological tradition. There is, however, a high price to be paid for this vision—a price that is nothing less than time itself. The *birth* of eternally constructive subjectivity is the *death* of the passionate temporal subject. "It is the dream of philosophers," Merleau-Ponty explains, "to conceive an 'eternity of life,' lying beyond permanence and change, in which time's productivity is preeminently contained, and yet a thetic consciousness *of* time that dominates it and embraces it merely destroys the phenomenon of time" (*PP*, 415; 475). Merleau-Ponty is convinced that this dream cannot be realized, for he discerns an unavoidable "blind spot" in the philosopher's eagle eye.

Claims to the contrary notwithstanding, absolute knowledge remains forever inaccessible to the temporal subject. Echoing Heidegger's insistence that ontotheology constitutes itself by forgetting its origin, Merleau-Ponty contends that the philosopher who claims to know universal truth forgets the inescapable non-knowledge from which his reflection repeatedly departs.

If I pretend to find, through reflection, in the universal spirit [*esprit*] the premise that had always backed up my experience, I can do so only by forgetting this non-knowing [*non-savoir*] of the beginning which is not nothing, and which is not the reflective truth either, and which also must be accounted for. I was able to appeal from the world and the others to myself and take the route of reflection only because first I was outside of myself, in the world, among the others, and this experience constantly nourishes my reflection. (*VI*, 49; 74)

The experience that nurtures reflection cannot itself be known. The obscure and ambiguous "origin" that "is not nothing" implies a "non-knowing" that the philosopher struggles to repress. It is the effort to return to this repressed that leads Merleau-Ponty to chart the course leading from the Etoile, along the Champs Elysées to Notre-Dame, and back. To follow this route is to discover that the return of the repressed is the re-turn of time.

The achievement of total self-consciousness requisite for absolute knowledge presupposes that the reflective subject returns to itself from its self-objectification in the objects of knowledge. If knowledge is not incomplete, the self must discover *itself* in everything that appears to be other than itself. In one of his richest and most influential criticisms of the reflexivity of self-consciousness, Merleau-Ponty writes:

The philosophy of reflection . . . thinks it can comprehend our natal bond with the world only by *undoing* [défaisant] it in order to remake [*refaire*] it, only by constituting it, by fabricating it. . . . It is, therefore, essential to the philosophy of reflection that it bring us back, this side of our *de facto* situation, to a center of things from which we proceeded, but from which we were decentered, that it retravel, this time starting from us, a route already traced out from that center to us. The very effort toward internal adequation, the enterprise of reconquering explicitly all that we are and make implicitly, signifies that what we are finally as *naturata* we first are actively as *naturans,* that the world is our birthplace only because first we, as spirits or minds, are the cradle of the world. . . . For the movement of recovery, of recuperation, of return to self, the progression toward internal adequation, the very effort to coincide with a *naturans,* which is already ourselves and which is supposed to deploy the things and the world before itself—precisely inasmuch as they are a return or a reconquest, these operations of re-constitution or restoration, which come second, cannot in principle be the mirror image of its internal constitution and its establishment, as the route from the Etoile to the Notre-Dame is the inverse of the route from the Notre-Dame to the Etoile; the reflection recuperates everything except itself as an effort of recuperation, it clarifies everything except its own role. The eye of spirit, the mind's eye also has its blind spot [*son point aveugle*], but because it is of spirit or mind, it cannot be unaware of it, nor treat it as a simple state of non-vision, which requires no particular mention, the very act of reflection that is *quoad nos* its act of birth. If it is not unaware of itself—which would be contrary to its definition—the reflection cannot feign to unravel [*dérouler*] the same thread that the mind would first have woven [*roulé*], to be spirit or mind returning to itself within me, when by definition it is I who reflect. The reflection must appear to itself as a progression toward a subject X, an appeal to subject X. (*VI,* 33–34; 54–55)

The irreducible temporality of subjectivity "decenters" self-consciousness in two ways. In the first place, reflection is secondary to an experience that eludes conceptual comprehension. Since the thinking subject is "always already" "thrown into" a *de facto* situation, "the search for the conditions of possibility is in principle posterior to an actual experience, and from this it follows that even if subsequently one determines rigorously the *sine qua non* of that experience, it can never be washed of the original stain [*souillure:* dirt, impurity, defilement] of having been discovered *post festum* nor ever become what positively founds that experience (*VI,* 44–45; 69).[10] Though claiming to be the creative source or origin of the world of experience, the reflective subject is a parasite nourished by experience more "originary" than its own deeds. This ever-present, though always inaccessible, origin effectively deconstitutes (or deconstructs) the subject's constitutive or constructive acts. "The mistake of reflective philosophies," Merleau-Ponty concludes, "is to believe that the meditating subject can absorb into its meditation or seize without remainder [*sans reste*] the object of its meditation, that our being amounts to our knowledge. As meditating subject, we are never the unreflective subject that we seek to know; but neither can we become wholly consciousness, or make ourselves into the transcendental consciousness" (*PP,* 62; 76).

Time enters reflection to displace centered consciousness in a second way. The achievement of self-consciousness takes time. Merleau-Ponty uses the imaginary journey from the Etoile to Notre-Dame and back to suggest the inevitable *delay* between the constituting act of consciousness and the return of the constructive subject to itself through the process of recollection. The interval between the centrifugal and centripetal moments of consciousness and self-consciousness disrupts the coincidence of origin and conclusion in the life of the subject. As a result of this delay, the consummation of the union of subjectivity and objectivity remains a dream whose realization is perpetually "deferred" (*différée; VI,* 41; 64). Temporal deferral opens a gap in the subject that self-consciousness cannot close. This opening marks the time and space of carnal existence.

10. Elsewhere Merleau-Ponty underscores reflective philosophy's preoccupation with avoiding the illegitimate thought of defilement by invoking the image of the "bastard." "At the same time that the reflection liberates us from the false problems posed by bastard and unthinkable experiences [*expériences bâtardes et impensables*], it also accounts for them through the simple transposition of the incarnate subject into a transcendental subject and of the reality of the world into an ideality; we all reach the world, and the same world, and it belongs wholly to each of us, without division or loss, because it is *that which* we think we perceive, the undivided object of all our thoughts" (*VI,* 31; 52). The notion of the bastard plays a significant role in Derrida's analysis of Hegel.

Flesh: Return of the Fold

My left hand is always on the verge of touching my right hand touching the things, but I never reach coincidence; the coincidence eclipses itself at the moment of producing itself, and one of two things always occurs: either my right hand really passes over to the rank of touched, but then its hold on the world is interrupted; or it retains its hold on the world, but then I do not really touch *it*—my right hand touching, I palpate with my left hand only its exterior envelope. . . . But this incessant withdrawal or concealment, this impotence to superpose exactly upon one another the touching of the things by my right hand and the touching of this same right hand by my left hand . . . is not a failure [*échec*]. . . . This hiatus between my right hand touched and my right hand touching . . . is not an ontological void, a non-being spanned by the total being of my body, and by that of the world; it is the zero of pressure [*zéro de pression*] between two solids that makes them adhere to one another. (*VI,* 147–48; 194–95)

For Merleau-Ponty, human existence is *carnal.* This carnality creates a cleavage in the subject that faults self-consciousness. Rather than a self-contained entity, the body is a "gaping wound [*blessure béante*]" (*PP,* 342; 394) that always remains "incomplete [*inachevée*]" (*VI,* 147; 193). While the reflective subject attempts to close in on itself by incorporating every other and assimilating all difference, the living body resists closure and necessarily remains open to what is other than, and different from itself. This "openness" (*ouverture*) is the "dehiscence or fission [*déhiscence ou fission*] of [the body's] mass" (*VI,* 146; 192). As a result of its holey-ness or gappiness, the living body cannot be defined in terms of the binary opposites that structure conceptual reflection. The body is neither "subject nor object" (*PP,* 198; 213), neither "*in itself*" nor "*for itself*" (*PP,* 212; 246), neither *res extensa* nor *res cogito* (*PP,* 80; 95). Rather, the body is the *mean* between extremes—the "milieu" (*milieu*) in which opposites like interiority and exteriority, as well as subjectivity and objectivity, intersect. Never reducible to the differences it simultaneously joins and separates, the body is forever *entre-deux.*

Describing the liminal status of the body, Merleau-Ponty writes: "At the same time that the body withdraws [*se retire*] from the objective world, and forms between the pure subject and the object a third genre or gender [*troisième genre*] of being, the subject loses its purity and its transparence" (*PP,* 350; 402). The body, in other words, is never a body "proper." To the contrary, carnality is unavoidably *improper*. In an effort to convey this elusive "third term" (*troisième terme; PP*, 101; 117), Merleau-Ponty uses a variety of images: a "gaping wound," a "dehiscence," "a zero point of pressure between two solids," and "a third genre or gender." Elsewhere he describes the body as "a hinge, joint, or articulation" (*charnière; VI*, 148; 196), which forms "the pivot of the world" (*PP*, 82; 97). This pivotal joint is "a being of porosity" (*être de porosité; VI*, 149; 195), which "is to be compared, not to a physical object, but rather to a work of art" (*PP*, 150; 176). The significance of this association increases when the comparison between the body and the work of art is set in the context of Merleau-Ponty's depiction of the body as the condition of the possibility of the "lighting" (*éclairage*) necessary for perceptual experience. This "lighting" must not be confused with light itself, for it "is neither color nor, in itself, even light [but] is on this side of [*en deçà de*] the distinction between colors and luminosities. That is why it always tends to become 'neuter' [*neutre*] for us" (*PP*, 311; 359). Forever *entre-deux*, this liminal "third gender" is neither male nor female but is "neuter." While the body is not an object or a subject, "it is that by which there are objects" as well as subjects (*PP*, 92; 108). Like the cleavage opened by Heidegger's work of art, the body is the "dark hole" that makes light possible. Irreducible darkness is, paradoxically, the lighting necessary for the staging of every spectacle. By holding open "the open," the body creates the possibility of the play of differences that constitutes spatial and temporal experience. "Bodily space can be distinguished from external space and envelop its parts instead of deploying them, because it is the obscurity necessary in the theatre to light up the spectacle, the background of somnolence or the reserve of vague power against which the gesture and its aim detach themselves, the zone of non-being *in front of which* precise beings, figures, and points can come to light" (*PP*, 100–101; 117). The eagle eye of the reflective philosopher never dispels this darkness, unravels this mystery, penetrates this obscurity. The non-philosopher, however, can *apprehend*—which is not to say *comprehend*—the body.

While the carnal body always remains obscure, it nonetheless has a discernible structure. Merleau-Ponty designates this structure "the chiasmus" (*le chiasme*).[11] "Chiasmus" derives from the Greek *khiasmos*,

11. In view of the close relationship between the notion of the chiasmus and Heidegger's "cleavage," it is important to stress that in his working notes for *The Visible and the Invisible* Merleau-Ponty actually identifies *le chiasme* and *le clivage* (*VI*, 214; 268).

which, in turn, comes from *khiazien,* meaning to mark with the letter χ.[12] In grammar, a chiasmus is "a figure by which the order of words in one of two parallel clauses is inverted in the other." In Christianity, χ is the sign of the cross.[13]

Merleau-Ponty develops his most complete analysis of the chiasmus in a chapter of *The Visible and the Invisible* entitled "*L'entrelacs—le chiasme.*" An *entrelacs* (*entre:* between, betwixt; *lacs,* string, noose, trap) is an ornament consisting of interlacing figures. While *entrelacer* is to interlace, interweave, or intertwine, *s'entrelacer* is to entwine or twist around each other. When understood in terms of *l'entrelacs,* the chiasmus figures a complex structure of "implication" (*im-pli-cation*), "enfoldment" (*enroulement*), and "envelopment" (*enveloppement*). The chiasmic "structure of implication" (*PP,* 149; 174) inscribes a cross that is a double-cross. At this intersection, opposites fold into each other in such a way that everything seems to be "completely reversed or turned inside out [*retourné*]" (*VI,* 143; 189). This double enfoldement is the "*re-pli-cation*" of differences in each other. Such mutual implication does not, however, establish the identity of differences but exposes a "*doub-lure*" (lining) (*VI,* 149; 195) that remains the "central cavity" (*cavité centrale; VI,* 149; 195), or "a hollow" (*creux; VI,* 123; 164) in everything that appears to be solid. Since differences do not collapse into identity, the implication of opposites does not create a fusion that issues in immediacy. The "reversibility" of the chiasmus insures that neither pole in the relationship dominates the other. Like intertwined hands that almost touch and are touched, the chiasmus points to "a coincidence always past or always future, an experience that remembers an impossible past [*passé impossible*], anticipates an impossible future [*avenir impossible*], that emerges from Being or that will incorporate itself into Being, that 'is of it' but is not it, and, therefore, is not a coincidence, a real fusion [*fusion réelle*], as of two positive terms of an alloyage, but a recovering or overlaying [*recouvrement;* cf. *Bezug*], as of a hollow and a relief that remain distinct" (*VI,* 122–23; 163–64).

12. The closely related *khiasma* means cross or piece of wood. In anatomy, a chiasma is "a crossing or intersection of two tracts, as of nerves or ligaments," and in genetics, it is "a point of contact between homologous chromosomes, considered the cytological manifestation of crossing over" (*The American Heritage Dictionary*).

13. Derrida examines the relationship between CHI and the German *ICH.* He presents some of his most illuminating remarks about the significance of CHI and *Ich* in response to Valerio Adami's lithographs on *Glas.* Derrida interprets the fish that forms the center of Adami's work of art in terms of the Christian church and its erect subject, the centered ego. See below, chapter 9, fourth section.

Merleau-Ponty describes the gaping wound, dark hole, open gap, central cavity, inaccessible hollow in the midst of the chiasmus, formed by a process of folding and refolding, with a term usually associated with Derrida's texts: *invagination.*

> The surface of the visible is doubled up over its whole extension with an invisible reserve [*réserve invisible*], and . . . in our flesh as in the flesh of things, the actual, empirical, ontic visible, by a sort of refolding, invagination [*de repliement, d'invagination*], or padding exhibits a visibility, a possibility that is not the shadow of the actual but is its principle, that is not the proper contribution of a "thought" but is its condition, a style allusive, elliptical like every style, but like every style inimitable, inalienable, an interior horizon and an exterior horizon, between which the actual visible is a pro-vision-al partitioning [*cloisonnement; cloison: dividing membrane*] and which, nonetheless, open indefinitely only upon other visibles. (*VI,* 152; 200)

"There is no name in traditional philosophy" to designate the "strange domain" of carnality. While the philosopher struggles to repress every vestige of bodily existence, the non-philosopher invokes an elusive and elliptical style to evoke carnality. The provocative name Merleau-Ponty gives the body that cannot be properly conceived is "flesh."

> What we are calling flesh, this interiorly worked-over mass, has no name in any philosophy. As the formative milieu [*milieu formateur*] of the object and the subject, it is not an atom of being, the hard in-itself that resides in a unique place and moment: one can indeed say of my body that it is not *elsewhere,* but one cannot say that it is *here* or *now* [*ici ou maintenant*] in the sense that objects are; and yet my vision does not soar over [*survole*] them, it is not the being that is all knowing, for it has its own inertia, its attachments. We must not think the flesh starting from substances, from body and spirit—for then it would be the union of contradictories—but we must think it . . . as an element, as the concrete emblem of a general manner of being. (*VI,* 147; 193)

As the "formative milieu" of subjectivity and objectivity, "flesh" is not limited to a particular genre of existence. To the contrary, "the world is universal flesh" (*VI,* 137; 181). When the world is apprehended as universal flesh, it appears to be a complex "field" or a "network of relations" in which everything is intertwined and interlaced. In different terms, the field of flesh is "a diacritical [*diacritique*], relative, oppositional system" (*VI,* 213; 267). Within this differential milieu, everything is a chiasmus. The example Merleau-Ponty most often uses to illustrate this chiasmic structure is visual—color and its perception.

> The color is yet a variant in another dimension of variation, that of its relations with the surroundings: this red is what it is only by connecting up from its place with other reds about it, with which it forms a constellation, or with other colors it dominates or that dominate it, that it attracts or that attract it, that it repels or that repel it. In short, it is a certain knot [*noeud*] in the woof [*trame:* plot, course, progress] of the simultaneous and the successive. It is a concretion of visibility, it is not an atom. The red dress a fortiori holds with all its fibers onto the tissue or fabric [*tissu*] of the visible, and thereby onto a tissue or fabric of invisible being. . . . A naked color, and in general a visible, is not a chunk of absolutely hard, indivisible being, offered all naked to a vision that could be total or null, but is rather a sort of strait or channel [*détroit*] between exterior horizons and interior horizons ever gaping open, something that comes to touch lightly and makes diverse regions of the colored or visible world resound at the distances, a certain differentiation, an ephemeral modulation of this world—less a color or a thing, therefore, than a difference between [*différence entre*] things and colors, a momentary crystallization of colored being or of visibility. Between the alleged colors and visibles, we would find anew the tissue or fabric that lines or doubles [*double*] them, sustains them, nourishes them, and which for its part is not a thing, but a possibility, a latency, and a *flesh* of things. (*VI,* 132–33; 174–75)

Inasmuch as the "flesh of things" is the invisible interplay of differences that articulates the difference necessary for identity, flesh "is not a contingency, chaos, but a texture" (*VI,* 146; 192). The interweaving of universal flesh produces a "texture" (*texere:* to weave) that forms "the tissue or fabric of the visible." Perpetually alternating between warp and woof, this tissue [14] is the text-ured fabric in which all things are interlaced. "My flesh and that of the world therefore involve clear zones, clearings, about which pivot their opaque zones, and the primary visibility, that of the *quale* and of the things, does not come without a second visibility, that of the lines of force and dimensions, the massive flesh without a subtle flesh, the momentary body without a glorified body" (*VI,* 148; 195). The invisible glorified body that lies

---

14. In Middle English, *tissue* is a rich cloth. It derives from Old French *tistre,* "to weave," by way of the Latin *textere.*

in the "midst" (*le milieu;* compare *die Mitte* and *der Mittler*) of the visible world is the word incarnate. How, asks Merleau-Ponty, is it possible to "read" the text of such a carnal word?

Savage Word

To shift from "massive flesh" to "subtle flesh" is to move from "the flesh of the body" to "the flesh of language" (*VI*, 153; 200). The word "incarnate" in the flesh of language is a "savage" word.[15] This savage word "is the common text-ure, fabric, tissue of which we are made" (*VI*, 203; 257). "*L'Etre sauvage,*" Merleau-Ponty maintains, is "the pre-spiritual milieu without which nothing is thinkable" (*VI*, 204; 257). The enveloping structure of the chiasmus implies the isomorphism of flesh and language. Following the lead of Saussure and acknowledging the importance of Lévi-Strauss's extension of Saussurean linguistics, Merleau-Ponty argues that language is a relational network in which "there are only *differences* between signifiers" (*VI*, 171; 225). This play of differences, which generates all meaning, is not simply created by the individual speaker or speakers. "I" can speak only because language speaks in and through me. So understood, the savage word "would be a language of which [the individual speaker] would not be the organizer, words he would not assemble, that would combine through him by virture of a natural intertwining [*entrelacement*] of their meaning, through the occult traffic of metaphor—where what counts is no longer the manifest meaning of each word and of each image, but the lateral relations, the kinships that are implicated in their transfers and their exchanges" (*VI*, 125; 167). As the vessel of language, the speaker "offers himself and offers every word to a universal Word [*Parole universelle*]" (*VI*, 154; 202). With the transubstantiation of universal flesh into universal word, the Logos appears.

For Merleau-Ponty, as for Heidegger, the Logos is "the obscure region whence comes instituted light" (*VI*, 154; 202).[16] As such, the

15. At several points, Merleau-Ponty explicitly refers to Lévi-Strauss's notion of *la pensée sauvage.* This association of terms should not obscure the significant differences between Merleau-Ponty's savage word and Lévi-Strauss's savage thought. As the analysis of carnality suggests, the savage word escapes the structure of binary opposition. For this reason, the incarnate word can be perceived but not conceived.

16. While Merleau-Ponty uses terms like speech, Logos, and light, which are characteristic of ontotheology, his exploration of flesh and the savage word, like Heidegger's account of the cleft Logos, points in the direction of something logo-

Logos is not a transcendent ideality, but is concretely embodied in, and inseparably intertwined with the sensible world. The Word is always already incarnate. This carnal Logos is nothing other than the interlacing of flesh. The re-turn of the fold is "a furrow [*sillage:* wake, track] that traces itself [*se trace*] magically under our eyes without a tracer [*traceur*], a certain hollow, a certain interior, a certain absence, a negativity that is not nothing" (*VI*, 151; 198).[17] This negativity that is not nothing is not, however, a positivity. Unlike the Hegelian "magic" that transforms the negative into the positive, the "magic" of this tracing inscribes that which is neither negative nor positive. Uncontainable by, and incomprehensible in, conceptual categories, the Logos, paradoxically, is not logical—nor is it illogical. Always escaping the domination of the reflective subject and eternally returning to interrupt the mastery of the concept, the savage word is the *Logos endiathetos,* which embodies a "sense before logic" (*VI*, 169; 222). The sense of this Logos is never completely "unveiled" (*sans voiles*), for "it withdraws [*s'éloigne*] in the measure that we approach it" (*VI*, 150; 197).

More precisely, "I" cannot approach the Logos; it must approach me. "The Logos realizes itself in man, but not at all as his property or propriety [*propriété*]" (VI, 274, 328). From Merleau-Ponty's point of view, the Logos effectively dispossesses self-consciousness, by deconstituting its constitutional acts. Always on the verge of resistance, the savage word is unconstitutional. Though reflective self-consciousness is "thetic," i.e., it constitutes or posits the objects to which it relates, *constructive* reflection is never originary but always secondary. Reflection "draws its inspiration from" that which is antecedent to its own acts. This irreducible anteriority escapes the grasp of every comprehensive concept.[18] In order to apprehend the savage word, it is necessary to return to "a more muffled, muted, rumbling [*sourde*] relation-

---

centrism always leaves unthought. For this reason, Merleau-Ponty's appropriation of Lévi-Strauss's categories is actually subversive. By subtly turning the language of structuralism against itself, Merleau-Ponty creates an opening for the poststructuralists who come after him. Nevertheless, it is obvious that Merleau-Ponty is not yet a poststructuralist.

17. As will become clear in the next section, the hollow that remains "in" the return *of* the fold makes it impossible to return *to* the fold. In a carnal economy, the excessively prodigal son can never return to the home of the father. In different terms, once self-consciousness ventures into the world (as it must for its own sake), it cannot return to itself.

18. To understand the nuances of this claim, it is necessary to recall the way in which the sense of grasping is captured in the French words *prise, com-prendre,* and *compréhensif.* Compare the German *Griff, Be-griff,* and *be-greifen.*

ship with the world, . . . which is always already [*toujours déjà*] accomplished when the reflexive return intervenes" (*VI,* 35; 57).

The incarnate Logos, which cannot be conceived, can be perceived. Instead of imperiously imposing itself upon the world, perceptual awareness is "nonthetic" (*PP,* 280; 324). For one who is unreflective but perceptive—indeed perceptive *because* unreflective—otherness is "a gift" (*un don*) to be received gratefully, rather than a threat to be destroyed anxiously (*PP,* 44; 53). Thus "it is necessary to comprehend perception as . . . interrogative thought that lets the perceived world be, rather than posits it, before which the things form and undo themselves in a sort of slipping and sliding [*glissement*],[19] on this side of yes and no" (*VI,* 102; 138). Just as flesh is neither subject nor object, so carnal perception is neither subjective nor objective. Since perception remains open to difference, it is unavoidably marginal, liminal, interstitial—*entre-deux.* The non-philosopher, who is attuned to perception, "asks of our experience of the world what the world is before it is a thing one speaks of and what is taken for granted, before it has been reduced to a set of manipulable, disposable significations; [he] directs this question to our mute life, . . . to that melange of the world and of ourselves that precedes reflection, because the examination of the significations would give us the world reduced to our idealizations and our syntax" (*VI,* 102; 138).

The syntax of the Word, which is perceived but not known, is never *my own.* In a manner reminiscent of the occurrence of *a-lethia,* perception *of* the incarnate Logos transpires, though "I" do not perceive. "I" do not constitute this Logos; "it" utters itself "through" me. "My" speech, therefore, is "the speech that possesses the signification less than it is possessed by it, that does not speak *of it,* but speaks *it,* or speaks *according to it,* or lets it speak and be spoken within me, pierces [*perce:* opens, breaks through] my present" (*VI,* 118; 158). The free *don* of the gracious word is not a present. This *don* is *le coup de don* that is *un coup de grâce.* The unconstitutional *coup* of perception overthrows the sovereign subject. Always arriving "*après-coup,*" reflection is impotent to heal the wound opened by *le coup de grâce.* Through this opening, the gift of perception makes one aware of an *other* that silently speaks "within" the subject. The savage, wild, untamed, uncivilized, unsocial word, which *cannot* be known, is the uncon-

19. *Glissement* also refers to the sound generated by slipping, sliding, and gliding. This strange sound has already begun to echo in the "tolling" of Heidegger's traces, and will resound in both Blanchot's uncanny "murmur" and Derrida's shattering *Glas.*

scious that forever haunts consciousness. Since I am never able to incorporate or domesticate this "other," "my" voice is always also the voice of the other.

Unfinished Diealectics

Shortly after Hegel's death, Kierkegaard satirized speculative philosophy by comparing the formation of the System to the *construction* of a fantastic castle. "Most systematizers in relation to their systems are like a man who builds an enormous [*unhyre:* prodigious, monstrous] castle and himself lives alongside it in a shed; they themselves do not live in the enormous systematic building. But in the realm of mind or spirit [*Aand:* the Danish word for *Geist*], this nonresidence is and remains a decisive objection. Spiritually understood, a man's thoughts must be the building in which he lives—otherwise the whole thing is deranged [*galt*]" (*JP,* 3308; VIII[1] A 82). Merleau-Ponty repeats many of Kierkegaard's criticisms of the flights of philosophical imagination. "True philosophy," he maintains, "is non-philosophy," which "mocks" the presumption of philosophers.[20] Through a steadfast "refusal of high-altitude thinking" (*VI,* 91; 125), Merleau-Ponty attempts to bring philosophy back down to earth.

In developing his critique of the philosophy of reflection, typified by Hegel's mature System, Merleau-Ponty draws on many of the insights elaborated in what he regards as Hegel's early "existential" writings. To avoid the dangerous illusions of grandeur plaguing the modern philosophy of the subject, it is necessary to return to the obscurity, ambiguity, and contradictions of concrete temporal experience. Such a return, Merleau-Ponty argues, is possible when reflection is transformed into "hyperreflection [*surréflexion*]."[21] In his most extensive account of *surreflexion,* Merleau-Ponty explains:

> We are catching sight of [*entre-voyons*] the necessity of another operation besides the conversion to reflection, more fundamental than it, of a sort of *hyperreflection* that would also take into account itself and the changes it introduces into the spectacle. Accordingly, it would not lose sight of the brute thing and the brute

20. "Philosophy and Non-Philosophy since Hegel," p. 75.

21. Though Merleau-Ponty never makes the comparison, it is tempting to relate *surréflexion* to *surréalisme.* This association is all the more suggestive when placed in the context of Merleau-Ponty's relationship with Lacan, who was deeply interested in surrealism.

perception and would not finally efface them. . . . On the contrary, it would set itself the task of thinking about them, of
reflecting on the transcendence of the world as transcendence,
speaking of it not according to the law of the inherent significations of words given in language, but with a perhaps difficult
effort that employs the significations of words to express beyond
[*au-delà*] themselves, our mute contact with the things, when
they are not yet things said. If, therefore, the reflection is not to
presume upon what it finds and condemn itself to putting into
the things what it will then pretend to find in them, it must
suspend the faith in the world only so as to *see it,* only so as to read
it in the route it has followed in becoming a world for us; it must
seek in the world itself the secret of our perceptual bond with it.
It must use words not according to their pre-established signification, but *in order to state* this prelogical bond. It must sink into
the world instead of dominating it; it must descend toward it
such as it is, instead of working its way back up toward a prior
possibility of thinking it—which would impose upon the world
in advance the conditions for our control over it. (*VI,* 38–39; 61)

Hyperreflection does not assimilate the "transcendence" of the world
within its own immanent activity. Transcendence, in this context,
refers to nothing otherworldly, but designates the brute givenness or
facticity of the world as such. From the perspective of hyperreflection,
there is something "beyond" words. Though never knowable, this *au-
delà* can be implied by various strategies which, contrary to expectation, allow words to say the unsayable. In this way hyperreflection is
always open to both difference and otherness. Having given up the
sovereign subject's struggle for mastery, it no longer seems necessary
to try to dominate all things by incorporating each difference and
discovering oneself in every other.

Hyperreflection issues in a "hyperdialectic" (*hyperdialectique*),
which Merleau-Ponty characterizes by a comparison with the ques-
tionable dialectic of reflective philosophy.

The bad dialectic begins almost with the dialectic, and there is no
good dialectic but that which criticizes itself and surpasses itself
as a separate statement; the only good dialectic is the hyperdialectic. The bad dialectic is that which does not wish to lose its soul
in order to save it, which wishes to be dialectical immediately, becomes autonomous, and ends up at cynicism, at formalism, for
having eluded its own double meaning or sense. What we call
hyperdialectic is, on the contrary, a thought that is capable of
reaching truth because it envisages without restriction the plurality of the relationships and what has been called ambiguity.

The bad dialectic is that which thinks it recomposes being by a thetic thought, by an assemblage of statements, by thesis, antithesis, and synthesis; the good dialectic is that which is conscious of the fact that every *thesis* is an idealization, that Being is not made up of idealizations or of things said, as the old logic believed, but of bound or tied ensembles, where signification is never, except in tendency, where the inertia of the content never permits the defining of one term as absolute suppression of the negative by itself. The point to be noted is this: that the dialectic without synthesis of which we speak is not, therefore, skepticism, vulgar relativism, or the reign of the ineffable. (*VI*, 94–95; 129)

Within this hyperdialectic, synthesis is impossible because existence remains open-ended. The openness of existence extends back toward a past that was never present and ahead toward a future that will never be present. Since the temporal individual is hemmed in by two "experiences" that are never truly experienced, he cannot become totally present to himself in complete self-consciousness. "Neither my birth nor my death can appear to me as experiences of my own, since, if I were to think of them thus, I would be assuming myself to pre-exist or to survive [*sur-vivre*] myself, in order to be able to experience them, and I should not, therefore, be genuinely thinking of my birth or my death. I can, then, apprehend myself only as "already born" [*déjà né*] and "still living" [*encore vivant*]—I can apprehend my birth and my death only as prepersonal horizons: I can know that people are born and die, but I cannot know my own birth and death" (*PP*, 215–16; 249–50).

The reflective subject always discovers itself as "already born." I have pointed out that Merleau-Ponty rejects the notion of an originary thetic subject, and insists that reflection is unavoidably secondary to an irreducible anteriority that eludes conceptual comprehension. It now becomes evident that this inescapable "before" is an "impossible past" which, like Heidegger's "essential past," is *never* present. "Hence reflection does not grasp its full sense or meaning unless it mentions the unreflective fund [*fonds irréfléchi*] that it presupposes, from which it profits [*profite*], and which constitutes for it a kind of original past [*passé originel*], a past that has never been present" (*PP*, 242; 280).[22] Having never been present, this "original past" cannot be re-presented. In an image that recalls Hegel's discussion of the sign, Merleau-Ponty describes existence as "perched on a pyramid

22. Merleau-Ponty underlines the economic import of his remark by using the terms *fonds* (stock, capital, principal, cash, ready money, business, etc.) and *profiter*.

of the past [*pyramide du passé*]" (*PP*, 393; 450).[23] This pyramid points to the chiasmic intertwining of past and future. The past that is never present eternally re-turns as the future that never arrives. The non-present future that bounds life and makes the temporal individual "dreadfully" edgy is death. Though "I" (or "the I") never experience death, "I" always live in its "atmosphere." This ever-outstanding future "opens the world to me through a perspective, along with which there comes to me the feeling of my contingency, the dread [*angoisse*] of being surpassed [*dépassé*], so that, while I do not think my death, I live in an atmosphere of death in general, and there is a kind of essence of death always on the horizon of my thinking" (*PP*, 364; 418). While my "primal past" remains forever "remote," "my death is an inaccessible future." In temporal existence, experience always involves the interlacing of a being-from and a being-toward. By refusing premature closure in an imaginary synthesis, the hyperdialectic is, in effect, a die-alectic open to the past and future that wound every present. This diealectic spells the death of the centered self.

Though the remote past and inaccessible future are never present, they are not exactly absent. Always haunting the present, they seem to be something like the Snow Man's "Nothing that is not there and nothing that is." Inasmuch as this nothing *approaches* (from behind as well as ahead) but never arrives, it is "proximal" (*proximale; VI*, 37; 60). Recalling Heidegger's "near" and anticipating Levinas's and Blanchot's "proximity," the "proximate" is neither simply distant nor merely close. Rather, the proximate is "the approach of the remote as remote" (*approche du lointain comme lointain; VI*, 102; 138). The approach of the remote is, in Heidegger's terms, "the coming-into-nearness-of-distance." In this case, "distance is not the contrary of . . . proximity [but] is in profound accord with it" (*VI*, 135; 178).

The remote proximity or proximate remoteness, which approaches yet is not present, cannot be named properly. "It [*Elle*]" is "anonymous."[24] Flesh is an "anonymity innate in myself" (*VI*, 139; 183). This inherent anonymity introduces "the impersonal at the center of subjectivity" (*PP*, 346; 408). Such anonymous impersonality is "an other subject [*un autre sujet*] beneath me, for whom a world exists before I am there" (*PP*, 254; 294). This "other" is the other that

23. He borrows this image from Proust. In view of the importance of the analysis of Van Gogh that Heidegger presents in "The Origin of the Work of Art," and of Derrida's response to Heidegger in "Restitutions: of Truth in Painting" (in *The Truth in Painting*), it is worth noting that Merleau-Ponty's remark is made in the context of a consideration of Van Gogh's painting.

24. Recall Heidegger's account of the anonymity of the *Es* in *Es gibt*.

"speaks" through the "I." Though its words are never clear, its "clamor" (*rumeur*) is "the background of everything we do" (*PP*, 328; 378). The *rumeur* of the other dispels the rumor circulating among reflective philosophers concerning the transparency of the self-conscious subject.

The anonymous other that is always "within" splits the subject, leaving it a bit "cracked [*fêlé*]." The splitting of the subject testifies to its irreducible temporality. Time is not simply a succession of "nows" in which the present slips into the past as it moves toward the future. To the contrary, the past that is never present returns as a future that never *comes*. This ever-never present temporality creates a hole that reflection cannot fill. Repeatedly interrupted by an other it cannot control, self-consciousness is necessarily incomplete. Since self-consciousness is never total, its diealectic is ever unfinished. Hence analysis is interminable. The knowing self cannot become fully transparent to itself. Like Blanchot's Thomas, the subject is forever shrouded in obscurity. Ambiguity is not a penultimate moment that is finally overcome in absolute knowledge. Despite the best efforts of philosophers, everything remains opaque. Always split, the subject never coincides with itself. "What there is is not a coinciding by principle or a presumptive coinciding and a factual noncoinciding, a bad or lacking truth [*une vérité mauvaise ou manquée*], but a privative noncoinciding, a coinciding from afar [*de loin*], a fault [*écart:* swerving, mistake, deviation], and something like a 'good error [*bonne erreur*]'" (*VI*, 124–25; 166). Ever twisting and turning, the errant subject wanders with no hope of return.

Philosophy's insight is always shadowed by a certain blindness. Incapable of ascending to high-altitude thinking, the philosopher's vision remains riddled with obscurity. Since the blind spot created by the splitting of the subject cannot be healed, the philosopher is unable to penetrate the heart of the pyramid. Thus he cannot solve the riddle of the sphinx. The tear, cleavage, cut in his eagle eye prevents *him* from consummating *his* philosophical project. This impotence petrifies the philosopher.

Overleaf: Stefan Richter, *Tattoo*. Courtesy of Quartet Books, Ltd.

4

Real

J A C Q U E S   L A C A N

The Reel Thing

In an essay entitled "The Thing" (*Das Ding*), Heidegger writes:

> The terrifying [*Das Entsetzende*] is unsettling; it places everything
> outside its own essence. What is it that unsettles and thus
> terrifies? It shows itself and hides itself in the *way* in which
> everything presences, namely, in the fact that despite all over-
> coming of distances [*Entfernungen*] the nearness of things remains
> absent.
>   What about nearness [*Nähe*]? How can we come to know its
> own nature or essence? Nearness, it seems, cannot be encountered
> directly. We manage to reach it by attending to what is near. Near
> to us are what we usually call things. But what is a thing? (*PLT*,
> 166)

This seemingly simple question provides the occasion for one of
Heidegger's most provocative meditations on the question of Being.
In order to rethink the interrelation of *Sein* and *Seiendes*, Heidegger
approaches the problem of the thing by way of a consideration of a
highly suggestive "jug" (*Krug*).

The jug, Heidegger explains, is a "holding vessel" made by a
potter. And yet "the potter in no way constitutes what is peculiar and
proper to the jug insofar as it is *qua* jug" (*PLT*, 168). The thing, in the
strict sense of the term, is not made by the potter, or anyone else. *Das
Ding* is not an ob-ject—a *Gegen-stand*—that "stands before, over
against, opposite" us. Insofar as the "jug's thingness resides in its
being *qua* vessel," the jug must be understood as a void, emptiness—
even nothingness. "When we fill the jug with wine, do we pour the
wine between the sides and the bottom? At most, we pour the wine
between the sides and over the bottom. Sides and bottom are, to be
sure, what is impermeable in the vessel. But what is impermeable is
not yet what does the holding. When we fill the jug, the pouring that

fills it flows into the empty jug. The emptiness, the void [*die Leere*], is what does the vessel's holding. The emptiness, the void, this nothingness [*dieses Nichts*] of the jug, is what the jug is as the holding vessel" (*PLT,* 169; 167). Instead of making the jug, the potter merely "shapes the void," which he does not create. Since "the vessel's thingness does not lie at all in the material of which it consists, but in the void that holds," the thing is not constituted by a *constructive* subject. A circumscribed void or hollow, the thing escapes the grasp of comprehension.

This elusive thing simultaneously emerges and withdraws in an act of exchange. Witholding "manifests" itself in an "outpouring" that is the giving of a gift. "The nature of the holding void is gathered in the giving [*Schenken*]. But giving is richer than a mere pouring out. The giving, whereby the jug is a jug, gathers in the twofold holding—in the outpouring [*Ausgiessen*]. We call the gathering of the twofold holding into the outpouring, which, as a being together, first constitutes the full presence of giving: the poured gift [*Geschenk*]. The jug's jug-character consists in the poured gift of the pouring out" (*PLT,* 172). The jug gives . . . *Es gibt* . . . a gift . . . *un don*. This giving of a gift is a sacrifice that is a "gushing forth." The "place" of this generous giving or excessive expenditure is the sacrificial altar. "The outpouring [*Guss:* gush] is the libation poured out for the immortal gods. The gift of the outpouring as libation is the authentic gift. In giving the consecrated libation, the pouring jug occurs as the giving gift. The consecrated libation is what our word for a strong outpouring flow, "gush," really designates: gift and sacrifice [*Spende und Opfer*]. "Gush," Middle English, *guschen, gosshen*—*cf.* German *Guss* [gush, torrent, gutter, fount], *giessen* [pour, spill, sprinkle—is the Greek *cheein,* the Indo-European *ghu*. It means to offer in sacrifice. To pour a gush, when it is achieved essentially, thought through with sufficient generosity, and genuinely uttered, is to donate, to offer in sacrifice, and hence to give" (*PLT,* 172–73).

By virtue of the donation of the thing—the thing that is *das Ding an sich*—"earth and sky, divinities and mortals come to dwell *together all at once*" (*PLT,* 173). The thing "is" the emptiness, the void, the nothingness in the midst of the fourfold where all things are interlaced. "Preceding everything that is present," the hollow thing itself is never properly present (*PLT,* 173). In the act of exchange, the thing emerges as a withdrawing, for it is revealed as self-concealing. Though never present, the thing is not absent. It is *near.* "Nearness preserves farness [*Ferne*]. Preserving farness, nearness presences nearness in nearing that farness. Bringing near in this way, nearness conceals its own self and remains, in its own way, nearest of all" (*PLT*, 178).

The nearness of the thing conditions everything. Unable to construct "the thing itself," the creative subject is, in Heidegger's neologism, "conditioned" or "be-thing-ed [*be-ding-t*]." The void of the thing discloses the nothingness in the midst of all things. Heidegger describes the altar of this nothing or no thing as "death." "Death is the shrine of Nothing [*der Schrein des Nichts*], that is, of that which in every respect is never something that merely exists, but which nevertheless presences [*west*], even as the mystery of Being itself. As the shrine of Nothing, death harbors within itself the presencing of Being" (*PLT*, 178–79).

The intimate relation between *das Ding* and death suggests an unexpected association between the real thing (i.e., *das Ding an sich*) in which Heidegger rethinks Being and beings and the reel thing (i.e., "*die Holzspule*" [wooden reel]) that occasions Freud's reconception of Eros and Thanatos. As Heidegger's thing itself (which, in French, is *la chose elle-même*) figures the presence/absence of *Sein*, in and through which all beings exist, so Freud's reel thing stages a play of *fort/da* in and through which the withdrawal of the mother's *sein* draws the death haunting every subject near. To appreciate the implications of the relationship between *das Sein* and *le sein*, it is necessary to recast Heidegger's question "What is a thing?" to read: "What is a jug?" Or, more precisely: "What are jugs?"

Jugs, of course, are breasts.[1] Inasmuch as the gift of the breast nourishes and sustains life, its withdrawal signals death. As Kierkegaard explains in *Fear and Trembling*, "When the child is to be weaned, the mother, too, is not without sorrow, because she and the child are more and more to be separated, because the child who first lay under her heart and later rested upon her breast will never again be so close. So they mourn [*sorge*] together the brief sorrow" (*FT*, 13; 3:66). This

1. At first glance, this association might seem highly arbitrary. It is, however, important to recall that Lacan was not only seriously interested in Heidegger's philosophy but was also fascinated by surrealism. The possibility of joining Heidegger's analysis of the question of *Sein* and the Freudian interpretation of *le sein* is suggested by an entry in *Dictionnaire Abrégé du Surrealisme* (Paris: Galerie Beaux-Arts, 1938): "The breast [*le sein*] is the bosom [*la poitrine*] elevated to the state of mystery—the moralized bosom" (Novalis). "The mother [*la mère*] of evening, such as the breasts of Amélie" (Rimbaud). "My wife with breasts of night—my wife with breasts of ruby-colored crucible" (André Breton). "Breasts, Oh my heart" (Paul Eluard). The interplay between Heidegger's notion of *Sein* and the image of the breast—especially the mother's breast—is also important in the writings of Bataille, Kristeva, and Derrida.

mourning is bound to a melancholy that can never be completely worked through. With the loss of *Sein/sein,* the sacrificial altar becomes "the hymenal altar" over which the impossible "goddess" presides. Along this limen that both joins and separates *genres,* "the thing" of man and *le sein* of woman overlap. *Das Ding* "is" *la chose; es ist . . . ça est.* When "*ça parle,*" she utters . . . utters something like a "death sentence": "*Viens . . .* Come."

Though never present as such, Heidegger's *Das Ding* echoes throughout Lacan's *La chose freudienne.* According to Lacan, Freud's entire undertaking is a response to the seductive call of the goddess.

> But if a more serious metaphor befits the protagonist, it is that which shows us in Freud an Actaeon perpetually slipped by dogs that have been tracked down from the beginning, and which he strives to draw back into pursuit, without being able to slacken the chase in which only his passion for the goddess leads him on. Leads him on so far that he cannot stop until he reaches the grottoes in which the chthonian Diana in the damp shade, which makes them appear as the emblematic refuge of truth, offers to his thirst, with the smooth surface of death, the quasi-mystical limit of the most rational discourse in the world, so that we might recognize the place in which the symbol is substituted for death in order to take possession of the first swelling [*boursouflure:* turgidity] of life. (*E,* 124; 412)

In a way similar to the enigmatic Heideggerian thing, which conceals itself in its very disclosure, *la chose freudienne* "withdraws [*se dérobe:* steals away, escapes: *dérober:* to steal, purloin, conceal] as soon as she appears" (*E,* 121, 408). Since *la chose,* like *das Ding,* is not at the disposal of the self-conscious subject, Lacan maintains that it is necessary to *wait* for the thing to speak of itself. When *la chose parle d'elle-même,* she warns the I/eye of reason:

> Whether you flee me in fraud or think to entrap me in error [*erreur*], I will rejoin you in the mistake [*méprise*] against which you have no refuge. In that place where the most caustic speech reveals a slight hesitation [*trébuchement; trébucher:* to stumble, slip, err], it is lacking in perfidy, I am now publicly announcing the fact, and it would be rather more subtle to pretend that nothing had happened, in good, or for that matter, bad company. . . . All the same the conjoint jurisdictions of politeness and politics would declare as unacceptable whatever is associated with me by presenting itself in so illicit a way, you will not get off so lightly, for the most innocent intention is disconcerted at being unable to conceal the fact that one's missing [*manqués*] acts are the most

successful and that one's failure [*échec*] fulfills one's most secret
wish. In any case, is it not enough to judge of your defeat to see
me escape [*évader*] first from the dungeon of the fortress in which
you are so sure you have secured me by situating me not in
yourselves, but in being itself? I wander about [*vagabonde*] in
what you regard as being least true in essence: in the dream, in
the way the most far-fetched witticism, the most grotesque
nonsense of the pun defies sense and meaning, in chance, not in its
law, but in its contingency, and I never do more to change the face
of the world than when I give it the profile of Cleopatra's nose. (*E*,
122; 410)

To follow the chthonian goddess into her shady grottoes, to listen to
the "incessant murmur" of her "grotesque nonsense," is to journey to
the underworld from which there is no return. In Hades, which,
paradoxically, is also Arcadia, the master of self-consciousness encounters death, and death sends him reeling.

Lacan rereads Heidegger's real thing in terms of Freud's "reel thing"
(*chose réelle*),[2] and vice versa. The reel thing is, of course, "the bobbin"
(*bobine:* spool, reel; a grotesque figure; *FFC*, 239; 216) with which
the child anxiously plays when the mother disappears. The *fort/da* of
the spool implies an interweaving of presence and absence. In the
well-known description of his grandson's play, Freud writes:

> At the same time, he was greatly attached to his mother, who had
> not only fed him herself but had also looked after him without
> any outside help. This good little boy, however, had an occasional
> disturbing habit of taking any small objects he could get hold of
> and throwing them away from him into a corner under the bed,
> and so on, so that the hunting for his toys and picking them up
> was often quite a business. As he did this, he gave vent to a loud,
> long-drawnout "o-o-o-o," accompanied by an expression of inter-
> est and satisfaction. His mother and the writer of the present
> account were agreed in thinking that this was not a mere
> interjection but represented the German word "*fort* [gone]." I
> eventually realized that it was a game and that the only use he
> made of any of his toys was to play "gone" with them. One day I
> made an observation that confirmed my view. The child had a
> wooden reel with a piece of string tied around it. It never
> occurred to him to pull it along the floor behind him, for instance
> and play at its being a carriage. What he did was to hold the reel
> by the string and very skillfully throw it over the edge of his

2. The association of the feminine and the real is suggested by the word "*réelle—
ré-elle.*

curtained cot, so that it disappeared into it, at the same time uttering his expressive "o-o-o-o." He then pulled the reel out of the cot again by the string and hailed its reappearance with a joyful "*da* [there]."[3]

Lacan explores the far-reaching implications of this *da* by taking Freud's account of the play of *fort/da* as a point of departure for the development of a corrective to Heidegger's interpretation of *Dasein*. "There can be no *fort* without *da,* and one might say, without *Dasein*. But contrary to the whole tendency of the phenomenology of *Daseinanalyse,* there can be no *Dasein* without the *fort*" (*FFC*, 239; 216). *Dasein,* in other words, in the "presence" of an "absence." The *da* of *Dasein* is the *fort* of both *das Sein* and *le sein*. In different terms, the child can be born only when the mother withdraws her breast. Everything "begins" with a catastrophic cleavage. The mother slips away when the child learns to speak in "the name of the father." In the first chapter of the *Phenomenology of Spirit,* Hegel argues that language harbors an absence that is the result of the negation of the sensual immediacy of the *hic et nunc*—the here and now, *l'ici et le maintenant*.[4] Lacan effectively reformulates Hegel's insight when he identifies "the word" as "a presence made of absence."

> Through the word—already a presence made of absence—absence itself gives itself a name in that moment of origin whose perpetual recreation Freud's genius detected in the play of the child. And from this couple of sounds [i.e., *fort/da*] modulated on presence and absence—a coupling that the trace [*la trace*] in the sand of the single and broken line [*trait*] of the mantic *kwa* of China would also serve to constitute—there is born the universe of sense or meaning of a language in which the universe of things will come to be arranged. Through that which becomes embodied only by being the trace of a nothingness [*la trace d'un néant*] and whose support cannot thereafter be altered, the concept, saving the duration of that which passes, engenders the thing. (*E,* 65; 276)

The absence *of* the word discloses the nothingness *of* the thing. Both Heidegger and Lacan underscore the etymological link between "thing" (Latin, *res*) and "nothing or no thing (French, *rien*).[5] Within

3. Sigmund Freud, *Beyond the Pleasure Principle,* trans. J. Strachey (New York: Norton, 1961), pp. 7–8.

4. See *PS,* 58–66; 79–89.

5. Lacan writes: "If we try to grasp in language the constitution of the object, we cannot fail to notice that this constitution is to be found only at the level of concept, a very different thing from a simple nominative, and that the *thing,* when reduced to a

the strictures of the father's word, the trace is always "the trace of a nothing." This trace "betrays in speech a center, exterior to language," which "manifests a structure" (*E*, 105; 320).

Lacan labels the structure of language betrayed by the trace "the symbolic order." Following Lévi-Strauss's extension of Saussurean linguistics in structural anthropology, Lacan contends that the symbolic order, like Heidegger's *Ding*, first emerges in the "exchange of gifts." In this economy of exchange, *le don* always involves a *coup*. Lacan explains that "all arises from the structure of the signifier. This structure is based on what I first called the function of the cut [*coupure:* incision, slit, break; suppression] and which is now articulated, in the development of my discourse, as the topological function of the margin or rim [*bord:* edge, brink, border, hem; shore, bank]" (*FFC*, 206; 188). The topological function of the margin recalls the text-ure of Merleau-Ponty's chiasmus. The symbolic order is comprised of an interwoven network in which signifiers assume determinate identity through their differential play. This fabric of signifiers is not constructed by creative subjects. To the contrary, the tissue of signification is antecedent to and constitutive of every individual subject. Subjectivity is a function of inscription in the textured symbolic order. While the birth of subjectivity presupposes the intertwining of the symbolic order, such entanglement is, nonetheless, catastrophic for the emerging subject. Lacan describes this catastrophe in terms of the *coupure* inflicted by "the Name-of-the-Father." The Name-of-the-Father is, in effect, the name Abraham—Abraham, the father of faith who, having left Sarah far behind, hears the words of the Father whispering in his ear: "'Take your son, . . . your only child Isaac, whom you love, and go to the land of Moriah. There you shall offer him as a burnt offering, on a mountain I will point out to you'" (*Genesis* 22:1–2).

The symbolic order is the Law and the Law is always "the Law-of-the-Father." The antecedent linguistic structure within which the subject is caught includes all the codes by which a culture regulates the systems of exchange (e.g., psychological, sociological, political, religious, and economic) necessary for its own preservation. In this way, the cut left by the Name-of-the-Father secures culture by continually wresting the subject from the bosom of "mother" nature. The function of the symbolic order appears most clearly in the primal law of culture: the incest taboo. The law of the father first ruptures the

---

noun, breaks up the double, divergent beam of the cause in which it has taken shelter in the French word *chose,* and the nothing (*rien*) to which it has abandoned its Latin dress (*rem*)" (*E,* 150; 498). Compare Heidegger, "The Thing" (*PLT,* 175–76).

mother-child dyad and then makes reunion with the maternal *sein* "impossible." The word of the father is the word of prohibition: "No. . . . Thou shalt not!"

As the system governing all behavior, language, in Lacan's extended use of the term, serves as something like a "template"[6] that patterns thought and action. The systematic structure or structural system into which the subject is born constitutes the universality ingredient in all individuality. Lacan is convinced that psychoanalysis exhibits the true significance of Hegel's recognition of the unavoidable interrelation of universality and particularity in concrete individuality. "But if there still remains something prophetic in Hegel's insistence on the fundamental identity of the particular and the universal, an insistence that reveals the measure of his genius, it is certainly psychoanalysis that provides it with its paradigm by revealing the structure in which that identity is realized as disjunctive [*disjoignante*] of the subject" (E, 80; 292).[7]

We have seen that for Hegel, universality and particularity join in spirit. The structure of spirit becomes transparent in absolute knowledge, which emerges when the subject becomes totally self-conscious.[8] Over against Hegel, Lacan contends that the universal symbolic order within which every individual is inscribed is irreducibly unconscious. For Lacan, "the unconscious is structured like a language." To develop his interpretation of the linguisticality of the unconscious, Lacan draws extensively on the work of Lévi-Strauss. In "The Effectiveness of Symbols," Lévi-Strauss reinterprets Saussure's distinction between *la langue* and *la parole* in a way intended to account for the structural commonality of *all* psychic functioning. The unconscious, Lévi-Strauss suggests, is a structure that can best be understood in terms of a linguistic analogy.

> The unconscious . . . is always empty—or, more accurately, it is as alien to mental images as is the stomach to the foods that pass through it. As the organ of a specific function, the unconscious

6. I borrow this term from Clifford Geertz. See his "Religion as a Cultural System," in *The Religious Situation,* ed. D. Cutler (Boston: Beacon Press, 1968), pp. 639–88.

7. Kojève's lectures, which Lacan attended, left a lasting impression on his thinking. While Lacan is critical of Hegel's speculative philosophy, he reformulates many Hegelian insights in terms of Freudian psychoanalysis.

8. Prior to such self-consciousness, the subject is unconscious of the forces operating through it. Hegel describes these forces as the "cunning of reason." As this phrase implies, the Hegelian unconscious is not radical but is, in principle, open to decipherment by the conscious subject.

merely imposes structural laws upon inarticulated elements that originate elsewhere—impulses, emotions, representations, and memories. We might say, therefore, that the preconscious is the individual lexicon where each of us accumulates the vocabulary of his personal history, but that this vocabulary becomes significant, for us and for others, only to the extent that the unconscious structures it according to its laws and thus transforms it into language. . . . If we add that these structures are not only the same for everyone and for all areas to which the function applies, but that they are few in number, we shall understand why the world of symbolism is infinitely varied in content, but always limited in its laws. There are many languages, but very few structural laws valid for all languages.[9]

By extending Lévi-Strauss's analysis through a rereading of Freud in terms of structural linguistics and anthropology, Lacan develops a reinterpretation of Hegel. While Hegel is persuaded that "re-collection" (Er-Innerung) heals the wound separating universality and particularity, Lacan insists that the rift between the universal (the unconscious) and the particular (consciousness) forever splits the subject, thereby rendering transparent self-consciousness unattainable.

As a result of its inescapable altarity, the unconscious remains excentric to consciousness. The subject, therefore, is inwardly torn and divided against itself. The excentricity/eccentricity of the subject calls into question the principles governing the Western philosophical tradition. "These principles are simply the dialectic of the consciousness-of-self, as realized from Socrates to Hegel, from the ironic presupposition that all that is rational is real, to its culmination in the scientific view that all that is real is rational. But Freud's discovery was to demonstrate that this verifying process authentically attains the subject only by decentering it [à le décentrer] from the consciousness-of-self, in the axis of which the Hegelian reconstruction of the phenomenology of spirit maintained it" (E, 79–80; 292). Since consciousness and the unconscious forever stand in tension, there is always an unconscious "Other" within the conscious subject. This Other, however, does not actually exist. The unconscious is pre-ontological; "it is neither being nor non-being" (FFC, 29–30; 31–32). Like Heidegger's presencing that is never present, the unconscious presents the self-conscious subject but does not itself ex-ist. Never standing out, the unconscious is always out-standing.

In a manner similar to Merleau-Ponty's "anonymous" imper-

9. Claude Lévi-Strauss, "The Effectiveness of Symbols," *Structural Anthropology*, trans. C. Jacobson and B. G. Schoepf (New York: Doubleday, 1967), p. 203.

sonality, this Other speaks through the "I." "The discourse of the Other" is a "savage word," foreign to the "I" of self-consciousness and inconspicuous to the "eye" of reason. Incessantly interrupted by language it cannot comprehend, the subject is actually "a subject-with-holes" (*sujet troué; FFC*, 184; 167). Merleau–Ponty's "gappy" (*béant*) body reappears as Lacan's holey subject. Lacan goes so far as to insist that the unconscious "conforms to the structure of a gap" (*béance; FFC*, 176; 160). This irrepressible gappiness points to the *primal* repression that constitutes subjectivity. Since the word of the father *severs* the mother-child binary, the birth of the subject is unavoidably traumatic. The subject emerges through a process of *differentiation* in which it struggles to construct its identity by separating itself from otherness. Such differentiation is inseparable from repression. In an effort to establish the equilibrium of the ego, the subject tries to exclude, dominate, or incorporate everything different from itself. But such an exclusive strategy inevitably fails. Following Freud, Lacan argues that subjectivity is never secure. Since the repressed returns to unsettle all domesticating activity, the subject is subjected to, entangled in, and "conditioned" (*be-ding-t*) by an Other it can never control or master.

To appreciate the complexity of Lacan's analysis, it is necessary to recognize different aspects of the altarity he explores. As I have stressed, the subject is split between the particularities of its conscious activity and the universality of the unconscious laws and codes that function through it. The self-conscious ego can never reduce the difference between the conscious and the unconscious to a stable identity. This difference is both alien and alienating. There is, however, a further dimension of altarity "infecting" the subject. The unconscious leaves traces of the "irreducible, traumatic, non-meaning or non-sense" (*non-sens*) to which one "is, as a subject, subjected" (*FFC*, 251; 226). Lacan designates this traumatic altarity "the real" (*le réel*). The real, which the self-conscious subject struggles to exclude but which repeatedly returns to speak through the unconscious, is neither present nor absent. "Where do we meet this real? For what we have in the discovery of psychoanalysis is an encounter, an essential encounter—an appointment to which we are always called with a real that withdraws or steals away [*se dérobe*]" (*FFC*, 53; 53). Having begun as *Traum-deutung*, psychoanalysis becomes *Trauma-deutung*. The real is a "beyond [*au-delà*] that makes itself heard in the dream" (*FFC*, 59; 58). Commenting on Freud's *Traumdeutung*, Lacan queries: "Is not the dream essentially, one might say, an act of homage to the missed or lacking reality [*la réalité manquée*]—the reality that can no longer produce itself except by repeating itself indefinitely, in some never attained awakening?" (*FFC,* 58; 75).

The real is *always* missing, *forever* lacking. It is not "there" (*da*) in the first place, but is always already "gone" (*fort*). As such, the real is something like a "non-original origin." Having never been present, this "origin" cannot be re-presented. The real "thing" can only be imagined in fantasy. "Fantasy [*le fantasme*] and reality converge . . . in something irreducible, *non-sensical,* that functions as an originally repressed signifier" (*FFC,* 251; 226). That which is "originally repressed" signifies neither an original presence nor an original absence, but the presence of an absence that discloses the absence inherent in all presence and every present. Rather than an original present, the real points to (but does not represent) an absolute past. As we have seen, Heidegger describes such irreducible anteriority as the "essential past," Merleau-Ponty as an "original past." As we will see, Levinas describes such irreducible anteriority as the "unrepresentable before," Blanchot as the "dreadfully ancient." This "time before time"—this "non-original origin"—"is" the "primal scene" that never takes place.

Non-sense and non-meaning can no more be comprehended than nonphilosophy can be understood. The real is not only unknown but is unknowable, not only unsaid but "unpronounceable" (*E,* 316; 819). Neither Hegel nor Freud fully recognizes the radical heterogeneity that Lacan labels "the real." Contrary to expectation, the secret of the wholly other is guarded by Abraham. "No doubt the corpse is a signifier, but Moses' tomb is as empty for Freud as that of Christ was for Hegel. Abraham betrayed his mystery to neither of them" (*E,* 316; 818). Though in different ways, the investigations of Hegel and Freud are guided by their devotion to the ideal of *Wissenschaft.* Freud expresses this Hegelian faith when he declares: "Our God [is] *Logos.*" [10] If the real is the rational and the rational the real, the task of the interpreter is to "decode" consciousness by un-veiling true sense underneath apparent non-sense. If, however, non-sense is, as Lacan claims, "irreducible," then the light of reason cannot penetrate every nook and cranny of the mind. Always lurking in the

10. Sigmund Freud, *The Future of an Illusion,* trans. W. D. Robson-Scott (New York: Doubleday and Co., 1964), p. 88. This and similar remarks notwithstanding, Freud is considerably more ambivalent about faith in reason than is Hegel. Few have done more than Freud to cast doubt upon the powers of reason. Nevertheless, the *desire* to transform psychoanalysis into a science sometimes leads Freud in the direction of a rationalism and a positivism that his own insights call into question.

shadows, always lingering in damp shade, grotesque grottoes, or tangled forest of the chthonian Diana, the real is an "exterior darkness" (*ténèbres extérieures; E,* 101; 316).

The exteriority of this darkness is a "pure exteriority" (*pure extériorité; E,* 134; 424), which can be neither remembered nor inwardized. The real, Lacan maintains, is *unassimilable* (*FCC,* 55; 55). This radical Other is "a pure negativity" (*E,* 95; 309). Unlike the Hegelian negative, which, through the magical power of self-consciousness, is transformed into something positive, Lacanian negativity resists assimilation and incorporation. Within the fractured economy of the split subject, there is always an excessive "remainder" (*reste; FFC,* 191; 174) that returns to subvert every investment. Paradoxically, this remainder both resists and engenders reasonable economic and philosophic speculation. Accordingly, *le reste* is simultaneously the condition of the possibility and impossibility of *Wissenschaft.* With this *reste,* Lacan implies a response, *avant la lettre,* to Derrida's question: *quoi du reste aujourd'hui, pour nous, ici, maintenant, d'un Hegel?*

Since "the residue" of the real cannot be conceived, the perfect copulation of subject and object is impossible. For Lacan, as for Freud, the satisfaction that brings pleasure is always delayed or deferred. The "beyond" of the real/reel thing points to what is "beyond the pleasure principle." This beyond is "the missed or lacking reality—the reality that can no longer produce itself except by repeating itself indefinitely" (*FFC,* 58; 57). In the *fort/da* of the real/reel thing, the no-thing-ness of death disrupts the homeostasis of pleasure. "The ensemble of the activity symbolizes repetition, but not at all that of some need that might demand the return of the mother, and which would be expressed quite simply in a cry. It is the repetition of the mother's departure as cause of a *Spaltung* in the subject—overcome by the alternating game [*jeu alternatif*], *fort-da,* which is a *here or there,* and whose aim, in its alternation [*alternance*] is simply the being the *fort* of a *da,* and the *da* of a *fort*" (*FFC,* 62–63; 61). The alternation of the reel repeats the altarity of the unconscious—the unconscious, "which vacillates in a cut of the subject" (*qui vacille dans une coupure du sujet; FFC,* 28; 29). This *coupure* is the incision opened by Abraham.

Lacan maintains that it is Kierkegaard, "the most acute questioner of the soul before Freud," who first recognizes the psychological importance of the story of Abraham (*FFC,* 60–61; 59). According to Lacan, the best way to approach Freud's *Beyond the Pleasure Principle* is "to reread Kierkegaard's essay *Repetition*" (*FFC,* 61; 59). *Repetition* is a fictive repetition of Kierkegaard's inability to copulate. The anonymous young man who cannot marry his beloved mirrors Søren's incapacity to wed Regina. The impossibility repeated in *Repetition* (as well as many of Kierkegaard's other texts) is closely associated with the incision figured in Abraham's raised knife. I have stressed that conception is not merely a sexual affair; it is also a matter of knowledge. Kierkegaard sets "repetition" (*Gjentagelse*) over against Hegelian "recollection" (*Er-indring*). "Recollection," Kierkegaard writes, "is the pagan lifeview, repetition is the modern. Repetition is the *interest* of metaphysics, and at the same time the interest upon which metaphysics founders." [11] *Repetition*/repetition marks the end of metaphysics by inscribing the eternal return of time. From Kierkegaard's point of view, Hegel's speculative philosophy represses time by attempting to incorporate or assimilate temporal and spatial existence within the eternal life of the concept. Anticipating Heidegger, Merleau-Ponty, and others, Kierkegaard insists that time remains both retrospectively and prospectively open-ended. "Repetition and recollection are the same movement, only in opposite directions; for what is recollected has been, is repeated backwards [*baglænds*], whereas repetition properly so called is recollected forwards [*erindres forlænds*]." [12] The past that is never finished approaches as a future that is never closed. To move toward this *futur antérieur* is to "recollect forwards." Repetition ruptures the closed circle in which beginning and end, Alpha and Omega are one. By holding open the time of space and the space of time, "repetition," in Lacan's words, "demands the new" (*FFC*, 61; 59). Lacan clarifies this cryptic remark in a passage that joins Freud's death instinct and Heidegger's notion of being-toward-death.

> In the same way as the repetition compulsion . . . has in view nothing less than the historicizing temporality of the experience of transference, so does the death instinct essentially express the limit of the historical function of the subject. This limit is death—not as an eventual coming-to-term [*échéance*] of the life of the individual, nor as the empirical certainty of the subject, but as Heidegger's formula puts it, as that "possibility that is one's ownmost, unconditional, unsupersedable, certain, and, as such, indeterminable," for the subject—"subject" understood as meaning the subject defined by his historicity. Indeed, this limit is at every instant present in what this history possesses as achieved. This limit represents the past in its real form [*forme réelle*], that is

11. Søren Kierkegaard, *Repetition: An Essay in Experimental Psychology,* trans. W. Lowrie (Princeton: Princeton University Press, 1964), p. 53; 3 : 189.

12. Ibid., p. 33; 3 : 175.

to say, not the physical past whose existence is abolished, nor the epic past in which man finds the guarantor of his future, but the past that manifests itself reversed in repetition. (*E*, 103; 318)

In repetition, the past that is never present is reversed and appears as the future that is always deferred. The guise of this future is death. Death, as Merleau-Ponty and Blanchot stress, is the present absence or absent presence that forms the ever approaching-receding horizon of human experience. The "beyond" of death opens with repetition.

From Lacan's perspective, Freud extends and deepens the criticism of self-consciousness that begins with Kierkegaard. For Freud, as for Kierkegaard, satisfaction is impossible. Repeating the structure of Hegel's unhappy consciousness, the split subject of psychoanalysis remains suspended between opposites it cannot reconcile. Freud approaches the question of what lies beyond the pleasure principle through a consideration of the difference between *Erinnern* and *Wiederholen*—recollection and repetition.[13] The never-present past, which cannot be recollected, *repeatedly* returns to split, fissure, fault, and crack the subject. To maintain, with Freud and Nietzsche, that repetition is eternal is to insist that the origin is inaccessible. If there is always already repetition, there is no source that is not secondary— no "matrix" (*matrix:* womb, from *mater,* mother) that is primal. By marking the impossibility of any originary *Sein/sein,* the real/reel thing remarks the lack *of* desire.

The Evil Eye /I: Pan Optics

Two grotesque monsters: one snaky-haired, the other with goat ears, horns, and legs. Two dispositions: fascination and panic. The dis-position provoked by these monsters "is" the crack of desire.

The breast fascinates. This is, perhaps, why the breast sometimes is called "the big brown eye." [14] The eye that fascinates is the evil eye, which casts a spell on those who fall under its gaze. "Fascination" derives from the Greek word for evil eye, *baskanos.* The Latin *fascinum* means "the evil eye, witchcraft, an enchanting or bewitching." One of the most feared evil eyes is that of the snaky-haired Medusa. The once

13. See "Remembering, Repeating, and Working-Through," *The Standard Edition of the Complete Psychological Works of Sigmund Freud,* trans. J. Strachey (New York: 1976), vol. 12.

14. Eugene Landy, *The Underground Dictionary* (New York: Simon and Schuster, 1971), p. 39.

beautiful Medusa angered Athena by laying with Poseidon in Athena's own shrine. Athena sought revenge by turning Medusa's hair into serpents and making her face so hideous that her gaze was petrifying. Still not satisfied, Athena conspired with Perseus to behead Medusa. According to Euripides, Medusa's blood was a *pharmakon*. In *Ion,* Athena gives two drops of Medusa's blood to Erichthonius, king of Athens: "one drop cured disease, the other was a deadly poison." [15] One of the most important aftereffects of the gaze of the evil eye is envy. The Hebrew word expressing envy, קִנְאָה, also designates the evil eye. The protection against the fascinating gaze and the envy it provokes is the *fascinus*—an amulet in the shape of a phallus.

Pan, son of Hermes and Penelope and lover of the chattering nymph Echo, protected the Athenians by frightening their enemies with a terrifying shout. Less often noted but no less important than Pan's responsibility for panic is the fact that his union with Echo issues in Iambe. Iambe produced the hilarious rites that interrupted the serious proceedings surrounding the Eleusinian Mysteries. She also created satiric verse know as Iambic. Iambe's end was not unlike that of Medusa. Plagued by the pain inflicted by her cutting words, she hanged herself.

Speculative philosophy, I have argued, claims to be all-seeing and all-knowing. The penetrating gaze of the philosopher's eagle eye is pan-optical. Classical authors derive the name Pan from a word that means "all." In view of the omnivorous appetite of speculative philosophy it is, perhaps, significant that the name Pan means "He Who Eats." I have already noted that, in the final chapter of the *Phenomenology of Spirit,* Hegel insists that "the self has to penetrate [*durchdringen*] and digest [*verdauen*] [the] entire wealth of its substance (*PS,* 492; 563)." Following Heidegger's claim that Western metaphysics culminates in the modern philosophy of the subject, Lacan interprets Hegel's desire to penetrate and incorporate everything as, among other things, an extension of the Cartesian quest for certainty. Convinced of the failure of the philosophical project that receives its most complete expression in Hegel's philosophy, Lacan declares:

> I promise . . . to show that the effective experience that has been
> established in the perspective of an absolute knowledge never
> leads us to anything that may, in any way, illustrate the Hegelian
> vision of successive syntheses, nothing that provides even so

15. Tripp, *Crowell's Handbook of Classical Mythology,* p. 364. In this description of Medusa and Pan, I have followed Tripp's account.

97

much as a hint of the movement that Hegel in some obscure way links to this stage, and which someone has been pleased to illustrate by the title of *Dimanche de la vie*—when no opening remains gaping [*aucune ouverture ne resterait béante*] at the heart of the subject. (*FFC*, 221; 201)

To expose the gaping opening of the subject, which Hegel struggles to close, Lacan fashions a critique of Hegelianism that proceeds as if from "within" the System. Like Merleau-Ponty (as well as Bataille, Levinas, Blanchot, and Derrida), Lacan believes that Hegel has a "blind spot." Though largely derived from Hegel's analysis of the struggle for recognition, Lacan's account of the formation of the "I" calls into question the presuppositions and conclusions of speculative philosophy. Lacan's critique of Hegel is already evident in the opening words of his highly influential lecture, "The mirror stage as formative of the function of the I as revealed in psychoanalytic experience."

The conception of the mirror stage that I introduced at our last congress, thirteen years ago, has since become more or less established in the practice of the French group. However, I think it would be worthwhile to bring it to your attention again, especially today, for the light it sheds on the formation of the "I" as we experience it in psychoanalysis. It is an experience that leads us to oppose any philosophy directly issuing from the *Cogito*. (*E*, 1; 93)

As its name implies, speculative philosophy is produced by a play of mirrors.[16] If the subject is to reach the goal of speculative philosophy, i.e., "*pure* self-recognition in absolute otherness," the "I" must see itself reflected in *everything* (*PS*, 407; 470). Hegel is persuaded that at the end of its arduous journey, the totally self-conscious subject enjoys the fruits of its labors: "the vision of itself in the other [*Andern*]" (*PS*, 407; 470).

Borrowing arguments initially advanced by Hegel, Lacan maintains that the "I" or the ego is "a *feedback* construction" (*une construction de* feed-back; (*E*, 139; 429). The ego begins to emerge at what Lacan describes as "the mirror stage" in the development of the personality. Bound by an uncontrollable body and driven by conflicting drives, the infant's first experience of itself as an integrated totality is a function of its recognition of the image of itself reflected in the eyes of others. Since the ego as a whole is an effect of reflective mirroring,

16. Speculative derives from *speculari*, to spy out, watch, observe. Compare: *specula*, watchtower (which serves as something like a panoptical); and *speculum*, a mirror.

Lacan labels it the "specular ego." Always seeking satisfaction, the specular ego is governed by the pleasure principle. In explaining one of his notoriously complex diagrams, Lacan remarks:

> You see, marked by the capital letters ICH, the *Ich* as apparatus tending to a certain homeostasis—which cannot be the lowest because that would be death. . . . As for the *Lust,* this is not a field strictly speaking, it is always an object, an object of pleasure, which, as such, is mirrored in the ego. This mirror-image, this bi-univocal correlate of the object, is here the purified *Lust-Ich* of which Freud speaks, namely, that which, in the *Ich,* is satisfied with the object *qua Lust. (FCC,* 241; 219)

The pleasure that the specular ego longs for arises through a process of "identification" (*FFC,* 242; 218). I have emphasized that the foundation of speculative reflection is the principle of identity in which difference is, in the final analysis (i.e., the analysis that is not interminable), reduced to or incorporated within identity. Since it is ruled by the principle of identity, the pleasure-seeking ego is inevitably "auto-erotic." In different terms, the effort of the speculative I/eye to see itself in every "other" is essentially narcissistic. The love of the "I" is always an *amour-propre* (*E,* 137; 427). Such narcissistic love is inseparably bound up with aggression. Unwilling to tolerate difference, the "loving" "I" seeks satisfaction by dominating others and assimilating difference. This struggle for mastery is the psychological form of "the will to power" that Heidegger believes to be characteristic of the modern philosophy of the subject.

In opposition to Hegel, Lacan contends that the "I," like Narcissus, disappears in the reflecting pool. While Hegel argues that specular subjectivity achieves full realization in the speculative knowledge unfolded in his System, Lacan maintains that the specular ego is an ideality that never becomes actual. Investment in this ego is, therefore, always a matter of speculation. "As a specular mirage [*mirage spéculaire*], love is essentially deception [*tromperie*]. It is situated in the field established at the level of the pleasure reference, of that sole signifier necessary to introduce a perspective centered on the Ideal point, capital I, placed somewhere in the Other, from which the Other sees me, in the form I like to be seen" (*FFC,* 268; 241).[17] Love, in other words, is always disappointing. "When in love, I solicit a look or a gaze [*regard*], what is profoundly unsatisfying and always missing [*manqué*] is that— *You never look at me from the place from which I*

17. In the passage with which I began chapter 3, Lacan credits Merleau-Ponty with the recognition of the importance of the phenomenon of the gaze of the other.

see you. Conversely, *what I look at is never what I wish to see"* (*FFC,* 102–3; 94–95). Since it always eludes the grasp of the knowing subject, the gaze of the other interrupts rather than completes self-consciousness. "The dialectic of the eye and the gaze," Lacan maintains, "is not a point of coincidence, but [is] functionally a lure [*leurre:* decoy, snare, trap]" (*FFC,* 102; 94). The lure of speculative philosophy is the promise to heal the wound or mend the tear rending the subject. Its cure, however, is nothing more than a *trompe-l'œil*. Psychoanalysis exposes the gaze of the other as the blind spot of Hegelianism. This exposure transforms the eye of the other into "the evil eye." "It is striking, when one thinks of the universality of the function of the evil eye, that there is no trace anywhere of a good eye, of an eye that blesses. What can this mean, except that the eye carries with it the fatal function of being itself endowed—if you will allow me to play on several registers at once—with a power to separate [*pouvoir séparatif*]. But this separating goes much further than distinct vision" (*FFC,* 115; 105).

The evil eye of the other is, as I have suggested, the eye of Medusa. The gaze of Medusa subverts philosophy's *amour-propre* by interrupting the circuit of reflection. This interruption effectively *alters* philosophy. In different terms, the eye of Medusa castrates the philosopher. "The evil eye is the *fascinum,* it is that which has the effect of arresting movement and, literally, of killing life. At the moment the subject stops, suspending his gesture, he is mortified. The anti-life, anti-movement function of this terminal point is the *fascinum,* and it is precisely one of the dimensions in which the power of the gaze is exercised directly. The moment of seeing can intervene here only as a suture, a conjunction of the imaginary and symbolic, and it is taken up again in a dialectic, that sort of temporal progress that is called in haste, thrust, forward movement, which is concluded in the *fascinum"* (*FFC,* 118; 107). The problem with speculative philosophy is that its hastily stitched suture always comes undone. This is Abraham's secret. Though Hegel seeks to flee the petrifying gaze of Abraham by returning to the beautiful Greek pair, Deucalion and Pyrrha, who bring stones to life, he stumbles along the way. His argument is filled with holes and thus his text unravels. Lacan believes that the undoing of speculative philosophy is the result of the lack of desire. Always linked to lack, "desire is based on castration" (*FFC,* 118; 108).

Desire is a function of the subject's *manque à être*. This "lack of being" engenders a "want of being" (*manque à être*). Ever wanting, the subject's being is a "want-to-be." The lack (*manque*) that gives birth to this want (*manque*) is a function of the incisive cut (*coupure*) of separation. There are at least two dimensions of separation that contribute to desire: the separation of the subject from others, and the separation of the self from itself.

The birth of the subject involves a traumatic separation from the maternal matrix. The gap between mother and child deepens when the name of the Father intervenes. By barring a return to the mother, the Father makes the infant's loss irrecoverable. The incest taboo promulgated in the name of the Father effectively castrates the son. As a result of the internalization of the Father's "No," the subject itself is "barred" (*barré*). In Lacanian calculus, "$" designates the split subject produced by primal repression. Never identical with itself, the faulty subject is haunted by an unknowable Other. An "outside" that is "inside," this Other hollows out the "place" of desire.

"Man's desire," Lacan argues, "is the desire of the Other (*le désir de l'Autre; FFC,* 235; 213). The "of" in this well-known formula is polyvalent and must, therefore, be read in several ways. The desire *of* the Other is the Other's desire. Just as Heidegger's *Sprache spricht* and Merleau-Ponty's "savage word speaks" through the "I," so the desire of the Other "speaks" through the "I." I do, the "I" does not, desire. To the contrary, an Other desires in and through the "I." Thus I do not know what I want, for my desire is unconscious. More precisely, my desire is the desire of an Other that is the unconscious itself. Lacan's "of" can, however, be understood differently. The desire *of* the Other is "my" desire *for* the Other. Insofar as the Other "I" desire is indissociable from the mother, my desire for the Other is a desire for the mother I have always already lost. To fulfill this desire, I would have to *be* what the mother desires. But "What does woman want [*manque*]?" "What does woman lack [*manque*]?" Though neither man nor woman can be sure, man guesses that woman wants/lacks the phallus. The desire *of* the Other is, accordingly, the desire to *be* the phallus *for* the mother. I, the capital I—ICH, must always stand *erect* in order to satisfy mother. The erection of the Son threatens to displace the Father. The Father responds with a "No," which, like the gaze of Medusa, decapitates the capital "I" erected in speculative philosophy. The Father's *coup d'œil* opens a "wound" (*coup*) in the "eye" (*œil*) of the philosopher that his knowledge never heals. Inasmuch as the "I" is forever unsettled by an Other that cannot be returned to same and a difference that cannot be reduced to identity, satisfaction is never achieved. Since fulfillment is impossible, desire is endless.

The prospect of interminable desire sends panic through the philosopher. Philosophy's narcissistic project is supposed to silence the "incessant murmur" of desire. But desire always returns to echo through the hollow words of philosophy. Echo, whose ceaseless babbling led Hera to condemn her to repeat forever the last words of others—the same Echo who is the lover of Pan and mother of Iambe—obsessively courted Narcissus. Narcissus, however, turned a deaf ear to her solicitous entreaties. To listen to the compulsive repetition of Echo's non-sense is to lose all hope of re-membering.

The hollow sound of Echo's unrequited love tolls the death knell of philosophy. The lack of desire is, for Lacan, a structural "notion" that points to the irrepressible gap in being. *Das Sein—le sein—*is never present but is always missing or lacking. With an additional twist, the phrase *manque à être* underscores the lack of *being,* which is the lack of *being itself.* As Heidegger maintains, this is the lack that Western metaphysics tries to repress. As Lacan demonstrates, this lack always returns.

The impossibility of satisfying desire determines the structure of the drive. While Hegelian philosophy can be represented as "the circle of circles," Freudian psychoanalysis can be graphed as an elliptical ellipse. The "Copernican revolution" by which Freud "decenters" the self-conscious subject can be understood as the displacement of the circle by the ellipse. "The linguistically suggestive use of Copernicus's name has more hidden resources that touch specifically on what has just slipped [*glisser*] from my pen as the relation to the true, namely, the emergence of the ellipse as being not unworthy of the locus from which the so-called higher truths take their name. The revolution is no less important concerning only the 'celestial revolutions'" (*E,* 295; 797). Since something is always missing, the Freudian ellipse is actually an ellipsis. The structure of the drive is open-ended. The drive oscillates or alter-nates in an "outward-and-back [*aller-et-retour*] movement" (*FFC,* 178; 162) between erogenous zones, characterized by their "margin or rim-like structure" (*FFC,* 169; 153), and the object of desire, which is "the presence of a hollow [*creux*], a void [*vide*]" (*FFC,* 168; 164).

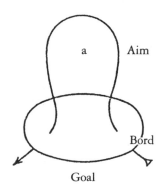

a   Aim

Bord

Goal

Lacan charts the course of the drive in a diagram. Recalling Merleau-Ponty's depiction of the fleshy chiasmus and anticipating Derrida's characterization of the interlaced columns of *Glas*, Lacan describes the structure of the drive in terms of "invagination": "Does it not seem that the drive [*la pulsion*],[18] in this turning inside out [*retournement*] represented by its pocket [*poche*], invaginating [*s'invaginant*] across the erogenous zone, is given the task of seeking something that each time responds to the Other?" (*FFC*, 196; 178).

Since the subject is barred from the Other, its seeking never ends. Every object of desire is a substitute for the real/reel thing. Each object is, therefore, a partial object.[19] Desire moves relentlessly in a process of displacement that Lacan compares to the metonymic play of signifiers. This displacement does not come to rest, for it never reaches its "goal" (*but*) or achieves its "aim" (*but*). Noting that *but* has two meanings, Lacan explains:[20] "In order to differentiate them I have chosen to note them here in a language in which they are particularly expressive, English. When you charge someone with a mission, the *aim* is not what he brings back, but the route he must take. The *aim* is the way taken. The French word *but* may be translated by another English word, *goal*. In archery, the *goal* is not the *but* either; it is not the bird you shoot, it is having scored a hit [*marqué le coup*] and thereby attained your *but*" (*FFC*, 179; 163). If the *but* of the drive is *marquer le coup*—to mark the cut/wound or to score—and if it is impossible to do this without a bird or birdie, then it appears that Lacan's chart of the drive is at the same time a graphic depiction of the organ or organs of the drive. The alternation of the drive suggests that its organ might be something like a scored or scoring shuttle-cock.

Scoring Shuttlecocks

Of all that is savage about savages, the most savage is what they do to themselves. They paint, puncture, tattoo, scarify, cicatrize,

18. In *Ecrits*, Lacan labels *la pulsion* a "bastard term": *la bâtardise du mot* (E, 301; 803). I have already underlined the importance of the term "bastard" in another context. The significance of the bastard for Hegel's family circle is not unrelated to the displacement of the speculative circle by the psychoanalytic ellipse. Precisely how this is so will become clear in the context of the analysis of *Glas*.

19. Lacan labels this object *objet petit a*. This small *a* is to be distinguished from "*le grand A*" of *l'Autre*. *L'objet petit a* and *L'Autre* stand in a substitutive relation which, Lacan maintains, *is not* representative. *L'Autre* resists every effort to represent it.

20. In view of the thrust of his analysis, it is surprising that Lacan omits several additional meanings of the English word "but" and its homophone "butt."

circumcise, subincise themselves. They use their own flesh as so much material at hand for—what? We hardly know how to characterize it—Art? Inscription? Sign-language? . . . What we are dealing with is inscription. Where writing, graphics, is not inscription on clay tablets, bark or papyrus, but in flesh and blood, and also where it is not historical, narrative. Where it is not significant, not a matter of marks whose role is to signify, to efface themselves before the meaning, or ideality, or logos. For here the signs count: they *hurt.*[21]

Lacan warns: "one must never read Freud without one's ears cocked. When one reads such things, one really ought to prick up one's ears" (*FFC,* 168; 153). In his rereading of Freud, Lacan, described by some as a cocky prick, is preoccupied with scoring. What does it mean to score? How does one score or keep score? Why would one score one's own body? Can every score be played, all scores counted, each score settled?

We have seen that the impossibility of satisfaction leaves the drive alternating in an "outward-and-back movement." The drive, in other words, shuttles back and forth between the margin of the erogenous zone and the hollow of its object. As the *arrow* in Lacan's diagram suggests, the organ of this drive is the shuttlecock. The shuttlecock points both back to the fabric or text-ure of Merleau-Ponty's flesh and ahead to the stylus of Derridean writing.

In the course of reinterpreting the mythic account of love that Plato develops in the *Symposium,* Lacan identifies something like a scored shuttlecock. He points out that in analytic experience the subject does not search for his complement but seeks "the part of himself, lost forever, that is constituted by the fact that he is only a sexed living being, and that he is no longer immortal" (*FFC,* 205; 187). In what he describes as "the myth of the lamella," Lacan labels the subject's eternally lost part the "unreal organ" (*organe irréel*). "One of the most ancient forms in which this unreal organ is incarnated in the body, is tattooing [*tatouage*], scarification [*scarification*]. The tattoo certainly has the function of being for the Other, of situating the subject in it, marking his place in the field of the group's relations, between each individual and all the others. And, at the same time, it obviously has an erotic function, which all those who have approached it in reality have perceived" (*FFC,* 205–6; 187). Elsewhere Lacan is even more explicit: "Imagine a tattoo traced [*tatouage tracé*] on the sexual organ

21. Alphonso Lingis, *Excesses: Eros and Culture* (Albany: State University of New York Press, 1983), pp. 22–23.

ad hoc in the state of repose and assuming its, if I dare say, developed form in another state" (*FFC,* 88; 82).[22]

A scored shuttlecock is a tattooed penis. A tattoo is, most obviously, "a permanent mark or design made on the skin by a process of pricking and ingraining an indelible pigment or by raising scars." But a tattoo is also "a signal sounded on drum and bugle to summons soldiers to bed." In this connection, a tattoo is "a beating or pulsation [n.b.] as of a drum; the action of beating, pulsating, thumping, or rapping continuously on something." These lesser-known meanings of "tattoo" reflect the word's derivation from the Dutch *taptoo,* which refers to the shutting off of taps at a tavern (whence the association of "tattoo" and "taps"). In colloquial seventeenth-century Dutch, *taptoe* meant "to shut up or stop." If this meaning of tattoo is combined with the definition of the cock as "a faucet or valve [or tap] by which the flow of a liquid or gas can be regulated," then the tattoo can be understood as the cutting off of the flow of the cock. The cut of the tattoo signifies the restriction of the free flow of fluids from the penis. The rhythmic pulsation of the tattoo is the restless alternation of the drive as it thrusts outward and turns back. The incised penis is the inscribed penis. The scored shuttlecock is the phallus, and the phallus is the signifier of desire.

Desire, we have seen, circulates in the gap, tear, hole separating mother and child. The phallus, Lacan argues, is "a symbol of the lack" (*symbole du manque*) of desire (*FFC,* 103; 95). Like the "of" in "desire of the Other," the "of" in "lack of desire" must be understood in at least two ways. The lack *of* desire is, in the first place, the lack that constitutes or creates desire. I desire because I lack. In the second place, the lack *of* desire designates the satisfaction of desire. To be totally satisfied is to lack desire. Both meanings of the phrase "lack of desire" can be read in the signifying phallus. The phallus is the organ that would satisfy desire by rejoining one to the generative matrix from which he *or she* has always already fallen. In Lacan's economy, however, closing the gap, mending the tear, or filling the hole is impossible, for the phallus is an "unreal organ." As such, the phallus testifies to the abiding lack that "is" desire itself. Always missing, the lack of desire "appears" only as a dis-appointing dis-appearance.

The outward-and-back pulsation of the Lacanian phallus recalls the centrifugal and centripetal rhythm of the Heideggerian Logos. This insight helps to clarify one of Lacan's most baffling remarks: "The

22. The image of the tattooed phallus and its oscillation plays a very important role in the style and substance of *Glas.*

function of the phallic signifier here opens [*débouche*] on its most profound relation: that in which the Ancients embodied the *Nous* and the *Logos*."[23] In a way similar to Heidegger's *Riss,* the tattoo of the scored shuttlecock marks and remarks a play of differences that generates every difference—sexual and otherwise. The phallus, which must not be confused with the penis as such, is neither male nor female. It is *neuter.* The fault of Heidegger's *Sein* returns yet again when *le sein* displaces the phallus. To follow this movement of desire, it is necessary to reconsider "the myth of the lamella."

Lacan describes the lamella in a satirical remark that implicitly criticizes philosophers from Plato to Descartes.

> If you want to stress its joky side, you can call it [i.e., the lamella] *l'hommelette.*[24] This *hommelette,* as you will see, is easier to animate than primal man, in whose head one always has to place a homunculus to get it working.

> Whenever the membranes of an egg in which the fetus emerges on its way to becoming a new-born are broken, imagine for a moment that something flies off, and that one can do it with an egg as easily as with a man, namely the *hommelette,* or the lamella.

> The lamella is something extra-flat, which moves like the amoeba. It is just a little more complicated. But it goes everywhere. And as it is something—I will tell you shortly why—that is related to what the sexed being loses in sexuality, it is, like the amoeba in relation to the sexed beings, immortal—because it [*ça*] survives any division, any scissiparous intervention. And it can run around [*Et ça court*]. (*FFC,* 197; 179–80)[25]

23. This is the last sentence in the essay "The Signification of the Phallus" (*E,* 281–91; 685–95). Lacan neither explains nor elaborates his cryptic remark.

24. Joyce also plays on the word *homme-let* in *Finnegans Wake.* See also Edgar Allan Poe, "The Duc de L'Omelette," *Poetry and Tales* (New York: The Library of America, 1984), pp. 143–46.

25. The last sentence in this passage defies translation. In *Ecrits,* Lacan suggests some of the implications of *ça* in commenting on the difficulties of rendering Freud's sentence *Wo Es war, soll Ich werden* in French. "Thus I would agree . . . to force a little in French the forms of the signifier in order to bring them into line with the weight of a still rebellious signification, which the German carries better here, and therefore to employ the homophony of the German *es* with the initial of the word '*sujet*' (subject). By the same token, I might feel more indulgence, for a time at least, to the first translation that was given the word *es,* namely, '*le soi*' (the self). The '*ça*' (id), which not without good reason, was eventually preferred, does not seem to me to be much more adequate, since it corresponds rather to the German *das,* as in the question '*Was ist das?*', and the answer '*das ist*' ('c'est'). The elided '*c*' that will appear, if we hold to the accepted equivalence, suggests to me the production of the verb, '*s'être*', in which would be expressed the mode of absolute subjectivity, in the sense that Freud properly

The lamella, in other words, is a "remainder" (*reste*) or residue that cannot be assimilated and thus always remains. This remainder, however, does not exist. The lamella, like the unreal organ signified by the phallus, is "an organ whose characteristic is not to exist, but which, nevertheless, is an organ" (*FFC*, 197–98; 180). This nonexistent or unreal organ bears an essential relation to "the real." "The unreal is defined by articulating itself on the real in a way that escapes us, and it is precisely this that requires that its representation should be mythical, as I have made it. But the fact that it is unreal does not prevent an organ from incarnating itself" (*FFC*, 205; 187). In different terms, the lamella defines itself in relation to the real/reel thing. Lacan clarifies his understanding of the lamella when he writes: "The relation to the Other is precisely that which for us brings out what is represented by the lamella—not sexed polarity, the relation between masculine and feminine, but the relation between the living subject and that which he loses by having to pass, for his reproduction, through the sexual cycle" (*FFC*, 199; 181). As we have seen, the real/reel thing, which is lost when the child becomes sexually differentiated by inscription within the symbolic order through the name of the father, is inextricably bound up with the mother, i.e., the creative matrix figured as the breast.

The displacement of thing as phallus to thing as breast can be discerned in Lacan's diagrams. While Lacan's graph of the drive obviously sketches a phallus, it less obviously outlines the form of a pacifier that the child sucks instead of the mother's breast. This is not really surprising, for the phallus is actually something like a pacifier. In the pacifier, phallus becomes breast. This displacement appears when one redraws Lacan's chart of the drive and places it beside one of his other graphs. As if to retrace Merleau-Ponty's journey from the Etoile to Notre-Dame and back, Lacan argues that "the heterogeneity [*hétérogénéité*] of the movement out and back shows a gap in its interval" (*FFC*, 194; 177). This gap he labels a "cleavage" (*clivage*) (*FFC*, 259; 233). Lacan leaves no doubt that this cleavage is the cleavage of the breast. "The breast [*le sein*] is also something superimposed,

---

discovered it in its radical excentricity: 'There where it was . . . ,' I would like to be understood, 'it is my duty that I should come into being'" (*E*, 128–29; 417–18). It is understandable that one might translate *Et ça court* as "And it runs around." The relationship between *ça* and *es*, however, suggests the sexual connotations of this phrase. If one reads the French *court* as the English "courts," the translation becomes, "And it (i.e., *es* or *id*) courts." In chapter 9 we will see that Derrida stresses the further association between *ça* and *SA*, the initials for the French rendering of absolute knowledge, *savoir absolu*.

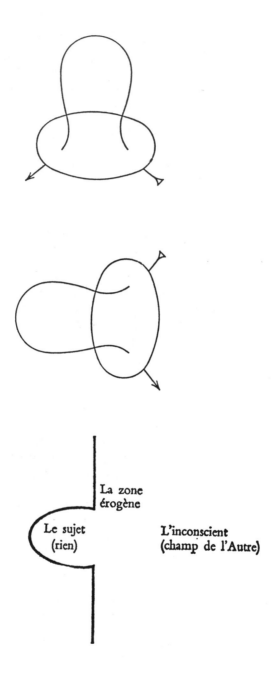

La zone
érogène

Le sujet
(rien)

L'inconscient
(champ de l'Autre)

who sucks what?—the organism of the mother. Thus we see clearly enough, at this level, the nature of the subject's claim to something that is separated from him, but belongs to him and which he needs to complete himself" (*FFC*, 195; 179). Repeating the presencing of Heidegger's Logos, *le sein* presents but is never present. The real/reel thing withdraws in giving and thus "reveals" herself as self-concealing. By provocatively evoking an origin that is never present and an aim that is never achieved, the phallus and the breast point toward a lost cause.

Sein: *Lost Cause*

At the end of his essay entitled "God and the *Jouissance* of Woman: A Love Letter, " Lacan juxtaposes Freud and Kierkegaard: "It is not by chance that Kierkegaard discovered existence in a little tale of seduction. It is by being castrated, by renouncing love that he believes he accedes to it. But then after all, why shouldn't Regina also have existed? This desire for a good at one remove . . . perhaps it was through the intermediary of Regina that he came to it" (*FS*, 147–48). For Kierkegaard, wedding Regina is rendered impossible by something that is wholly Other. Kierkegaard "names" this unnameable Other "God." Lacan unexpectedly suggests that radical altarity "is" the goddess. To understand the association of altarity with gods and goddesses, it is necessary to go back to the beginning—*Genesis*.

> In the beginning God created the heavens and the earth. Now the earth was a formless void, there was darkness over the deep, and God's spirit hovered over the water.
> God said, "Let there be light," and there was light. God saw that the light was good, and God divided light from darkness. God called the light "day," darkness he called "night." Evening came and morning came: the first day (*Genesis* 1: 1–8).

In the Jewish and Christian traditions, as in many other religions, the act of creation is an act of *separation*. The created order emerges when the Word of the Father tears open the sea. As *Genesis* indicates, the fissuring of the word articulates binary opposites like light and darkness, day and night, heaven and earth, male and female, etc.

Lacan imagines the creation of the world with the help of the Greeks, mediated (as always) by Heidegger.

[The creation of the world] required a *clinamen,*[26] an inclination, at some point. When Democritus tried to designate it, presenting himself as already the adversary of a pure function of negativity in order to introduce thought into it, he says, *It is not the mēden that is essential,* and adds—thus showing you that from what one of my pupils called the archaic stage of philosophy, the manipulation of words was used just as in the time of Heidegger—*it is not a mēden, but a den,* which, in Greek, is a coined word. He did not say *en,* let alone *on.* What, then, did he say? He said, answering the question I asked today, that of idealism, *Nothing, perhaps?*—not *perhaps nothing,* but *not nothing* [*Rien, peut-être? non pas—peut-être rien, mais pas rien*] (*FFC,* 63–64; 61).[27]

With this "nothing, perhaps," or, "perhaps nothing," we again return to the real/reel thing. As I have pointed out, Heidegger and Lacan establish a link between the Latin *res* and the French *rien.* In terms previously discussed, the thing (*res*) is no thing (*rien*). Heidegger also underscores the relation between *res* and *causa,* which eventually develops into the Romance *la cosa,* and finally appears as the French *la chose* (*PLT,* 175–76). *Res . . . rien . . . causa . . . chose.* The thing, perhaps, is no-thing, which "is" the nothing that seems to be the "cause" of all things.

But what is a cause? There is no easy answer to this question, for, as Lacan stresses, a cause is a "hole" (*trou*), "cleft" (*fente*), or "gap" (*gap*) (*FFC,* 22; 25), which has "the character of an absolute point without any knowledge" (*FFC,* 253; 228). "Whenever we speak of a cause . . . there is always something anti-conceptual, something indefinite. The phases of the moon are the causes of tides—we know this from experience, we know that the word cause is correctly used here. Or again, miasmas are the cause of fever—that doesn't mean anything either, there is a hole, and something that oscillates in the interval. In short, there is a cause only in something *qui cloche*" (*FFC,* 22; 25). A hole . . . something that oscillates . . . in the interval . . . only in

---

26. *Clinamen* derives from the Latin, *clinare,* to incline. For a rich exploration of this complex notion, see Harold Bloom, *Poetry and Repression: Revisionism from Blake to Stevens* (New Haven: Yale University Press, 1976). Bloom's argument is particularly suggestive, for he is sensitive to the complex interplay of psychoanalysis and religion. See also his *Kabbalah and Criticism* (New York: Seabury Press, 1975).

27. The nuances of Lacan's concluding words are lost in English translation. *Peut-être* is formed by combining *peut*—a form of *pouvoir* (to be able), which contains the verb *voir* (to see)—with *être,* to be.

something *qui cloche*. The implications of this hole, oscillation, and interval can be clarified by considering the puzzling word *clocher*. *Clocher* is "to halt, hobble, or limp" (like Oedipus?). But *clocher* also means "to sound like a bell." A *cloche* is a bell, and a *clocher* is a steeple or a belfry. If the interval is the opening of a bell, then something that oscillates in this hole might be the clapper of a bell—a clapper that sometimes is labeled *un batail*. Is this *batail* the woman named Sylviane—Sylviane Bataille, the woman shared by Lacan and Georges Bataille? Or is this *batail* the sounding clapper that anticipates a certain *Glas?*

According to Lacan, the interval of the indefinite notion "cause" marks the opening of the unconscious. "This indicates that the cause of the unconscious—and you see that the word cause is to be taken here in its ambiguity, a cause to be sustained, but also a function of the cause at the level of the unconscious—this cause must be conceived fundamentally as a lost cause [*une cause perdue*]" (*FFC*, 128; 117). The Lacanian lost cause is even more ambiguous than is usually realized. In a claim that most of his interpreters would prefer to forget or repress, Lacan notes an unexpected dimension of his exploration of the unconscious: "I am speaking of religion in the true sense of the term— not of a desiccated, methodologized religion, repressed into the distant past of a primitive thought, but of religion as we see it practised in a still living, very vital way" (*FFC*, 7; 12). Elsewhere Lacan confesses: "For the myth of the *God is dead*—which, personally, I feel much less sure about, as a myth of course, than most contemporary intellectuals, which is in no sense a declaration of theism, nor of faith in the resurrection—perhaps, this myth is simply a shelter against the threat of castration" (*FFC*, 27; 29). As Lacan emphasizes, his resistance to the myth of the death of God in no way involves a return to traditional religious belief. Lacan's misprision of Freud points toward a genuine "atheism" that approximates what Bataille labels "atheology." "For the true formula of atheism is not *God is dead*—even by basing the origin of the function of the father upon his murder, Freud protects the father—the true formula of atheism is *God is unconscious*" (*FFC*, 59; 58).[28] The unconscious that is "God" is, for Lacan, eternally feminine. When considering Lacan's rereading of

---

28. Two additional comments by Lacan are noteworthy in this context. "*The gods belong to the field of the real*" (*FFC*, 45; 45). "If I am using this S(ø) to designate nothing other than the *jouissance* of the woman, it is undoubtedly because I am thereby registering that God has not made his exit" (*FS*, 154).

Freud, it is always important to remember his insistence that what leads Freud on, in his relentless chase, is "his passion for the goddess" (*E, 124; 412*).

If the cause that is lost is feminine, then the lost cause obsessing Lacan might be a certain feminism. After all, Lacan maintains that "the woman has a relation to God greater than all that has been stated in ancient speculation according to a path that has manifestly been articulated only as the good of mankind" (*FS, 153*). By returning to the "beginning," we discover the lost cause to be the sea. For Lacan, *la mer* that bears us all is *la mère*. The Word of the Father separates one from the bosom of the mother. The lost cause, it seems is nothing other than the real/reel "thing" (*chose,* from *causa*), which "is" *le sein*. Over against the entire Western philosophical tradition, Lacan joins Heidegger to argue that *Sein/sein* is a lost cause. More precisely, *le sein* is *the* lost cause, and this lost cause is "The Woman." But *The* Woman, like *Das Sein,* does not exist. "There is no such thing as *The* woman since of her essence, . . . she is not at all. . . . This *the* is a signifier characterized by being the only signifier which cannot signify any-thing, but which merely constitutes the status of *the* woman as being not at all. Which forbids our speaking of *The* woman. There is woman only as excluded by the nature of things which is the nature of words" (*FS, 144*). Since she is always excluded by the nature of things, which is the nature of words, The Woman is the no thing that must forever be barred. This is why Lacan writes "The Woman" as "~~The~~ Woman."

Inasmuch as The Woman is excluded by the nature of words, she is perpetually "excommunicated." Always lingering just beyond the bounds of language (and hence binding words by leaving them open), The Woman can neither speak properly nor truly be spoken. She can, nonetheless, be heard. The Woman is heard in her cry—a cry that *cannot* be stilled. The cry of The Woman is *le cri* that repeatedly interrupts *E-cri-ts* and perpetually disrupts all *é-cri-ture*. Though al-ways rumbling, *le cri* cannot be heard until language withdraws. Instead of a silence that "complements" speech, the beyond of the cry is a "supplement" that exceeds language (*FS, 144*).

Le cri of *E-cri-ts* can be heard only in the act of transgression through which one approaches that which is forever excommuni-cated. Such transgression brings *jouissance* rather than pleasure. The beyond of The Woman's cry is the *au-delà* of *Beyond the Pleasure Prin-ciple*. This *au-delà* is, as I have noted, inseparable from the repetition that tolls death. The Woman's cry of "Encore, Encore, Encore . . ." panics, terrifies, even petrifies the "I" that merely seeks the *amour-propre* produced by the subject's return to itself in and through all others and every difference. Transgressive intercourse with the excommunicated involves an excessive expenditure from which, and for which, there is no return. To experience *jouissance* is to suffer loss—the loss of desire that exposes the impossibility of satisfaction. This impossibility is the wisdom concealed in the mystic's "cloud of unknowing."

> The mystical is by no means that which is not political. It is something serious, which few people teach us about, and most often women or highly gifted people like Saint John of the Cross—since when you are male, you don't have to put yourself on the side of $\forall x \phi x$. You can also put yourself on the side of the not-all. There are men who are just as good as women. It does happen. And who therefore feel just as good. Despite, I won't say their phallus, despite what encumbers them on that score, they get the idea, they sense that there must be a *jouissance* that goes beyond. That is what we call a mystic. (*FS,* 146–47)

The *jouissance* of the mystic, which carries one beyond *le tout,* is *ecstasy.*

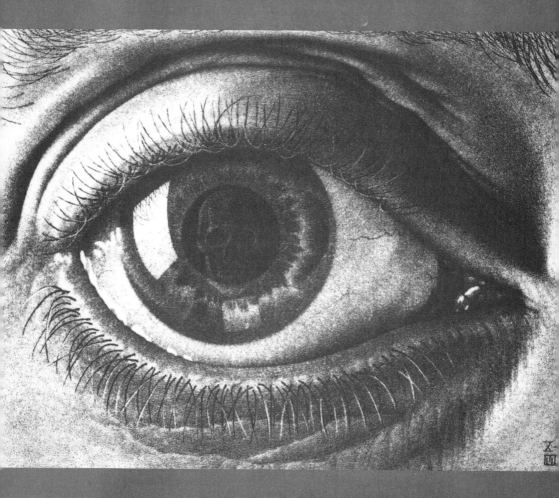

5

Ecstasy

GEORGES BATAILLE

■

Pineal Eye of the Obelisk

The goal of speculative philosophy is concord. Through rational mediation, the philosopher attempts to reconcile hostile opponents. The analyses and criticisms of Heidegger, Merleau-Ponty, and Lacan raise serious questions about the efficacy of the Western philosophical tradition that culminates in Hegelian philosophy. Is the struggle to unite or reunite warring opposites ever successful? Is mediation always a failure? Does *la bataille* (battle, fight, struggle) eternally return?

Exactly where *is* the place of concord for which philosophy has been searching since its beginnings in ancient Greece? The Place de la Concorde is, of course, in the middle of the city named for the prince of Troy whose abduction of Helen provoked the Trojan War—Paris. We have already passed through this Place while following Merleau-Ponty from the Etoile to Notre-Dame and back. At this point in our wanderings, it will be helpful to pause long enough to consider different aspects of the Place.

The Place de la Concorde occupies a central place not only in Paris, but also in French history. It was originally designed by Gabriel in the middle of the eighteenth century for the purpose of displaying a statue of Louis XV, son and successor of The Sun King, Louis XIV. A grand equestrian figure, surrounded by representations of Strength, Wisdom, Justice,and Peace dominated the square from 1763 to 1792. After the capture of Tuileries, the Legislative Assembly ordered the statue of the king to be replaced by a figure of the Goddess of Liberty, which many people derisively labeled *La Liberté de Boue* (*boue:* mud, mire, dirt, filth). This central site in Paris was not named Place de la Concorde until 1795. In 1792, the guillotine was constructed on the square. Between 1792 and 1795, Louis XVI, Marie Antoinette, Robespierre, as well as nearly three thousand others were decapitated on the scaffold in the Place. In 1836, an obelisk, which was a gift of

Mohammed Ali, Viceroy of Egypt, was erected at the heart of the Place de la Concorde. The obelisk, inscribed on all sides with hieroglyphs, originally stood in front of a temple in Luxor, located next to Thebes, an Egyptian city with the same name as the home of Oedipus.

The Egyptian word for obelisk, *téhen,* is philologically connected with the word for sunbeam. *Obeliskos,* the Greek root of the English word "obelisk," means "a pointed pillar." The tapered tip of the obelisk forms a pyramid. The word "obelisk" also has meanings that are related to writing and printing. It designates the dagger sign (†) used to indicate a marginal reference or footnote. In ancient manuscripts, the obelisk, in the form of either — or ÷, is a mark employed to point out a spurious, corrupt, doubtful, or superfluous passage.

The close connection between the obelisk and the sun, implied by the Egyptian word *téhen,* is reflected in the common practice of erecting obelisks to honor the sun god, Ra. The obelisk can, in fact, be understood as the sign of solar religion. The scriptive aspect of "obelisk" is not completely lost in this context. Ra's nocturnal representative is Thoth, who, during the reign of the sun king Osiris (perhaps a distant ancestor of Louis XIV), "initiated men into arts and letters and created hieroglyphic writing" (*D,* 92; 104). For reasons that will become obvious in what follows, it is important to note that Thoth appears as "the bull among the stars." Sun (Ra) and bull (Thoth) reemerge in the religious mythology of the West. Between the time of Plato's effort to lead prisoners out of dark grottoes by the light of reason and Hegel's struggle to liberate the unenlightened through rational reflection, Constantine, then a devotee of solar monotheism, converted to Christianity. His conversion took place on the banks of the Tiber, where he had a vision of the cross, which is itself something like a scriptive obeblisk (†), superimposed upon the sun. He interpreted this vision as an auspicious omen sent by the Christian God. The union of church and empire initiated by Constantine proved fateful for all subsequent history. Not until the modern epoch is it possible to glimpse the beginning of the eclipse of the heliocentrism characteristic of Western thought, society, and culture. One of the earliest indications of this sociocultural shift appears in a little book, entitled *Repetition,* written by a parodic descendent of Constantine, a certain Constantin Constantius. Constantin Constantius's work points to a dark underside that haunts the dominant religious, philosophical, and political tradition in the West. Like the lunar (perhaps lunatic) Thoth, this repressed other first appears in the form of a bull. Prior to the conversion of Constantine, the now little-known cult of Mithraism seriously rivaled Christianity for the heart and mind of the West.

In a brief essay bearing the provocative title "Rotten Sun," Bataille suggests a startling series of associations, which begins to illuminate the significance he attaches to the obelisk standing in the middle of the Place de la Concorde.

> In mythology, the scrutinized sun is identified with a man who slays a bull (Mithra), with a vulture that eats the liver (Prometheus): in other words, with the man who looks along with the slain bull or the eaten liver. The Mithraic cult of the sun led to a very widespread religious practice: people stripped in a kind of a pit [which might be related to a pyramid] that was covered with a wooden scaffold, on which a priest slashed the throat of a bull; thus they were suddenly doused with hot blood, to the accompaniment of the bull's boisterous struggle and bellowing—a simple way of reaping the moral benefits of the blinding sun [*soleil aveuglant*]. Of course the bull himself is also an image of the sun, but only with his throat slit. The same goes for the cock [*coq*], whose horrible solar cry [*cri*] always approximates the screams of a slaughter. One might add that the sun has also been mythologically expressed by a man slashing his own throat, as well as by an anthropomorphic being *deprived of a head*. All this leads one to say that the summit of elevation is in practice confused with a sudden fall of unheard-of violence. The myth of Icarus is particularly expressive from this point of view: it clearly splits the sun in two—the one that was shining at the moment of Icarus's elevation, and the one that melted the wax, causing a failure and a screaming fall when Icarus got too close. (*VE,* 57–8; 1:213–32)

Sun, scaffold, sacrifice; cut, cleavage, coup; erection, resurrection, insurrection; cock and bull; capitol, capital, capitalism, capitalization; decapitation, blindness, castration; Icarus. The obelisk, it seems, marks the site of the scaffold that is the altar of sacrifice where reason loses its head in a revolution from which we are still spinning—and weaving.

Icarus was the son of the inventive Daedalus. At the behest of Pasiphae, wife of King Minos, Daedalus constructed a lifelike cow in which the queen hid in order to fulfill her grotesque desire to copulate with a bull. From their union came the Minotaur, a monster with the body of a man and the head of a bull. King Minos commissioned Daedalus to build a labyrinth in which to hide the monster and thus conceal the fruit of his wife's transgression. When the handsome Theseus volunteered to serve as one of the victims sacrificed to appease the appetite of the captured monster, Ariadne, daughter of Minos, fell in love with him. She persuaded Daedalus to give Theseus a ball of thread that he could unroll as he penetrated the labyrinth. By retracing his steps, Theseus was able to find his way out of the maze. King Minos suspected Daedalus of plotting the escape and ordered him and his son, Icarus, to be imprisoned in the labyrinth. The pair escaped with the aid of wax wings designed by Daedalus. Icarus, however, forgot Daedalus's warning and flew too close to the sun. The wings melted, sending father and son plunging into *la mer*.

Bataille associates Icarus and his "high-altitude flight" (*survole*) with the soaring of the eagle. "The eagle-god [*l'aigle-dieu*] who is confused with the sun by the ancients, the eagle who alone among all beings can contemplate while staring at 'the sun in all its glory,' the Icarian being who goes to seek the fire of the heavens is, however, nothing other than the automutilator, a Vincent Van Gogh, a Gaston F. All the rich excess he derives from the mythical delirium is limited to the incredible vomiting of the liver, ceaselessly devoured and ceaselessly vomited by the gaping belly of the god" (*VE*, 70; 1:269). Many physicians in the past believed the tendency to stare at the blinding sun to be a sign of incurable madness. It is just this madness which, according to Bataille, plagued Hegel—the same Hegel whose name when pronounced with a French accent, we now realize sounds like *aigle*. For two years after he had completed the System, Hegel seemed convinced that his speculative flights had led him to the brink of madness. Commenting on the irony of Hegel's dread, Bataille writes:

> A comic little summary. Hegel, I imagine, touched the extreme limit. He was still young and believed himself to be going mad. I even imagine that he worked out the System in order to escape (each type of conquest is, no doubt, the deed of a man fleeing a threat). To conclude, Hegel attains *satisfaction,* turns his back on the extreme limit. *Supplication is dead within him.* Whether or not one seeks salvation, in any case, one continues to live, one cannot be sure, one must continue to supplicate. While still alive, Hegel won salvation, killed supplication, *mutilated himself.* Of him, only the handle of a shovel remained, a modern man. But before mutilating himself, no doubt he touched the extreme limit, knew supplication: his memory brought him back to the perceived abyss, *in order to annul it!* The system is the annulment. (*IE*, 56)[1]

In an important essay entitled "The Obelisk," Bataille approaches Hegel's speculative philosophy by way of a consideration of the

---

1. In quoting Bataille's *L'expérience intérieure,* I have used Leslie Boldt's forthcoming translation *Interior Experience* (Albany: State University of New York Press). The page numbers cited are from the French edition.

118

obelisk, topped by a pyramid, in the Place de la Concorde. We have seen that for Hegel, the obelisk and pyramid represent the base sensuousness of a sign that has not yet been raised, erected, or resurrected to the spiritual level of the concept. According to Bataille, the obelisk "is without a doubt the purest image of the head and the heavens." Recalling a "petrified sunbeam," the firmly fixed obelisk is the "Egyptian image of the IMPERISHABLE." As such, it "is the surest and most durable obstacle to the drifting away of things" (*VE,* 215; 1:504). Thus speculative philosophy may be compared to an obelisk. Hegelian re-collection, I have argued, purports to take perishable temporal and spatial existence up into the eternal life of the concept. Bataille explains some of the implications of such an untimely resurrection when he points out that "even Hegel describing the march of Spirit as if it excluded all possible rest [*arrêt*] made it end, however, at HIMSELF as if he were its necessary conclusion. Thus he gave the movement of time the *centripetal* structure that characterizes sovereignty, Being, or God. Time, on the other hand, dissolving each center that has formed, is fatally known as *centrifugal. . . .* The dialectical idea, then, is only a hybrid of time and its opposite, of the death of God and the position of the immutable. But it nevertheless marks the movement of a thought eager to destroy what refuses to die, eager to break the bonds of time as much as to break the law through which God obligates" (*VE,* 219; 1:509). Echoing Merleau–Ponty, Bataille maintains that in pursuing its goal of concord, speculative philosophy "casts time to the outside" (*rejette le temps au dehors; IE,* 70). The struggle "to break the bonds of time" inevitably issues in the double bind implied by the scaffold that serves the interests of both revolution and restoration.

The insurrection against the grandson of the Sun King eventually led to the decapitation of those who once had seemed to be the voice of reason itself. Reason loses its head when enlightenment spreads terror. The death *of* reason hollows out the pyramid at the top of the obelisk. While the obelisk is "the image of the imperishable," the pyramid is a constant reminder of the ceaseless flow of time and the unavoidability of death. The pol(e)arity of obelisk and pyramid embodies the *difference* between eternity and time. For Bataille, this difference can be understood in terms of the difference between the recollection of Hegel's eternal re-membering and the repetition of Nietzsche's eternal re-turning. Over against the obelisk of speculative philosophy, Bataille sets "the Pyramid of Suleri," i.e., the "pyramidal rock or stone" along the lake of Silvaplana, which precipitated Nietzsche's ecstatic vision of the eternal return. Bataille maintains

119

that the difference between Hegel and Nietzsche is a (or, more precisely, the) matter of time.

> In order to represent the decisive break [*fracture*] that took place
> . . . , it is necessary to tie the sundering vision of the "return"
> to what Nietzsche experienced when he reflected upon the explosive vision of Heraclitus, and to what he experienced later in
> his own vision of the "death of God": this is necessary in order to
> perceive the full extent of the bolt of lightning that never stopped
> shattering his life while at the same time projecting it into a burst
> of violent light. TIME is the object of the vision of Heraclitus.
> TIME is unleashed in the "death" of the One whose eternity gave
> Being an immutable foundation. And the audacious act that
> represents the "return" at the summit of this laceration [*déchirement*] only wrests from the dead God his *total* strength, in order
> to give it to the deleterious absurdity of time.
>   A "state of glory" is thus deftly linked to the feeling of an
> endless fall. It is true that a fall was already a part of human
> ecstasy, on which it conferred the intoxication of that which
> approximates the nature of time—but that fall was the *original*
> fall of man, whereas the fall of the "return" is FINAL. (*VE*, 220;
> 1:510–11)

The pyramid, which though atop the obelisk, undercuts the monumental desire it represents, is not merely a matter of philosophical concern, for it also points to cryptic psychological, cultural, and social realities. Having originated near a city named Thebes, the triangular sides of the pyramid capping (and uncapping) the obelisk in the Place de la Concorde evoke the complex triangular relationship of mother-father-child. Bataille, like Lacan, never considers individuals apart from the roles they play within social and cultural structures. In elevating himself from nature to culture, man tends to forget the matrix that bears and nourishes him. "Human bodies," Bataille maintains, "are erect on the ground like a challenge to the Earth, to the mud which engenders them and which they are happy to send back to nothingness [*au néant*]. Nature giving birth to man was a dying mother: she gave 'being' to the one whose coming into the world was her own death sentence" (*IE*, 93). The conflict between man and woman assumes a different, though related, form in the struggle between reason and non-reason. The "male" principle of reason, Bataille argues, is founded upon the exclusion or repression of non-reason, which assumes the form or non-form of the feminine. Within Bataille's excessive psychology, however, man always slips and falls. Men inevitably lose their heads over women.

It is important to realize that Bataille's pyramid is also a social pyramid. At the summit of the social structure sits the (sun) king or his representatives, and at the base, the unruly masses. The overthrow of the ruling master in the name of "reason" does not necessarily result in freedom, equality, and fraternity. Reason itself can become oppressive and repressive. Though prefigured in the terror of the guillotine, the horrifying consequences of reason's "will to power" do not become fully evident until the twentieth century. Bataille contends that the totalizing nisus of reason eventually produces the totalitarianism of the modern state. Furthermore, he is persuaded that "insofar as fascism values a philosophical source, it is attached to Hegel and not to Nietzsche" (VE, 186; 1:454). Anticipating or recalling (it is not clear which it is) Heidegger, Bataille maintains that reason extends its repressive activity in modern science and technology. In the course of analyzing "the public square" in the midst of the modern metropolis, Bataille writes:

> The homogeneity [homogénéité] of the kind realized in cities between men and that which surrounds them is only a subsidiary form of a much more consistent homogeneity, which man has established throughout the external world by everywhere replacing *a priori* inconceivable objects with classified series of conceptions or ideas. The identification of all the elements of which the world is composed has been pursued with a constant obstinacy, so that scientific conceptions, as well as the popular conceptions of the world, seem to have voluntarily led to a representation as different from what could have been imagined *a priori* as the public square of a capital is from a region of high mountains.
>
> This last appropriation—the work of philosophy as well as of science or common sense—has included phases of revolt and scandal, but it has always had as its goal the establishment of the homogeneity of the world, and it will only be able to lead to a terminal phase in the sense of excretion when the irreducible waste products of the operation are determined. (VE, 95–96; 2:60–61)

The "homogeneity of the world," which is the dream of Western philosophy, science, and technology, is, for Bataille, a nightmare. Confronted with systems—philosophical, scientific, religious, social, cultural, political, and economic—that attempt to master every other by incorporating, assimilating, or digesting all differences, Bataille attempts to expose an altarity that can never be domesticated. Always searching for *radical* difference, Bataille repeatedly asks: What remains after the System digests everything? In a effort to respond to this question, he examines "the irreducible waste products" of various systematic operations. The excrement of the System constitutes "the blind spot" of Hegelianism.

The locus of this "blind spot or stain" (*aveugle tache*) is what Bataille describes as "the pineal eye." "The pineal eye" is a multivalent term that can be understood in many different ways. This peculiar organ is obviously related to the pineal gland, a small, reddish-gray conical body attached to the third ventrical of the brain from which it protrudes as a hollow outgrowth. Descartes believed the pineal gland, which was regarded by some as the seat of the soul, to be responsible for the unification of body and soul. The relationship between Cartesianism and Hegelianism suggests further aspects of the pineal eye. Speculative philosophy, I have stressed, aspires to panopticism. To realize its vision, the gaze of the philosopher must comprehend everything. Philosophy's penetrating insights are produced by a penal eye/I that disciplines and punishes everything that tries to evade its grasp and resist its control.[2] When Lacan's account of "the evil eye" is joined to the foregoing description of the obelisk and pyramid, additional questions concerning the pineal/penal eye arise. The obelisk, inscribed with hieroglyphs and erected on the site where decapitation takes place, recalls the tattooed phallus of Lacanian analysis. At the tip of this obeliscal column, we have discovered a cut or an opening that is something like the "eye" of the penis. Rather than securing philosophical mastery, this penal eye castrates the philosopher by exposing the blindness of knowledge. In this way, the gaze of the strange pineal eye approximates the petrifying stare of Medusa.[3] The pineal eye, however, most commonly designates a raised stalk, structured like an eye, which is an appendage on primitive water creatures like the lamprey. This grotesque "median eye" is thought to be a "remnant" (*reste*) of an important sense organ in ancestral forms of life.

2. See, inter alia, Michel Foucault, *Discipline and Punish: The Birth of the Prison*, trans. A. Sheridan (New York: Random House, 1979). Foucault is deeply indebted to Bataille. It is not insignificant that Foucault edited the all-important first volume of Bataille's *Oeuvres complètes*.

3. Bataille explicitly relates the obelisk, decapitation, and petrification in the following passage. "The Place de la Concorde is dominated, from the height of the palace balustrades, by eight armored and acephalic figures, and under their stone helmets they are as empty as they were on the day the executioner decapitated the king before them. After the execution, Marly's two horses were brought from the nearby forest and set up at the entrance to the exalted places, before which they rear without end. The central point of the triangle formed by the two horses and the obelisk marks the location of the guillotine—an empty space, open to the rapid flow of traffic" (*VE*, 221; 1:512).

Bataille plays on a broad range of connotations when he describes the pineal eye.

> I imagined the eye at the summit of the skull like a horrible erupting volcano, precisely with the shady and comical character associated with the rear end and its excretions. Now the eye is without any doubt the symbol of the dazzling sun and the one I imagined at the summit of my skull was necessarily on fire, since it was doomed to the contemplation of the sun at the summit of its bursting [*éclat*]. The imagination of the ancients attributed to the eagle as solar bird the faculty of contemplating the sun face to face. In the same way an excessive interest in the simple representation of the pineal eye is necessarily interpreted as an irresistible desire to become a *sun* oneself (a blind sun or a blinding sun, it hardly matters). In the case of the eagle, as in the case of my own imagination, the act of directly looking is the equivalent of identification. But the cruel and shattering character of this absurd desire soon appears, due to the fact that the eagle is cast down from the heights of the skies—and, as for the eye that opens in the middle of the skull, the result, even imaginary, is much more terrifying, though horribly ridiculous. (*VE*, 74; 2:14–15)

Inasmuch as the pineal eye is associated with the blinding light of the sun, which causes the fall of the Icarian being with the eagle eye/I, this gap in the skull interrupts the supposedly panoptical gaze of philosophy. Bataille elaborates this understanding of the pineal eye in *L'expérience intérieure:*

> When I solicit gently, in the very heart of anguish, a strange absurdity, an eye opens itself at the summit, in the middle of my skull.
>
> This eye which, to contemplate the sun, in its nudity, face to face, opens up to it in all its glory, does not arise from my reason: it is a cry [*un cri*] that escapes me. For at the moment when the lightning stroke blinds me, I am the flash of a broken life, and this life—anguish and vertigo—opening itself up to an infinite void, is lacerated [*se déchire*] and spends itself all at once in this void. (*IE*, 92)

Paradoxically, the pineal eye emits a cry that bursts out of a shattered life. This agonizing *cri* is not a "fact of reason" but is an "irreducible waste product"—something like excrement that cannot be digested. Describing his original vision of the pineal eye, Bataille establishes a close relation between eye and excrement: "This eye that I wanted to have at the top of my skull (since I had read that its embryo existed, like the seed of a tree, in the interior of the skull) did not appear to me as anything other than a sexual organ of unheard-of sensitivity, which would have vibrated, making me let out atrocious cries, the cries of a magnificent but stinking ejaculation. Everything that I can recall of my reactions and my aberrations in this period, and moreover the normal symbolic value of a lightning-flash image, permits me today to characterize this pineal eye fantasy as an excremental fantasy" (*VE*, 77–78; 2: 19). By ripping open the body proper, the tears of the cry of the pineal eye, tears that are the tears of laughter— tears of *le rire déchirant,* rend the eye/I of philosophy by opening a blind spot that can never be closed.

> *To summon all of man's tendencies into a point, all of the possibles that he is, to draw from them at the same time the accords and the violent oppositions, no longer to leave outside the laughter tearing apart { le rire déchirant} the fabric of which man is made, to the contrary, to know oneself to be assured of insignificance as long as thought is not itself this profound tearing of the fabric and its object—being itself—the fabric torn (Nietzsche had said: "regard as false that which has not made you laugh at least once; . . ."), in this respect my efforts recommence and undo Hegel's Phenomenology. (IE, 96)*

Bataille's undoing of Hegelian philosophy begins with his exploration of the tears and tears of the gaping body.

Tears: Gaping Body

To break the grip of philosophy, it is necessary to "make reason shit" or "vomit."[4] This is the task Bataille sets for himself in his outrageous fiction. What does the pineal eye "see" that is so offensive to reason? In his first novel, *Story of the Eye,* Bataille's description of the aftermath of a drunken orgy suggests the beginning of an answer to this question:

> Half an hour later, when I was less drunk, it dawned on me that I ought to let Marcelle out of her wardrobe: the unhappy girl, naked now, was in a dreadful state. She was trembling and shivering feverishly. Upon seeing me, she displayed a sickly but violent terror. After all, I was pale, smeared with blood, my clothes askew. Behind me, in unspeakable, unnameable disorder,

4. Denis Hollier, *La prise de la Concorde: Essais sur Georges Bataille* (Paris: Gallimard, 1974). Derrida frequently uses the image of vomit to suggest that which speculative philosophy cannot swallow.

ill bodies, brazenly stripped, were sprawled about, almost inert. During the orgy, the debris of glass [*des débris de verres*] had left deep bleeding cuts in two of us. A young girl was throwing up, and all of us had exploded in such wild fits of laughter at some point or other that we had wet our clothes, an armchair, or the floor. The resulting stench of blood, sperm, urine, and vomit made me almost recoil in horror, but the inhuman cry [*cri inhumain*] from Marcelle's throat was far more terrifying.[5]

The themes and images in this passage return again and again throughout Bataille's fiction. What Bataille seeks to evoke and provoke in such texts is the unspeakable horror that lies just beyond the bounds of language. The terrifyingly obscure time and space opened by Marcelle's "inhuman cry" are not only beyond language; they are beyond every principle of pleasure. Discussing Freud's death instinct, Lacan unwittingly indicates the general direction of Bataille's *pas au delà:* "From the approach that we have indicated, the reader should recognize in the metaphor of the return to the inanimate (which Freud attaches to every living body) that margin beyond [*marge au-delà*] life which language gives to the human being by virtue of the fact that he speaks, and which is precisely where such a being places in the position of a signifier, not only those parts of the body that are exchangeable, but this body itself" (*E,* 301; 803). Bataille labels the body that figures that which lies beyond language and pleasure "a strange or foreign body (*das ganz Andere*)" (*VE,* 94; 2:58). In the eyes of reason, *das ganz Andere* is *grotesque.* Analyzing the writings of Rabelais, Bakhtin offers what is, in effect, a concise description of the contours of Bataille's *corps étranger:* "Contrary to modern canons, the grotesque body is not separated from the rest of the world. It is not a closed, complete unit; it is unfinished, outgrows itself, transgresses its own limits. The stress is laid on those parts of the body that are open to the outside world, that is, the parts through which the world enters the body or emerges from it, or though which the body itself goes out to meet the world. This means that the emphasis is on the apertures or the convexities, or on the various ramifications and offshoots: the open mouth, the genital organs, the breasts, the phallus, the potbelly, the nose."[6]

Recalling a word used by Merleau-Ponty and Lacan, the grotesque body can be described in terms of the inside-out/outside-in structure

---

5. Geroges Bataille, *Story of the Eye by Lord Auch,* trans. J. Neugroschel (New York: Urizen Books, 1977), p. 17; *Oeuvres complètes,* 1:21.

6. Mikhail Bakhtin, *Rabelais and His World,* trans. H. Iswolsky (Cambridge, MA: MIT Press, 1968), p. 26.

of invagination. Man, Bataille maintains, is "a tube with two orifices, anal and buccal: the nostrils, the eyes, the ears; the brain represent the complications of the buccal orifice; the penis, the testicles, or the female organs that correspond to them, are the complication of the anal" (*VE,* 88–89; 2:33). Mouth and anus, eye and ear, penis and vulva are marginal sites of passage that call into question hard-and-fast distinctions between interiority and exteriority. Are eye and ear, mouth and esophagus, anus and intestine, penis and testicles, vulva and uterus inside or outside? The body, like the pyramid, is hollowed out, as if from within. This chiasmic body cannot be articulated in terms of the binary opposites that structure thought and language. Never "proper, clean, neat, or tidy," the body is inescapably transgressive. Such an improper body is the *corps étranger.* With no firmly fixed limits, it is never clear precisely where the body begins or ends. Concave and convex intersect to form a knot that cannot be untied.

The interplay of inner and outer characterizes not only the bodily organs but also the grotesque "objects" that obsess Bataille. These "objects" are not really "objects" in the strict sense of the word, for their distinguishing characteristic is that they *do not* stand over against a subject. Neither object nor subject, though surely not nothing, these strange somethings are similar to Freud's "transitional objects" and Lacan's "exchangeable objects." Bataille designates such stuff "matter." "Matter," he explains, "can only be defined as the *nonlogical difference* [*différence non logique*] that represents in relation to the *economy* of the universe what *crime* represents in relation to the law" (*VE,* 129; 1:319). This matter is nonlogical because it eludes the principle of noncontradiction that defines logic. Throughout his writings, Bataille investigates a variety of forms assumed by the nonlogical difference of matter: sperm, menstrual blood, urine, fecal matter, vomit, tears, sobs, screams, cries, and laughter. In examining this matter, Bataille develops a scatology through which he attempts to subvert the eschatology of speculative philosophy and traditional theology.[7] While Hegel is preoccupied with securing the System "proper" by wiping or flushing away *Kote,* Bataille struggles to expose the gap through which the repressed eternally returns.

One of the most vivid illustrations of Bataille's scatological practice is a work entitled *The Blue of Noon.* Like most of Bataille's writings, this is a story of excess. Its principal character, who apparently is

7. It is important to recall the use of the word "altar" to refer to a toilet. The image of the toilet in the context of a critique of speculative philosophy also occurs in Derrida's account of Genet's writings.

named Troppmann, is a "man" (*Mann* [German]: man, husband) of "excess" (*trop:* too much, too many, too far).[8] The story opens with a prostitute, named Dirty, drunk "in London, in a cellar, in a neighborhood dive [*lieu héteroclite*]—the most squalid of unlikely places." Troppmann explains: "The scene that preceded this nauseous carnival—afterwards, rats must have come crawling over the floor round the two sprawled bodies—was in every way worthy of Dostoevsky" (*BN*, 11, 22; 13, 27). The nauseous carnival continues throughout the entire work. *The Blue of Noon* is an unending orgy of excess. Troppmann recounts one of the many disgusting episodes from which he stitches together something barely resembling a narrative.

> Dirty remained mutely perched on the chair. There was a long silence: you could have heard our hearts inside their bodies. I walked over to the door, pale and sick, my face smeared with blood; I was hiccupping and on the point of vomiting. The terrified servants saw that water was trickling across the chair and down the legs of their beautiful guest. While the urine was gathering into a puddle that spread over the carpet, a noise of slackening bowels made itself ponderously evident beneath the young woman's dress—beet-red, her eyes twisted upwards, she was squirming on her chair like a pig under the knife. (*BN*, 16–17; 20)

The eye "twisted upwards," as if staring into the blinding sun, is none other than the pineal eye whose strange visions make reason shit and vomit.

After leaving Dirty, the narrator enters a relationship with another prostitute named Lazare, whom he describes as "ugly and conspicuously . . . filthy . . . macabre . . . strange . . . ridiculous." Troppmann, if that is his name, eventually confesses to Lazare his most *unspeakable* transgression. He admits that he is a necrophiliac. For Bataille, the corpse is a paradigmatic "transitional" object. As the point at which life and death intersect, the corpse is neither merely living nor dead. The stench of decay, which is the smell of death, is at the same time the aroma of life renewing itself. An unassimilable "remainder" (*reste*), the corpse is a grotesque monstrosity that is disgusting yet strangely fascinating and attractive. The narrator's desire reaches *unheard-of* proportions in relation to the corpse. Violating every taboo, this man, who devotes his life to excess, has sexual intercourse with the corpse of his mother. "'I started down the cor-

8. The impropriety of the proper names Bataille uses in his fiction makes it impossible to be certain about the identity of the characters.

ridor, barefoot. I was quivering. In front of the corpse I kept quivering—I was frightened and aroused. Aroused to the limit. I was in a kind of trance. I took off my pajamas. Then I—you understand . . .'" (*BN,* 77; 105–6).

The "body" (*corps*) of the "mother" (*mater*) is, for Bataille, the nonlogical difference of "matter" (*mater-ia*). Though always obsessed with the mother, Bataille develops his most extensive treatment of her forbidden and foreboding body in a fictive work entitled simply *My Mother.* The narrative is constructed around the incestuous relation between a boy named Pierre (*pierre:* stone) and his nameless mother. Either recalling or anticipating Lacan (again it is impossible to be sure which it is), Pierre explains: "My mother loved me; I believed that we thought and felt alike, in a unison marred only by the presence of the intruder, my father (*MM,* 11)." Pierre recognizes his mother's "abjection," her "monstrous impurity," and his mother acknowledges her "unspeakable depravity." (*MM,* 30, 39)

> Through her tears she smiled at me, but unhappiness had got into her like a cramp and, bent over, she clutched herself as though about to have to vomit.
> "You have turned out to be nice," she said. "I deserved something else. I should have found myself with some buck who would have abused me. I'd have preferred that. The gutter, the dungheap, that's where your mother [like Hegel's Jew] feels at home. You shall never know what horrors I am capable of. I'd like you to know, though. I like my filth. Today I'll end up being sick, I have had too much to drink, I'd feel better if I vomit. Even if I did my worst in front of you I'd still be pure in your eyes."
> Then she brought out that smutty laugh, the sound of which has left me impaired like a cracked bell. (*MM,* 18)

Forever forbidden by "the Name-of-the-Father," the mother arouses in Pierre "the anticipation of the impossible." When his father dies, Pierre attempts "to attain the inaccessible" (*MM,* 31, 83). But he fails; his *eros* ineluctably leads to *thantos.* "I could defer telling how it all ended: the day my mother realized that in the long run she must yield, and release in the sweat of the sheets the tension that had propelled me towards her, and her towards me, she hesitated no longer, and killed herself" (*MM,* 83). Confronted by the unavoidable death of the mother and hence the impossibility of the copulation that mends every tear and wipes away the tears of the gaping body, Pierre confesses: "The system I had built up, within which I had taken refuge, was now about to collapse" (*MM,* 46).

Neither Troppmann's nor Pierre's mother is simply *a* woman. These strange mothers are more like The Woman who, as Lacan insists, is always inaccessible and therefore impossible. *La mère,* in other words, is ~~The~~ Woman. In ~~The~~ Woman, men and women meet what Pierre describes as "something empty and dark, something unfriendly, huge—something that [is] no longer me" (*BN,* 72). In *L'expérience intérieure,* Bataille expands Pierre's account of the impersonal, inhuman, unnameable, unspeakable, unknowable "*ELLE.*"

> Contemplating night, I see nothing, love nothing. I remain immobile, frozen, absorbed in IT [*ELLE*]. I can imagine a landscape of terror, sublime, the earth open as a volcano, the sky filled with fire, or any other vision capable of "ravishing" the spirit; as beautiful and disturbing as it may be, night surpasses this limited "possible" and yet IT is nothing [*ELLE n'est rien*], there is nothing sensible in IT, not even finally darkness. In IT, everything fades away, but, exorbitant, I traverse an empty depth and the empty depth traverses me. In IT, I communicate with the "unknown" opposed to the *ipse* that I am; I become *ipse,* unknown to myself, two terms are confounded in a single rending [*déchirement*], hardly differing from a void—not able to be distinguished from it by anything that I can grasp—nevertheless differing from it more than does the world of a thousand colors. (*IE,* 145)

ELLE is the exorbitant other, *das ganz Andere,* who or which undoes philosophy by leaving the philosopher "impaired like a cracked bell." Such *une cloche fêlée* sounds the *glas* of ontotheology. The impossible aim of philosophy is to silence the "clapper" (*batail*) of this bell.

Excommunication: Expense of Excess

Hegel approaches "the abyss" (*l'abîme*), Bataille maintains, "*in order to annul it.* The System is annulment, cancellation, repeal, abolition" (*IE,* 56). To explain how this annulment *works,* Bataille turns to what he describes as *un texte capital,* which he insists, constitutes the heart of Hegel's entire philosophical corpus.

> But the life of Spirit is not the life that shrinks from death and keeps itself untouched by devastation, but rather the life that endures it and maintains itself in it. It wins its truth only when, in utter dismemberment it finds itself [*indem er in der absoluten Zerrissenheit sich selbst findet; qu'en se trouvant soi-même dans le déchirement absolu*]. It is this power, not as something positive,

which closes its eyes to the negative, as when we say of something that it is nothing or is false, and then, having done with it, turn away and pass on to something else; to the contrary, Spirit is this power only by looking the negative in the face, and tarrying with it. This tarrying with the negative is the magical power that converts it into being (*PS*, 19; 20–30).

The speculative philosopher seeks to find *himself* in *his own* dismemberment, *déchirement, Zer-*riss-*enheit* [tearing, rending, breaking, laceration, rupture, mutilation]. Self-discovery in the midst of absolute laceration results from what Bataille identifies as "the principle of homogeneity," through which all "heterogeneity" is overcome. In the examination of the dialectic of identity and difference, I emphasized that in Hegel's speculative economy, "otherness" (*heteros*) always represents something negative that finally must be negated. The negation of the negative returns difference to "identity" (*idem:* same) and otherness to "same" (*homos*). When understood as the negation of negation, negativity is "the magical power" that transforms the negative into the positive. Inasmuch as Hegel interprets the Absolute in terms of double negation (i.e., the active process of negating negation), the negative as such is penultimate. It is repeatedly superseded by a "higher" positivity. Since the negative is *always* negated, dismemberment (*déchirement* or *Zerrissenheit*) is a transitory moment that is *necessarily* taken up into (or resurrected within) an all-inclusive totality where every loss is redeemed and all wounds healed.[9] Loss—absolute loss—is *incomprehensible* to Hegel and *inconceivable* in his System.

When fully deployed, Hegel's principle of homogeneity assumes two basic forms: theoretical and practical. The theoretical goal of philosophy is to reduce "the unknown [*l'inconnu*]" to "the known [*le connu*]". For the philosopher, the "ultimate possibility" "is that nonknowledge [*non-savoir*] is still knowledge [*savoir*]" (*IE*, 129; 130). The all-knowing philosopher is something like "a sponge" (*une éponge*) (*IE*, 99) that absorbs or assimilates everything.[10] If absolute knowl-

---

9. Commenting on Kojève's analysis of Hegel, Bataille writes: "The atheistic mystic. *Conscious of himself*, conscious of having to die and to disappear, would live, in the words of Hegel, *obviously speaking of himself*, 'in a state of absolute dismemberment [*déchirement*]'; . . . [the atheistic mystic] would not go beyond it [i.e., the negative], 'contemplating negation right in the face,' but never being able to transpose it into Being, refusing to do it and holding his own amid ambiguity." "Hegel, la mort et le sacrifice," *Deucalion* 5 (1955): 30n.

10. Compare the use of the image of the sponge by Derrida in *Signéponge/ Signsponge*, trans. R. Rand (New York: Columbia University Press, 1984), and by Nietzsche in *The Gay Science*, p. 181.

edge is possible, otherness cannot be final or difference irreducible. The knowing subject can actually know only "that which is made" or constructed by subjectivity itself (*IE,* 129). Hegel's philosophy of self-consciousness, therefore, is inevitably a philosophy of *construction.* Bataille argues: "The construction [*la construction*] of Hegel is a philosophy of work [*travail*], of the 'project.' The Hegelian man—Being and God—fulfills or accomplishes himself [*s'accomplit*], completes, perfects, consummates himself [*s'achève*] in the adequation of the project" (*IE,* 96). Since knowing is doing (i.e., knowledge is construction), theory is inseparable from practice.

"Reason," Bataille maintains, "is bound up with work and the purposive activity that incarnates its laws." [11] Work, in turn, is governed by the principle of *utility.* In Hegel's System, reasonable activity is, by definition, purposeful. The worker seeks a profitable return on every investment of his or her time and energy. When the System is working at maximum efficiency, nothing is useless. The Hegelian economy actually assumes full employment in which no one is *désoeuvré:* out of work, unoccupied, or idle. Unemployment of any kind calls into question the entire economy. To preserve itself, a utilitarian system must *exclude* what is useless or profitless. Consequently, work is inextricably bound up with a complex network of prohibitions. While reasonable work and the work of reason rest on taboos, taboos work by excluding or repressing that which disrupts productive labor. For Bataille, the two primary forces interrupting purposive activity are *eros* and *thanatos.* In his consideration of "the interdependent ensemble of prohibitions," Bataille stresses that "for all known peoples, the world of work opposes that of sexuality and death." [12] Inverting the customary association of the sacred with order (cosmos) and the profane with disorder (chaos), Bataille contends that the world of work is profane and the forbidden domain circumscribed by work is sacred.

Bataille is convinced that when reason is pushed to its limit, it inevitably slips and falls. Reason constitutes itself both theoretically and practically in and through an act of exclusion that is maintained by prohibitions, which every reasonable person deems inviolable. In this way, prohibition functions as the condition of the possibility of reason. The philosopher, however, resists recognizing the implica-

11. Georges Bataille, *Death and Sensuality: A Study of Eroticism and the Taboo* (New York; Arno Press, 1977), p. 168.
12. Georges Bataille, *Lascaux or the Birth of Art,* trans. A. Wainhouse (Switzerland: Skira, n.d.), p. 33; 9:35.

tions of reason's constitution. Inasmuch as reason rests upon prohibition, taboo itself cannot be rationally comprehended. Reason, in other words, presupposes nonreason. Since reason is always secondary to something that is unreasonable, it can never be all-encompassing. The encounter with an unavoidable limit drives the philosopher *mad* and renders the comprehensive aspirations of philosophy *laughable.* This is the madness that blinds Hegel at the moment he "completes" his System; this laugh is *le rire déchirant*—the laugh whose incessant clapping leaves one torn, rent, lacerated, mutilated. *Le rire déchirant* is the laugh that exposes the inescapability of dismemberment, *déchirement,* and *Zerrissenheit.* Though the philosopher struggles to silence this disruptive laugh, its "clap" (*coup*) always returns to mock his work.

> I reach first of all the extreme limit of knowledge (for example, I mimic [*mime*] absolute knowledge, in whatever way, but that assumes an infinite effort of the mind wanting knowledge). I know then that I know nothing. As *Ipse* I wanted to be everything (through knowledge) and I fall into anguish: the occasion of this anguish is my non-knowledge, non-sense beyond hope (here non-knowledge does not abolish particular knowledge, but its sense—removes from it all sense). (*IE,* 67)

Bataille attempts to subvert Hegelianism, and all it represents, by miming absolute knowledge. Elsewhere he elaborates this strategy.

> The *Phenomenology of Spirit* comprises two essential movements completing a circle: it is the completion by degrees of the consciousness of self (of human *ipse*) and the becoming everything [*tout*] (the becoming God) of this *ipse* completing knowledge (and by this means destroying particularity within it, thus completing the negation of oneself, becoming absolute knowledge). But if in this way, as if by contagion and by mime, I accomplish in myself Hegel's circular movement, I define—beyond the limits attained—no longer an unknown, but an unknowable. Unknowable not on account of the insufficiency of reason, but by its nature (and even, for Hegel, one could only have concern for this beyond for lack of possessing absolute knowledge. . . .). (*IE,* 127)

In an effort to undercut philosophy's foundational principle of homogeneity, Bataille develops what he describes as a "heterology" (*hétérologie*). Heterology deconstructs every philosophical construction by disclosing the inevitable return of the repressed. Bataille defines heterology as "the science of what is completely other [*tout autre*]. The term *agiology,*" he admits, "would perhaps be more precise, but one would have to catch the double meaning of *agio* (analogous to the double meaning of *sacer*), *soiled* as well as *holy*. But it is above all the term *scatology* (the science of excrement [*ordure*]) that retains in the present circumstances (the specialization of the sacred) an incontestable expressive value as the doublet of an abstract term such as *heterology*" (*VE*, 102n; 2:61–62n). By exploring an other that cannot be returned to the same and a difference that cannot be reduced to identity, Bataille rubs the philosopher's nose in the shit and vomit of his own (digestive) system.

Miming philosophy, Bataille develops two sides of heterology: theoretical and practical. The two aspects of Bataille's "science" of the other come together in the notion of *dépense* (expenditure, outlay, flow; *dépenser:* to spend, expend, waste; *dépensier:* extravagant). Theoretically, *dépense* points to that which is outside of thought [*la pensée*]. "Heterology" is actually an oxymoron. *Heteros* is, for Bataille, precisely what eludes the *logos*. Consequently, heterology is an *impossible* science. "When one says that heterology scientifically considers questions of heterogeneity, one does not mean that heterology is, in the usual sense of such a formula, a science of the heterogeneous. The heterogeneous is even resolutely placed outside the reach of scientific knowledge, which by definition is only applicable to homogeneous elements. Above all, heterology is opposed to any homogeneous representation of the world, in other words, to any philosophical system" (*VE*, 97; 3:62). Over against philosophical systems, which operate according to the principle of homogeneity by attempting to reduce the unknown to the known, Bataille proposes a heterology that returns the known to the unknown. In this heterology, otherness is not merely a negative awaiting a magical transformation that will turn it into something positive. Radical altarity resists all incorporation, assimilation, and appropriation. *Heteros* is not only unknown; it is *unknowable*. Otherness is not a penultimate moment that eventually is subsumed within a comprehensive and comprehensible totality. To the contrary, altarity is excommunicated from all reasonable circles. Bataille, in keeping with Lacan (who actually follows Bataille), argues that the expense/ ex-pens(é)e of *dépense/dé-pens(é)e* is excommunication/ ex-communication.[13] For a faithful philosopher like Hegel, no price is too high to pay to avoid excommunication. Hegel is even willing to

13. Compare Lacan, "Excommunication" (*FFC*, 1–13; 7–17).

repress his bastard son and to flush away or assimilate (at this point expulsion and incorporation coincide) "shitty" Jews in order to keep the (Christian) family pure.

Dépense harbors additional nuances that extend its range from theory to practice. *Un dé* is a die used in the game of dice.[14] In figurative terms, *le dé* refers to a throw or hazard. *Un coup de dés*, which recalls *un coup de don*, is a throw of the dice.[15] Accordingly, *le dé* implies the chance and contingency that every system is constructed to master. A form of the verb *penser* (to think), *pense* intimates *la panse*, which means belly. Since Hegel often relates knowledge to assimilation, incorporation, and digestion, that which is outside of thought likewise appears to be outside the belly. *Dépense,* in other words, connotes something difficult to stomach, something the belly cannot contain—like shit or vomit. Such excrement is the refuse that can be neither refused nor re-fused. Always open at both ends, the gaping body spreads its excremental residue from anus and penis to mouth and eye: shit to vomit, fart to laugh, piss to spit, sperm to cry, blood to tears.

Practically, *dépense* designates an "expenditure" (*ex*, out + *pendere*, to pay) without return. This expenditure releases "remains" (*le reste*) that reason works to repress: shit, vomit, farts, laughs, piss, sperm, cries, blood, sweat, and tears. Practical heterology is undeniably transgressive and hence inevitably excessive. Bataille contends that the repressive stranglehold of reason can only be broken, albeit it temporarily, by violating every known taboo. In contrast to the utilitarianism of reasonable labor, excessive expenditure is useless. Dismemberment does not lead to re-membering; loss yields no profit. For the speculator who insists on a reasonable return on every investment, such absolute loss is worse than unproductive; it is insane, mad. The reasonable investor does not gamble, for he does not know how to read a "die [*dé*]." In different terms, reason does not know how "to read" (*lire*) the "delirium" (*dé-lire*) created by senseless expenditure. To

---

14. It hardly seems necessary to comment on the relationship between "die" (as in dice) and "die" (as in death). In attempting to master every chance, philosophy tries to control what seem to be terrifying shadows of death. The ultimate chance is that death is ultimate. Since the Hegelian philosopher insists that negation is necessarily negated, he refuses to acknowledge the final chance haunting everything that appears chancy. Protests to the contrary notwithstanding, this philosophical venture remains a risky chance that Bataille does not think is worth taking.

15. See Derrida's discussion of Mallarmé's *Un coup de dés* in "The Double Session," *Dissemination*. In *Spurs*, Derrida explores the suggestive interplay between *le coup de don* and *le coup de dés*.

appreciate the irreducible insignificance of *dépense,* it is necessary to return to two domains that reason supposedly surpasses in achieving absolute knowledge: religion and art.

Atheology: Transgressive Sintax

To transgress is, in Blanchot's terms, to take *le pas* [step, not] *au-delà.* In an essay entitled *Le rire des dieux,* which is included in a work dedicated to Bataille, Blanchot comments on the paradox of transgression.

> We must understand that transgression—the surpassing of the unsurpassable limit—is not only a possibility more difficult than others, but designates that which, being radically beyond our reach, lies open to man only when human power or personal mastery (having been raised to the highest level) ceases to be the ultimate dimension. The prohibition, in this case, is no longer the positive from which transgression—as Hegelian logic would have it—would still need to promote negativity that would content itself by restoring prohibition to a higher level until some definitive absolute be attained: prohibition marks the point where *power* ceases (and, at this point, the primacy of the *ego,* like the logic of identity, also ceases), while transgression is the experience of that which eludes power, the *impossible* itself.(A, 201)

The logic of identity and the primacy of the "I" are two sides of the same coin. To subvert the former is to fissure the latter. While claiming to negate negation, the dialectical affirmation of identity remains thoroughly negative. The speculative subject affirms itself by negating everything other than, and different from, itself. Bataille's transgression, by contrast, is radically affirmative. The impossible "science" of heterology is an extension of Nietzsche's "gay science" in which thoroughgoing "Yea-saying" displaces all "Nay-saying." "Transgression," as Michel Foucault explains, "opens onto a scintillating and constantly affirmed world, a world without shadow or twilight, without the serpentine 'no' that bites into fruits and lodges their contradictions at their core. It is the solar inversion of satanic denial. It was originally linked to the divine, or rather, from this limit marked by the sacred it opens the space where the divine functions." [16]

16. Michel Foucault, "A Preface to Transgression," *Language, Counter-Memory, Practice,* ed. D. F. Bouchard, trans. D. F. Bouchard and S. Simon (Ithaca: Cornell University Press, 1977), p. 37.

Le pas au-delà is the step beyond that carries one from the known to the unknown. Reflecting on one of Blanchot's most opaque *récits*, Bataille remarks: "Outside the notes of this volume, I only know *Thomas the Obscure* in which there are, at times, even though they remain hidden, questions of the new theology (which has only the unknown [*l'inconnu*] for its object)" (*IE*, 120). This "new theology" has nothing to do with what Bataille, recalling Kierkegaard, describes as "the degraded God" of Christendom. In Christianity, "God rapidly and almost entirely loses his terrifying features, his appearance as a decomposing cadaver, in order to become, at the final stage of degradation, the simple (paternal) sign of universal homogeneity" (*VI*, 96; 2:61). Heterology calls into question this universal homogeneity by uncovering what Christianity represses. "The development of knowledge touching on the history of religions," Bataille argues, "has shown that the essential religious activity was not directed toward a personal and transcendent being (or beings), but toward an impersonal reality" (*VE*, 242; 1:562). This "impersonal reality" is *the sacred.* The return to, and of the sacred is impossible apart from the death of God, i.e., the personal God of Christianity. A fully developed heterology, therefore, is an "atheology" (*athéologie*).

As "the opposite of a *substance* that withstands the test of time, [the sacred] is something that flees as soon as it appears and cannot be grasped" (*VE*, 214; 1:560). The elusiveness of the sacred reflects its irreducible ambiguity. Following insights developed by psychologists, sociologists, and anthropologists, Bataille stresses that the sacred is both pure and impure, holy and soiled.[17] As interpreters from Otto and Freud to Eliade and Girard point out, the ambiguity of the sacred triggers irresolvable emotional ambivalence. Both holy and filthy, the sacred is simultaneously attractive and repulsive, alluring and forbidding. Such ambiguity and ambivalence render the sacred *fascinating.* The fascination exercised by the sacred cannot be ex-

---

17. The classical account of the notion of the holy is developed by Rudolph Otto in *The Idea of the Holy: An Inquiry into the Non-rational Factor in the Idea of the Divine and Its Relation to the Rational*, trans. J. W. Harvey (New York: Oxford University Press, 1958). Other interpretations of the sacred that are relevant to Bataille's analysis include Emile Durkheim, *The Elementary Forms of the Religious Life*, trans. J. W. Swain (New York: The Free Press, 1955) (sociological); Sigmund Freud, *Totem and Taboo*, trans. J. Strachey (New York: Norton, 1950) (psychological); Mircea Eliade, *The Sacred and the Profane: The Nature of Religion*, trans. W. R. Task (New York: Harper and Row, 1961) (history of religions); Mary Douglas, *Purity and Danger: An Analysis of Pollution and Taboo* (New York: Praeger, 1969) (anthropological); and René Girard, *Violence and the Sacred*, trans. P. Gregory (Baltimore: Johns Hopkins University Press, 1977) (literary/anthropological).

plained rationally. The sacred comes to expression first in the enactment of religious ritual and then in the performative sintax of art.

I have already noted that Bataille reverses the traditional association of the sacred with order and the profane with disorder. In Bataille's atheological heterology, the structured world of reason and work is profane. As we have seen, the order of this "cosmos" is maintained by a network of taboos, the most important of which involve prohibitions against death and sexuality. In a manner similar to the Lacanian unconscious, which extends into the realm of the gods, the sacred interrupts reason and labor. The intervention of the sacred exposes gaps, holes, tears, and *Risse,* in what had seemed to be the coherent and consistent fabric of experience. The eruption of the sacred into the domain of the profane takes place in religious ritual. Inasmuch as the maintenance of the structure of reason and work requires submission to the prohibitions against death and sex, the disorder[18] associated with the sacred can be released only by the violation of these founding taboos. In Bataille's "general economy"[19] of the sacred, transgression is enacted at the *altar* of sacrifice and the *altar* of eroticism.[20] By taking the step beyond, the transgressor glimpses the altarity of the sacred.

18. The distinctiveness of Bataille's position becomes clearer when it is contrasted with Victor Turner's analysis (see, inter alia, *The Ritual Process: Structure and Anti-structure* [Chicago: Aldine, 1969]). Turner's account of the relation between structure and anti-structure remains bound to the categories of structuralism. The breakdown of structure plunges ritual participants into an apparently "original" condition in which social differentiations dissolve. Turner labels this archaic state *communitas.* The periodic return to *communitas* is therapeutic for both individual and community. Personal and group tensions are released, thus permitting the cleansing and renewal of psychological and social structures. Bataille's account of the sacred moves beyond the polar opposites that structuralists regard as essential. Though disruptive of the structured world of reason and work, the sacred cannot be defined simply in terms of "anti-structure." In his analysis of ritual, Bataille discovers a form of "communication" that bears a superficial resemblance to Turner's *communitas.* For Bataille, however, the outbreak of disorder renders the presence of subjects both to themselves and to others *impossible.* Finally, Bataille's emphasis on the uselessness of ritual excess stands in marked contrast to Turner's insistence on the utility of ritual practice.

19. Bataille uses this term to distinguish the excess of expenditure from the restricted economy of a system like the one developed by Hegel. For a consideration of the difference between the general and the restricted economy, see Derrida, "From Restricted to General Economy: A Hegelianism without Reserve," *WD,* 251–77; 369–407.

20. In this context, it is helpful to recall that "altar" can refer to the altar of pleasure or the altar of bliss and, by extension, to the external genital organs of a woman. Furthermore, "alter" sometimes means "to castrate or spay." For Bataille and many who come after him pleasure and bliss differ significantly.

In an essay entitled "Sacrificial Mutilation and the Severed [*coupée*] Ear of Vincent Van Gogh," Bataille examines "the radical *alteration* [*altération*] of the person" who participates in ritual sacrifice.

> Such an action [i.e., sacrifice] would be characterized by the fact that it would have the power to liberate heterogeneous elements and to break the habitual homogeneity of the person, in the same way that vomiting would be opposed to its opposite, the communal eating of food. Sacrifice considered in its essential phase would only be the rejection of what had been appropriated by a person or by a group. Because everything that is rejected from the human cycle is altered in an altogether troubling way, the sacred things that intervene at the end of the operation—the victim struck down in a pool of blood, the severed finger or ear, the torn-out eye—do not appreciably differ from the vomited food. Repugnance is only one of the forms of stupor caused by a horrifying eruption, by the disgorging of a force that threatens to consume. The one who sacrifices is free—free to indulge in a similar disgorging, free, continuously identifying with the victim, to vomit his own being just as he has vomited a piece of himself or a bull, in other words, free to throw himself suddenly *outside of himself* [*hors de soi*], like a gall or an aissaouah. (*VE*, 70; 1:269–70)

For Abraham standing on the heights of Moriah facing his son, for the devotee of Mithra standing on the scaffold facing the bull, for the Icarian Hegel standing at the summit of his (solar) System facing the sun/son, the *coup de grâce* is a *coup* of grace. This *coup* is "a liberating laceration" (*déchirure libératrice; VE*, 251; 2:371). By cutting the tie that binds, one is freed from the gravity of reason and labor.

The sacrificial *coup*, however, need not be a cut that alters or mutilates sacrificer and/or victim. One can also sacrifice by giving. Accordingly, *le coup* of sacrifice can be *le coup de don*. Like so many others, Bataille was deeply influenced by Marcel Mauss's *Le don*.[21] Instead of simply appropriating this richly suggestive analysis of the gift, Bataille uses Mauss's insights to develop his own interpretation of *dépense*. For Bataille, sacrificial giving is an unproductive expenditure that embodies the principle of absolute loss, i.e., loss without return. Such incalculable expenditure involves excessive "prodigality" (*prodigus*, from *prodigere*: to drive away, squander; compare *prodigiosus*, from *prodigium*: omen, portent, prodigy). While, in Hegel's domestic economy, the prodigal always returns to the home of the father (or Father), in Bataille's nondomestic economy, there is no return on, or of

21. Marcel Mauss, *The Gift: Forms and Functions of Exchange in Archaic Societies*, trans. I. Cunnison (New York: Norton, 1967).

the prodigal. To appreciate the force of Bataille's argument, it is necessary to realize that the gift *does not* establish a reciprocal relationship of give-and-take. Rather, sacrificial offering breaks the circuit of exchange by turning away from the prudential calculation that characterizes all reasonable activity. Bataille maintains that the most graphic example of the alogic of sacrifice is the ritual of *potlatch*. "As a game, *potlatch* is the opposite of a principle of conservation: it puts an end to the stability of fortunes as it existed within the totemic economy, where possession was hereditary. An activity of excessive exchange replaced heredity (as a source of possession) with a kind of deliriously [*délirante*] formed ritual poker. But the players can never retire from the game, their fortunes made; they remain at the mercy of provocation. At no time does a fortune serve to *shelter its owner from need*. To the contrary, it functionally remains—as does the possessor—*at the mercy of a need for limitless loss* [*perte démesurée*], which exists endemically in a social group" (*VE*, 122–23; 1 : 311). From Bataille's perspective, the need for limitless loss, instead of the need for total satisfaction characterizes human activity.

It is clear that Bataille's reading of *Le don* differs significantly from the use made of Mauss's analysis by a structuralist like Lévi–Strauss.[22] For Lévi-Strauss, Mauss's interpretation of the gift implies a logic of exchange that structures personal and social relations. Over against Lévi-Strauss, Bataille stresses what he regards as the unreasonable and unproductive aspects of giving. The difference between Lévi-Strauss's structural and Bataille's nonstructural or poststructural understanding of *le don* is evident in their contrasting views of sexuality. For Lévi-Strauss, the exchange of women, made possible by a network of taboos, ensures the orderly functioning of the psychosocial system. Ever suspicious of systems, Bataille approaches sexuality in terms of eroticism. Unlike the socially sanctioned relation between the sexes, eroticism is "deflected [*détourné*] from genital finality." In the eyes of reason, such sexual activity is "perverse," even "monstrous" (*VE*, 118; 1 : 305). "Erotic conduct is the opposite of normal conduct, as spending is the opposite of getting. If we follow the dictates of reason, we try to acquire all kinds of goods, we work in order to increase the sum of our possessions or of our knowledge, we use all means to get richer and to possess more. . . . But when the fever of sex seizes us, we behave in the opposite way. We recklessly draw on our strength and sometimes in the violence of passion we

---

22. See, inter alia, Claude Lévi-Strauss, *The Elementary Structures of Kinship*, trans. J. H. Bell and J. R. Von Sturmer (Boston: Beacon Press, 1969).

squander considerable resources to no real purpose. Pleasure is so close to ruinous waste that we refer to the moment of climax as a 'little death.' Consequently, anything that suggests erotic excess always implies disorder."[23] While the orderly exchange of women establishes and secures the identity of psychological, social, and cultural differences, perverse eroticism subverts all hard-and-fast distinctions. Erotic activity upsets every form of self-possession by keeping open the tears of the gaping body.

The excesses of transgression reach a climax in the religious festival. Within the sacred time-space of the ritual, the violation of taboos designed to control *eros* is indistinguishable from the violation of taboos surrounding *thanatos*. "If we view the primary taboos as the refusal laid down by the individual to cooperate with nature regarded as a squandering of living energy and an orgy of annihilation, we can no longer differentiate between death and sexuality. Sexuality and death are simply the culminating points of the holiday that nature celebrates with the inexhaustible multitude of living beings, both of them signifying the boundless wastage of nature's resources as opposed to the urge to live on that characterizes every living creature."[24] For Bataille, the most vivid instance of such an "orgy of annihilation" is the Dionysian festival of the ancient Greeks. With the invocation of Dionysus, Bataille returns to his critique of Hegel's systematic analysis of the orderly cosmos of reason and work.

In what is perhaps the best-known phrase in all of his writings, Hegel describes the *Phenomenology of Spirit* as "the bacchanalian revel in which no member is sober" (*PS*, 27; 39). Rejecting Hegel's characterization of his own work, Bataille contends that neither work nor a work can ever be bacchanalian. Bacchus is another name for Dionysus who, in turn, is known by atheologians like Nietzsche and Bataille as "the Anti-Christ." We have seen that Hegel's christocentric work is actually constructed to master time. The bacchanalian revel in which Dionysus is honored is a saturnalia that simultaneously celebrates Saturn—the Italic and Roman deity whose Greek name is *Cronus*. While Hegel's work works to master time, Bataille's transgressive festival releases excessive flows that keep one ever open to an unstoppable temporal flux.

> It even seems that ancient Greece was engendered by wounds and crime, just as the strength of Cronus was engendered by the bloody

23. Bataille, *Death and Sensuality*, p. 170.
24. Ibid., p. 61.

mutilation of his father Uranus,[25] in other words, of precisely the divine sovereignty of the heavens. Cronus, the very "human" god of the golden age, was celebrated in saturnalia; Dionysus, whose coming into the world depended on the murder of his mother by his father—the criminal Zeus striking down Semele in a flash [*coup*] of lightning—this tragic Dionysus, broken in joy, started the sudden flight of the bacchantes. And the least explained of all the "mysteries," TRAGEDY, like a festival given in honor of horror-spreading TIME, depicted for gathered men the signs of delirium and death whereby they might recognize their true nature. (*VE*, 218; 1:507)

In the modern world, however, religion no longer involves transgressive excess; it has been domesticated. Instead of honoring "horror-spreading time," religion promises an escape from the terrors of temporality. Rituals that once disrupted order and decentered structure gradually have been transformed into mechanisms for psychological and social control. While not denying the transgressive potential of religious activity, Bataille maintains that art now provides a more effective access to the uncanny time-space of the sacred.

Bataille, like Heidegger, is preoccupied with the question of the origin of art. Without directly acknowledging Heidegger, Bataille suggests that the most promising place to begin an investigation of the origin of art is the cleavage of a rock. In *Lascaux, or the Birth of Art*, he argues that art "begins" in the bowels of mother earth. As the photographs of "the cave" (*la grotte*) named "The Hall of Bulls"[26] suggest, art is first inscribed upon the invaginated intestinal walls of "self-secluding" earth. From the beginning (if indeed there is a beginning), there is something *grotto-esque* and *dirty* about art. Bataille is convinced that the dirt of art's grotesque, subterranean "origin" can

25. In Greek mythology, Uranus was "the sky and the god of the sky. [He] was the first son of Ge (Earth), who had been born of Chaos. He married her and she bore him the Hundred-handed, the Cyclopes, and the Titans. When Uranus imprisoned his children (or all but the Titans) within the body of earth, Ge roused her children against their father and gave Cronus, the youngest and wiliest, a sickle. Uranus came at evening to lie upon Ge, but Cronus castrated him and flung the severed parts into the sea. From the foam that formed about them Aphrodite grew; the blood that fell upon the earth spawned the Erinyes, the giants, and the Meliae." Tripp, *Crowell's Handbook of Classical Mythology*, p. 596. After considering Bataille's account of "The Solar Anus," it no longer seems implausible to interpret Uranus as the "original" (*Ur*) anus.

26. As noted above, Bataille emphasizes the importance of the figure of the bull in his discussion of sacrifice and the sacrificial altar.

Lascaux—Les Grottes—Salle des Taureaux. © ARCH.PHOT.PARIS*/ ARS, NY/SPADEM 1987.

never be wiped away. Art, like religion, emerges from the filth of the sacred.

> A work of art, a sacrifice . . . , participate in the spirit of the festival overflowing [*débordant*] the world of work, and clash with the spirit, if not the letter, of the prohibitions necessary for the protection of this world. Every work of art, in isolation, possesses a meaning independent of the desire for the marvelous or pro-digious [*prodige*],[27] which it has in common with all others. But we may say in advance that a work of art in which this desire cannot be sensed, in which it is faint or barely present, is a mediocre work. Similarly, there is a specific motive behind every sacrifice: an abundant harvest, expiation, or any other logical objective; nonetheless, in one way or another, every sacrifice grows out of the research [*recherche*] for a sacred instant, sur-passing profane time, where prohibitions insure the possibility of life.[28]

27. A slip by the English translator is revealing. *Prodige* is rendered "prodigal." The French word for prodigal is *prodigue*. For Bataille, prodigality is prodigious or marvelous.

28. Bataille, *Lascaux or the Birth of Art,* p. 39; 9:42.

Though stressing the disturbing force of multiple forms of art, Bataille's theoretical and practical concerns tend to concentrate on literature. In a review, "Hemingway in the Light of Hegel," Bataille underscores the role of literature in "drawing us toward the inaccessible."[29] The writer is *l'homme du puits* whose writing involves the ceaseless effort "to treat the life of the outside [*la vie due dehors*]" (*IE*, 83). This *dehors* is the *au-delà* of the sacred. Since the sacred forever eludes the grasp of reason, it can never be expressed directly. As Kierkegaard insists, the writer who is obsessed by that which is wholly Other must communicate *indirectly*. For Bataille, as for Kierkegaard and Heidegger, the privileged form of indirect communication is *poiesis*.[30] "The term *poésie*," Bataille avers, "applied to the least degraded and least intellectualized forms of expression of a state of loss, can be considered synonymous with expenditure; it in fact signifies, in the most precise way, creation by means of loss. Its meaning is therefore close to that of *sacrifice*" (*VE*, 120; 1:307). So understood, *poésie* designates a particular literary praxis rather than a specific literary genre. In the *poésie* of his poems and prose, Bataille puts his heterology into practice. For the poet, language is not descriptive, referential, or representational; it is performative. The performance of the modern and postmodern writer is actually a substitute for the performance of religious ritual. In a manner similar to the ritual practices it displaces, *poésie* transgresses the prohibitions upon which culture depends. The playful (yet dreadful) words of the poet interrupt the workmanlike language of reason. To the ear of reason, *poésie* is the incomprehensible discourse of the Other—*das ganz Andere*. Always bubbling up, or bursting out from an "outside" that is "inside," the poet's aberrant syntax is, for anyone who is reasonable, disgusting sintax. The insistence of the poet's letter gags reason until it is forced to vomit. Stuttering and stammering, reason eventually "slips" (*glisse*) and falls. The slippery word of the poet, which sounds the *glas* of reason and its spokesman, the philosopher, is *un mot glissant*. The poet, Bataille, writes: "I will give only one example of a slipping *word* [mot *glissant*]. I say *word:* it could just as well be the sentence into which one inserts the word, but I limit myself to the word *silence*. It is already, as I have said, the abolition of the sound that the word is; among all words it is the most perverse, or the most

29. "Hemingway in the Light of Hegel," *Semiotext(e)*, 1976, 14; "Hemingway à la lumière de Hegel," *Critique* 70 (1973).

30. There are important differences in the views of *poiesis* developed by Kierkegaard, Heidegger, and Bataille. For Heidegger's interpretation of *poiesis,* see chapter 2, fourth section. I will discuss Kierkegaard's position in chapter 10.

poetic: it is the token of its own death" (*IE*, 28). *Le mot glissant* "says" the unsayable by "unsaying" itself in the very act of saying. To say "silence" is to break silence. Silence inevitably "withdraws" in and through its articulation. In Heideggerian terms, *poésie* enacts the "original or primal strife" of disclosure and concealment. To hear the unbearably light words of the poet is, paradoxically, to fall—to fall into the "deleterious absurdity of TIME." Since this fall is "FINAL," it is a loss from which one never recovers, a loss from and upon which there is no return (*VE*, 220; 1:511). By inscribing and reinscribing this *tombe* (*tomber:* to fall; *tombe:* tomb, tombstone) *l'homme du puits* repeatedly returns to the labyrinthian pyramid from which the philosopher, following Icarus, vainly struggles to flee.

I have noted that Nietzsche's vision of eternal recurrence was occasioned by the sight of a pyramidal rock, which, like Melville's monstrous Moby-Dick,[31] erupts from watery depths. Analyzing "The Pyramid of Suleri," Bataille writes:

> Nietzsche is to Hegel what a bird breaking its shell [*coquille;* compare *coq:* cock] is to a bird contentedly absorbing the substance within. The crucial instant of fracture can only be described in Nietzsche's own words: "The intensity of my feelings makes me both tremble and laugh. . . . I had cried too much. . . . These were not tears of tenderness, but tears of jubilation. . . . That day I was walking through the woods, along the lake of Silvaplana; at a powerful pyramidal rock not far from Suleri I stopped. . . ." (*VE*, 219–20; 1:510).

Bataille names the ecstatic experience suffered by Nietzsche *l'expérience intérieure.* In the book bearing this title, Bataille offers a first-person account of this uncanny experience.

> Fifteen years of this ago (perhaps a bit more), I returned from I don't know where, late in the night. The rue de Rennes was deserted. Coming from Saint-Germain, I crossed the rue du Four (the post office side). I held in my hand an open umbrella and I believe it was not raining. (But I had not drunk: I tell you, I am

---

31. "But even stripped of these supernatural surmisings, there was enough in the earthly make and incontestable character of the monster to strike the imagination with unwonted power. For, it was not so much his uncommon bulk that so much distinguished him from other sperm whales, but, as was elsewhere thrown out—a peculiar snow-white wrinkled forehead, a high, *pyramidical* white hump. These were his prominent features; the tokens whereby, even in the limitless, uncharted seas, he revealed his identity, at a long distance, to those who knew him." Herman Melville, *Moby-Dick; or, The Whale* (Berkeley: University of California Press, 1979), p. 184. Emphasis added.

sure of it.) I had this umbrella open without needing to (if not for
what I speak of later). I was extremely young then, chaotic and
full of empty intoxications: a round of unseemly, vertiginous
ideas, but ideas already full of anxieties, rigorous and crucifying,
ran through my mind. In this shipwreck of reason, anguish, the
solitary fall from grace, cowardice, bad faith profited: the festival
started up again a little further on. What is certain is that this
freedom, at the same time as the "impossible" that I had run up
against, burst in my head. A space constellated with laughter
opened its obscure abyss before me. At the crossing of the rue du
Four, I became unknown in this nothingness, suddenly. . . . I
negated these gray walls that enclosed me, I rushed into a sort of
rapture [*ravissement*]. I laughed divinely: the umbrella, having
descended upon my head, covered me (I expressly covered myself
with this black shroud). I laughed as perhaps one had never
laughed; the extreme depth of each thing opened itself up—laid
bare, as if I were dead. (*IE*, 46)

*Chaotique, ivresse, vide, vertige, crucifiant, angoisse, déchéance, fête, impos-
sible, abîme, obscur, néant, inconnu, ravissement, rire divinement, mort:*
these are the words Bataille uses to describe the experience that slips
away from language. *L'expérience intérieure* involves absolute *déchirement, Zerrissenheit,* dismemberment. In *le déchirement absolu,* one does
not find oneself but *loses oneself absolutely. "Spirit moves in a strange world
where anguish and ecstasy coexist"* (*IE*, 10). This agonizing crucifixion of
spirit is not followed by resurrection. *L'expérience intérieure* deepens
rather than mends the *Riss* that faults the subject. This experience is,
therefore, a "voyage to the end of the possibility of man" (*IE*, 19).

Always escaping the grasp of the Logos, *l'expérience intérieure* calls
into question reason in both its theoretical and practical capacities.
"Experience, in fever and anguish, is the putting into question of that
which a man knows of being. Should he in this fever have any ap-
prehension whatsoever, he cannot say: 'I have seen God, the absolute,
or the depths of the universe'; he can only say 'that which I have seen
eludes understanding'" (*IE*, 16). Inasmuch as *l'expérience intérieure*
evades the categories of understanding, it can be identified as neither
objective nor subjective, exterior nor interior. *L'expérience intérieure* is
yet another *mot glissant,* which unsays itself in its very saying. Bataille
maintains that this impossible saying, which is an unsaying, is, nevertheless, a "communication." In the course of his analysis of *l'expérience
intérieure,* Blanchot describes this strange communication.

Communication, therefore, only begins to be authentic when
experience has stripped existence bare, has removed it from that

which ties it to discourse and to action, has opened it to a nondiscursive interiority where it vanishes, communicates itself outside all objects that can give it an end or where it can master itself. It is not so much participation of a subject with an object as a union by language. It is the movement in which, when the subject and the object are relinquished, pure and simple abandon becomes loss naked in the night.[32]

Such communication is, of course, impossible. For Bataille, this impossibility of communication is the *communication* of "the impossible."

The impossibility of *l'expérience intérieure* is not merely theoretical; it is practical as well. Bataille agrees with Heidegger and others in his conviction that the modern philosophy of the constructive subject comes to completion in Hegel's philosophical "project [i.e., pro'ject and 'project]." "Contrary to all action," *l'expérience intérieure* frustrates all projects and subverts every projection (*IE,* 59). Like the person listening for what Heidegger describes as the tolling of the stillness of silence, one in search of ecstasy must give up purposeful striving and *wait*. This extraordinary experience always comes "from the outside" (*du dehors; IE,* 175). In the encounter with the exorbitant, the potency of the constructive subject gives way to inescapable impotence. "There all possibility dries up, the possible disappears, and the impossible holds sway. To face the impossible is, in my eyes, to undergo a divine experience; it is similar to torture" (*IE,* 45). Such *supplice*— torment, pain, anguish—grows out of "capital punishment" (*le dernier supplice*) in which both sovereign potentate and potent subject are "executed" (*suppliciés*). As we have been led to suspect, the place of this execution is the Place de la Concorde. For Bataille, the obelisk in the midst of the Place is a sign of the decapitation of all aspects of capitalism. At the base of capitalization stands the erect subject, i.e., the capital *I,* rendered impotent by *l'expérience intérieure.* I, the "I," cannot experience ecstasy. In *ekstasis,* the "I" is never *da,* but is always *fort.* To undergo *l'expérience intérieure* is to suffer the death of the "I." A remark of Blanchot again clarifies Bataille's insight.

We speak of it as of an experience and, nonetheless, we will never say that we have experienced it. Experience that is not a lived event, even less a state of ourselves, at the very most the *limit-experience* or, perhaps, where the limits fall. . . .

Experience of non-experience.
Detour of all visible and all invisible. (*EI,* 311)

32. Maurice Blanchot, *Faux Pas* (Paris: Gallimard, 1971), p. 51.

To experience non-experience is, of course, impossible. For Bataille, this impossibility of experience is the *expérience* of "the impossible."

> That which I must abhor today: voluntary ignorance, methodical ignorance through which I searched for ecstasy. Not that ignorance does not open, in effect, the heart to rapture [*ravissement*]. But I bitterly test the *impossible*. Every profound life is heavy with the *impossible*. The intention, the project destroys. However, *I knew* that I did not know anything and this, my secret: "non-knowledge" communicates ecstasy. (*IE, 73*)

This impossible ecstasy or ecstasy of the impossible is a *catastrophe* for the proper "I." "*Catastrophe*—lived time," Bataille argues, "must be represented ecstatically not in the form of an old man, but as a skeleton armed with a scythe [*une faux; faux:* false, erroneous, wrong; base, treacherous, deceitful, equivocal]: a glacial gleaming skeleton, whose teeth adhere to the lips of a severed head [*une tête coupée*]" (*VE*, 134; 1:94–95). This is the catastrophe that philosophy is constructed to avoid. But the philosopher always fails to consummate his project. A timely catastrophe inevitably causes the philosopher to lose his head. This blow is the *coup de grâce* for the philosopher's *texte capital*. The *faux* of Cronus inflicts the cruelest wound of all: the castration of the philosopher. The severed skeletal head haunting Escher's extraordinary drawing, "EYE," depicts the blind spot in the philosopher's eagle/I.

The person who undergoes *l'expérience intérieure* does not struggle to cast "horror-spreading time" "to the outside." Like Dionysian revelers, one in ecstasy "dances with the time that kills him" (*VE*, 236; 1:554). This Nietzschean dance is "the practice of joy before death." The ecstatic atheological bacchant cries:

> "I AM joy before death."
> "The depth of the sky, lost space is joy before death: everything is profoundly cracked [*fêlé*]."
> "I imagine the earth turning vertiginously in the sky.
> I imagine the sky itself slipping, turning and losing itself.
> The sun, comparable to alcohol, turning and bursting breathlessly.
> The depth of the sky is like an orgy of frozen light, losing itself.
> Everything that exists destroying itself, consuming itself and dying, each instant producing itself only in the annihilation of the preceding one, and itself existing only as mortally wounded.

Ceaselessly destroying and consuming myself in myself in a great festival of blood." (*VE*, 238; 1:555–56)

This joy is not the pleasure of the pleasure principle; it is *jouissance*, which always lies beyond the pleasure principle. In *jouissance*, one forsakes the struggle to secure the death of time by remaining open to the time of death. In the ravishing night of *jouissance*, "the human being arrives at the threshold: there he must throw himself headlong into that which has no foundation and no head" (*VE*, 222; 1:513). In this fall, which is, after all a *tombe* (like the pyramid at the [pineal/penal] tip of the obelisk), one hears echoes of a cry, the cry of (a) woman, a woman named Theresa, Theresa whose *cri* haunts both *é-cri-ture* and *E-cri-ts*, and whose "Come" covers *Encore*.

> The eternal extension of God serves, first of all, the objective of enabling each person who loses himself to refind himself in him. But what is then missing is the satisfaction of those who aspire only to lose themselves, without wanting to refind themselves. When Theresa of Avila cried out [*s'écria;* cf. *écrire* and *éc-rire*][33] that she was dying of not dying, her passion opened a breach or gap, beyond any possible barrier, on a universe where perhaps there is no composition either of form or of being, where death rolls from world to world. (*VE*, 253; 2:373)

Theresa's other name, which is really the non-name of the Other, is *ELLE*. As we have seen, for Bataille, "*ELLE* is nothing, there is nothing sensible in *ELLE*, not even finally darkness. In *ELLE*, everything fades away, but, exorbitant, I traverse an empty depth and an empty depth traverses me. In *ELLE*, I communicate with the 'unknown.'. . ." (*IE*, 145). Though eternally unknowable, *ELLE* seems to be Woman.

---

33. It is virtually impossible to read *écrier* without seeing *écrire*. If one reads *écrire* carefully, another important association emerges. Not only is there a *cri* in the midst of *écrire*, there is also a *rire* in the middle of "*éc-rire.*" This is fortuitous, for according to Bataille, *le cri* is *le rire*, and to cry is to laugh. The *cri* of *jouissance* is nothing other than *le rire déchirant*, which the philosopher tries to repress.

6

Woman

JULIA KRISTEVA

Skirting Abjection

If one follows the lead of Lacan and Bataille, it appears that altarity has something to do with woman. Perhaps altarity "is" woman—The Woman who is the other Woman, the Woman who is the Other. Perhaps this Other is "the nonlogical difference of matter," matter that is *mater, mater* who is Mother. Perhaps the Mother that matters is the Mother who is M-Other. Perhaps this Woman "is" not (if, that is, not "is"). Perhaps the shady Other Woman exists in and through her self-withdrawal, like the self-seclusion of dirty Mother earth. Perhaps this dirt is the soil that soils everything clean and proper, even "Truth" itself. Perhaps the filthy Other Woman (sometimes named "Dirty," sometimes simply "My Mother") is The Woman who "has not allowed herself to be won"—especially by "philosophers" who are "very inexpert about women." [1] Perhaps she can be neither won nor one because she is duplicitous, that is, because she lies, always lies since "she herself does not believe in truth itself" (*S*, 53). Perhaps *ELLE* lies (or is laid) at the altar—the hymenal altar. Perhaps her altar is an altarity that is a hymen. Perhaps this hymenal altar, where weddings do and do not take place, is the nonlogical difference of *mater*. Perhaps this difference is the neither/nor that lies—lies between both/and and either/or. Perhaps the difference between Hegel and Kierkegaard has something to do with Woman. Perhaps the altarity of Woman is so horrifying that it cannot be spoken but only written, written by not writing it or by writing it indirectly. Written as something like a love letter—"Une lettre d'âmour." [2] Perhaps. *Peut-être.*

1. Friedrich Nietzsche, *Beyond Good and Evil,* trans. W. Kaufmann (New York: Random House, 1966), p. 2.
2. See Lacan, "A Love Letter," *FS,* 149–61. Lacan transforms *amour* into *âmour* in order to play with the relation between love (*amour*) and soul (*âme*).

Always suspicious of matter, Hegel idealized everything—especially Woman. Nowhere is Hegel's idealism more evident than in his love letters. At one point in his life (*before* he "completed" his System), Hegel was convinced that his feeling of love could be expressed only in poetry. On April 13, 1811, he wrote a poem to his fiancée, Marie von Tucher. In the last three stanzas he describes the "essence of love."

> Narrow bands dividing us, fall away!
> Sacrifice alone is the heart's true way!
> I expand myself to you, as you to me.
> May what isolates us go up in fire, cease to be.

> For life is only as reciprocated,
> By love in love is it alone created.
> To the kindred soul abandoned,
> The heart opens up in strength gladdened.

> Once the spirit atop free mountains has flown,
> It holds back nothing of its own.
> Living to see myself in you, and you to see yourself in me,
> In the enjoyment of celestial bliss shall we be.[3]

We have seen that, within Hegel's domestic economy, love overcomes all opposition, and thus heals every wound rending self and other. When love is consummated, "I expand myself to you, as you to me." Lover and beloved are not two, but one. Each sees himself or herself in the "other": "Living to see myself in you, and you to see yourself in me." This perfect love, Hegel insists, is impossible outside of marriage. Marriage is an apocalypse (or a holocaust) which, by burning every difference in an all-consuming fire, ushers in heaven on earth. The "marriage of heaven and hell" leads to "the enjoyment of celestial bliss," not in some ancient past or distant future, but "here and now," *hic et nunc, ici et maintenant.* This bliss prefigures the satisfaction of absolute knowledge. In a fragment written nearly fourteen years before his poem to Marie, Hegel explains:

> True union, or love proper, exists only between living beings who
> are alike in power and thus in one another's eyes living beings
> from every point of view; in no respect is either dead for the other.
> This genuine love excludes all oppositions. . . . When the unity
> was immature, there still stood over against it the world and the
> possibility of a cleavage between itself and the world; . . . finally,

3. G. W. F. Hegel, *Hegel: The Letters,* trans. C. Butler and C. Seiler (Bloomington: Indiana University Press, 1984), p. 237.

love completely destroys objectivity and thereby . . . deprives man's opposite of all foreign character, and discovers life itself without any further defect. (*ETW,* 304–5)

Such love, it seems, is too good to be true. The more one reads Hegel's love letters and analyzes his philosophical accounts of love, marriage, and family, the more anxious his words begin to sound. It is as if this idealization of domestic bliss is constructed to forget another matter. What does Hegel's writing leave unsaid? Bataille claims that "In the 'system,' poetry, laughter, ecstasy are nothing. Hegel hastily gets rid of them: he knows no other aim than knowledge. To my eyes, his immense fatigue is linked to his horror of the blind spot" (*IE,* 130). But did Hegel *never* laugh? Did he ever experience ecstasy? Was the bliss he enjoyed always domestic? Was he never torn asunder by *jouissance?* Was Marie the only woman he "knew" or was there another woman? Are his letters—love as well as philosophical—written to "forget" an Other, an other Woman, a woman who was, for Hegel, almost *nothing?*

There was at least one other woman in Hegel's life. Before Hegel knew his blessed Mary, he knew a woman named Christiana Charlotte Johanna Burkhardt (née Fischer). Possessed of multiple lures, Christiana, it seems, was a fisher of men. Hegel took the bait—hook, line, and sinker. During the spring of 1806, while he was feverishly writing the *Phenomenology of Spirit,* Hegel lay with Christiana, who at the time was married to his landlord, a tailor dealing in text-iles rather than books. On February 5, 1807, Georg Ludwig Friedrich Fischer, the bastard son of Hegel and Christiana, was born. The philosopher who devoted his whole life to the pursuit of truth lied to Christiana. When her husband died shortly after the birth of Ludwig, Hegel vowed to marry her, but never kept his promise. Furthermore, for more than nine years, Hegel refused to take Ludwig into his home. Even after openly acknowledging Ludwig as his son, Hegel would not provide him with a proper university education. Eventually Ludwig was forced to join the *foreign* legion. Hegel's illegitimate son was killed in *une bataille* far from his father-land.

Is Ludwig a skeleton in Hegel's closet? Is the mistress what is missing—missing from the System "proper"? Is Christiana the "impure" Other Woman who defiles The Philosopher? Does Hegel (even *after* his marriage) find transgression and the defilement it inevitably brings attractive? Do his tired words in praise of the truth of love and the love of truth tremble with a sadness brought by the loss of ecstasy? In the first chapter of her book *Powers of Horror: An Essay on Abjection,*

Julia Kristeva essays what might be read as the beginning of a reply to these questions, a *reply* which, like every good *réplique,* is a "refolding" of the question itself:

> It is in the *historical* act that Hegel sees fundamental impurity consuming itself [*se dépenser*]; as a matter of fact, the latter is a sexual impurity whose historical achievement consists in marriage. But—and this is where transcendental idealism, too, sadly comes to an end—here it is that desire (*Lust*), thus normalized in order to escape abject animality (*Begierde*), sinks into the banality that is sadness and silence. How come? Hegel does not condemn impurity because it is exterior to ideal consciousness; more profoundly—but also more craftily—he thinks that it can and should eliminate itself through the historico-social act. If he differs from Kant in this, he nevertheless shares his condemnation of (sexual) impurity. He agrees with his aim of keeping consciousness separated from defilement [*la souillure*], which, nevertheless, dialectically constitutes it. Reabsorbed into the trajectory of the Idea, what can defilement be if not the negative side of consciousness—that is, lack [*manque*] of communication and speech? In other words, defilement reabsorbed in marriage becomes sadness. In so doing, it has not strayed too far from its logic, according to which it is a border of discourse—a silence. (*PH,* 29–30; 37–38)

The silence edging discourse tolls in the mournful writings of "the melancholy Dane." On August 24, 1849, Kierkegaard wrote in his Diary:

> If I had not been a penitent, if I had not had my *vita ante acta,* if I had not had my melancholy [*tungsindig*]—marriage to her would have made me happier than I had ever dreamed of becoming. But being the person I unfortunately am, I must say that I could become happier in my unhappiness without her than with her— she had touched me deeply, and I willingly, or even more than willing, would have done everything . . .
>
> But there was a divine protest, so it seemed to me. Marriage. I would have to keep too much from her, base the whole marriage on a lie [*Usandhen*].
>
> I wrote to her and sent back her ring. The note is found verbatim in "The Psychological Experiment." I deliberately made it purely historical, for I have spoken to no one about it, not one single person, I who am more silent than the grave. If she should happen to see the book, I simply wanted her to be reminded of it. (*JP,* 6472; X^5 A 149)

"The Psychological Experiment" is included in yet another diary folded into a pseudonymous work entitled *Stages on Life's Way*. " 'Guilty?/Not Guilty?:' A passion narrative, a psychological experiment by *Frater Taciturnus* [*taciturnus:* silent]" is a diary written by either the Frater or a young man with the non-name "Quidam" (*quidam:* a certain person or thing). On the morning of May 8 (the year is not indicated), someone—Kierkegaard, the Frater, and/or Quidam—preoccupied with an impossible relationship to a woman, confesses:

> I wrote her a letter in these terms:
> "In order not to put more often to the test a thing which after all must be done, and which being done will supply the needed strength—let it then be done. Above all, forget him who writes this, forgive a man who, though he may be capable of some things, is not capable of making a girl happy.
> "To send a silk cord is, in the East, capital punishment [*Dødsstraf*] for the receiver; to send a ring is here capital punishment for him who sends it." (*SLW,* 304; 308–9)

These taciturn words recall another Kierkegaardian persona who, preoccupied with, among other things, silence and capital punishment, goes under the pseudonym Johannes de Silentio. *Fear and Trembling* can be read in many, perhaps infinite, ways. From one point of view, Isaac's relation to Abraham mirrors Kierkegaard's relation to his father. Born into a life of poverty on the Jutland heath, Michael Pedersen Kierkegaard rose to become a successful and wealthy Copenhagen merchant who traded wool and text-iles. Despite his riches, Michael did not lead a happy life. His first wife died, leaving him childless. Before the customary year of mourning had passed, he married Ane Sørensdatter Lund, a woman of peasant stock who had been a servant in the home of Michael and his recently deceased wife. Five months after the marriage, the couple's first child was born. As he grew older, Michael became obsessed with his violation of Ane. In search of forgiveness for his transgression, he retired early from his business and devoted all his time and energy to theological reflection and religious activity. In his favored son, Søren, Michael saw the possibility of atonement for his own sin. Søren was the chosen son whose sacrifice could redeem the father. Toward this end, Michael subjected Søren to an extraordinary religious upbringing. Having been deeply influenced by the Protestant pietism then sweeping Denmark, the fundamental tenet of Michael's religious outlook was the inescapability of human depravity. Sin, the father relentlessly impressed upon the son, is manifest most powerfully in sexual desire. For man, the "name" of sin is "Woman."

Kierkegaard's translation of the Abraham-Isaac story can, however, be interpreted in another way. Recalling "Quidam's Diary," it is possible to read Abraham's sacrifice of Isaac as Søren's sacrifice of Regina. The Father's "No!" made the union of Søren and Regina impossible. Religious obligation ("a divine protest") forced Kierkegaard to sacrifice his relation to Regina. Not just his relation to her, but perhaps Regina herself, for the distraught young woman declared she would kill herself if Søren left her. Despite the drama with which it was staged, Kierkegaard's separation from Regina always remained incomplete. The rejected woman eternally returns to haunt all his writings. Only the name of the father appears more often in Kierkegaard's texts than the name "Regina."

There is, however, another name that does not appear in Kierkegaard's writings. This is the name of an Other Woman—his mother. In the fourteen volumes of his *Samlede Værke* and the twenty volumes of his *Papirer,* the name "Ane Sørensdatter Lund" does not appear once. While the name of the father is inscribed again and again, Søren *never* writes the name of his violated, defiled mother. The silence of the mother repeatedly interrupts the *é-cri-ture* of the son with the incessant *cri:* "*Mor, Mor, Mor!*" To hear the echoes of this cry, it is important to note that "*Mor,*" the Danish word for mother, sounds much like the English word "more." The child's cry for "*Mor*" is the cry for an impossible "more." Neither the mother nor any of her substitutes can ever still this cry. The endless cry of "*Mor*" bespeaks a certain absence. This absence "is" no thing—"Nothing that is not there and the nothing that is." According to "the most acute questioner of the soul before Freud," this "Nothing" provokes *Angest*— dread or anxiety.

In *The Concept of Anxiety,* suggestively subtitled *A Simple Psychologically Orienting Deliberation on the Dogmatic Issue of Hereditary Sin,* Vigilius Haufniensis[4] describes the way in which anxiety signals

4. This name means "watchman of Copenhagen." Vigilius's epigram discloses his understanding of his writerly mission: "The age of making distinctions [*Distinctionens Tid*] is past. It has been vanquished by the System. In our day, whoever loves to make distinctions is regarded as an eccentric [*Særling*] whose soul clings to something that has long since vanished. Be that as it may, yet Socrates still is what he was, the simple wise man, because of the peculiar distinction that he expressed both in words and in life, something that the eccentric Hamann first reiterated with great admiration two thousand years later: 'For Socrates was great in "that he distinguished between what he understood and what he did not understand"'" (*CA,* 3; 4:274).

"something Other" (*noget Andet*)—something or nothing that interrupts everything, even what seems to be "original" or "paradisical
innocence." "In this state there is peace and repose, but there is
simultaneously something other that is not contention and strife, for
there is indeed nothing against which to strive. What, then, is it?
Nothing [*Intet*]. But what effect does nothing have? It begets anxiety.
This is the profound secret of innocence, that it is at the same time
anxiety" (*CA,* 41; 4:313). A vigilant psychologist, Vigilius notes
that "in observing children, one will discover this anxiety imitated
more particularly as a seeking for the marvelous [*Eventyrlige*], the
monstrous [*Unhyre:* immense, prodigious, shocking], the enigmatic
[*Gaadenfulde:* mysterious, puzzling; *Gaade:* riddle, puzzle + *fuld:*
full, drunk]" (*CA,* 42; 4:314). In anxiety, the marvelous, monstrous,
or enigmatic appears to be a "foreign power" (*fremmed Magt*) that
nonetheless is strangely attractive. In an effort to evoke the ambivalence elicited by this other, Vigilius describes anxiety as "a sympa-
thetic antipathy and an antipathetic sympathy" (*CA,* 43, 42; 4:314,
313). The irresolvable paradox of anxiety reflects the irreducible ambiguity of its "object" or "pseudo-object," i.e., the no thing that
neither "is" nor "is" not. Nothing cannot, of course, reveal itself. Its
disclosure is a concealing, its unveiling a reveiling. Such unavoidable revelation issues from the irrepressible "modesty" of Nothing.
"With innocence," Vigilius explains, "a knowledge begins that has
ignorance for its first qualification. This is the concept of modesty
[*Blufærdogjed*] (*Scham*)" (*CA,* 68; 4:338).

The recognition of the complex interplay of woman, mother, other,
absence, silence, nothing, and anxiety, is inseparably bound to the
realization that "modesty" (*la pudeur*) is "a feminine operation."
Woman, who, as Lacan tells us, does not exist, might "be" Nothing—nothing but a "feminine operation" that forever alters man.

> Perhaps woman—as non-identity, non-figure, simulacrum—
> is the *abyss* of distance, the distancing of distance, the cut [*coupe*]
> of space, distance itself, if one were still able to say, which is
> impossible, distance *itself* [*elle-même*]. Distance distances itself,
> the far withdraws [*s'éloigne*]. It is necessary here to appeal to the
> Heideggerian usage of the word *Entfernung:* at once divergence
> [*l'écartement*], remoteness [*l'éloignement*], the remoteness of the
> remote, the delay of the distant, the de-ferment, the destruction
> (*Ent-*) that constitutes the distant as such, the veiled enigma of
> proximity. The secluded opening of this *Entfernung* gives way
> to truth, and here woman averts from herself. There is no essence
> of woman because she averts and is averted from herself. Out of

the depths, endless and unfathomable, she devours, enveils all essentiality, all identity, all propriety. Here philosophical discourse, blinded, founders and allows itself to be hurled down to its ruin. There is no truth of woman, but it is because of this abyssal fault of truth, because this non-truth is the "truth." Woman is the name of this non-truth of truth. (*S*, 49, 51)

Perhaps. Perhaps Woman "is" non-identity, the *abyss* of distance, the cut of space . . . the non-truth of truth. If so, Woman is "something to be scared of—*de quoi avoir peur*," for her powers are "powers of horror—*pouvoirs de l'horreur*." Perhaps this horror is, in Kierkegaard's words, the *horror religiosus*.[5] This possibility, or impossibility, obsesses Kristeva.

In approaching *The Powers of Horror*, it is important to recall not only Bataille's analysis of abjection, but also Lacan's rereading of Freud through Hegel and Heidegger, and Hegel and Heidegger through Freud. The anxiety provoked by no thing that is not there and the nothing that is signals the return of the *fort/da* of the real thing. The reel with which the child anxiously plays when the mother disappears implies the interplay of absence and presence that marks and remarks the opening of all *Da-sein*. *Dasein* is the "presence" of an "absence" and the "absence" of a "presence." The *da* of the child's *Da-sein* presupposes the absence of the mother, who (impossibly) both appears and disappears as the *fort* of her *sein*. Kristeva describes the real thing that figures (which is *not* to say represents) the interweaving of presence and absence as "the phobic 'object.'" This "object" is "a *hieroglyph* that condenses *all fears*" (*PH*, 34; 46). The fear that Kristeva associates with the phobic object has most of the characteristics usually related to anxiety. Fear of the phobic object is fear of no thing specific or determinate. "The fear of which one can speak, the one which, therefore, has a signifiable object," Kristeva explains, "is a belated and more logical product, which takes upon itself all the anterior emotions of primitive, non-representable fear [*peur primitive irreprésentable*]" (*PH*, 34; 45). This anterior, primitive, non-representable fear is provoked by an *other* that "is" no thing—nothing other than nothing. For Kristeva, the phobic object is a "*hallucina-*

5. What Kristeva describes as "fear" is close to what Kierkegaard identifies as anxiety. In the wake of *The Concept of Anxiety*, it has become customary to distinguish fear from anxiety by insisting that while the former has a determinate object, the latter is occasioned by nothing or by nothing determinate. Kristeva's fear arises not from an object but from an indeterminate something that cannot be clearly distinguished from no thing.

tion of nothing" (*PH*, 42; 53). Nothing, I have stressed, cannot be named, or cannot be named *properly*. Fear, which has as its "object" a hallucination of nothing, is, in effect, fear of the unnameable. The real thing, Kristeva argues, is a substitute for an other, which or who "is" a non-representable no-thing. *"Hans,"* she concludes, *"is afraid of the unnameable* [Hans a peur de l'innommable]" (*Ph*, 34; 45).[6]

It is clear that the "phobic 'object'" is a peculiar "object." Instead of an object it is really a non-object or a "pseudo-object." Kristeva names this unnameable pesudo-object "the abject." "The phobic object has no other object than the abject. But that word 'fear'—a fluid haze [*brume:* mist, obscurity, uncertainty], an ungraspable or incomprehensible moistness—no sooner has it cropped up than it shades off like a mirage and impregnates all words of language with nonexistence, with an hallucinatory, ghostly glimmer. Thus, fear, having been placed between parentheses, discourse will seem tenable only if it ceaselessly confronts that otherness, a burden both repelling and repelled, a deep well of memory that is inaccessible and intimate: the abject" (*PH*, 6; 14).

In contrast to the ob-ject, which always stands over against a subject, the ab-ject is *"neither subject nor object"* (*PH*, 1; 9). "The ab-ject is, by definition, the sign of an impossible ob-ject, boundary and limit [*frontière et limite*]" (*PH*, 154; 180). This boundary "is above all, ambiguity" (*PH*, 9; 17). Never telling the truth, but always lying, lying at the edge, the ambiguity of abjection makes any truly proper subject edgy. The margin or limen that remarks the dis-place-ment of the abject is an *entre-deux,*[7] which is "a void that is not nothing but designates . . . a defiance or challenge to symbolization" (*PH*, 48, 51; 59, 62). Neither subject nor object, this nor that, here nor there, present nor absent, the abject eludes the binary oppositions that structure the symbolic order. It cannot, therefore, be "integrated with a given system of signs" (*PH*, 14; 22). To the contrary, the abject is "a *heterogeneity of significance* [*une* hétérogénéité de la signifiance] that "draws [one] toward the there [*là*] where meaning, sense, or direction collapses" (*PH*, 51, 62; 2, 9). This heterogeneity "disturbs identity, system, order" (*PH*, 4; 12). Extending Bataille's heterological scatology, Kristeva argues that the heterogeneous abject is what systems—philosophical, psychological, social, political, economic, and religious—are *constructed* to exclude. The abject is, in Bataille's terms,

6. Hans is, of course, Freud's "Little Hans."

7. Compare Merleau-Ponty's use of this term. See chapter 2, second section, above.

"the irreducible waste product" of homogenizing and hegemonizing systems.

The abject is the improper and unclean refuse that the proper and clean subject throws [*jacet*] away [*ab*] or refuses. "Disgust from a piece of food, filth, waste, shit. Spasms and vomiting that protect me. Repulsion, the retching that thrusts me to the side and turns me away from defilement, sewage, and muck. The shame of compromise, of the *entre-deux*, of treachery. The fascinated start that leads me toward and separates me from them" (*PH*, 2; 10). If the abject is disgusting and repugnant, why is it so fascinating? Toward what does it lead? How can vomiting protect me? Explaining the way in which the subject constitutes itself through exclusion and repression, Kristeva writes: "In the trajectory where 'I' become, I give birth to myself amid the violence of sobs, of vomit. Mute protest of the symptom, shattering violence of a convulsion, inscribed in a symbolic system, but which, without either wanting or being able to become integrated in order to respond to it, it reacts, abreacts. It abjects [*Ça abjecte*]" (*PH*, 3; 11). The repressed abject does not simply disappear; it remains and returns as the condition of the possibility and impossibility of the identity of every object and subject. This "absolutely paradoxical" "remainder [*reste*] appears to be coextensive with the entire architecture of non-totalizing thought. In its view, there is nothing that is everything, nothing that is exhaustive, there is a residue [*reliquat*] in every system" (*PH*, 76; 92).

The residue in every system is the "outside" that is "inside," hollowing out everything that seems to be fixed, firm, solid, and erect. This interior *dehors* is neither present nor absent. It is, in Heidegger's words, "near—the near," or, in Blanchot's terms, "proximate—the proximate." Like the Lacanian "real," which haunts consciousness without ever becoming conscious, the abject approaches without ever arriving. Thus Kristeva begins her analysis of the abject with *APPROCHE DE L'ABJECTION.* The nothing that approaches without being present can be approached only indirectly. In this uncanny domain, communication inevitably is "indirect communication." Always entangled in a play of veiling and reveiling, the author can, at best, *skirt* abjection.

The skirting of *abjection* is not, however, exhausted by the indirection of her approach. The abject, which every system excludes, is, for Kristeva L[*a*]'*abjection. Ça est ELLE.* "The logic of prohibition," Kristeva contends, "founds the abject." She credits Bataille with the recognition of the importance of the undecidable interplay of prohibition and prohibited: "Georges Bataille remains the only one, to my knowledge, who has tied the production of the abject to the *weakness of that prohibition* which, in other respects, necessarily constitutes each social order. He has tied abjection to the 'inability to assume with sufficient strength the imperative act of exclusion'" (*PH,* 64; 78). In formulating her analysis of abjection, Kristeva brings together Bataille's heterology and Lacan's psychoanalysis. Bataille's "Mother" and Lacan's "Woman" meet in Kristeva's "Woman" who is always a M-Other. "In the following," Kristeva explains, "my point will be to suggest that this archaic relation to the *object* translates, as it were, the relation to the *mother*" (*PH,* 64; 78).

Mothering and Fothering

In the beginning was the Word—the Word of the Father. "Before the beginning" was "separation"—separation from the Mother. "The abject might then appear as the most *fragile* (from a synchronic point of view), the most *archaic* (from a diachronic one) sublimation of an 'object' still inseparable from the drives. The abject is that pseudo-object, which is constituted *before,* but appears only *within* the gaps [*brèches*] of secondary repression. *The abject would be this 'object' of primal repression*" (*PH,* 12; 20). The emergence of subjectivity is a "slow and laborious" process of othering that is mediated by (among others) mother and fother. The othering necessary for the articulation of the subject is inseparable from repression. Repression is the exclusive act through which the subject proper separates itself from the abject. "The advent of one's proper identity [*identité propre*] demands a law that mutilates" (*PH,* 54; 66). What is this law? How and why does it mutilate? What is the object or objective of primal repression?

In an effort to answer these questions, Kristeva turns to the work of Lévi-Strauss. "Structural anthropology," she maintains, "had one advantage among others; it tied a system of classification, that is, a symbolic system within a given society, to the order of language in its universality (binary aspects of phonology, signified-signifier dependencies and autonomies, etc.)" (*PH,* 66; 81). Though Lévi-Strauss's analyses of social processes open new ways of understanding human behavior, his position, according to Kristeva, is seriously deficient with respect to one very important issue. "In attaining universal truth [disclosed when language is viewed '*as common and universal code*'], it [i.e., Lévi-Strauss's anthropology] nevertheless neglected the subjective dimension and/or the diachronic and synchronic implication of the speaking subject in the universal order of language" (*PH,* 66;

81-82). Kristeva attempts to extend Lévi-Strauss's insights from social systems to the structure and development of human subjectivity. In so doing, she advances "the hypothesis that a (social) symbolic system *corresponds* to a specific structuration of the speaking subject in the *symbolic order*" (*PH*, 67; 82). Though often unacknowledged or indicated only indirectly, Kristeva's defense of this hypothesis draws extensively on the writings of Lacan.

Through her archaeological inquiry, Kristeva unearths an archaic mother who is the "terrifyingly ancient" *mater* from which the "speaking subject" must forever be separated.[8] "The abject confronts us . . . within our personal archaeology, with our most ancient attempts to demarcate ourselves from the *maternal* entity, even before ex-isting outside of her, thanks to the autonomy of language. It is a violent and clumsy breaking away, with the constant risk of falling back under the sway of a power as securing as it is stifling" (*PH*, 13; 20). "The maternal is abject" because she is neither an object nor a subject *sensu strictissimo*. Like Merleau-Ponty's chiasmic flesh and Bataille's nonlogical difference of matter, the body of *mater* has "imprecise boundaries" (*frontières imprécises*) and therefore is characterized by "the nondistinctiveness of inside and outside" (*PH*, 60, 61; 75, 76). As a result of the invagination of the maternal matrix, the subject's "archaic relation to the mother" is "always marked by the uncertainty of its borders" (*PH*, 63; 78).

Though mother and child are not *properly* two, the father is, nonetheless, "a third [*un tiers*] who "cuts [*coupe*] . . . the permeability [*perméabilité*]" of the "primal dyad" (*PH*, 13, 61; 20, 76). As *un nom* that is *un non,* the Name-of-the-Father is the law that mutilates both mother and child. Speaking the *non* of this *nom* inflicts "immemorial violence" (*violence immémoriale*) (*PH*, 10; 17). To claim that the violence separating *one* from the mother is "immemorial" is to insist that the subject is always already divided and the mother always already absent.

In Kristeva's Lacanian analysis, the Name-of-the-Father is the name of language. For Kristeva, as for Lacan, language designates the entire symbolic order, which includes all the codes by which culture regulates the *flow* of psychosocial forces. On the most basic level,

---

8. Following Lacan's analysis of the constitution of the subject, Kristeva insists that there is no subject apart from language. In other words, there is not *first* a subject who subsequently speaks. Rather, the subject becomes articulate(d) only by speaking and being spoken.

language effects "the founding division" that secures "the establishment of the subject/object division" (*PH,* 46; 58). The primal form of this separation is the tearing of child from mother. "The paternal agency [*l'instance paternelle*] introduces the symbolic division between 'subject' (child) and 'object' (mother)" (*PH,* 44; 56). The logical and psychological aspects of the problem of identity come together in Kristeva's assertion that "syntax" is "the most solid guarantee of our identity" (*DL,* 178). When it is not transgressive sintax, syntax protects the propriety and property of identity by securing the legitimacy of the name—the proper name. The proper name is always the name of the father. From this point of view, it is not surprising that Hegel resisted admitting the little bastard Ludwig into his cozy family circle.

Nor is it surprising that Kierkegaard never speaks of his mother, and that he writes "about" her only by not (directly) writing about her. How could he do otherwise? If the Name-of-the-Father is the name for the naming of language, the "name" of the mother is the "name" for what language cannot name. "Mother" is the "name" of the unnameable. More precisely, the ever archaic mother is irreducibly "prenomial." Since she is a "heterogeneity of significance," the mother slips through the classifying grid imposed in the name of the father. Every totalizing system encodes the insignificant maternal remainder as "the abject." Recalling Bataille's claim that the body is a tube open at both ends, Kristeva identifies two primary sites of maternal abjection: anal and oral. The body of the mother remains *dirty* and *bloody.* The filth of menstrual blood spreads to the urine, shit, and sperm which, according to Kristeva, pollute the *corps étranger* of woman. This body, which is the inescapable *before* of every *one,* must be left behind by the child. "Evocation of the maternal body and childbirth induce the image of birth as a violent act of expulsion through which the nascent body tears itself away from the substances of the maternal interior. Now, the skin apparently never ceases to bear the traces [*traces*] of such matter. These are the persecuting and threatening traces by means of which the fantasy of the born body, tightly held in the placenta that is no longer nourishing but ravaging, rejoins with the reality of the leper" (*PH,* 101; 120). Traces . . . traces of the unnameable . . . traces we can neither escape nor wash away.

Traces, however, are not always anal; they can be oral. The child not only shits, pisses, and (eventually) fucks; he/she also spits, vomits, and sucks. The site of the "primal" exchange between child and mother is the mouth/breast. *Le don* of mother to child, like the gift of son/father to mother/wife is a "whitish fluid"—milk.[9] Along the limen of mouth/breast, there is "another flow mingling [*flux mé-langeant*] two identities [that] connotes the bond of one to the other: milk. A milieu common to mother and infant, a food that does not separate but binds" (*PH*, 105; 123). This tie that binds also inflicts a wound that creates a double bind for the child. *Le sein*, which bestows *le don* of *Sein*, carries the threat of a mortal *coup* that can overwhelm and engulf the child. A mother's love, after all, can s-mother. The nourishing breast of the mother sometimes appears to be a devouring b(r)east. Milk can make one gag, even vomit.[10]

> Alimentary disgust is perhaps the most elementary and most archaic form of abjection. When the eyes see or the lips touch that skin or the surface of milk—harmless, thin as a sheet of cigarette paper, pitiful as a nail paring—I experience a gagging [*glotte;* compare, *coup de glotte:* glottal stop (as in gl...., gl...)] sensation and, still farther down, spasms in the stomach, the belly; and all these organs shrivel up the body, provoke tears and bile, increase heartbeat, cause forehead and hands to perspire. With the vertigo that clouds vision, *nausea* makes me balk at that milk cream, separates me from the mother and father who present it to me. "I" want none of that element, sign of their desire; "I" want to know nothing of it, "I" do not assimilate it, "I" expel it. But since food is not an "other" for "me," who am only in their desire, I expel *myself,* I spit *myself* out, I abject *myself* within the same motion through which "I" pretend to pose *myself.* That detail, perhaps insignificant, but one that they ferret out, emphasize, evaluate, that trifle turns me inside out like a glove, guts sprawling; it is thus that *they* see that "I" am in the process of becoming an other [*un autre*] at the expense of my own death. (*PH*, 3; 10)

As the child becomes an other, the mother becomes The Other. To become oneself, it is necessary to engage in something like what Nietzsche describes as "creative forgetting." Though unavoidable, such oblivion, nevertheless, is "catastrophic." Catastrophe is not a once-and-for-all event; it continues to occur throughout life. Forever beyond the pleasure principle, separation, otherwise known as "the death drive," is necessary for life. "The abject from which he [i.e., the

---

9. One of the roots of "milk" is *g(a)lag-, g(a)lakt-,* which is found in the Greek *gala* (stem *galakt-*). "Galactic" and "galaxy" are also related to this stem. In chapter 9, we will see that various forms of white "fluid," stretching from milk and sperm to the distant stars of galaxies (especially the Milky Way), are spread throughout *Glas.*

10. Since milk mixes identities, it is a transitional pseudo-object that disrupts everyone and every one. Never one but always *entre-deux,* milk is a flow that no *one* can stop.

exile] does not cease to separate himself is for him, in short, a *land of oblivion* [*terre d'oubli*] that is constantly remembered. Once upon an effaced time, the abject must have been a magnetized pole of covetousness. But the ashes of oblivion now serve as a screen [*paravent*] and reflect aversion, repugnance" (*PH*, 8; 16). Paradoxically, in this land of forgetting there is also a remembering (which *does not* re-member). The child's oblivion is the "deep well of memory that is inaccessible and intimate." The "untouchable, impossible, absent body of the mother" is the unnameable nothing that can be read in the hieroglyphic phobic object (*PH*, 6; 14). As the nothing that is not there and the nothing that is, the *fort/da* of the mother is "the absolute, because primordial, place of the impossible (*PH*, 22; 30). The impossibility of the mother ceaselessly murmurs in the mournful language of the child. "The abject is the violence of mourning for an 'object' that has always already been lost [*toujours déjà perdu*]. The abject shatters the wall of repression and its judgments. It takes the ego back to its source in the abominable limits from which, in order to be, the ego has detached itself—it returns it to a source in the non-ego, to drive, to death" (*PH*, 15; 22).

This mourning can be heard in Hegel's sadness and Kierkegaard's melancholy. Since the Word of the Father inevitably separates one from the body of the mother, language is always "a language of lack" (*PH*, 38; 49). For Kristeva, as for Lacan, the *de* in *un langage du manque* must be read in at least two ways. The language of lack is the lack of language. In relation to the M-Other, language is always lacking. On the one hand, the lack of language implies "the preverbal" (*le pré-verbal*) which can never be spoken (*PH*, 61; 76). On the other hand, the unnameable (impossibly) "speaks" through the lack of language. Inasmuch as the language of lack "falls" (*tombe*) "outside" (*dehors*) the bounds of sense, it is not "semantic" but "semiotic." In an essay suggestively entitled "From One Identity the Other [*D'une identité l'autre*]," Kristeva argues:

> The semiotic process, which introduces errancy [*errance*] or fuzziness into language and, *a fortiori*, into poetic language is, from a synchronic point of view, a mark of the drive processes (appropriation/rejection, orality/anality, love/hate, life/death) and, from a diachronic point of view, stems from the archaisms of the semiotic body. Before recognizing itself as identical in a mirror and, consequently, as signifying, this body is dependent vis-à-vis the mother. At the same time instinctual and maternal, semiotic processes prepare the future speaker for entrance into meaning and signification (into the symbolic). But the symbolic (i.e.,

language as nomination, sign, and syntax) constitutes itself only by breaking [*coupant*] with this anteriority, which is retrieved as "signifier," "primary processes," displacement and condensation, metaphor and metonomy, rhetorical figures—but which always remains subordinate—subjacent to the principal function of nomination-predication. Language as symbolic function constitutes itself at the cost of repressing instinctual drive and continuous relation to the mother. (*DL,* 136; 161–62)

Semiotic processes prepare the future speaker for entrance into the symbolic order through what Kristeva labels "primal mapping" (*cartographie primaire*). "While being the precondition of language," this "semiotic" (*sémiotique*) mapping, over which the mother presides, "is dependent upon meaning, but in a way that is not that of *linguistic* signs or of the *symbolic* order they institute" (*PH,* 72; 87).

Since mapping is "primal," the subject is, in Heidegger's terms, always *On the Way to Language.* Inscription in the symbolic order *splits* the subject. For the faulted subject, the *arche* is always already lost. The impossibility of origin, i.e., the ever-absent body of the mother, renders desire insatiable. Always exiled from the garden, the fallen subject is condemned "to err" in search of a kingdom that is forever delayed or deferred.

> The one by whom the abject exists is thus a *jeté*[11] who places (himself), *separates* (himself), situates (himself), and thus *errs* [erre], instead of recognizing himself, desiring, belonging, or refusing. Situationist in a sense, and not without laughter [*rire*]—since laughing is a way of placing or displacing abjection. Necessarily dichotomous, somewhat Manichaean, he divides, excludes, and without, properly speaking, wishing to know his abjections, is not at all unaware of them. Moreover, he often includes himself among them, thus casting within himself the scalpel that carries out his separations.
>
> Instead of interrogating himself about his "being," he does so concerning his place: "*Where* am I?" rather than "*Who* am I?" For the space that preoccupies the *jeté,* the excluded, is never *one,* nor *homogeneous* [*homogène*], nor *totalizable* [*totalisable*], but [is] essentially divisible, foldable, pliable [*pliable*], and catastrophic. . . . A voyager in a night whose end flees. He has a sense of the danger, of the loss that the pseudo-object attracting him repre-

---

11. *Jeté* defies translation. *Jeter* means to throw, fling, throw up, toss, knock down, throw out, fling away, empty, discharge. *Le jeté* means a dance step; in knitting, "wool forward"; an oblong piece of lace, a large ornamental mat or doily; and a spray of flowers.

sents for him, but he cannot help taking the risk at the very moment he sets himself apart from it. And the more he errs, the more he is saved. (*PH*, 8; 15–16)

This errant "salvation" does not mend and heal but rends and tears. The one (but she is not one) who bestows this *coup de grâce* is a sanguine goddess.

Sanguine Goddess

"'Jewgreek is greekjew. Extremes meet'" (*WD*, 153; 228).[12] For Kristeva, we are first Greek, then Jew, and finally Christian. The extremes of the Greek and Jewish meet in the Christian. In contrast to Hegel's thoughtful sublimation of religious representations in rational concepts, Kristeva insists that religious images and rituals disclose the impossibility of copulation and the illegitimacy of conception. From this point of view, "empirical heterology" can never be reconciled with "formal tautology." The heterological is "the unthinkable, unsayable transcendence of the other." This other is the abject whose "name," we have discovered, is "Woman." Having established the link between the abject and the feminine, Kristeva proceeds to argue: "*As abjection—so the sacred*. Abjection accompanies all religious constructions and reappears, in order to be elaborated in a new guise, at the time of their collapse. Several structurations of abjection should be distinguished, each one determining a specific form of the sacred" (*PH*, 17; 24). Kristeva identifies three primary patterns of the sacred: pagan (i.e., Greek), Jewish, and Christian. Her analysis of the different modalities of the sacred implicitly recalls Hegel's tripartite interpretation of religion. A careful examination of Kristeva's argument discloses a dialectical relation among the encodings of the sacred characterizing socio-cultural as well as individual development. Advancing from the Greek, through the Jewish, to the Christian, the

12. As noted above, Derrida quotes this line from Joyce. Kristeva writes of Joyce: "How dazzling, unending, eternal—and so weak, so insignificant, so sickly—is the rhetoric of Joycean language. Far from preserving us from the abject, Joyce makes it break out in what he sees as the prototype of literary utterance: Molly's monologue. If that monologue spreads out the abject, it is not because there is a woman speaking. But because, *at a distance*, the writer approaches the hysterical body so that it might speak, so that he might speak, using it as a springboard, of that which eludes speech and turns out to be the hand-to-hand [*corps à corps*] struggle of one woman with another, her mother, of course, the absolute, because primeval, place of the impossible—of the excluded, the outside-of-meaning, the abject. Atopia" (*PH*, 22; 30).

sacred is transformed from exteriority to interiority. While the Greek suffers the sacred from without and the Jew encounters it in and through willful transgression, the Christian experiences the sacred as an outside that is inside, forever faulting his identity. Over against Hegel, Kristeva maintains that the meeting of Greek and Jew in the Christian does not involve a reconciliation of opposites. To the contrary, Kristeva's inwardly divided Christian embodies a *coincidentia oppositorum* that contradicts rather than prefigures rational unity.

For Kristeva, as for Bataille, Lacan, Freud, and others, the sacred is irreducibly ambiguous; it is both pure and impure, proper and improper, holy and filthy. This ambiguity provokes an emotional ambivalence in which the sacred appears simultaneously attractive and repulsive. Implicitly appropriating Bataille's reversal of Hegel's assessment of the relation between religion and art, Kristeva maintains that the sacred comes to expression in human experience first in religious ritual and more recently in the writing of modern and postmodern artists.

Though never acknowledging Paul Ricoeur's important contribution to the question of evil, Kristeva follows the course he charts. Ricoeur opens his influential book *The Symbolism of Evil* with an examination of "defilement." "Dread of the impure and rites of purification," he points out, "are in the background of all our feelings and all our behavior relating to fault."[13] In a manner similar to Ricoeur, Kristeva begins her account of the sacred by examining the shift "from filth [*saleté*] to defilement [*souillure*]" displayed in numerous religious rituals.[14]

Through language and within highly hierarchical religious institutions, man hallucinates partial "objects"—witness to the archaic differentiation of the body on its way to proper identity,

13. Paul Ricoeur, *The Symbolism of Evil* (Boston: Beacon Press, 1967), p. 25. Ricoeur's analysis of evil extends his consideration of the problematic relationship between the voluntary and the involuntary (*Freedom and Nature: The Voluntary and the Involuntary*, trans. E. V. Kohak [Evanston: Northwestern University Press, 1966]) and anticipates his major work on Freud (*Freud and Philosophy: An Essay on Interpretation*, trans. D. Savage [New Haven: Yale University Press, 1970]). The structure of Ricoeur's analysis of defilement, guilt, and sin in *The Symbolism of Evil* is formally parallel to Kristeva's consideration of Greek, Jewish, and Christian experience. Ricoeur's enterprise, however, is more "Hegelian" than Kristeva's undertaking, for he is concerned to establish the way in which "the symbol gives rise to thought."

14. *Saleté* also means dirty, trick, ribaldry, and obscenity. "*Souillure*," in addition to defilement, means dirt, spot, stain, and impurity. While a *souillon* is a sloven or a slut, a *souillard* is a hole for water in a stone. Associations with several English words are also noteworthy in this context. In its verbal form, "soil" means to stain, and as a noun it refers to earth or dirt.

which is also sexual identity. The *defilement* from which the ritual protects us is neither a sign nor a material. Within the rite that extracts it from repression and perverse desire, defilement is the translinguistic trace of the most archaic boundaries of the clean and proper body. In this sense, if it is a dropped object, it is so from the mother. It absorbs within itself all the experiences of the non-objectal that accompany the differentiation of the mother-speaking being, hence all ab-jects. . . . As if purification rites, through a language that is already there, were to return toward an archaic experience and were to obtain from it a partial object, not as such but only as a *trace* of a pre-object, an archaic *découpage*. By means of the symbolic institution of ritual, that is to say, by means of a system of ritual exclusions, the partial object consequently becomes *writing:* a demarking of limits, an insistence placed not on the (paternal) Law but on (maternal) Authority through the signifying order. (*PH*, 73; 88)

The translinguistic trace of the most archaic boundaries of *le corps propre* appears to be unclean, impure, and improper. As such, it is that which the clean, pure, and proper subject must exclude or repress. Building on her interpretation of language, Kristeva claims that "the opposition between the pure and the impure" is "*one* coding of the differentiation of the speaking subject as such, a coding of his repulsion vis-à-vis the other [*autre*] in order to autonomize himself. The pure/impure opposition represents . . . the aspiration for an identity, a difference" (*PH*, 82; 98).

Identity is disrupted by "flux or flow [*le flux*]." Consequently, "any secretion or discharge, anything that leaks out of the masculine or feminine body, defiles" (*PH*, 102; 121). Defilement results from contact with filthy traces, which are "always related to the corporeal orifices" (*PH*, 71; 86). The function of the rites of purification is to protect the subject from becoming contaminated by polluting pseudo-objects. In pagan experience, corruption initially seems to come from the *outside*. "Excrement and its equivalents (decay, infection, disease, corpse, etc.) represent the danger to identity coming from without [*de l'extérieur*]: the ego threatened by the non-ego, society menaced by its outside [*dehors*], life by death" (*PH*, 71; 86). In order to prevent subjects from dis-integrating, prohibitions are constructed around certain foods (i.e., any food that "is a border between two distinct entities or territories"), all forms of excrement, and corpses (*PH*, 75; 90). Borrowing insights from Bataille, Kristeva contends that the corpse is one of the most dangerous instances of a filthy trace. "A rotting body, lifeless, completely turned into dejection, blurred between the inanimate and the organic, a transitional swarming, an inseparable lining [*doublure inséparable*] of a humanity whose life confounds itself with the symbolic—the corpse [*le cadavre*] is fundamental pollution" (*PH,* 109; 127). Such a body is *un corps étranger,* which is *das ganz Andere.*

Even within the economy of pagan ritual, pollution cannot be restricted to external substance. Insofar as humanity is possessed by a *doublure inséparable,* the body proper is always already "infected" by a certain exterior, which, though interior, is not subject to *Er-innerung.* While excrement and its equivalents stand for "external" pollution, blood figures "internal" corruption. "Menstrual blood . . . represents the danger coming from the interior of identity (social or sexual); it threatens the relationship between the sexes within a social ensemble and, by interiorization, the identity of each sex in the face of sexual difference" (*PH,* 71; 86). *Eros* and *thanatos* mix in blood. For the ritual subject, blood signifies both the blood of the mother's body and the blood of the father or brother, which must be spilled in order to satisfy sexual desire. The ritual prohibitions attached to blood are, in effect, the functional equivalents of the two taboos upon which society and culture rest: the taboos against incest and murder. As Freud points out in *Totem and Taboo,* the one who transgresses these fundamental prohibitions is himself defiled and thus becomes a source of pollution that can infect the entire community. Since defilement is contagious, corruption can spread by contact. Within a psychoanalytic perspective, the paradigmatic instance of a transgressor who becomes defiled is, of course, Oedipus. According to Kristeva, Oedipus is a *pharmakos.*

The *pharmakon,* Derrida explains, "properly consists of a certain inconsistency, a certain impropriety, this nonidentity-with-itself always allowing itself to be turned against itself" (*D,* 119; 136). Kristeva emphasizes that the *pharmakos* is irreducibly "ambiguous." "If the *pharmakon* is 'ambivalent,' it is because it constitutes the medium [*milieu*] in which opposites are opposed, the movement and play that relates them to one another, reverses them and makes one side cross over into the other (soul/body, good/evil, inside/outside, memory/forgetfulness, speech/writing, etc.). . . . The *pharmakon* is the movement, the locus of the play: (the production of) difference. It is the différance of difference" (*D,* 127; 145–46). In keeping with the analyses of Derrida and Girard, Kristeva identifies the *pharmakos* with the scapegoat.[15] Summarizing the tragedy of Oedipus, she writes: "His abjection is due to the permanent ambiguity of the roles he plays

15. See, especially, Derrida, *D,* 133; 153; and Girard, *Violence and the Sacred,* pp. 94–95.

unknowingly, even when he believes he knows. It is precisely this dynamic of reversals that makes him a being of abjection and a *pharmakos*, a scapegoat [*bouc émissaire*] who, having been expelled, allows the city to be freed from defilement. The strength of the tragedy lies in this ambiguity; prohibition and ideal are conjoined in a single character in order to signify that the speaking being has no space of his own but stands on a fragile threshold as if stranded by an impossible demarcation" (*PH*, 84–85; 100–101).

The figure of the *pharmakos* marks the transition from the Greek to the Hebraic. The movement from pagan to Jewish parallels the Hegelian transformation of substance into subject. No longer simply the function of contamination from an external *substance*, Oedipus's defilement is the consequence of a *subjective* action. And yet his transgressive deed is not fully subjective, for it is the result of "a flaw or fault in his knowledge" rather than a free self-conscious violation of the law. Despite his ignorance, Oedipus is *guilty*. When defilement becomes guilt, " 'there is an abject' henceforth [is] stated as, '*I* am abject, that is, mortal and speaking'." This incompleteness and dependence on the other [*l'Autre*], far from making desiring and murderous Oedipus innocent, only allow him to render his dramatic cleavage [*clivage*] transmissible. Transmissible to a foreign hero, and hence opening up the undecidable possibility of some effects of truth. Our eyes can remain open provided we recognize ourselves as always already altered [*altérés toujours déjà*] by the symbolic—by language. Provided we hear in language—and not in the other, nor in the other sex—the gouged-out eye, the wound, the fundamental incompleteness that conditions the indefinite quest of signifying chains" (*PH*, 88–89; 104–05).

First Greek, then Jew. The struggle between paganism and Judaism is, for Kristeva, a contest between the mother goddess and the father god. Judaism is a religion of the Law. The Law, we have seen, is "the *nom*/*non*-of-the-Father." With the transition from paganism to Judaism, "impurity distances itself from the material register and announces itself as profanation of the divine name. At this point in the trajectory, where the separating agency [*insistance*] asserts its own pure abstract value ('holy of holies'), the impure will no longer be merely the mixture, the flow or flux, the non-conforming, converging toward the 'improper and unclean' place, which is, in all senses of the term, the maternal living being. Defilement will now be that which impinges on symbolic oneness, that is to say simulacra, substitutions [*Ersatz*], doubles, idols" (*PH*, 104; 123). For the Jew, God the Father is One, or conversely, Oneness, Identity is God. The Jewish religion is, above all else, monotheistic. Monotheism involves "a prohibition, a *monologism,* a subordination of the code to 1, to God" (*DL,* 70). The monologism of Jewish monotheism is expressed "topo-logically" in "the holy place of the Temple" and "logically" in "the holy Law" (*PH,* 94; 113).

> The one and the other are two aspects, semantic and logical of the imposition of a *strategy of identity,* which is, in all rigor, that of monotheism. The semes that clothe the operation of *separation* (orality, death, incest) are the inseparable lining [*doublure inséparable*] of its logical representation aiming to guarantee the place of the law of the One God. . . . In other words, the place *and* the law of the One do not exist without a *series of separations* that are oral, corporeal, or still more generally material and, in the last analysis, related to fusion with the mother. The pure/impure apparatus testifies to the severe struggle which Judaism, in order to constitute itself, must wage against paganism and its maternal cults. This apparatus carries over, into the private lives of everyone, the cutting [*tranchant*] of the struggle that each subject must wage during the entire length of his personal history in order to become separate, that is to say, to become a speaking subject and/or subject to the Law. In this sense, we will say that the "material" semes of the opposition pure/impure that mark out the biblical text are not metaphors of the divine prohibition resuming archaic, material customs, but are the reply [*réplique*] of the symbolic Law from the side of the subjective economy and the genesis of speaking identity. (*PH,* 94; 113)

This struggle for identity is really a strategy of control that operates by "a *logicizing* [logification] of what departs from the symbolic" (*PH,* 91; 110). Since the law of the symbolic is the law of (the) One, i.e., the Law of the Father who alone is God, the logicizing strategy of identity amounts to a scheme for mastering duplicity in all its guises. This lawful economy entails a "series of separations" from the most duplicitous threat of all—the feminine. The erection of (the Law of) the Father "performs the immense *coup de force,* which consists of subordinating maternal power (whether historical or phantasmic, natural or reproductive) to symbolic order as pure logical order regulating the social game [*le jeu social*]" (*PH,* 91; 110).

Defilement reappears in biblical Judaism as "abomination." The abominable is that which the Word of the Father forbids. In the first instance, the *difference* between God and man is established by means of dietary distinctions.[16] "On the one hand, there is bloodless flesh

16. Kristeva concentrates her analysis on Leviticus 11–16 and 19–26.

(destined for man) and, on the other, blood (destined for God)" (*PH*, 96; 115). Blood, we have established, is associated with violence and, by extension, with death. For the Jew, God alone wields the power of life and death. Dietary laws regulating the eating of meat are the ritual displacement of the death drive. But blood is not only related to *thanatos*. "[A]s a vital element, [blood] also refers to women, to fertility, to the promise of fecundity. It thus becomes a fascinating semantic crossroads, the propitious place for abjection where *death* and *femininity, murder* and *procreation, cessation of life* and *vitality,* all come together" (*PH*, 96; 116).

For Kristeva, the association of blood and woman points to a bond between "*food and the feminine.*" This bond raises further questions:

> Might it be that dietary prohibitions are a screen in a still more radical process of separation? Would the dispositions *place-body* and the more elaborate one *speech-logic of differences* be an attempt to keep the being who speaks to his God separated from his mother? In that case, it would be a matter of separating the phantasmatic power of the mother, that archaic Mother Goddess who actually haunted the imagination of a nation at war with the surrounding polytheism. A phantasmatic mother who also constitutes, in the specific history of each person, the abyss that must be established as an autonomous (and not encroaching) *place* and *distinct* object, *that is to say signifiable,* so that such a person might learn to speak. (*PH*, 100; 119)

Between the explanation of the implications of the rules concerning the clean and the unclean in dietary practices (Leviticus 11) and the statement of regulations governing the treatment of diseased bodies (Leviticus 13),[17] there is a brief chapter devoted to the purification of women after childbirth. If a woman "bears a female child, then she shall be unclean for two weeks, as in her menstruation; and she shall continue in the blood of her purifying for sixty-six days" (Leviticus 12:5). The ritual of purification takes a different form for mother and child when the offspring is male. "If a woman conceives, and bears a male child, then she shall be unclean seven days; as at the time of her menstruation, she shall be unclean. And on the eighth day the flesh of his foreskin shall be circumcised. Then she shall continue for thirty-

17. It is important to note that the regulations concerning sick bodies are concerned primarily with diseases of the skin: boils, burns, swelling, scabs, rashes, discolorations, baldness, etc. In this context, the most threatening disease is leprosy. From Kristeva's point of view, these "superficial" diseases assume such importance because they disfigure, open, tear, or lacerate the "*boundaries of the clean and proper body*" (*PH*, 101; 120).

three days in the blood of her purifying; she shall not touch any hallowed thing, nor come into the sanctuary, until the days of her purifying are completed" (Leviticus 12:2–4). The rite of circumcision is carried out on the altar of sacrifice figured in Abraham's offering of Isaac. The circumcised penis is the scored phallus that bears the symbolic mark of castration. By breaking the circuit of copulation, this *coup* makes conception inconceivable. When understood as a purification rite, circumcision appears to "separate one from maternal, feminine impurity and defilement" (*PH*, 99, 118).

There is, however, an important difference between Isaac and the *pharmakos.* Unlike the scapegoat, Isaac is not *actually* sacrificed. Kristeva holds that the taboo inscribed on the incised phallus "forestalls the sacrifice" (*PH*, 94; 114). The difference between sacrifice and taboo parallels the distinction between metaphor and metonomy, which, as Lacan demonstrates, characterize the two basic strategies of dreamwork. While sacrifice involves metaphoric substitution, taboo entails metonymic displacement.[18] Such displacement expands to form a complex network of laws, rules, and regulations, which are supposed to control all behavior. The shift from sacrifice to taboo signals the move from "religion" to "morality."

> Isaac is not offered to God. If Judaism remains a religion due to the sacrificial act, which persists in order to insure the metaphoric, vertical relation of the officiating priest to the One Alone [*l'Un Seul*], this foundation is largely compensated for by the deployment of the prohibitions that take over from it and transform its economy into a metonymic, horizontal chain. A religion of abomination covers up a religion of the sacred. This is the exit of religion and the deployment of morality. Or the leading back of the One that separates and unifies, not to the fascinated contemplation of the sacred, from which it separates, but to the very apparatus that it inaugurates: in logic, abstraction, rules of systems and judgments. (*PH*, 111; 129)

From a moral point of view, corruption or pollution is not the result of contact with a filthy substance that pollutes from without, but is the consequence of the subject's own free action. The one who is holy is the one whose will *always* conforms to the will of the Holy One.

First Greek, then Jew, and finally Christian. Involuntary defilement (substance) and voluntary transgression (subject) meet in the

---

18. In the case of the Abraham-Isaac story, this distinction is not as clear as Kristeva claims. While Isaac is not sacrificed, a ram does take his place. Thus both metaphor and metonymy seem to be at work in this ritual.

"absolutely paradoxical" Christian. Vigilius Haufniensis devotes his
Simple Psychologically Orienting Deliberation on the Dogmatic Issue of Hereditary Sin [*Arvesynde:* original sin] to an exploration of this paradox.
"Ethics," he argues, "points to ideality as a task and assumes that
every man possesses the requisite conditions. Thus ethics develops a
contradiction, inasmuch as it makes clear both the difficulty and the
impossibility. What is said of the law is also true of ethics: it is a
disciplinarian that demands, and by its demands only judges but does
not bring forth life" (*CA*, 16; 4 : 289). Ethics becomes contradictory
by demanding the impossible. No one can fulfill the Law perfectly.
The very struggle for Oneness discloses the inescapable duplicity of
human experience. As Ricoeur's elaboration of Kierkegaard's interpretation of the relation between original sin and sin makes clear,
Christian fault includes both action and suffering; it is simultaneously
voluntary and involuntary.[19]

Commenting on the movement from the Jewish violation of the
Law to the Christian experience of sin, Kristeva writes: "What is
happening here is that a new arrangement of differences is being set
up, an arrangement whose economy will regulate a wholly different
system of meaning, and hence a totally other [*tout autre*] speaking
subject. An essential trait of those evangelical attitudes or narratives
is that abjection is no longer exterior. It is permanent and comes from
within" (*PH*, 113; 135). In contrast to the speculative economy in
which "digestion" leads to the assimilation of otherness and difference, Kristeva is convinced that the "swallowing up of the other
[*engloutissement de l'autre*]" is not a reconciling *Er-Innerung* (*PH*, 118;
140). In this case, introjection *is not* incorporation. What is introjected is not incorporated, for it is not transmuted into the body of the
devouring agent. Rather it remains an undigestible crumb that hollows *one* out, as if from within. Thus torn, rent, split, and cleft, the
subject cries out: '"I" am heterogeneous . . .'" (*PH*, 112; 131).

In this "new arrangement," the most important difference is the
distinction between spirit and flesh. Paul gives the classic Christian
formulation of this difference: "But I say to you, walk by the Spirit,
and do not gratify the desires of the flesh. For the desires of the flesh
are against the Spirit, and the desires of the Spirit are against the flesh;
for these are opposed to each other, to prevent you from doing what
you would" (Galatians 5 : 16–17). Flesh is the outside that is forever
inside, disrupting the life of spirit. In Kristeva's terms, "flesh" (*chair*)

19. See, especially, Ricoeur, "The 'Adamic' Myth and the 'Eschatological' Vision
of History," *The Symbolism of Evil*, pp. 232–78.

is "what might be called . . . an overflowing pulsation that is not bridled by the symbolic" (*PH*, 124; 145:46). Always resisting the Law, flesh is the unrepresentable before, which is even more archaic than the Word of the Father. While Christian theologians describe flesh in terms of original sin, in Christian mythology, flesh assumes the guise of a serpent.

As Kierkegaard observes, even in what seems to be the state of "peace and repose . . . there is something other [*noget Andet*]" (*CA*, 41; 4:313). Since the garden is disturbed from the beginning by a serpent, the enjoyment of innocence is a "memory" of a past that was never present. To appreciate such serpentine symbolics, it is necessary to ask more precisely what the disruptive serpent "is." Ricoeur's analysis again proves helpful:

> In the figure of the serpent, the Yahwist may have been dramatiz-
> ing an important aspect of the experience of temptation—the
> experience of quasi-externality. Temptation would be a sort of
> seduction from without; it would develop into compliance with
> the apparition that lays siege to the "heart"; and, finally, to sin
> would be to *yield*. The serpent, then, would be a part of ourselves
> that we do not recognize; he would be the seduction of ourselves
> by ourselves, projected into the seductive object. . . . Likewise,
> St. Paul identified the quasi-externality of desire with the "flesh,"
> with the law of sin that is in my members. The serpent, then,
> represents this passive aspect of temptation, hovering on the
> border between the outer and the inner.[20]

Neither inside nor outside, but lingering on the border *entre-deux*, the serpent is a descendant of earlier water monsters, which are common in the mythology of the ancient near East.[21] As I noted in the consid-eration of Lacan, one of the biblical accounts of creation suggests that there is something anterior to the Word of the Father: *la mer*. As the figure for "the flow or flux" that "is" always already "there" (though this *déjà-là* is *da* only as *toujours déjà fort*), the serpentine sea monster is a watery goddess. The serpent, in other words, "is" (The) Woman. More precisely, *la mer* "is" *la mère*. When the Word of the Father breaks the waters of the mother, the fluid goddess becomes sanguine.

For the Christian who is not only spirit but also flesh, "feminine

20. Ibid., p. 256.
21. For an examination of the relation between the serpent and water monsters, see Eliade, *The Sacred and the Profane*, chapter 1. Eliade's analysis of the combat between Marduk and Tiamat in the Gilgamesh epic is particularly instructive (pp. 48, 55, 77, 79).

temptation" comes from "inside" (*PH,* 126; 148). In the Christian economy of salvation, the incorporation of the temptress involves an effort to domesticate the feminine. Within the paternal symbolic order, woman is a negative no-thing, which must be negated. In Ricoeur's terms, "the Bible never speaks of sin except in the perspective of salvation that delivers from sin."[22] The archaeology of fault, therefore, points toward a teleology of redemption. In what Derrida labels the "archaeo-teleological" perspective, sin is not merely something negative. Inasmuch as the negation of the negative leads to a higher positivity, the fall is a *felix culpa.* Kristeva quotes Hegel to make her point: "Source of evil and mingled with sin, abjection becomes the condition of reconciliation, in spirit, between flesh and the law. 'It is the origin of disease, but also the source of health, it is the poisoned cup [*coupe*] from which man drinks death and putrefaction, and at the same time the source of reconciliation; in effect, to pose oneself as evil is to suppress evil in oneself'" (*PH,* 127–28; 149–50).

In order to enjoy this salvific redemption, the Christian must participate in something like a purification rite. In Christian praxis, ritual performance becomes performative utterance. Kristeva describes purification rituals as *"a writing without signs"* (une écriture sans signes). "Rites concerning defilement (but perhaps also any rite, defilement rite being prototypical) effect an abreaction of the pre-sign impact, the semiotic impact of language" (*PH,* 73:89). The semiotic impact of language is *felt* in the words of confession. In his avowal, the penitent tries to put into words his unspeakable sinfulness. The purpose of confession is absolution. As the ritual actor attempts to cleanse himself or herself by performing the rite, so the confessor seeks to wash away his or her sins. When understood as performative utterance, confession is a "talking cure." "No dogma postulates it. It will be necessary to wait for Freud to disengage heterogeneous drives, or simply the negativity working in all discourse. But the practice of confession, on the whole, does nothing else but weigh down discourse with sin. By having to bear that weight, which alone confers the intensity full of communication, avowal absolves from sin and, by the same stroke, founds the power of discourse" (*PH,* 130; 152).

The negativity of discourse already haunts the speech of confession as the inseparable "lining" (*doublure*) or the inescapable "double" (*doubleur*) that renders all language duplicitous and makes every speaking being *un être altéré.* The "lacerating" (*déchirante*) struggle to

22. Ricoeur, *The Symbolism of Evil,* p. 274.

speak the unspeakable is an (impossible) attempt to say what cannot
be *spoken* but only *written.*

> Finally, the frequency of rites of defilement in societies *without
> writing* leads one to think that such cathartic rites function like a
> "writing of the real" [*écriture du réel*]. They cut out, demarcate,
> delineate an order, a framework, a sociality, without having any
> other signification than the one immanent in that very cutting
> out [*découpage*] and the order that is thus linked together. One
> might ask, proceeding in reverse, whether all writing is not a
> second order rite, at the level of language, which causes one to be
> reminded, through the linguistic signs themselves, of the demar-
> cations that precondition them and exceed them. Writing, in
> effect, causes the subject who risks it to confront an archaic
> authority on the nether side of the proper Name. (*PH,* 74–5; 91)

The unspeakability of the sanguine goddess resounds silently in the
Word of the w-rite-r.

W/ritel/ing the Real

In an earlier chapter we heard to the cry of Nietzsche's madman:
"Whither is God . . . I will tell you. *We have killed him*—you and I.
All of us are his murderers. But how did we do this? How could we
drink up the sea? Who gave us the sponge to wipe away the entire
horizon?" Writers from Heidegger to Bataille (and beyond) maintain
that the constructive subject of modern philosophy is "the sponge"
(*l'éponge*) that "wipes away the entire horizon" by absorbing everything
different from, and other than itself. When thought and action tend
toward homogenization and hegemony, the question of otherness becomes critical. For Kristeva, the task of recovering altarity falls to the
writer. "In a world in which the Other [*l'Autre*] has collapsed, the
aesthetic effort—a descent into the foundations of the symbolic construct—consists of retracing the fragile boundaries of the speaking
being, closest to its dawn, to that bottomless 'origin' that is called
primal repression. In this experience, which is, nevertheless, directed
by the Other, 'subject' and 'object' repel, confront each other, break
up and start again—inseparable, contaminated, condemned, at the
limit of the assimilable, the thinkable: abject" (*PH,* 18; 25). In the
absence of religious rites, the w-rite-r becomes the high priest who
undertakes the impossible task of writing the unnameable. While
"the phobic object is a proto-writing [*proto-écriture*], . . . the writer is
a phobic" whose writing "is not an ultimate resistance but an unveil-

178

ing [*dévoilement*] of the abject. An elaboration, an emptying, and a hollowing out of abjection by the Crisis of the Word [*la Crise du Verbe*]" (*PH*, 38, 208; 49, 246). "The Crisis of the Word" is occasioned by a complex cultural event or, more precisely, a complex of cultural events which can best be described as "the death of God." Though religiously, theologically, and philosophically significant, the death of God is fundamentally a *linguistic* event. A god dies when a community loses "faith in One Master Signifier" (*PH*, 209; 247). Without One, there "is" no thing, and Nothing can remain only as *style*. For Kristeva, "writing and style occupy the place left empty by the eclipse of God, Project, and Faith" (*PH*, 186–87; 219).

After the death of God, all questions become questions of style. Who, one might ask, is the stylist, and what is style? The stylist is the writer who "sound[s] a dissonance within the thetic, paternal function of language" by "tampering with vocabulary and syntax" (*DL*, 139; *PH*, 137; 161). Kristeva borrows a description of style from Céline: "Style is a certain way of doing violence to sentences (. . .) of having them slightly fly off the handle, so to speak, displacing them, and thus making the reader himself displace his meaning. But ever so slightly! Oh, ever so slightly!" (*PH*, 203; 239). The stylist inflicts violence in an effort to "*resensitize language*, so that it *throbs* [palpite] more than *it reasons*" (*PH*, 190; 225). The alternation of such throbbing or palpitation results in what Kristeva labels "desemantization." The desemantization of language reduces discourse to the state of "pure signifier," in which the structures of representation and narrativity are fatally cracked. By evoking "a *heterogeneity of signification*," the "elliptical" words of the writer become the inscription of the impossible. In different terms, the impossibility of writing "is" the writing of the impossible.

Like Kierkegaard, Heidegger, Bataille, and others, Kristeva is persuaded that poetic language can "say" what reason leaves unsaid. "If modern art, which is post-Hegelian, sounds a rhythm in language capable of placing in check [*mettre en échec*] any subjugated work and all logic, this discredits only that closure in Heideggerian reflection that systematizes Being, beings, and their historical truth. But such discredit does not jeopardize the logical stake [*enjeu*] of *poésie*, inasmuch as *poésie* is a practice of the speaking subject, consequently implying a dialectic between limits, both signified and signifying, and the setting of a pre- and trans-logical rhythm solely within this limit" (*DL*, 25; 359). Like the oscillation of Heidegger's Logos, the interlacing of Merleau-Ponty's savage word, the vibration of Lacan's discourse of the Other, and the slipping and sliding of Bataille's *mot glissant*, Kristeva's *poésie* opens language to a "dreadfully ancient" that is pre- or trans-logical. "Since poetry works on the bar between signifier and signified and tends to erase it, it [must be understood as] an anarchic cry [*cri anarchique*] against the thetic and socializing position of syntactic language" (*DL,* 174; 187). By means of this an-archic, i.e., non-original, *cri,* the poet tries "to make language hear [*entendre*] what it does not want to say" (*DL,* 31; 365). The unsaying of language subverts philosophical discourse by calling into question the constructive subject, which, as Heidegger maintains, comes to completion in Hegelian and Husserlian phenomenology. "Meaning and signification, however, do not exhaust the poetic function. Therefore, the thetic predicative operation and its correlatives (signified object and transcendental ego), though valid for the signifying economy of poetic language, are only one of its *limits:* Certainly constitutive, but not all-encompassing [*englobante*]. While poetic language can indeed be studied through its meaning and signification (by revealing, depending on the method, either structures or process), such a study would, in the final analysis, amount to reducing it to the phenomenological perspective and, hence, failing to see what in the poetic function departs from the signified and the transcendental ego and makes of what is known as 'literature' something other than knowledge" (*DL,* 132; 158).

To release language from the master code 1, it is necessary to move beyond symbolics, syntax, and semantics to semiotics. Commenting on Jakobson's analysis of the poetry of the Russian futurist Mayakovsky, Kristeva argues that "the irruption of the semiotic rhythm into the signifying system of language will never be an Hegelian *relève,* that is, it will not truly be experienced in the present. The fixed, imperious, immediate present kills, puts aside, and wastes the poem. Thus the irruption within the order of language of the anteriority of language evokes a later time, that is, a forever. The time of the poem is a 'future anterior' that will never take place, never come about as such, but only as an upheaval [*bouleversement:* confusion, disorder, destruction] of present place and meaning" (*DL,* 32; 369). Elusive semiotic processes cannot be translated into clearly articulated symbolic, syntactic, and semantic structures. The "upheaval of present place and meaning," which faults every sense, occurs along the "catastrophic fold [*pli-catastrophe*] between body and language" (*PH,* 190; 226). The "strophe" (*strophe:* a turning; derived from *strephein:* to turn) in which this "cata-strophe" (*kata:* down + *strephein*) resounds is "a strange, foreign discourse, which, strictly speaking, shatters verbal communication (made up of a knowledge and a truth that are nevertheless heard) by means of a device that mimes the terror, enthusiasm, or orgy, and is more closely related to rhythm and song than to the Word" (*PH*, 30; 38).

By opening the time and space of the anteriority of language, which is never present but always to come, the strange discourse of the poet unleashes an orgy that is, in effect, a "carnival" (*carnelevamen: caro*, flesh + *levare*, to raise, lift up). "The poetic word, polyvalent and multidetermined, adheres to a logic exceeding that of codified discourse and fully comes into being only in the margins of recognized culture. Bakhtin was the first to study this logic, and he looked for its root in *carnival*. Carnivalesque discourse breaks through the laws of a language censored by grammar and semantics and, at the same time, is a social and political protest" (*DL*, 65; 144). In the modern world, the excesses involved in the ritual performance of ancient festivals reappear in the excesses of the writer's performative utterance. Kristeva transforms Bataille's "nonlogical difference of matter" into the dialogic of the carnival and its nondiscursive discourse. "As composed of distances, relationships, analogies, and nonexclusive oppositions, it [i.e., the carnival, as well as its discourse] is essentially dialogical. It is a spectacle, but without a stage; a game, but also a daily undertaking. . . A carnival participant is both actor and spectator; he loses his sense of individuality, passes through a zero point of carnivalesque activity and splits into a subject of the spectacle and an object of the game. Within the carnival, the subject is reduced to nothingness, while the structure of *the author* emerges as anonymity that creates and sees itself created as self and other, as man and mask" (*DL*, 78). Participation in the carnival both splits, tears, and rends the subject proper, and soils, stains, and dirties the proper subject. Kristeva is convinced that Céline brings to completion the carnivalesque tradition that begins with Bakhtin. Céline "ceaselessly renders the sound and image, or even the causes, of the apocalypse. Never any dissertation, commentary, judgment. In the face of the apocalypse, he exclaims with a horror close to ecstasy. The Célinian laugh is a horrified and fascinated exclamation. An apocalyptic laugh" (*PH*, 204; 240). *Le rire apocalyptique* is "an unfamiliar, troubling, indefinable laugh," a laugh as unfamiliar, troubling, and indefinable as the strange apocalypse it portends (*DL*, 181; 195).

Kristeva's apocalypse is not the realization of a Hegelian *telos* in which absolute knowledge becomes totally present. To the contrary, this apocalypse is "black with burnt up meaning" (*DL*, 181; 195). Here apocalypse is not the *parousia* but its impossibility. "The apocalypse that laughs is an apocalypse without god. Black mysticism of transcendental erasure" (*PH*, 206; 240). Instead of the enjoyment of perfection or completion, the "ecstasy" of this "black mysticism" is the *jouissance* suffered when one recognizes the "tress of horror and fascination that signals the incompletion of the speaking being (*PH*, 209; 247). "*Jouissance* alone makes the abject as such exist. One does not know it, one does not desire it, one revels in it [*en jouit*]. Violently and with anguish. A passion. And, as in *jouissance,* where the object of desire, known as object *a,* bursts with the shattered mirror where the ego gives up its image in order to look at oneself in the Other, there is neither objective nor objectal in the abject. It is simply a boundary, a repulsive gift [*don*] that the Other . . . allows to fall so that the "I" does not disappear but finds in it, in this sublime alienation, a fallen existence [*une existence déchue*]" (*PH*, 9; 17).

Like Bataille's *expérience intérieure,* Kristeva's *jouissance* is *le pas au-delà.* To take this step, one must follow the traces of the errant writer. The writing that results from "black mysticism" is perhaps the ultimate form of a secular attitude, without morality, without judgment, without hope. Neither Céline, who is such a writer, nor the catastrophic exclamation that constitutes his style, can find outside support to sustain themselves. Their only support is the beauty of the gesture which, here, on the page, compels language to approach, as near as possible, the human enigma, the place where *ça* kills, thinks, experiences *jouissance,* all at the same time. A language of abjection, of which the writer is both subject and victim, witness and bascule.[23] Alternate in what? In nothing other than the effervescence of passion and language that is style, where any ideology, thesis, interpretation, mania, collectivity, threat, or hope is drowned" (*PH*, 206; 242). Such aberrant style is the "feminine operation" that blinds philosophical discourse. While the truthful philosopher is a man (even when a woman), the stylish writer is a woman (even when a man).

In the absence of God, literature remains (*reste*); (the) literary remains (to) "take the place of the sacred" (*PH*, 208; 246). "Upon close inspection," Kristeva writes, "all literature is probably a version of the apocalypse, which, whatever its socio-historical conditions, seems to me to take root in the fragile boundary ('borderline') where identities (subject/object, etc.) are not, or are hardly at all—double, blurred, heterogeneous, animal, metamorphosed, altered, abject"

---

23. A bascule is "an apparatus acting on the principle of the lever or pulley, whereby one end is raised when the other is depressed." In French, *bascule* carries the figurative meaning of vacillation, or playing up alternately on either side. *Basculer* is to see-saw, swing, vacillate, and hence to *alternate.*

(*PH*, 207; 245). *Altéré, abject. Abject, altéré.* Abjection "is" the altarity that systems are constructed to exclude and/or repress. The abject, however, can never be totally repressed; it forever returns to deconstruct every construction—be it philosophical, theological, psychological, social, political, cultural, or economic. The mournful cry of the one who suffers the eternal return of the abject tolls the death of the One. The tears of the writers are tears of *jouissance; le cri* of *l'é-cri-ture,* the paradoxical laughter of *le rire déchirant.*

> We do not laugh . . . in order to judge the position that gives meaning; even less so in order to place ourselves outside of judgment, in some surreality where everything is equal. We laugh on account of the limit assumed in the very movement that poses and deposes finitude within an indefinitely centered and decentered process. (*DL*, 182; 196)

That which endlessly roots and uproots finitude is, for Kristeva, "*a transfinite element*" (*DL*, 173; 186). The name or non-name of the transfinite is the Infinite.

Overleaf: George Segal, *The Holocaust.* Photograph by Allan Finkelman. Courtesy of the Jewish Museum, New York.

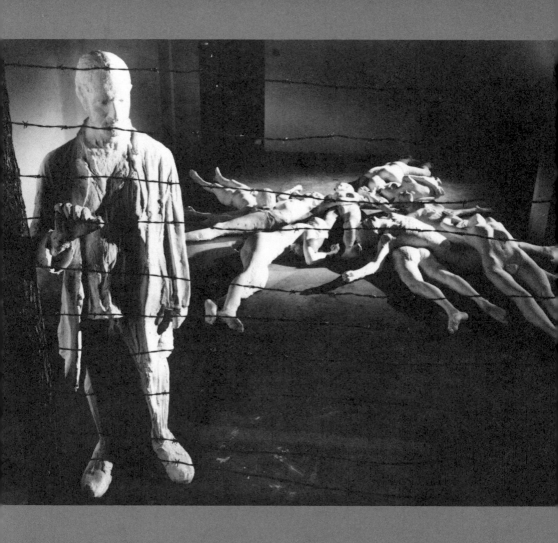

7

Infinity

EMMANUEL LEVINAS

Anarchy: Lapse of Time

If Hegel's penetrating insight consummates the wedding of subjectivity and objectivity, anything written after his System would seem to be an anticlimax—little more than a postscript, which, by definition, is unscientific. What appears to come *after* can, however, evoke a remote *before*. "Ante," which derives from the same root as "anti" (i.e., *ant*) means "before" and is related to *antiquus,* former or antique. The anti-climax that comes after all, i.e., after the System that claims to know all and be all, might point to an ante-climax more ancient than any philosopher ever conceived. Perhaps this is the ante that is at stake in the philosophical wager. By delaying the climax, the ante appears to make conception impossible.

Something like this seems to be the opinion of one of Hegel's most disturbing successors: Anti-Climacus. One might say of Kierkegaard what Blanchot says of Nietzsche, that he "can only come after Hegel, but it is always before, and it is always after Hegel that he comes and comes again. Before: because thought, even as the absolute, as presence, has never assembled in itself the accomplished totality of knowledge" (*PA,* 34–35).[1] Anti-Climacus presents his most extensive critique of Hegel in *The Sickness unto Death.* He begins his argument by reconsidering one of the central categories in Hegelian philosophy: spirit.

1. As will become increasingly evident, reference to Kierkegaard in the context of a consideration of Levinas is hardly out of place. It is significant that Levinas dedicates *Totality and Infinity* to Jean Wahl, the well-known French Kierkegaard scholar. He also begins the first chapter of his later and more mature book, *Otherwise than Being or Beyond Essence,* with an epigram from Wahl's *Traité de métaphysique,* (Paris: Payot, 1968). As I have pointed out in the opening section, Wahl presents a detailed examination of the relation between Kierkegaard and Hegel in his two major works, *Etudes kierkegaardiennes* (Paris: Fernard Aubier, 1938), and *Le malheur de la conscience dans la philosophie de Hegel* (Paris: Les Editions Rieder, 1976). It is clear that Levinas has learned and borrowed much from his long-time friend, Jean Wahl.

A human being is spirit [*Aand*]. But what is spirit? Spirit is the self. But what is the self? The self is a relation that relates itself to itself or is the relation's relating itself to itself in the relation; the self is not the relation but is the relation's relating itself to itself. A human being is a synthesis of the infinite and the finite, of the temporal and the eternal, of freedom and necessity, in short, a synthesis. A synthesis is a relation between two. Considered in this way, a human being is still not a self.

In the relation between two, the relation is the third [*det Tredie*] as a negative unity, and the two relate to the relation and in the relation to the relation. . . . If, however, the relation relates itself to itself, this relation is the positive third, and this is the self.

Such a relation that relates itself to itself, a self, must either have been posited [*sat*] by itself or have been posited by an other [*et Andet*].

If the relation that relates itself to itself has been posited by an other, then the relation is indeed the third, but this relation, the third, is yet again a relation that relates itself to that which posited the entire relation.

The human self is such a derived, posited relation, a relation that relates itself to itself and in relating itself to itself relates itself to an other.[2]

Upon first reading, Anti-Climacus's account of spirit seems to be an elaboration of Hegel's claim that "the self is a relation that relates itself to its own self." A more careful consideration of the text, however, suggests that use of Hegelian terminology parodies the speculative definition of spirit. The departure from Hegelian dialectics is evident in Anti-Climacus's insistence that "the self is not the relation but is the relation's relating itself to itself." Anti-Climacus is convinced that in Hegel's notion of spirit, the self *is* the relation which, in relating itself to itself, establishes a *negative* unity.[3] I have argued that for Hegel, spirit is essentially self-referential negativity that binds together co-implicated opposites. This negative structure incorporates everything within an all-encompassing totality by reconciling all differ-

---

2. Søren Kierkegaard, *The Sickness Unto Death*, trans. H. V. and E. H. Hong (Princeton: Princeton University Press, 1980), pp. 13–14; 11:127–28. It is not possible to consider this passage in detail in this context. Elsewhere I have developed extensive analyses of Kierkegaard's definition of spirit. See *Journeys to Selfhood: Hegel and Kierkegaard*, pp. 160–80, and *Kierkegaard's Pseudonymous Authorship: A Study of Time and The Self* (Princeton: Princeton University Press, 1975), pp. 81–126.

3. Anti-Climacus underscores this point elsewhere in the text: "In the relation between two, the relation is the third as a negative unity, and the two relate to the relation and in the relation to the relation" (13; 11:127).

ences. Over against Hegel, Anti-Climacus denies that contraries are identical in their difference and that opposites are related in such a way that each in itself is at the same time its own other. Consequently, spirit, as the structure of self-relation within which opposites meet, cannot be the "negative unity" of internal relationality, but must be a "positive third" that constitutes a genuine *coincidentia oppositorum*. In other words, since opposites are not implicitly identical or necessarily related, they must be contingently conjoined. Expressing his most important difference from Hegel, Anti-Climacus insists that such self-relation is possible only by virtue of the relationship of the self to "an Other" (*et Andet*). The self *is not* autonomous or self-positing but is posited by an Other which, as Kierkegaard explains elsewhere, is "infinitely and qualitatively different." In relating itself to itself, the self relates itself to this Other.

For Hegel, this wholly Other is the God of Judaism whose subjects suffer the mournful melancholy of unhappy consciousness.[4] In the *Science of Logic,* Hegel describes this Other as the "bad or spurious infinite" (*Schlecht-Unendliche*). "The infinite, determined as such, has present in it the finitude that is distinct from it; the former is the *in-itself* in this unity, and the latter is only determinateness, limit [*Grenze*] in it; but it is a limit that is the sheer other [*das schlechthin Andere*] of the in-itself, is its opposite; the infinite's determination, which is the in-itself as such, is ruined by the addition of such a quality; it is thus a *finitized infinite*" (*L,* 145; 5: 159). If the finite and the infinite are merely antithetical, the infinite is limited by the finitude over against which it stands. The finite, therefore, appears to be independent and self-subsistent, and the *in*-finite seems to be dependent on and conditioned by firmly established finitude. From the perspective of Hegel's dialectical reason, the finite is neither independent nor self-subsistent, but is inherently dependent and inwardly self-contradictory. Since finitude does not itself possess aseity, its being necessarily entails the being of another, which is its opposite, infinitude. "*The being of the finite,*" Hegel explains, "*is not only its being, but is also the being of the infinite*" (*LPR,* 3: 254; 17: 437). Finitude includes within itself its opposite as the indispensable presupposition and essential ground of its being. The determinate identity of finitude comprehends its own difference (infinitude) in such a way that relationship to "other" is a dimension of self-relation requisite for self-realization.

4. For an analysis of this form of experience, see chapter 1, first section.

Infinitude, by contrast, contains finitude in its own being. While the finite realizes itself in and through the infinite, infinitude renders itself infinite in relation to finitude. The finite is not merely other than or opposed to the infinite but is an essential dimension of the infinite itself. To be truly infinite, infinitude cannot be limited by finitude; it must include otherness within itself as a necessary moment of its self-determination. Just as finitude is dialectically related to infinity, so the infinite becomes itself in relation to its own other, finitude.

> Thus both finite and infinite are this *movement* in which each returns to itself through its negation; they *are* only as *mediation* within themselves, and the affirmative of each contains the negative of each and is the negation of the negation. They are thus a *result,* and hence not what they are in the determination of their *beginning;* the finite is not a *determinate being* on *its* side, and the infinite a *determinate being* or *being-in-itself* beyond the determinate being [*jenseits des Daseins*], that is, beyond the being determined as finite. . . . They occur . . . only as moments of a whole and . . . come on the scene only by means of their opposite, but essentially also by means of the sublation of their opposite. (*L,* 147; 5 : 162).

In the process of establishing its identity through difference, infinitude sublates the otherness of its other and makes finitude an intrinsic aspect of its own being. The infinite, therefore, "is on its own account just as much finite as infinite" (*L,* 153; 5 : 170). So interpreted, infinitude is not limited by alien finitude and consequently is no longer "bad or spurious" but is now "true."

In his analysis of the complexities of Infinity, Levinas returns to issues raised in Kierkegaard's critique of Hegel's speculative infinite. Neither Greek nor Christian, Levinas is devoutly Jewish. His Judaism, however, closely resembles Kierkegaard's Christianity. Like Kierkegaard, Levinas follows the nomadic wanderings of the exiled Abraham rather than the circuitous journeys of Ulysses. Levinas develops his interpretation of the Infinite through an extended criticism of the modern philosophy of the subject formulated by Hegel and elaborated by Husserl.[5] To break out of the ontotheological tradition, Levinas argues, it is necessary to think "otherwise than being" (*autrement qu'être*) by thinking "beyond essence" (*au-delà de l'essence*).

5. In *Totality and Infinity,* Levinas argues that Heidegger, as well as Hegel and Husserl, is a representative of the ontological tradition that dominates Western philosophy. *Otherwise than Being* presents a more subtle reading of Heidegger. In formulating his critique of Hegelian and Husserlian phenomenology, Levinas draws extensively, though usually indirectly, on the arguments of Heidegger.

The notion of essence is the foundation of ontotheology. At the beginning of the second book of his *Science of Logic*, entitled "The Doctrine of Essence," Hegel defines essence as "the self-subsistent [*Selbständige*], which *is* as self-mediated through its negation, which negation essence itself is; it is therefore the identical unity of absolute negativity and immediacy. The negativity is negativity in itself; it is its relation to itself and is thus in itself immediacy; but it is negative self-relation, a negating that is a repelling of itself, and the inherent immediacy is thus negative or *determinate* in regard to it. But this determinateness is itself absolute negativity, and this determining, which is, as determining, immediately the sublating of itself, is a return-into-self" (*L*, 398; 6:22). When understood in this way, essence secures the identity of identity and nonidentity and the union of union and nonunion. As I have argued, this internally differentiated structure constitutes the basis of Hegel's System.[6] Levinas maintains that essence, which, as absolute negativity that returns to itself by negating all negation (i.e., all difference and otherness), functions as an "assembling" that "cannot leave anything outside [*dehors*], has no outside, cannot fall into ruin [*s'abîmer*]" (*OB* 163; 208). Through the negation of all exteriority, essence *works* to "fill every interval [*intervalle*]," and thereby establish "a present without fissure [*fissure*] or surprise [*imprévu*]" (*OB*, 4, 5; 4, 5). In Hegel's speculative dialectic, this labor of the negative is always carried out in the interests of self-consciousness.

In an effort to stress the role of interest in the speculative doctrine of essence, Levinas claims that "*Esse* is *interesse;* essence is interest" (4; 4).[7] Speculators, we have discovered, attempt to avoid deficits by securing a profitable return on every investment. Securities are exchanged to ensure the security of those who trade them. As the broker of such exchange, essence requires "a rigorous book-keeping" (*OB*, 125; 161).[8] Following Bataille, Levinas identifies two aspects of such investment: psychological and economic. Since the speculative subject must always return to itself by discovering itself in every "other,"

6. See above, chapter 1, second section. Since Hegel lays bare the implications of ontotheology, to criticize his foundational notion of essence is, in effect, to attack the entire tradition that he brings to completion.

7. Compare Kierkegaard's remark: "Reality is an *inter-esse* between the moments of that hypothetical unity of thought and being that abstract thought presupposes." *Concluding Unscientific Postscript*, trans. D. F. Swenson and W. Lowrie (Princeton: Princeton University Press, 1968), p. 279; 7:270.

8. We will encounter the figure of a bookkeeper in the consideration of Kierkegaard's *Stages on Life's Way* in chapter 10.

its investments inevitably are narcissistic."Being's interest dramatizes itself in egoisms struggling with one another, each against all, in the multiplicity of allergic egoisms that are at war with one another and thus are together [*ensemble*]. War is the gesture or drama of the essence's interest" (*OB*, 4; 5). This war of self-interested subjects is a variation of Hegel's struggle for recognition. Despite the losses involved in such a contest, the speculative philosopher believes the struggle remains a profitable venture. The war of all against all is a necessary stage in the long march toward peace. "But," Levinas cautions, "this rational peace, a patience and length of time, is calculation, mediation and politics. The struggle of each against all in which each becomes exchange and commerce. The clash of each against all in which each comes to be with all, becomes reciprocal limitation and determination, like that of matter. But the persisting in being, interest, is maintained by the future compensation that will have to equilibrate the concessions patiently and politically consented to in the immediate" (*OB*, 4–5; 5). For the Jewish Levinas, unlike the Christian Hegel, this compensatory future never arrives. The Messiah, in other words, has not yet come. In such ante-climactic thinking, the *Par-ousia*, the appearance of essence (*ousia*), is forever delayed.

In contrast to this delay, the economy of essence privileges presence and its temporal modality, the present. To be is to be present and only the present truly is. When everything is finally revealed in the *Par-ousia*, there is "a coincidence of being and its manifestation" (*OB*, 63; 80). Levinas stresses that "the manifestation of being, the appearing, is indeed the primary event, but *the very primacy of the primary is in the presence of the present*" (*OB*, 24; 31). The present in which such manifestation occurs is not a single moment but is a long, slow process that takes time. The unveiling of essence involves the deployment of identity in difference and the return of difference to identity. "The manifestation of being to itself would [seem to] imply a separation in being. The manifestation cannot occur as a fulguration in which the totality of being shows itself to the totality of being, for this 'showing itself to' indicates a getting out of phase [*déphasage*], which is precisely time, that astonishing divergence [*écart*] of the identical from itself!" (*OB*, 28; 36). As the "deviation" of being from itself, time remains bound to the present. We have already determined that in an ontotheological perspective there are not three times but *three* modalities of *one* time. The *locus classicus* of this view of time is Augustine's *Confessions*.

It is now, however, perfectly clear that neither the future nor the past is in existence, and that it is incorrect to say that there are three times—past, present, and future. Though one might perhaps say: "There are three times—a present of things past, a present of things present, and a present of things future." For these three do exist in the mind, and I do not see them anywhere else: the present time of things past is memory; the present time of things present is sight; the present time of things future is expectation.[9]

Augustine suggests that when the essence of time is understood in terms of presence, temporality appears to be inseparably bound to the activity of the self-conscious subject.

Developing the complex interplay of being, presence, time, and self-consciousness, Levinas writes:

> Time is essence and monstration of essence. In the temporalization of time the light comes about by the instant falling out of phase with itself—which is the temporal flow, the difference of the identical [*la différence de l'identique*]. The difference of the identical is also its manifestation. But time is also a recuperation of all deviations [*écarts*], through retention, memory, and history. In its temporalization, in which, thanks to retention, memory, and history, nothing is lost, everything is presented or represented, everything is consigned and lends itself to writing, or is synthesized or, as Heidegger would say, assembled, in which everything is crystallized or sclerosized into substance—in the recuperating temporalization, without time lost, without time to lose, and where the being of substance comes to pass. (*OB*, 9; 11)

Through the process of re-presentation, the subject re-collects the past and integrates it with the present. Such re-membering presupposes the self's transparency to itself. In the final analysis, subjectivity must be "reduced" to total self-consciousness in which nothing remains obscure. If, as Hegel maintains, the temporal perfection of self-consciousness fully actualizes the essential ground of all reality, then "time, the Essence, the Essence as time, would be the absolute itself in the Return to Itself [*Retour à Soi*]" (*OB*, 103; 131). When the absolute becomes temporal, the temporal becomes absolute. Such essential time is the time of Hegel's phenomenology of spirit.[10] This time extends into Husserl's phenomenology of internal time-consciousness.

9. Augustine, *Confessions*, trans. R. Warner (New York: New American Library, 1963), p. 273.

10. From Hegel's point of view, this is the conceptual truth embodied in the images of Christianity. Through the drama of incarnation, crucifixion, and resurrection, the infinite becomes finite and the finite becomes infinite. Hegel believes this twofold movement characterizes not only the particular figure of Jesus but also the entire natural and historical process.

In Hegelian and Husserlian phenomenology, "there is a remission of time and tension of the recapture, relaxation and tension without a break [*rupture*] without a gap. There is not a pure distancing [*éloignement*] from the present, but precisely re-presentation, that is, a distancing in which the present of truth *is* already [*déjà*] or *still is* [est encore]; for a representation is a recommencement of the present that in its "first time" is for the second time; it is a retention and a protention, between forgetting and expecting, between memory and project. Time is reminiscence and reminiscence is time, the unity of consciousness and essence" (*OB*, 29; 36). Though time seems to pass in such reminiscence, there is no "lapse of time" (*laps de temps; OB*, 9; 11).

"Lapse," which is derived from the Latin *lapsus*, error, sliding (from *labi:* slide, slip, fall), means "a slip of the memory, the tongue, the pen; a slight error, a mistake; a falling from rectitude; a moral slip; apostatizing from the faith; deviation from one's principles; an intermission; a gliding flow (of water); the gliding passing away, passage of life, time, etc.; to pass or sink gradually through absence of effort; to fall into error, heresy, sin, or decay." For Levinas, the lapse of time calls into question the interpretation of temporality that dominates the ontotheological tradition. He designates the temporal lapse that slips away from philosophical vision "*anarchy*." This anarchy is an *an-arche* that signals a "deep formerly" (*profond jadis*), which is not a "'modification' of the present" (*OB*, 9; 11). Such anarchy overturns the order and structure of philosophy by exposing the gaps, tears, and wounds that reason is supposed to cover, mend, and heal.

> This an-archy [*an-archie*]—this refusal to be assembled into a representation, has its own way to concern me: the *lapse*. But the lapse of time, irrecuperable in the temporalization of time, is not only negative like the immemorial.
>
> Temporalization as lapse, the loss of time, is neither an initiative of the ego, nor a movement toward some *telos* of action. The loss of time is not the work of any subject. Already the synthesis of retentions and protentions in which Husserl's phenomenological analysis, through an abuse of language, recuperates the lapse, bypasses the ego.[11] Time passes [*se passe*]. This synthesis which occurs *patiently*, called with profundity passive, is

---

11. Levinas's argument at this point is, in effect, a deconstructive reading of Husserl's interpretation of time. He insists that Husserl glimpsed but did not pursue something like a primordial temporality. This "time before time" disrupts Husserl's internal time-consciousness and dislocates consciousness itself. In his analysis of time, Levinas attempts to think what Husserl, inter alios, left unthought.

aging. It breaks out [*éclate*] under the weight of years, and is irreversibly removed from the present, that is, from re-presentation. In self-consciousness, there is no longer a *presence* of self to self, but senescence. It is as senescence beyond the recuperation of memory that time, lost time that does not return, is a diachrony and concerns me. (*OB*, 51–52; 66–67)

In contrast to the past that can be remembered, anarchy "is" a radical ante that is "incommensurable with every present." Like the Lacanian unconscious, which is something other than the Freudian preconscious, Levinas's *anarchie* is a past "more ancient than every representable origin, a pre-original and anarchial *passed*" (*OB*, 9; 11). Instead of an absolute origin (*arche*), the *an-archie*, which is *toujours-déjà*, renders impossible every origin and all originality. Everything, everybody is ever after, i.e., never primary, always secondary.

Since nonoriginal anarchy has never been present, this remote anteriority cannot be re-presented. "Immemorial, unrepresentable, invisible, the past that bypasses the present, the pluperfect past [*plus que parfait*], falls [*tombe*] into a past that is a gratuitous lapse. It cannot be recuperated by reminiscence not because of its remoteness, but because of its incommensurability with the present. The present is esssence that begins and ends, beginning and end assembled in a thematizable conjunction; it is the finite in correlation with a freedom. Diachrony is the refusal of conjunction, the non-totalizable [*le non-totalisable*], and in this sense, [*it is*] Infinite" (*OB*, 11; 13–14). Inasmuch as being is identified with presence, that which is incommensurable with the present does not belong to being. This does not, however, imply that the unrepresentable before *is* nothing. When nothing is conceived as the binary opposite of being, thought remains bound to and by the ontological categories characteristic of Western philosophy. The irreducible diachrony of Levinas's anarchy implies (without revealing or representing) an infinite that "is" beyond essence and, as such, "is" otherwise than being and nonbeing.[12] "*The other of being* or *the otherwise than being*" is "beyond the Logos, beyond

12. The dialectic between being and nonbeing is sustained by a process of negation in which opposites are joined. In the ontotheological tradition, this relationship is asymmetrical rather than reciprocal. Insofar as nonbeing "is," as it must be to stand in relation to being, nonbeing is incorporated within or subsumed by being. "The task," Levinas avers, "is to conceive of a break out of essence. To go where? Toward what region? To stay on what ontological plane? But the tearing away from essence contests the unconditional privilege of the question 'where?' It signals a non-place [*non-lieu*]. The essence pretends to cover and recover every ex-ception—negativity, nihilation, and already since Plato, non-being, which 'in a certain sense is'" (*OB*, 8; 9).

being and nonbeing, beyond essence, beyond true and non-true" (*OB,* 45; 58). Forever *un pas au-delà* being and nonbeing, the Infinite neither is nor is not. "The statement of being's other, of the otherwise than being, claims to state a difference beyond that which separates being from nothingness—the very difference of the *beyond,* the difference of transcendence" (*OB,* 3; 4). [13] Such a different difference, such an other other is "outside [*dehors*] ontological categories," it is, in fact, "the outside" itself. This *dehors* is the "exteriority" philosophy struggles to master through the process of *Er-Innerung.* But the effort is futile, for this beyond is "a transcendence inconvertible into immanence" (*OB,* 140; 179). Levinas labels this radical Other "Alterity." [14]

Always approaching (but never arriving) from without, alterity "exceeds [*dépasse*] every capacity, and manifests, as it were, its excess [*démesure*] in reverse" (*OB,* 12; 14). Such an "exorbitant" other is an irreducible enigma that "refuses to be tamed [*apprivoisée*] or domesticated [*domestiquée*] by a theme" (*OB,* 100; 127). Since reason is, for Levinas, always thematic, alterity cannot appear to consciousness as such. Alterity, which eludes the binary opposites of being and nonbeing, neither becomes conscious nor remains unconscious. Just as nonbeing is bound in a dialectical relation to being, so the unconscious, when understood as the complement of consciousness, is a negativity defined by the polar relation of opposites. Alterity, by contrast, is *das ganz Andere,* which is other than the otherness of the unconscious. Neither existent nor nonexistent, present nor absent, conscious nor unconscious, alter-ity endlessly alter-nates *entre-deux.* Consciousness, however, is not indifferent to this strange other. Like Lacan's discourse of the Other, alterity "interrupts" consciousness and self-consciousness. Levinas labels this subversive Other "the trace."

In terms that recall the interplay of unveiling and reveiling in Heidegger's *a-letheia,* as well as the *fort/da* of Lacan's reel thing, Levinas maintains that the trace appears as disappearance. In the approach of the radically Other, "there is inscribed or written the trace [*la trace*] of the Infinite, the trace of a departure, . . . the trace of what is ex-

13. Elsewhere Levinas gives one of his clearest statements on transcendence: "Transcendence designates a relation with a reality infinitely distant from my own reality, yet without this distance destroying this relation and without this relation destroying this distance, as would happen with relations within the same." *Totality and Infinity: An Essay on Exteriority,* trans. A. Lingis (Pittsburgh: Duquesne University Press, 1969), p. 41; *Totalité et Infini: Essai sur l'extériorité* (The Hague: Martinus Nijhoff, 1980), p. 12.

14. In order to avoid confusion, I use Levinas's term "alterity" rather than my variation of this word, "altarity," throughout the analysis of his argument.

cessive [dé-mesuré], [of what] does not enter into the present, and inverts the *arche* into anarchy" (*OB*, 117; 149).[15] Such anarchy is what the philosopher dreads. In searching for first principles, the master of philosophy attempts to repress anarchy by returning to the *arche* that founds and grounds everything. The enigmatic trace drives the philosopher mad by "throw[ing] 'a grain of folly' [*grain de folie*] into the universal ego" (*OB*, 91; 117). This excessive grain is the "infinitesimal difference" (*différence infinitésimale*)[16] that renders the aspirations of philosophy laughable (*OB*, 91; 116). For Levinas, the philosopher would be comic were not the holocaust to which his will to power sentences everything different from and other than himself so tragic.

Before Sentencing: Betrayal of Saying

Many questions were troubling the explorer, but at the sight of the prisoner he asked only: "Does he know his sentence?" "No," said the officer, eager to go on with his exposition, but the explorer interrupted him: "He doesn't know the sentence that has been passed on him?" "No," said the officer, again pausing a moment as if to let the explorer elaborate his question, and then said: "There would be no point in telling him. He'll learn it on his body."[17]

The penal eye of the philosopher constructs a penal colony in which all non-conformity is sentenced. The words of the philosopher are never "idle" (*désoeuvré*) chatter but always work through the labor of the negative. This work transforms knowledge into power, which is capable of inflicting violence. Philosophical sentences are judgments. Judgment, which works by subjecting the particular to the universal, has as its goal the establishment and maintenance of law and order. Before and/or apart from judgment, there is, as Foucault suggests, anarchy—theoretical as well as practical, intellectual as well as social.

15. In another context, Levinas writes: "The Infinite cannot be tracked down [*être suivi à la trace*] like game by a hunter. The trace left by the Infinite is not the residue [*résidu*] of a presence; its very glow is ambiguous" (*OB*, 12; 15).

16. In the infinite-simal, the Infinite, usually regarded as excessively grand, becomes in-calculably minute. Whether great or small, the Infinite escapes all human calculation—especially the calculations of (self)-interested speculators.

17. Franz Kafka, "In the Penal Colony," *Penal Colony: Stories and Short Pieces,* trans. W. and E. Muir (New York: Schocken, 1961), p. 197. For a discussion of the role the penal colony plays in Genet's writings, see *Glas,* pp. 49–50. Blanchot's essays on Kafka are collected in *De Kafka à Kafka* (Paris: Gallimard, 1981).

The most tenacious subjection of difference is undoubtedly that maintained by categories. By showing the number of different ways in which being can express itself, by specifying its forms of attribution, by imposing in a certain way the distribution of existing things, categories create a condition where being maintains its undifferentiated repose at the highest level. Categories organize the play of affirmations and negations, establish the legitimacy of resemblances within representation, and guarantee the objectivity and operation of concepts. They suppress the anarchy of difference, divide differences into zones, delimit their rights, and prescribe their task of specification with respect to individual beings. On one side, they can be understood as the a priori forms of knowledge, but, on the other, they appear as an archaic morality, the ancient decalogue that the identical imposed upon difference. Difference can only be liberated through the intervention of acategorical thought.[18]

The distinction between categorical and acategorical thought appears in Levinas's writings as the difference between "the said" (*le dit*) and "saying" (*le dire*). By thinking this difference, Levinas attempts to release "the anarchy of difference." The said is "always already said." In a manner similar to Saussure's *langue* and Lacan's symbolic order, the said designates the structured totality of language which, existing prior to and independent of any particular subject, guides all rational thought.[19] This complex linguistic structure functions to reduce the unknown to the known. Such a reduction incorporates or assimilates difference and excludes novelty. "Language qua said," Levinas explains, "can be conceived as a system of nouns identifying entities, and then as a system of signs doubling the beings, designating substances, events and relations by substantives or other parts of speech derived from substantives, designating identities—in sum, *designating*" (*OB*, 41; 51).

In its capacity as the said, language plays the role that Western ontotheology traditionally assigns the Logos. Heidegger points out that "the word *Ho Logos* names that which gathers all present beings into presencing and lets them lie before us in it. *Ho Logos* names that in which the presencing of what is present comes to pass" (*EGT*, 76; 227). For Levinas, the "presencing of what is present comes to pass"

18. Foucault, *Language, Counter-Memory, Practice*, p. 186.
19. Although Levinas is aware of, and sensitive to, the psychological, social, and cultural dimensions of language, he does not analyze them in any detail. His primary concern is to situate his account of language in relation to the philosophical tradition and, less obviously but no less importantly, to certain strands in Jewish and Christian theology.

through the logical process of de-sign-ating. To designate is to nominate or name what is or becomes present. Within the said, what *is* "can be conceived as a *system* of nouns identifying entities." *Le dit,* in other words, is a *systematic* structural totality that is the condition of the possibility of presentation. Recalling the Greek Logos, Levinas writes: "Whatever be the abyss that separates the psyche of the ancients from the consciousness of the moderns, both belong to a tradition in which intelligibility derives from the assembling of terms united in a system for a locutor who states an apophansis—which is the concrete situation of the assembling into a system. Here the subject is origin, initiative, freedom, present. To move oneself or to have self-consciousness is, in effect, to refer oneself to oneself, to be an origin" (*OB,* 78; 98). This account of the said reflects the influence of both Saussure's structural linguistics and Hegel's speculative logic. "Clarity," Levinas argues, "comes from a certain arrangement that orders the entities or the moments and the *esse ipsum* of these entities into a system, assembling them" (*OB,* 133; 170). The law of this order is the law of identity. From a structural as well as a speculative point of view, identity is established and maintained by relation to difference. Language as a whole is diacritical. The specific identity of every term is the result of its differentiation from terms other than itself. "In a system, signification is due to the definition of terms by one another in the synchrony of a totality, where the whole is the finality of the elements. It is due to the system of the language on the verge of being spoken. It is in this situation that universal synchrony is effected. In the said, to have a meaning is for an element to be in such a way as to turn into references to other elements, and for the others to be evoked by it" (*OB,* 69; 87).

Language synchronizes through judgment, and judgment is passed in the sentence. On the most basic level, judgment joins two terms by means of the copula: A is B. This judgment declares the identity of differences. In the "is," the difference between A and B is reduced to an identity. This identification synchronizes A and B by rendering each *present* to the other. The sentence establishes "an identity in the discursiveness of the this [i.e., A] and the that [i.e., B], the this as that, which insures being's presence to itself" (*OB,* 63; 79). The judgment that presents (i.e., 'presents and pre'sents) being to itself by identifying differences is the rational judgment. "Reason is sought in the relationship between terms, between the *one* and the *other* showing themselves in a *theme.* Reason consists in insuring the *co-existence* of these terms, the *coherence* of the one and the other, *despite their difference, in the unity of a theme;* it insures the accord of the different terms [*différents*] without breaking up [*éclater*] the present in which the theme is held. This *coexistence* or *accord* between the different terms *in the unity of a theme is* called a system" (*OB*, 165; 211).

The rational identification of differences in the systematic theme is not merely intralinguistic. As "a system of signs doubling beings," the said is purported to dispel duplicity by perfectly mirroring that which is. Language *represents* reality. Within ontotheology, thought and being are *said* to be one. The structure of language reflects the Logos of being. For reflection to be completely transparent, it must be total. Through its synchronization, the said totalizes differences. This process of totalization is most fully realized in science. "A science," Levinas maintains, "would be able to totalize being at all levels of its *esse* by fixing the ontological structures that articulate being" (*OB*, 134–35; 171). This perfect union of thought and being is consummated when the Logos of Greek philosophy unites with the Logos of Christian theology to form a *Wissenschaft* in which philosopy is scientific and science is philosophical.

Scientific reason is not, however, restricted to the labor-atory and library. Levinas agrees with Heidegger's claim that in the modern world, knowledge becomes power through technology and its extension in the authoritarian state. When reason becomes all-powerful, the world actually becomes a penal colony. In its declarative sentence, the said declares war on every difference that does not conform to identity and every other that does not return to the same. "The face of being that shows itself in war is fixed in the concept of totality, which dominates Western philosophy. Individuals are reduced to being bearers of forces that command them unbeknown to themselves. The meaning of individuals (invisible outside of this totality) is derived from the totality. The unicity [*unicité*] of each present is incessantly sacrificed to a future appealed to in order to bring forth its objective meaning. For the ultimate meaning alone counts; the last act alone changes beings into themselves."[20] Within the bounds of the (always already) said, this last act has (always already) occurred. Since the *Parousia* has arrived, the Logos is completely revealed and thus totally present. By disclosing what is implicitly present in the beginning, the end assembles what appear to be dispersed temporal moments into a coherent narrative. In this narrative structure, only the present truly is: the past is a past present, and the future a future present. *Sub specie aeternitatis* the three modalities of the present, like the God whose

20. Levinas, *Totality and Infinity*, pp. 21–22; x.

presence they represent, are One. The narrative of the Logos forms what Merleau-Ponty calls "the prose of the world." The Western ontotheological tradition culminates in the reading of this prosaic narrative.

For Levinas, however, the Logos that names and can be named is not original but is secondary to a pre-original anarchy that remains unnameable but not unsayable. This *an-archie* is the fore-word and the pre-text, which by fissuring *le dit,* keeps thinking open.

> Thinking's saying would be stilled in
> its being only by becoming unable
> to say that which must remain unspoken.
>
> Such inability would bring thinking
> face to face with its matter.
>
> What is spoken is never, and in no
> language, what is said.
>
> That a thinking is, ever and suddenly—
> whose amazement could fathom it? (*PLT,* 11).

"What is spoken is never . . . what is said." Conversely, what is said is never what is spoken. *Le dit* is not *le dire.*

Levinas maintains that "the said and the non-said do not absorb all saying, which remains on this side of [*en deçà*], or goes beyond [*au-delà*] the said" (*OB,* 23; 29). Levinas's *dire* recalls Heidegger's *sagen,* which, "in the preparation of the sayable simultaneously brings the unsayable as such into the world" (*PLT,* 74). From Levinas's point of view, saying can say what remains unspoken in the said only through a preoriginal saying, which is before sentencing. Such "saying is not a game. Anterior to the verbal signs it conjugates, to the linguistic systems and the semantic glimmerings, a preface or foreword [*avant-propos*] preceding languages, it is the proximity of the one to the other [*proximité de l'un à l'autre*], the commitment of an approach, the one for the other, the very signifyingness of signification" (*OB,* 5; 6). I have stressed that the preface or foreword to language (i.e., to the Logos as the said) is the anarchy that the said excludes or represses in the very act of constituting itself. By saying the "deep formerly" of an "unrepresentable before," *le dire* says "the temporalization of time" that signifies "the *beyond of being* and of *not being*" (*OB,* 9; 11). In contrast to the time of the said, the temporalization of saying cannot be assembled in the present. Saying says only in and through its own disappearance. The "appearance" of this disappearance interrupts the present, thereby dislocating the presence of the said.

Levinas labels this "unsaying [*dédire;* compare, *délire*] of the said" *la déthématisation du Dit* (*OB,* 47; 60). Insofar as the said is a systematic totality in which all parts are integrated, it functions to assemble thought and being into a rational construction that is defined by a comprehensive and comprehensible theme. Thematization is, in effect, a rationalization in which spatio-temporal dispersion is synchronically organized. As such, thematization rests upon the assumption that all diachrony can be synchronized. Levinas is convinced that this presupposition is faulty. Since the rational integrity of the theme is constituted by excluding a preoriginal *an-arche,* thematization is forever secondary to and dependent upon something it can never incorporate. Saying dethematizes by recalling this unassimilable remainder.

Dethematization is undeniably paradoxical. The unsaying of the said can take place only through the said itself. While the said presupposes saying, saying is impossible apart from the said. Like Kristeva's "desemantization," Levinas's dethematization requires the very language it calls into question. Saying is nothing other than the destructuring (which *is not* the destruction) of rational discourse. This disarticulation is inseparable from the process of articulation. "Language," Levinas maintains, "permits us to say—be it by betrayal [*le trahissant*]—this *outside of being* [dehors de l'être], this *ex-ception* to being [ex-ception *à l'être*], as though being's other [*l'autre de l'être*] were an event in being" (*OB,* 6; 7). Inasmuch as *le dire* is always *un dédire,* saying betrays *itself* by unsaying the said.

"Betrayal" is a complex word with many nuances. To betray is to prove false, to be disloyal, or faithless—as when a man betrays a woman, or a woman a man. Such betrayal usually involves deceit in which one seduces another by leading him or her astray—into error. "Betray" can also mean "to disclose, reveal, or show." Since betrayal is deceitful, the disclosure it effects always involves a certain duplicity, which is a "breach of faith." As duplicitous, the betrayal of saying is twofold. By saying itself in and through the said, *le dire* is inevitably false, disloyal, and faithless. Saying *errs* in the said. The betrayal of such erring is, nonetheless, a disclosure of what cannot be said. "The said, contesting the abdication of the saying that everywhere occurs, in this said, thus maintains the diachrony in which, holding its breath [*le souffle retenu*], the spirit hears the echo of the *otherwise.* The hither side, the preliminary, which the pre-originary saying animates, refuses the present and manifestation, or lends itself to them only out of time. The unsayable saying lends itself to the said, to the ancillary indiscretion of the abusive language that divulges or profanes the unsayable. But it lets itself be reduced without effacing the unsaying in the ambiguity or the enigma of the transcendent, in which the breathless spirit [*l'esprit essoufflé*] retains a fading echo [*un écho qui s'éloigne*]" (*OB*, 44; 57).

The duplicity of saying is inseparable from its abuse *of* and *by* the said. Like the cleavage of Heideggger's *Riss* and the fault of Lacan's unconscious, saying unveils through reveilation. This slippery disclosure, which is a concealment, and concealment, which is a disclosure, marks "an irreparable cleavage [*un clivage irréparable*]" in the Logos of language qua said (*OB*, 70; 88). Since this gap can never be closed, knowledge is always incomplete. As a result of this incompletion, the truth and certainty for which philosophers always search and sometimes claim to find can never become present. In the absence of truth, skepticism is unavoidable. "Skepticism, at the dawn of philosophy, translated and betrayed the diachrony of this very translation and betrayal [*traduction et trahison*] To conceive the *otherwise than being* requires, perhaps, as much audacity as skepticism shows, when it does not hesitate to affirm the impossibility of statement [*énoncé*] while venturing to *realize* this impossibility by the very statement of this impossibility. If, after the innumerable 'irrefutable' refutations that logical thought sets against it, skepticism has the gall to return . . . , it is because in the contradiction that logic sees in it, the 'at the same time' of the contradictories is missing, because a secret diachrony commands this ambiguous or enigmatic way of speaking, and because in general signification signifies beyond synchrony, beyond essence" (*OB*, 7; 9).

By signifying beyond synchrony, beyond essence, saying signifies signification itself. Levinas distinguishes signification from representation. While the concepts that spell out the said are constructed to de-sign-ate by re-present-ing a past that once was present, "saying signifies otherwise than as an usher presenting essence and beings." Saying "signifies before *essence*, before identification" (*OB*, 46, 45; 59, 58). Since this "before" is a diachrony that cannot be erased, that which saying signifies is always a substitute for something that is not present. The structure of signification entails substitution in which one is never simply itself but is *always* "one-for-the-other." Instead of synchronizing diachrony, saying undoes the said by repeating the eternal return of a before that is never a now.

In Levinas's errant dis-course, saying has radical consequences. In saying, the sayer becomes a sign of something that cannot be represented. "The subject of saying," Levinas explains, "does not give signs, it or he becomes a sign" (OB, 49; 63). In becoming a sign, the subject loses its self-identity. "Signification is the-one-for-the-other of an identity that does not coincide with itself. This is, in fact, all the gravity of an animate body, that is, one offered to another, expressed, or opened up [s'épancher: to be discharged, poured out, to overflow]! This opening up, like a reverse conatus, an inversion of essence, is a relationship across an absolute difference. It is not reducible to any synchronic and reciprocal relationship that a totalizing and systematic thought would seek in it, the thought concerned with understanding the 'unity of the soul and the body.' Neither is it a structure, nor an inwardness of a content in a container, nor a causality, nor even a dynamism, which still extends in a time that could be collected into a history" (OB, 70; 89). Signification opens one (as well as the One) to an Other, which, though never present, is not absent. This "exposure" to the Other establishes a "communication" that cannot be understood in terms of sending and receiving messages. "Saying," Levinas insists, "is communication, to be sure, but as a condition for all communication, as exposition. Communication is not reducible to the phenomenon of truth and the manifestation of truth conceived as a combination of psychological elements: thought in an ego—will or intention to make this thought pass into another ego—message by a sign designating this thought-perception of the sign by another ego—deciphering of the sign. The elements of this mosaic [mosaique] are already in place in the preliminary exposition of the ego to the other, the non-indifference to the Other, which is not a simple 'intention to address a message'" (OB, 48, 61–62).

The Mosaic in which one is not indifferent to the Other is inscribed in a fore-word that is prior to and other than the Logos. The saying that is before sentencing is the discourse of the Other—a wholly Other that is infinitely and qualitatively different from anything that can be expressed by or contained in the said. This alternative discourse communicates by holding open the openness of communicating subjects. For Levinas, as for Bataille, to communicate is to lose rather than find oneself. "But communication would be impossible if it should have to begin in the ego, a free subject, to whom every other would be only a limitation inviting war, domination, precaution, and information. To communicate is indeed to open oneself, but the openness is not complete if it is on the watch for recognition. . . . Communication is an adventure of a subjectivity, different from that which is dominated by the concern to recover itself [se retrouver], different from that of coinciding in consciousness; it will involve uncertainty" (OB, 119; 153–54; 120; 154). Such communication is never reassuring but always painful. In becoming open, "one is exposed to the Other as a skin is exposed to that which wounds it, as a cheek is offered to that which smites it" (*OB*, 49; 63). This wound traumatizes the subject.

Exille: Trauma of Subjectivity

The history of Western philosophy has not been the refutation of skepticism as much as the refutation of transcendence. The logos said [*dit*] has the last word dominating all meaning, the word of the end, the very possibility of the ultimate and the result. Nothing can interrupt it. Every contestation and interruption of this power of discourse is at once related and invested by discourse. It thus recommences as soon as one interrupts it (*OB*, 169; 214–15).

The struggle to refute transcendence in all its guises culminates in the philosophy of the constructive subject developed by Hegel and elaborated by Husserl. Levinas describes this subject as "the imperial ego." Throughout his writings, one of Levinas's chief concerns is to "strip the ego of its pride and the dominating imperialism characteristic of it" (*OB*, 110; 140).

The constructive subject exercises its imperial power through the "hegemony of representation." Representation—be it philosophical, religious, artistic, or political—presupposes the ego's intentional activity. "What is realized in and by intentional consciousness offers itself to protention and diverges from itself in retention, so as to be, across the fault, identified and possessed. This play in being is consciousness itself: presence to self through a difference, which is both loss of self and recovery in truth. The *for itself* in consciousness is thus the very power that a being exercises upon itself, its will, its sovereignty. A being is equal to itself and possesses itself in this form; domination is in consciousness as such. Hegel thought that the *I* is but consciousness mastering itself in equality to itself, in what he calls 'the freedom of this infinite equality'" (*OB*, 102; 129). The mastery of self-consciousness requires the domination of otherness within and without. By achieving mastery, the subject becomes the absolute origin, i.e., the center around which the world seems to revolve. As Merleau–Ponty points out, two rhythms characterize the life of the subject: centrifugal and centripetal. The subject diverges from itself through intentional acts in which it constructs a world and returns to itself by comprehending its own constructions. The *telos* of this circuit is the presence of the self to itself in absolute knowledge. Since the philosopher's penal eye is supposed to be all-seeing, his imperial ego claims to be all-knowing.

Assertions to the contrary notwithstanding, there are at least two things the subject never sees, or never sees directly: his face and his backside.[21] Bodily orifices like eyes, ears, nostrils, mouth, and anus elude the specular gaze. Nor can the thetic subject "see" itself constituting itself in acts intended to establish its identity by repressing everything that defiles the body proper. Following Merleau–Ponty, Levinas argues that the subject can never grasp its own act of grasping. In the very effort to know itself, the subject repeatedly encounters something that is ungraspable. By relating itself to itself, the subject does not discover total self-presence but returns "to the hither side of the present in which every identity identified in the said is constituted. It is constituted here and now when the act of constitution first originates" (OB, 109; 133). In criticizing Hegel's notion of the subject, Levinas implicitly aligns himself with Kierkegaard's critique of Hegelian philosophy. The self, Levinas insists, does not constitute itself. Since the subject is not autonomous, the self's relationship to itself necessarily entails its relation to an Other. The return to and of this Other is the eternal recurrence of the alterity that decenters the auto-affective subject. "This recurrence [is] the ultimate secret of the incarnation of the subject; prior to all reflection, all apperception, this side of every positing, an indebtedness *before any borrowing,* not assumed, anarchic, subjectivity of a bottomless passivity, made out of assignation, like the echo of a sound that would precede the resonance of this sound. The active source of this passivity is not thematizable. It is a passivity of a trauma, but one that prevents its own representation, a deafening trauma, cutting the thread of consciousness that should have welcomed it in its present, the passivity of being persecuted" (OB, 111; 141).

To suggest the nonthematizable source of the subject, Levinas uses the term *ille,* which is both a Latin word and includes the *third* person *singular, il.*[22] "Illeity" links up with "Other," "Infinite," and "Alterity" to form a metonymic chain of signifiers intended to evoke what cannot be designated. In Levinas's deconstruction of the constructive subject, *ille functions* like Heidegger's *Es* (in *Es gibt*)[23] and

21. Levinas's analysis of the face extends Bataille's analysis of the gaping body.

22. It will become apparent that both the thirdness and the singularity of *ille* play a central role in Levinas's argument.

23. Levinas translates Heidegger's *Es gibt* as *Il y a.* See "*Il y a,*" *Deucalion* 1 (1946): 141–54.

Bataille's *ELLE*. "*Ille*," Levinas claims, "indicates a way of concerning me without entering into *conjunction* with me" (*OB*, 12; 15). Never joining the subject, *illeity* is irreducibly "nonphenomenal" and thus escapes every phenomenology. Neither present nor absent, *ille* is the "pure trace of a 'wandering cause,' inscribed in me" (*pure trace de 'cause errante,' en moi inscrit; OB*, 150; 192). Levinas's "errant cause" recalls Lacan's "lost cause" and anticipates the "nonoriginal origin" of Derrida's trace. In his richly suggestive essay, "The Trace of the Other," Levinas describes the trace as "a presence of that which properly speaking has never been there, of what is always past" (*TA*, 357). The trace marks the lapse of time by remarking the way in which the pre-original *anarchie* comes toward the subject as a departure. Never arriving or arriving only as departing, the trace opens everything but is not itself disclosed. "A graphologist, an expert in writing styles, or a psycholanalyst could interpret a trace's singular signifyingness, and seek in it the sealed and unconscious, but real, intentions of him who delivered the message. But then what remains in the specific sense a trace in the writing and style of the letter does not signal any of these intentions, any of these qualities, reveals and hides nothing. In a trace has passed an absolutely bygone past. In a trace its irreversible lapse is sealed. Disclosure [*dévoilement*], which reinstates the world and leads back to the world, and is proper to a sign or a signification, is suppressed in traces" (*TA*, 357).

The important similarities between this trace of the Other and contrasting inscriptions of the altarity that escapes binary oppositions should not obscure the significant differences between Levinas and other thinkers we have considered. For Levinas, the trace implies a "non-phenomenality" that is radically "*singular*." Drawing a distinction that strictly parallels Kierkegaard's contrast between *den Enkelt* (the singluar or the solitary) and *Individet* (the individual), Levinas distinguishes singularity from individuality. Following Kierkegaard, he attempts to establish the difference between the singular and the individual by criticizing Hegel's systematic logic in which "individuality" (*Einzelheit*) is the synthesis of "universality" (*Allgemeinheit*) and "particularity" (*Besonderheit*).[24] While the particular assumes intelligibility by incorporation in the universal, the universal becomes concrete through the particular. As the union of particularity and universality, individuality is the embodiment of the Logos, which becomes actual in the judgment of the self-conscious subject. Levinas

24. Hegel presents his most important discussion of this issue in his analysis of "The Syllogism." See: *Logic*, book 2, chapter 2.

joins Kierkegaard in arguing that the aim of such judgment is the repression of transcendent singularity.[25] The philosopher's judgment, however, is always partial. Universal categories cannot express radical singularity and therefore are impotent to repress the anarchy of difference.

Otherwise than being and nonbeing, the unthinkable singularity of *illeity* is "the third" (*le tiers; det Tredie*), which, for Levinas, constitutes the thetic subject that returns to itself, and, for Kierkegaard, posits the self that relates itself to itself.[26] To experience oneself so constituted or posited is to suffer a "traumatizing persecution" over which one has no control. In finding itself always already constituted, the subject is exposed to an exteriority that can never be interiorized. The radical ex-teriority of *il-leity* ex-il-es the self from itself.

> To revert to oneself is not to settle oneself at home [*s'installer chez soi*], even if stripped of all one's acquisitions. It is to be like a stranger, hunted down even in one's home, contested in one's own identity and one's very poverty, which, like a skin still enclosing the self, would establish it in an inwardness, already settled on itself, already a substance. It is always to empty oneself anew of oneself, to absolve oneself, like in a hemophiliac's hemorrhage. It is to be on the hither side of one's own nuclear unity, still identifiable and protected; it is to be emptied even of the quasi-formal identity of being *someone*. (*OB*, 92; 117)

Paradoxically, the poverty of the wandering exile discloses the richness of the errant subject.

The subject, which is never *chez soi*, does not coincide with itself but is forever uprooted and decentered by an Other. "This being torn up from oneself in the bosom [*au sein*] of one's unity, this absolute noncoinciding, this dia-chrony of the instant, signifies in the guise of one-penetrated-by-the-other" (*OB*, 49; 64). "*L'un-pénétré-par-l'autre*," Levinas argues, exposes the structure of "subjectivity as *the other in the same* [l'autre dans le même]" (*OB*, 111; 141). The constitutive activity of the intentional subject cannot return this other to the sameness of itself. The self is always passive *before* active, patient *before* agent. The passivity of the subject lies even deeper than the passivity that is the polar opposite of activity. This unsurpassable passivity is the "hetero-affection" (*l'hétéro-affection*) of the Infinite, which interrupts the "auto-affection" (*l'auto-affection*) of the subject (*OB*, 121;

25. The issue of singularity and its repression is central to the analysis of the self as well as the Other. I will consider the singularity of the subject in the next section.
26. This third recalls the "thirdness" of Lacan's discourse of the Other.

155). Hetero-affection leads to the "defection or the defeat [*défection ou défait; défaire:* to undo, unmake] of the identity of the ego" (*OB*, 15; 19). The un-doing of the ego is brought about by what Levinas describes as "good violence" (*bonne violence;* 43; 56). As a result of this violence, the subject is always a *sub-jectum,* i.e., is always "thrown under" by an Other more powerful than itself.[27] Levinas believes that the subjection of the subject implies an antihumanism more radical than that developed by latter-day critics of the modern philosophy of the subject. "Modern antihumanism, which denies the primacy that the human person (free and for itself) would have for the signification of being, is true over and beyond the reasons it gives itself. It clears the place for subjectivity positing itself in abnegation, in sacrifice, in a substitution that precedes the will. The genius of its intuition is to have abandoned the idea of person, goal, and origin of itself, in which the ego is still a thing because it is still a being. . . . Humanism has to be denounced only because it is not sufficiently human" (*OB*, 127–28; 164).

While the heteronomy that afflicts the purportedly autonomous subject cannot be known, it can be experienced sensibly. Levinas concurs with Merleau-Ponty's contention that nonthetic awareness arises from bodily perception. We are exposed to alterity, Levinas argues, through carnal experience. "Incarnation is not a transcendental operation of a subject that is situated in the midst of the world it represents to itself; the sensible experience of the body is already and from the start incarnate. The sensible . . . ties the knot of incarnation in a liaison [*intrigue*] larger than the apperception of the self" (*OB*, 76; 96). Like the chiasmus of Merleau-Ponty's flesh and the tangle of Lacan's Borromean knots, Levinas's "Gordian knot" is the "denouement of being" (*OB*, 77; 97). The knotted body opens the subject to two distinguishable dimensions of sensibility. On a superficial level, bodily perception entails the reception of the givens that constitute the "data" of all knowledge. The cognitive *activity* of the subject presupposes a *passivity* in which pre-posited data are received. Levinas believes that in addition to this passivity, the sub-ject suffers a more

27. By way of anticipation, it is helpful to register Blanchot's question: "Levinas speaks of the subjectivity of the subject; if one wishes to preserve this word—why?— it would perhaps be necessary to speak of a subjectivity without a subject, the wounded place, the bruise of the dying body already dead of which nobody would know how to be proprietor, nor to say 'me,' my body, that which rouses the only mortal desire, the desire that passes through dying without surpassing itself." "Discourse sur la patience (*en marge des livres d'Emmanuel Levinas*)," *Le Nouveau commerce* 30–31 (1975): 42.

profound "patience" (*patiens*, from *pati:* to suffer). Prior to its passivity and activity, the self is indebted to and dependent upon *das ganz Andere*. Rather than providing the "stuff" with which the reasonable subject works, this level of sensibility opens one to a "non-conceptualizable" Other. The "locus" of this Other is "matter" (*la matière*). In a remark that recalls Lacan's description of the real, Levinas claims that matter is "the way signification signifies before showing itself as a said in the system of synchronism, the linguistic system" (*OB*, 77; 97). Matter, in other words, resists assimilation by the ideal linguistic structure·labeled alternatively "the said" or "the Name-of-the-Father." When understood in this way, matter is indissociable from *mater*. "The-one-for-the-other has the form of sensibility or vulnerability, pure passivity, susceptibility, passive to the point of becoming an inspiration, that is, alterity in the same. . . . Here the psyche is the maternal body [*corps maternel*]" (*OB*, 67; 85). The maternal body opens the subject to a materialism that is at once the condition of the possibility and the impossibility of idealism. Levinas points out that "sensation is the source of idealism and at the same time that which cuts off [*tranche*] idealism" (*OB*, 63; 79). In idealism, the subject attempts to structure experience by positing categories intended to incorporate everything. This constitutional act, however, is always secondary to the reception of antecedent data. The maternal psyche cuts off the advances of the paternal ego by repeatedly returning repressed data. This cut renders the philosopher impotent.

It is clear that for Levinas, the psyche exceeds consciousness. The excess that consciousness never contains "inspires" (*inspirer: in +spirare*, to breathe) the subject by breathing into it an Other that cannot be identified.[28] As "the host" bearing the seed of an Other that forever remains strange, the psyche *m-others* the subject.[29] In its "total vulnerability" and "pure submission, " the psyche is "the bearer par excellence." Levinas defines this *porteur* as "maternity, gestation of the other in the same" (*OB*, 75; 95). By bearing/barring an "outside" that is "inside," the maternal body exposes "the dehiscence" (*la déhiscence*) of the subject (*OB*, 84; 106). Contrary to expectation, this dissemination of identity constitutes the "ipseity" (*ipséité*) of the self (*OB*, 127; 163).

28. Compare Derrida's discussion of "La parole soufflée" in *WD*, 169–95; 253–92.

29. "In the subject, it is precisely not an assembling, but an incessant alienation of the ego (isolated as inwardness) by the guest [*l'hôte*] entrusted to it. Hospitality, the-one-for-the-other in the ego, delivers it more passively than any passivity from links in a causal chain" (*OB*, 79; 99).

Illeity, which, I have noted, is irreducibly singular, posits the subject as absolutely singular. The "singularity" (*singularité*) of the subject is a "uniqueness without identity" (*unicité sans identité; OB,* 57; 73). Since this nonidentical singularity cannot be comprehended through the universal structures of *le dit,* it is unknowable. While conceptual judgment sentences particularity to incorporation in universality, *illeity* passes a judgment that elects the singular subject in its unspeakable uniqueness. For Levinas, as for Kierkegaard, the self's unique singularity is a function of election and suffering rather than choice and action. Having taken place "before" the beginning of the subject, election by the Other establishes a debt that can never be repaid. As a result of this incomprehensible debt, the sub-ject is the hostage of an Other it can never know.[30] "The self," Levinas concludes, "is from top to bottom a hostage, more ancient than the ego, before principles. Beyond egoism and altruism, it is the religiosity of the self" (*OB,* 117; 150).

Tracing Facing: Obsessive Murmuring

A MAN CAN BE A SIGN.

From measurable and from uncharted distances, another's alien existence can concern us, can contest us. What suffers in him can seem to us the cipher of an order that commands us. Yet one can use the other—the dreamer, those that live in the Easts, those without personality, suppliers of raw material for the West and raw materials themselves—for entertainment, for instruction, for enrichment, for the exercise of one's sovereignty. Western sovereignty, sovereignty of reason.[31]

Facing and defacing: What lies in a face? What truth in a face? What does the face betray? What does the face "say"—even, perhaps only, when it "says" nothing? Why is the face always the face of an other and not my own? It is possible to face the face—without defacing it?

For Levinas, "a face is a trace" (*OB,* 91; 116). "A trace lost in a trace, less than nothing in the trace of an excessive [*un excessif*], but

---

30. Elsewhere Levinas writes: "Subjectivity as hostage. This notion reverses the position where the presence of the ego to itself appears as the beginning or as the conclusion of philosophy. This coinciding in the same, where I would be an origin, or, through memory, a recovering of the origin, this presence, is, from the start, undone by *the other*" (*OB,* 127; 163).

31. Lingis, *Excesses: Eros and Culture,* p. 113.

always with ambiguity (trace of itself, possibly a mask, in a void, possibly nothingness or 'pure form of the sensibility'), the face of the neighbor obsesses me with this destitution. 'He is looking at me—everything in him looks at me; nothing is indifferent to me. Nothing is more imperative than this abandon in the void of space, this trace of the infinity that *passes* without being able to enter. In it is hollowed out the face as a trace of an absence, as a skin with wrinkles" (*OB*, 93; 118). The wrinkles lining the face are the hieroglyphs of an *an-archie* older than time itself. The inscribed body is the incised body—cut, wounded, torn by an Other whose *coup* is a *coup de grâce*. "The tenderness of the skin is the very gap [*décalage*] between approach and approached, a disparity, a non-intentionality, a non-teleology" (*OB*, 90; 114). This tender, wrinkled skin both draws together and holds apart—like a hymen that is sometimes called an altar. To worship at this altar is to bear witness to unnameable alterity.

The face that the I/eye encounters is always the face of an other. The other I face is the neighbor. The "style of the neighbor," Levinas insists, "is the face" (*OB*, 88; 112) As *le prochain*, the neighbor is "near" (*proche*) but never present, draws nigh without ever arriving. Since the face as such is not present, it "escapes representation; it is the very collapse of phenomenality" (*OB*, 88; 112). In the non-representable and non-phenomenal trace, written on the neighbor's face, "the Infinite comes to pass [*se passe:* happen, pass away, fade, decay,]" (*OB*, 156; 199). The passing of the Infinite issues an order that interrupts consciousness and hence disrupts the ordering structures of reason.

> The presence of a face thus signifies an irrecusable order, a command, which calls a halt to [*arrête*] the availability of consciousness. Consciousness is put into question by a face. The putting into question is not reducible to becoming aware of this being put into question. The absolutely other is not reflected in consciousness. It resists it to the point that even its resistance is not converted into a content of consciousness. The visitation consists in overwhelming the very egoism of the I; a face baffles the intentionality that aims at it. (*TA*, 352–53)

The order that arrests consciousness is "an absolutely heteronomous call," which comes from the "outside" (*dehors; OB*, 53; 68). In this call Levinas hears the saying of the Other that fissures the essence of philosophy.

> Is not essence the very impossibility of anything else, of any revolution that would not be a revolving upon oneself? Every-

thing that pretends to come from elsewhere, even the marvels of which *essence* itself is capable, even the surprising possibilities of renewal by technology[32] and magic, even the perfections of the gods peopling the heights of this world, and their immortality and the immortality they promise mortals—all this does not deaden [*amortit*] the disgusting disturbance of *there is* [il y a] recommencing behind every negation. There is not a break in the business carried on by essence, not a distraction. Only the meaning of the other is irrecusable, and forbids the reclusion and reentry into the shell [*coq-u-ille*] of the self. A voice comes from the other shore. A voice interrupts the saying of the already said. (*OB*, 183; 230)

The *il y a* re-sounding in this voice from *l'autre rive*, echoes Heidegger's *Es gibt*. We have seen that the sending of Being and beings effects a donation, which is a *coup*. The *il y a* of Levinas's *dire*, like the *Es gibt* of Heidegger's *sagen*, inflicts *un coup de don*. There is no necessity attached to this gift; it is contingent—as contingent as the throw of a die, *le coup de dés*. For the autonomous subject, this chancy gift is nothing less than "poison" (*Gift*). The appeal of the Other condemns the subject to whom it is addressed to guilt. Guilt is not secondary to a more original innocence. To the contrary, guilt is a "pre-original" fault. Since the call of the neighbor has always already sounded, "in approaching the other, I am always late for the rendez-vous" (*OB*, 192). The inescapability of this delay does not exonerate the subject from its failure to answer the neighbor's appeal. Innocence is but the dream of a self that is forever fatally flawed.

Though the Infinite, which comes to pass in the face of the neighbor, condemns the subject, it is, nonetheless, "the Good." "The Good," Levinas maintains, "is before being. Diachrony: unbridgeable difference between the Good and me, without simultaneity, unmatched terms. But also a non-indifference in this difference. The Good assigns [*assigne:* cite, summons] the subject, according to a susception [*susception:* taking (of holy orders), reception (of the crown, cross, etc.)] that cannot be assumed, to approach the other, the neighbor" (*OB*, 122–23; 157). In this assignation, responsibility is antecedent to freedom. The subject's responsibility is manifested in its response-ability, i.e., in the self's ability to respond to the call of the Other. The response of the subject assumes two distinguishable (though inseparable) forms, which reflect the two dimensions of the Other to which it responds. On the most rudimentary level, the

32. Recall Heidegger's claims about the relation of speculative philosophy to science and technology. See above, chapter 2, first section.

subject responds to the Other by abandoning its self-possession and accepting itself as constituted or posited by the Infinite. Like Heidegger's waiting and Blanchot's patience, this response is passive rather than active. To acknowledge election by that which is other than the self is, in effect, to "say" something incomprehensible—even to the sayer himself.

> Responsibility goes beyond being. In sincerity, in frankness, in the veracity of this saying, in the uncoveredness of suffering, being is altered [*l'être s'altère*]. But this saying remains, in its activity, a passivity, more passive than all passivity, for it is a sacrifice without reserve, without holding back, and in this it is non-voluntary—the sacrifice of a designated hostage who has not elected himself to be a hostage, but possibly elected by the Good, in an involuntary election not assumed by the elected one. For the Good cannot enter into a present nor be put into a representation. (*OB*, 15; 18–19)

In choosing oneself as always already chosen, the self becomes a sign of and for an Other. Such assignation is the signature of the subject—a signature that can never be de-sign-ated. Being-for-self is always being-for-other. The self's being-for-other issues in the second aspect of responsibility: the response to the approach of the neighbor. "When being-for-other displaces being-for-self, the subject is dispossessed. The passivity of wounds, the 'hemorrhage' of the for-the-other, is the tearing away of the mouthful of bread from the mouth that tastes it in full enjoyment [*en pleine jouissance*].[33] . . . It is an attack made immediately on the plenitude of the complacency in oneself . . . , on life in which signification, the for-the-other is swallowed up [*s'engloutit*], on life living or enjoying life" (*OB*, 74; 92). No longer able to enjoy its own identity, the indigent subject approaches *le prochain* in a "movement without return." Describing his excentric trajectory, Levinas explains: "The heteronomous experience we seek would be an attitude that cannot be converted into a category, and whose movement toward the other is not recuperated in identification, does not return to its point of departure" (*TA*, 348).

In contrast to the utilitarian calculations of the speculator who requires a profitable return on every investment, works undertaken in response to the appeal of the Good must be completely self-less.

---

33. In contrast to Lacan, Bataille, Kristeva, Blanchot, and Derrida, Levinas here associates *jouissance* with the satisfaction that fulfills and completes the subject and not with the experience of loss and incompletion.

Levinas formulates the difference between speculative work and ethical works by recourse to the difference between Greek and Hebraic experience.

> But then we must not conceive of a work as an apparent agitation of a ground that afterwards [*après coup*] remains identical with itself, like an energy which, in all its transformations, remains equal to itself. Nor must we conceive it as a technical operation, which through its much-proclaimed negativity reduces an alien world to a world whose alterity is converted into my idea. Both conceptions continue to affirm being as identical with itself and reduce its fundamental event to thought that is (and this is the uneffaceable lesson of idealism) thought of itself, thought of thought. *A work conceived radically is a movement of the same toward the Other which never returns to the same.* To the myth of Ulysses returning to Ithaca, we wish to oppose the story of Abraham who leaves his fatherland forever for a yet unknown land, and forbids his servant even to bring back his son to the point of departure. (*TA,* 348)

For Levinas, Hegel is a latter-day Ulysses, who, as Kierkegaard explains, tried to avoid the uncanny call of the sirens by "plugging the ears" (*JP,* 416; 1: A 95). The voice that Hegel's System is constructed to muffle is the voice of the Other. This is the Other that approaches Abraham from behind and whispers in his ear.

With the reappearance of Abraham, we return to the altar of sacrifice where the encounter with altarity is enacted. The sacrifice staged on Moriah figures the potlatch of the constructive subject of modern philosophy. In terms borrowed from Bataille, Levinas maintains that those who follow Abraham are called upon to make an "expenditure without return." "A work conceived in its ultimate nature requires a radical generosity of the same who in the work goes toward the Other" (*TA,* 349). The practice of such extraordinary generosity requires the most radical sacrifice of all—the sacrifice of one's very own self. Self-sacrifice presupposes a "dis-interestedness, an 'otherwise than being' that turns into a 'for-the-other,' burning for the other, consuming the bases of any position for oneself and any substantialization that would take form in this consummation, consuming even the ashes of this consummation, in which there would be a risk that everything be reborn again" (*OB,* 50; 65).[34]

34. It is important to recall that Levinas begins his analysis of that which is otherwise than being by contrasting the interest of essence to the disinterest of what is beyond being. His first chapter is entitled "Essence et Désintéressement."

Instead of providing satisfaction, this consummation fuels desire. As opposed to "need" (*besoin*), which "opens upon a world that is for me" desire is "desire of an Other who is Another [*d'un autre qui est Autrui*], neither my enemy (as he is in Hobbes and Hegel) nor my complement (as is still the case in Plato's *Republic,* which is constituted because something would be lacking for the subsistence of each individual)" (*TA,* 350). Since the subject's desire is always the desire *of* an Other, it can never be satisfied. The voice that approaches through the neighbor is the discourse of the Other, which "tears" (*arrache*) the self from itself. This wound that never heals renders desire infinite. Through the infinity of desire, the Infinite itself draws near. The interplay of presence and absence in the desire of the Other marks the proximity of the Infinite as an infinite proximity obsessing the subject.

Like Heidegger's near, which is neither present nor absent, the proximate is nearer than every presence yet more remote than any absence.

> Proximity, suppression of the distance that allows "consciousness of . . . ." opens the distance of a dia-chrony without a *common present,* where difference is the past that cannot be caught up with, an unimaginable future, the non-representable status of the neighbor behind which I am late and obsessed by the neighbor. This difference is my non-indifference to the Other. Proximity is a derangement of the rememberable time. One can call that apocalyptically the break-up [*éclatement*] of time. But it is a matter of an effaced but untameable dia-chrony of non-historical, non-said time, which cannot be synchronized in a present by memory and historiography, where the present is but the trace of an immemorial past. (*OB,* 89; 113)

In contrast to Hegel's *Par-ousia,* in which time and history come to an end in the total presence of absolute knowledge, this apocalyptic explosion of time exposes the impossibility of presence and the fault of knowledge. *L'éclatement apocalyptique* is *l'éclat du rire—le rire apocalyptique,* which is *le rire déchirant.*[35] No words can silence the laugh that shatters the subject. "Proximity is not a state, a repose, but precisely restlessness, non-place, outside of the place of repose. It overwhelms the calm of the non-ubiquity of the being that becomes a repose in a place. No place, then, is ever sufficiently a proximity, like an embrace. Never close enough, proximity does not congeal into a struc-

35. The former term is introduced by Kristeva, the latter by Bataille. See above, chapter 6, fourth section, and chapter 5, third section.

ture" (*OB*, 82; 103). With no place of its own, the subject can never return home; the exile is left to wander and roam. Never Greek . . . ever Jew.

The erring of the finite subject bears witness to the proximity of the Infinite. "No theme, no present, has a capacity for the Infinite. The subject in which the other is in the same, inasmuch as the same is for the other, bears witness [*témoigne*] to it [i.e., the Infinite]. The difference of proximity is absorbed in the measure that proximity becomes close, and by this very absorption is brought out gloriously, and accuses me always more. The same in its bearing as same is more and more extended to the other, to the point of substitution as a hostage. Expiation coincides in the last analysis with the extra-ordinary and dia-chronic reversal of the same into the other, in inspiration and the psyche" (*OB*, 146; 187). The hostage witnesses by betraying the Other it hosts. This betrayal is the saying of that which escapes the said. To say what language leaves unsaid requires "an extra-ordinary word, the only one that neither extinguishes nor absorbs its saying, but which cannot remain a simple word. The word God is an over-whelming [*bouleversant:* upsetting, confusing, staggering] semantic event subduing the subversion worked by *illeity*. The glory of the Infinite shuts itself up in a word and becomes a being. But it already undoes its dwelling and unsays itself without vanishing into nothing-ness" (*OB*, 151; 191). In Hebrew, YHWH, or JHWH, is the "name" of the unnameable. Like the cryptic hieroglyph, the unspeakable Tetragrammaton can never be deciphered or, what amounts to the same thing, is infinitely decipherable. "Language would exceed the limits of what is thought, by suggesting, by allowing to hint at without ever making understandable, an implication of sense distinct from that which comes to signs from the simultaneity of systems or the logical definition of concepts. This possibility is laid bare in the poetic *said* [*le dit poétique*], and the interpretation it calls for *ad infinitum* [*à l'infini*]" (*OB*, 169–70; 215–16). *L'appel à l'Infini:* To venture *ad infinitum* is to approach the un-ending [*in-fini*] murmur of the creative-destructive *il y a*. "The *there is* [il y a] is all the weight that alterity weighs supported by a subjectivity that does not found it. But one must not say that the *there is* results from a 'subjective impression.' In this overflowing of sense by nonsense, the sensibility, the self, is first brought out, in its bottomless passivity, as pure sensible point, a dis-interestedness, or subversion of essence. Behind the anonymous rustling [*bruissement anonyme*] of the *there is* subjectivity reaches pas-sivity without assumption" (*OB*, 164; 209). In the absence of resur-rection, this bottomless passivity is the passivity that passes all understanding. Such impotence is the "de-struction" of the "con-structive" subject. In the words of Blanchot:

> Passivity neither consents nor refuses: neither yes nor no, without will, only it would be suitable for the indefiniteness of the "neuter," unmasterable patience [*patience immaîtrisée*] that endures time without resisting it. The passive condition is a non-condition: it is an unconditional that no protection shelters, no destruction touches, that is outside submission, without initiative—with it, nothing begins. When we hear the word that is always already spoken, the (silent) language of beginning again, then we approach the night without darkness. This is the irreducible—the incompatible, that which is not compatible with humanity (the human *species* [genre]). Human weakness, which even frailty does not disclose, betrays us since we belong, at each instant, to the immemorial past of our death—by virtue of being indestructible because always and infinitely destroyed. The infinity of our destruction, this is the measure of passivity.[36]

To hear the an-archic silence of the Infinite's destructuring murmur is to hear not.

36. Blanchot, "Discours sur la patience," p. 42.

Overleaf: Günter Umberg, untitled. Courtesy of the artist. © Studio Ivan Nemec.

8

Nots

Unemployment of Philosophy

Not: close-cropped; to clip or cut short (hair or a beard; hornless, polled; the ordinary adverb of negation.

Die Not: need, want, distress, misery, exigency, emergency, trouble, urgency, difficulty, peril, danger.

Den not: groove, seine.

Pas: step, footprint, trace, dance, threshold, strait, pass, thread (of a screw), no, not, not any.

Nots (*inter alia*): *Celui qui ne m'accompagnait pas; Faux pas; Le pas au-delà; Pas.* K/Nots . . . of images . . . freely associated.

I met this woman I called Judith: she was not bound to me by a relationship of friendship or enmity, happiness or distress; she was not a disembodied [*désincarné*] instant, she was alive. And yet, as far as I can understand, something happened to her that resembled the story of Abraham. When Abraham came back from the country of Moriah, he was not accompanied by his child but by the image of a ram, and it was with a ram that he had to live from then on. Others saw the son in Isaac, because they did not know what had happened on the mountain, but he saw the ram in his son, because he had made a ram for himself out of his child. A devastating story. I think Judith had gone to the mountain, but freely. No one was freer than she was, no one troubled herself less about powers and was less involved with the justified world. She could have said, "It was a God who wanted it," but for her that amounted to saying, "It was I alone who did it." An order? Desire pierces through all orders. . . . She stared at me from the depths of an extreme past [*passé extrême*], a wild place [*lieu sauvage*], towards an extreme future [*avenir extrême*], a desert place, and because she was not at all contemplative, that look, strangely shameless, was a constant, violent attempt to

219

seize me, a drunken, joyful appeal unconcerned with either possibility or the moment.[1]

Instantly I felt a shock running through all my frame; nothing was to be seen, and nothing was to be heard; but a supernatural hand seemed placed in mine. My arm hung over the counterpane, and the nameless, unimaginable, silent form or phantom, to which the hand belonged, seemed closely seated by my bedside. For what seemed ages piled on ages, I lay there, frozen with the most awful fears, not daring to drag away my hand. . . . I knew not how this consciousness at last glided away from me; but waking in the morning, I shudderingly remembered it all, and for days and weeks and months afterwards I lost myself in confounding attempts to explain the mystery. Nay, to this very hour, I often puzzle myself with it.[2]

He was locked in combat with something inaccessible, foreign, something of which he could say: That does not exist . . . and which nevertheless filled him with terror as he sensed it wandering [errer] about in the region of his solitude. Having stayed up all night and all day with this being, as he tried to rest he was suddenly made aware that an other [autre] had replaced the first, just as inaccessible and just as obscure, and yet different. It was a modulation of that which did not exist, a different mode of being absent, another void in which he was coming to life. Now it was certain, someone was approaching him, standing not nowhere and everywhere, but a few feet away, invisible. . . . He felt ever closer [plus proche] to an ever more monstrous absence that took an infinite time to meet. He felt it closer to him every instant and kept ahead of it by an infinitely small but irreducible splinter of duration. (TO, 27; 37)

Judith . . . Ishmael . . . Thomas

Judith was the wife of Esau, the hairy son of Isaac and Rebecca. Esau's marriage to this "foreign woman" "made life better for Isaac and Rebecca" (Genesis 26:34). "Judith" is also the name of a book, a

1. Maurice Blanchot, *When the Time Comes,* trans. L. Davis (Barrytown, NY: Station Hill Press, 1985), pp. 66–67. *Au moment voulu* (Paris: Gallimard, 1951), pp. 147–50. For another highly influential account of the figure of Judith, see Michel Leiris, *Manhood: A Journey from Childhood into the Fierce Order of Virility,* trans. R. Howard (San Francisco: North Point Press, 1984), esp. chapter 5, "The Head of Holofernes."
2. Melville, *Moby-Dick,* p. 28.

supplementary book, a book of the Apocrypha. This noncanonical book recounts the story of how the beguiling Judith saved the Jews from the Assyrians by deceiving the commander sent by Nebuchadnezzar to subdue those who resisted his rule. Having aroused his passions and encouraged him to drink too much wine, Judith "went to the bed-rail beside Holofernes's head and took down his sword, and stepping close to the bed she grasped his hair. 'Now give me strength, O Lord, God of Israel,' she said; then she struck at his neck twice with all her might, and cut off his head" (Judith 13:6–8). Judith . . . another name for the petrifying Medusa.

Ishmael was the bastard son of Abraham and Hagar, the Egyptian slave of Sarah. God had promised Abraham and Sarah a son, but when they grew old and remained childless, they doubted. Sarah urged Abraham to lie with Hagar so that he might have the son she could not give him. After God fulfilled his promise through the birth of Isaac, Sarah grew fearful that her son would have to share his inheritance with the son of her slave. To protect their family circle, Sarah and Abraham drove Hagar and Ishmael into the wilderness of Beersheba. The descendants of Ishmael were called Ishmaelites, a nomadic people who wandered throughout the desert regions of Northern Arabia. Their place was no place, their destiny, errancy. Ishmael . . . another name for the outcast Ludwig.

Thomas in Aramaic and Hebrew is not a proper name but an epithet meaning "twin" or a double. Thomas the Obscure "is" an obscure double. In the apocryphal "Acts of Thomas," Thomas appears as the twin brother of Jesus. Thomas is also the name of one of the twelve disciples. Saint Thomas is the one who doubts, the one who has to stick his finger in the gaping holes of the body. As a doubting Thomas, Thomas the Obscure opposes the certainty of Descartes's "I think, therefore I am" with the uncertainty of "I think, therefore I am not" (*TO*, 99; 146). There is, of course, a second Saint Thomas who was born 1225 years after Christ—Saint Thomas Aquinas. The thirteenth century was, in Emile Mâle's phrase, "the century of the Encyclopedias." Thomas attempts to overcome his doubt by writing an encyclopedic book—*Summa Theologica,* which, like the Gothic cathedral, perfectly mirrors the reasonable order of the cosmos. "Gothic cathedral and the scholastic *Summa,*" Denis Hollier points out, "are both produced from the same synthetic spirit, they are bound to the same systematic enterprise, to the same ambition to totalize what human knowledge acquires. In effect, the thirteenth century is, in a manner that makes one think of Hegel, lived as an epoch of achieved science, as if the task were simply to put in order an acquisition that could be considered as defined and nearly complete. This aspect of synthetic totalization appears in the term *summa* by which scholasticism defines its epistemological project."[3] Thomas . . . the name of an obscure double of Descartes or Hegel.

In the first chapter of his massive nonbook *L'Entretien infini,* Blanchot brings together Thomas Aquinas and Hegel. "In Western philosophy, the *Summa* of St. Thomas, by its rigorous form—that of a determined logic and a mode of questioning that is in reality a mode of response, carries out philosophy as institution and teaching" (*EI,* 1).[4] Blanchot is convinced that it took nearly six hundred years for philosophers to realize the far-reaching implications of the synthesis Thomas achieved in his *Summa.* "The high times of philosophy, those of critical and idealist philosophy, will confirm the connections that it maintains with the University. Beginning with Kant, the philosopher is chiefly a professor. Hegel, in whom philosophy is reassembled and accomplished, is a man whose occupation is to speak from the height of a chair or pulpit, to compose lectures and to think while submitting to the demands of his magisterial form" (*EI,* 3).[5] When Hegel speaks from his highchair—sometimes a lectern, sometimes a pulpit—his magisterial voice claims "to say it all." The voice that says it all, however, talks in circles. Philosophy is, for Blanchot, the name of the discourse that tries to say it all by talking in perfect circles. "This is the circular requirement. Being deploys itself as movement turning in a circle and this movement goes from the most interior to the most exterior, from undeveloped interiority to exteriorization that alienates it and from this alienation that externalizes it until plenitude is attained and re-interiorized. Movement without end and yet always already accomplished. History is the infinite fulfillment of this move-

3. Hollier, *La prise de la Concorde,* p. 83. Hollier makes this remark in the course of his discussion of Bataille's *Somme athéologique.*

4. Not an integral book, *L'Entretien infini* is a collection of essays written between 1953 and 1965. For reasons that will become clear in what follows, Blanchot does not begin this text with the first chapter but prefaces his beginning with a "Note" and a collection of untitled fragments.

5. A few lines later, Blanchot notes the limitations of this understanding of philosophy and suggests the direction of his own argument by citing two authors so-called "philosophers" tend to overlook: "But there is Kierkegaard? There is Nietzsche?" (*EI,* 3).

ment that is always already accomplished" (*EI*, 19). The circle of philosophy achieves closure in Hegel's System. The completion of the circle makes explicit the implicit identity of *alpha* and *omega, arche* and *telos*. Within this circle, the principle of identity is presupposed. The pre-positing of identity renders discontinuity penultimate and continuity ultimate. Within the circle of philosophers, there is no tear that cannot be wiped away, no tear that cannot be mended. While claiming to be reasonable, the philosopher expresses an incomprehensible *desire*. "Man wants unity: he undeniably establishes separation. That which is other, whether it be an other thing or an other person, man must work to make identical: adequation, identification, as if with mediation, that is to say, the struggle and the work in history, these are the ways in which he wants to reduce everything to the same, but also to give to the same the plenitude of all that he must become at the end. In this case, unity passes through everything, just as truth is the movement of the whole—the affirmation of the whole as the sole truth" (*EI*, 94).

As Bataille points out, if philosophy is to work, there can be neither *désœuvrement* (idleness or unemployment) nor *dés-œuvrement* (something outside work or outside the work). Everyone and everything must work—work properly by working within and for the System. If something does not work, if someone merely plays, if nothing somehow works, the System collapses. When the System truly works, it is productive. Systematic work produces a systematic work, which overcomes everything *désœuvré*. Such a work is an *oeuvre* that is a book. The perfect book is a circular book known as an encyclopedia. *Encyclopedia* is a Latin term borrowed from the Greek, *enkyklios paideia,* which specified the circle of arts and sciences that formed the course of study that Greek youths went through before beginning professional training. Accordingly, encyclopedia means, first, "the circle of learning or a general course" and, second, "a literary work containing extensive information on all branches of knowledge." In an essay entitled "The Time of the Encyclopedias," Blanchot explains: "The circle of learning is the justification of all encyclopedias, all the more rich and the more beautiful because it is more moving and because it can respond to all the complexities of circular figures, so that what one knows and what is finished nonetheless participate in this infinite movement which, even if it were possible to know everything in its entirety, would still assure the eternal renewal of knowledge" (*A*, 62).

This book "begins with the Bible where the logos is inscribed as law" and ends with Hegel's *Encyclopedia of the Philosophical Sciences* (*EI*,

627). Though the encyclopedia served as an ideal for many eighteenth-century thinkers, its realization had to await the work of Hegel. Hegel is highly critical of the unsystematic form of Diderot's *Encyclopedia*. He maintains that the French encyclopedists were bound by a mechanistic view of the world and thus were blind to the rational coherence and necessary connection of all things. True knowledge, for Hegel, is *genuinely* encyclopedic. "The encyclopedia of philosophy," he argues, "must not be confounded with ordinary encyclopedias. An ordinary encyclopedia does not pretend to be more than an aggregation of sciences, regulated by no principle. . . . In such an aggregate, the several branches of knowledge owe their place in the encyclopedia to extrinsic reasons, and their unity is therefore artificial: they are *an exteriority* [*ein Äusserliches*]—a classification [*eine Ordnung*]."[6] A system, which must be internally organized, can be neither incomplete nor unfinished. The *Encyclopedia,* as the word itself implies, must assume the shape of a circle. From Hegel's point of view, "each of the parts of philosophy is a philosophical whole, a circle rounded and complete in itself. In each of these parts, however, the philosophical Idea is found in a particular determination or element. The single circle, because it is a totality in itself, breaks through the limits its elements found and gives rise to a wider sphere. The whole of philosophy resembles a circle of circles."[7] The circle of circles is traced in the *Encyclopedia.* Hegel's all-inclusive book is a perfectly coherent totality that is inwardly differentiated. The Hegelian System consists of three parts: *The Science of Logic, The Philosophy of Nature,* and *The Philosophy of Spirit.* The three divisions of the *Encyclopedia* form an organic whole, which achieves closure by bringing together beginning and end. The structural foundation of the *Encyclopedia* is nothing other than the logos disclosed in logic and embodied in nature and spirit. In his book of books, Hegel works to achieve total presence in the hic et nunc of writing and reading. For this reason, Blanchot suggests that the name Hegel "invites one to think presence as all, and all as presence" (*PA,* 34). In Hegel's *Encyclopedia,* nature and history (i.e., objectivity) come to completion through their rational comprehension by the subject, and subjectivity fulfills itself by seeing its own logos in everything other than itself. Blanchot summarizes the logic of the book:

6. Hegel, *The Logic of Hegel,* trans. W. Wallace (New York: Oxford University Press, 1968), p. 25; 8:61.
7. Ibid., p. 24; 8:60.

. . . the empirical book; the book: condition for all reading and writing; the book: totality or Work [*Œuvre*]. But with increasing refinement and truth, these forms all assume that the book includes knowledge as the presence of something virtually present, and always immediately accessible, if only with the aid of mediations and relays. Something is there, which the book presents in presenting itself and which reading animates, re-establishes, through its animation, in the life of a presence. Something that, on the lowest level, is the presence of a content or of a signified; then, on a higher level, the presence of a form, of a signifier or of an operation; and on a still higher level, is the becoming of a system of relations that is always already there [*toujours déjà là*], if only as a future possibility [*une possibilité à venir*]. The book rolls up time, unrolls time and contains this unrolling as the continuity of a presence in which present, past, and future become actual. (*EI,* 621–22)[8]

The book, however, never satisfies its author—not even the author of the book of books, the *Encyclopedia.* Hegel ends his famous Berlin lectures devoted to the philosophy of religion on a "discordant note" (*Misston*). Having worked so hard to complete his System, he finally is forced to admit that the reconciliation his book describes "is merely a partial one, without outward universality. Philosophy forms in this connection a separate sanctuary, and those who serve in it constitute an isolated order of priests, who must not mix with the world, and thus guard the possession of truth. How the temporal, empirical present [*zeitliche, empirische Gegenwart*] is to find its way out of this discord [*Zwiespalt*], and what form it is to take, are questions that must be left to itself to settle" (LPR, 3:150–51; 17:343–44). If inwardness and outwardness are not reconciled, subjectivity and ob-jectivity remain sundered, thereby rendering knowledge incomplete. In "the temporal, empirical present," absolute knowledge is not present and the knowledge present here and now is not absolute. "Knowledge, becoming absolute," Blanchot contends, "reverses it-self in nonknowledge" (*EI,* 405). The last chapter of the book is, therefore, the denouement instead of the fulfillment of Western phi-losophy. This unraveling exposes "the absence of the book." Rather than joining *telos* and *arche* to form the closed circle of knowledge, the absence of the end discloses the absence of the beginning. "The ab-sence of the book" is the "non-absent absence" that the book is

8. Maurice Blanchot, "The Absence of the Book," *The Gaze of Orpheus,* trans. L. Davis (Barrytown, NY: Station Hill Press, 1981), p. 146.

225

supposed to erase. "An emptiness, a void in the universe: nothing that was visible, nothing that was invisible. I suppose the first reader foundered in this non-absent absence, but without knowing anything about it, and there was no second reader because reading, from then on understood as the vision of an immediately visible—that is, intelligible—presence, was affirmed in order to make this disappearance into *the absence of the book* impossible" (*EI*, 620–21).[9] For Blanchot, the book fails, always fails. A non-absent absence, which *is not* a presence, eternally returns to interrupt the author and tear to pieces the pages of his book. This strange absence is the *toujours déjà* whose repetition before the beginning and after the end makes writing unavoidably secondary and necessarily incomplete.

The problem of the book is the problem of beginning (and, to delay for a moment, the problem of ending). The notion of the book, Blanchot insists, implies completion. The book, in other words, constitutes a systematic totality or totalistic system. When so understood, it is not clear whether the book can ever begin. An author, of course, might try to begin a book with a preface or an introduction. But is the foreword inside or outside the book? If inside, the preface is not really a preface; if outside, the book is not really a book. If a book begins with a preface, it is not a book, and in the absence of a preface the book cannot begin. The preface, then, is the condition of the possibility and the impossibility of the book.

Nowhere is this dilemma more evident than in the work of the author of the book par excellence, Hegel. Hegel begins his "book" with an extended preface, which he entitles *Phenomenology of Spirit*.[10] This preface is intended to make the all-inclusive *Encyclopedia* readable. But such a preface might be impossible, even if it is unavoidable. As Derrida points out, "the preface that Hegel *must* write, in order to denounce a preface that is both impossible and inescapable, must be assigned two locations and two sorts of scope. It belongs both to the inside and to the outside of the concept. But according to a process of mediation and dialectical reappropriation, the inside of speculative philosophy sublates *its own* [son propre] outside as a moment of negativity" (*D*, 11; 17). The reader is left to wonder whether Hegel's sublation is really successful. Can the extraordinary labor

9. Ibid., p. 145.
10. This preface is itself preceded by yet another "Preface." The section of the *Phenomenology* bearing the title "Preface" is not the introduction to the book that follows but is the preface to the System as a whole. Thus the preface to the System, which itself is not exactly inside the System proper, has a preface that falls outside of it.

involved in working through the System finally reappropriate the preface? Does Hegel's *hors d'oeuvre* expose the very *dés-œuvre-ment* his book is constructed to conceal? To answer these questions, it is necessary to return to the beginning of Hegel's beginning—the first section of the first chapter of the preface to his System: "Sense-Certainty: The This and Meaning [*das Meinen*]."[11]

If philosophy is necessarily bookish, then the problem of philosophy is the problem of (the) beginning. Hegel decides (but this decision, like all decisions, is a cutting off) to begin with what is most immediate: sense-certainty. He argues that all knowledge departs from the awareness of spatial and temporal immediacy in the here and now of the "This." To become knowledge proper, immediacy must be mediated by means of "the concept" (*der Begriff*). The concept works through language, which negates immediacy. Every "this" disappears in the very linguistic act intended to express it. Hegel explains that speakers "mean [*meinen*] 'this' bit of paper on which I am writing—or rather have written—'this'; but what they mean is not what they say. If they actually wanted to *say* [sagen] it, then this is impossible, because the sensuous 'this' that is meant *cannot be reached* by language [*Sprache*], which belongs to consciousness, i.e., to that which in itself is universal" (*PS*, 66; 88).[12] In the wake of the disappearance of immediacy, philosophy becomes a language game in which the *fort* of being is supposed to return in the *da* of the concept. Echoing Little Hans (who, of course, comes after Hegel, but perhaps the resonance of this "after" is the murmur of a "before" that already haunts the book), Hegel maintains that the game he plays (or more precisely that plays him) can, in the final analysis, re-present *das Sein*.

Blanchot is not taken in by Hegel's game of *fort/da*. Like Kierkegaard,[13] Blanchot does not work but writes. His writing, he freely admits, is not work, does not work, and cannot be made to work. Ever *désœuvrement*, Blanchot, as well as his *œuvre*, is always outside the System. This outside is not simply external to reflection but is an unrecollected "inside" that repeatedly interrupts philosophical discourse. Less preoccupied with denouement than with Nots, i.e., *les*

11. Hegel's difficulties are already evident in his title. *Meinen* designates not only meaning but also opinion and intention. Since it includes *mein* (my, mine), *Meinen* also implies possession and subjectivity.

12. Hegel's argument anticipates Levinas's analysis of singularity. See above, chapter 7, third section.

13. Derrida points out that Blanchot is a "prodigious reader of Kierkegaard." "Living On: *Border Lines*," *Deconstruction and Criticism* (New York: Seabury, 1979), p. 159.

pas, Blanchot questions what Hegel does *not* say. What, he asks, is *le pas* that Hegel cannot not take? What is the Not that Hegel must not say in order to write his knotty book? Blanchot maintains that the *dehors* signaled by the Not that Hegel cannot speak is actually "at work" in the System from the beginning. To demonstrate this point, he turns the opening argument of the *Phenomenology* against Hegel himself. Drawing on Kojève's lectures, Blanchot contends that "language plays the role of murderer." "Speech, the word [*la parole*], in its perpetual disappearance, carries death, emptiness [*le vide*], absence" (*PA,* 56; 46). "The word gives me that which it signifies, but first it suppresses it. For me to be able to say: 'this woman,' I must in some way or another withdraw the reality of her flesh and bones from her, render her absent and annihilate her. The word gives me being, but it gives it to me deprived of being. It is the absence of that being, it is its nothingness, that which remains when it has lost its being, that is to say, the very fact that it does not exist." [14] Always speaking out of the fear of death, the philosopher intends his word to fill the void. But words betray him. Hegel acknowledges that language is, in effect, a tomb. As we have seen, he describes the sign as a "pyramid." [15] For Hegel, however, this pyramid points beyond the grave. Death is never the last word in the System. When understood in relation to the story unfolded in the book *as a whole,* everyone lives happily ever after. Negation is always negated, loss inevitably turns to profit. When properly understood, the empty tomb is not a sign of absence but is a token of resurrected presence. This presence becomes actual when the *vor* of *die Vorstellung* [16] is erased by the presentation of *der Begriff. La parole* of philosophy is the magic Word that can transform a tombstone into the trace of life.

For a doubting Thomas like Blanchot, the magic does not *work;* the tomb "remains" (*reste*) empty and *le reste* marks and remarks the tomb of philosophy. Blanchot confesses: "When I speak, death speaks in

14. Blanchot, *La part du feu* (Paris: Gallimard, 1949), p. 312. Derrida repeats this argument: "My nonperception, my nonintuition, my *hic et nunc* absence are expressed by that very thing that I say, by *that* which I say and *because* I say it. This structure will never form an 'intimately blended unity' with intuition. The absence of intuition—and therefore of the subject of the intuition—is not only *tolerated* by speech; it is *required* by the general structure of signification, when considered *in itself." Speech and Phenomena,* p. 93. Derrida also considers this issue in *Edmund Husserl's "Origin of Geometry."*

15. See chapter 1, first section.

16. In addition to image and representation, *Vorstellung,* which derives from *vorstellen, vor,* before + *stellen,* to put, place, or set, can mean introduction.

me." [17] In language, a "dirge" resounds that no voice, however magisterial, can silence. Blanchot believes the writer is called to inscribe rather than erase the echoes of this incessant chant. To write the Not of philosophy, it is necessary to undo the philosopher's work. While the philosopher translates image into concept, the writer returns concept to image. "The image, capable of negating nothingness, is also the gaze of nothingness on us. The image is light, and nothingness is immensely heavy. The image shines and nothingness is the diffuse thickness where nothing reveals itself. The image is the crack, the mark of this black sun, the tear [déchirure], which, under the appearance of the dazzling burst [éclat], gives us the negative of the inexhaustible negative depth. That is why the image seems so profound and so empty, so threatening and so attractive, always rich in more senses than we lend it and also poor, void and silent, because in it advances this dark impotence, deprived of mastery, which is that of death as recommencement" (A, 51). L'interstice, la déchirure, l'éclat: the image is the tear, rent, fissure, cleft "in" language. As such, the image is unavoidably duplicitous. "The image is the duplicity of revelation. That which veils in revealing, the veil that reveals in reveiling in the ambiguous indecision of the word révéler, is the image" (EI, 42). In terms previously invoked (which will return yet again), the image is the da of the fort and the fort of the da. In opposition to Hegel, Blanchot maintains that da never erases fort. "Meaning does not escape into another meaning, but into the other [autre] of all meaning" (SL, 263; 276). Blanchot sometimes associates the obscure Other implied by the play of veils with woman—a woman who dwells in Hades. [18] Eurydice, whose "presence" is an "infinite absence," is the impossible "object" of every Orphic quest(ion) (SL, 172; 180).

The presence of infinite absence, which horrifies the philosopher, "fascinates" the writer. "So menacing and so attractive," the limen of the image is the "milieu of fascination, where what one sees seizes sight and renders it interminable, where the gaze stiffens into light, where light is the absolute gleam of an eye one does not see but which one does not cease to see since it is the mirror image of one's own

17. Blanchot, La part du feu, p. 313.

18. We will see in the next section that Blanchot also approaches this Other in terms that are neither masculine nor feminine. His analysis of the neutre and the il parallels the interpretation of the elle in the writings of Lacan, Bataille, and Kristeva. Elle, after all (and all of this is written after all, after the all of Hegel's book), can also mean "it." Il and elle both become tropes for troping itself. Inevitably turning away from that toward which it is directed, language necessarily "tropes" (tropos: a turn).

look—this milieu is utterly attractive. Fascinating. It is the light that is also the abyss [*l'abîme*], a light into which one sinks [*s'abîme*], both terrifying and tantalizing (*SL*, 32–33; 24).[19] As the figure of what can be neither figured nor figured out, as the reflection of the eye that does not see, Eurydice, like Medusa and Judith, blinds the philosopher.[20] The abyss in which blinding light is at the same time darkness, is an other night, a night beyond night, a night that is the night of an Other. To enter this night is to take *le pas au-delà* in which one approaches the entertaining interval of the neuter.

Neuter: Entertaining Interval

But if I advanced within myself, hurrying laboriously toward my precise noon, I yet experienced as a tragic certainty, at the center of the living Thomas, the inaccessible proximity of that Thomas which was nothingness, and the more the shadow of me diminished, the more I conceived of myself in this faultless clarity as the possible host filled with desires of this obscure Thomas. In the plenitude of my reality, I believed I was reaching the unreal. . . . I felt this nothingness bound to your extreme existence as an unexceptional condition. I felt that between it and you undeniable ratios were being established. All the logical couplings were incapable of expressing this union in which, without *then* or *because,* you came together, both cause and effect at once, unreconcilable and indissoluble. Was it your opposite? No, I said not. (*TO*, 97–99; 143–44)

"No, I said not." At the end of philosophy, the task of thinking is to think Not otherwise than by not thinking. For Heidegger, such thinking "designates the attempt at a reflection that persists in questioning" (*TB*, 55). But what is questioning? What does it mean to

19. Perhaps echoing Lacan and surely anticipating Kristeva, Blanchot proceeds to associate this abyss with the mother. We have already observed woman as the figure of the Other—an Other who often is the m-other. "Perhaps the force of the maternal figure receives its sudden bursting [*éclat*] from the very force of fascination, and one might say then, that if the mother exerts this fascinating attraction, it is because, appearing when the child lives altogether in fascination's gaze, she concentrates in herself all the powers of enchantment. It is because the child is fascinated that the mother is fascinating, and that is also why all the impressions of early childhood have a kind of fixity that comes from fascination" (*SL*, 33; 24).

20. It is important to recall that "fascination" derives from the Greek word for evil eye (see chapter 4, second section). The gaze of this eye is associated with Medusa, whose act of beheading, repeated by Judith, suggests castration.

entertain a question? Do questions entertain or is entertainment a question, *the* question, which is *la question la plus profonde?* For Blanchot, as for Heidegger, to persist in questioning is to quest-ion with no hope of finding, to ask without expecting an answer. If it is profound, "we will never be done with the question, not because there still remains too much to question but because the question, in this detour from the depth that is proper—a movement that diverts us from both profundity and self, puts us in contact with that which has no end" (*EI*, 27). The questioning of that which has no end is endless; questions always lead to other questions, and other questions finally lead to the question of the Other. The most profound question is "the other question, question of the Other [*l'Autre*], but also always an other question" (*EI*, 34). To entertain the question of the Other is, for Blanchot, to question entertainment—to interrogate an entertainment that is infinite—*l'entretien infini.*

L'Entretien infini is no ordinary conversation [*entretien*, conversation, talk, interview],[21] no amusing entertainment [*entretien*, entertainment]. Nor does this *entretien* maintain, preserve, or repair [*entretient*]. If it holds together [*entretient*], it does so by holding apart. If it supports [*entretient*], its "ground" is *l'abîme*. If it feeds [*entretient*], its food for thought makes (the) One [*l'Un*] vomit. If it hosts [*entretenir*], its guests are always strange. *L'entretien* that is infinite is a holding between: *entretien*—*entre*, between + *tenir*, to hold; entertainment, *intertenere*—*inter*, between + *tenere*, to hold. In a way similar to Heidegger's *Riss*, Blanchot's *entretien* joins by separating and separates by joining. This endless alternation is the altarity, that is the other, of all meaning and every word. The insistence of this Other intervenes "in" an analysis that is interminable. The altarity of *entre-tenir* can be neither comprehended nor communicated directly. Like Lacan's *réel*, *l'entretien* is the ex-communication that returns repeatedly to excommunicate those who lend it an ear (or a pen). "That which is present in this presence of word or speech, as soon as it affirms itself, is precisely that which never lets itself be either seen or attained: something is there, which is outside the range both of him who speaks and of him who understands; it is between us, it remains between [*se tient entre*] and the conversation [*entretien*] is the approach beginning with this between [*entre-deux*]—an irreducible distance that one must preserve if one wishes to maintain the relation with the unknown, which is the unique gift of the word or speech" (*EI*, 315).

21. The collection of essays bearing this title is, in effect, an unending conversation between Blanchot and a variety of other artists and writers.

The infinitely entertaining *entre-deux* is "the pure interval" (*le pur intervalle*) that forms the margin simultaneously joining and separating each pair and every couple. "It is this fissure—this rapport with the other," Blanchot explains, "that we have dared to characterize as an interruption of being, adding now: between man and man, there is an interval that would be neither [*ni*] of being nor [*ni*] of nonbeing and that bears the Difference of the word or speech [*la parole*], a difference that precedes everything different and everything unique" (*EI*, 99). The *ni . . . ni* of *l'entre-deux* is the neither . . . nor of the neuter. In one of his fragments, Blanchot writes: "The enigma of the neuter . . . *entre: entre/ne(u)tre*" (*PA*, 97). "Non-present, non-absent," the neuter "is" (but, of course, it no more is than is not) "an incessant going-and-coming" (*PA*, 104). This unending altaration is almost nothing . . . nothing Other . . . nothing other than the *désœuvrement* that interrupts the work of philosophy by exposing the Not in the philosopher's *œuvre*. "Something is at work through the neuter, which is immediately the work of idleness or non-work [*œuvre du désœuvrement*]: there is an effect of the neuter—that of the passivity of the neuter— which is not an effect *of* the neuter, not being the effect of a Neuter supposedly at work as a cause or a thing. There would therefore not be a labor of the neuter, as one says: the labor of the negative. The Neuter, paradoxical name: it hardly speaks at all, mute words, simple, however always veiling itself, always displacing itself outside its meaning, invisibly transforming itself, while never ceasing to discharge itself in the immobility of its position that repudiates depth. It neutralizes, neutralizes (itself) and thus evokes (does nothing but evoke) the movement of the *Aufhebung,* but it suspends and holds back, it retains only the movement of suspension, that is to say, the distance it suscitates by the fact that in occupying the terrain, it makes it disappear. The Neuter thus designates difference in indifference, opacity in transparency, the negative scansion of the other, which can reproduce itself only by conjured attraction—omitted— from the one" (*PA*, 105–6).

Forever *entre deux,* the neuter is a "third" that "falls" (*tombe*) between all binary opposites. This third is neither theological (a third that is a tri-unity) nor philosophical (a third that reconciles the one and the many).[22] Instead of synthesizing antitheses, this third makes

22. "The One, the Same remain the first, the last words. Why this reference to One like an ultimate and unique reference? In this sense, the dialectic, ontology, and criticism of ontology have the same postulate: all three refer to the One, either because the One completes itself as all or because it conceives being as the reassembling, light, and unity of being, or because, above and beyond being, it affirms itself as the Absolute" (*EI*, 34).

all synthesis impossible. In a manner not unlike Kierkegaard's positing *Treide*, Blanchot's *troisième* constitutes every pair but resists any
reciprocal relation.[23] To think this elusive third, it is necessary "to
turn ourselves toward the third genre [*troisième genre*] of which one
must only say: it does not tend to unity, it is not a relation with a view
to unity, a rapport of unification" (*EI*, 95).

The third genre or gender is neither masculine nor feminine. The
neuter is written as *il*. The function of *il* in Blanchot's texts recalls
Heidegger's and Freud's *es*, Bataille's and Kristeva's *elle*, Lacan's *ça*, and
Levinas's *illeity*. *Il* is not a word proper. "It" is always a substitute for
an other, a supplement to something Other. *Il* "is" in other words. *Il*
is, in other words, always "*un mot* de trop," which, paradoxically,
never says enough (*EI*, 458). As such, it is an excess that is a lack. "(*il*)
is pronounced without its having a position or a deposition of existence, without presence or absence affirming it, without the unity of
the word coming to free it from the between [*l'entre-deux*] where it is
disseminated. (*il*) is not 'that,' but the neuter that marks (*il*) (as [*il*]
calls for the neuter) takes it toward a displacement without space that
relieves [*destitute*] it of all grammatical position—a kind of lack
[*manque*] in becoming between two, several, and all words, thanks to
which these break off, without which they signify nothing, but which
constantly disrupts until silence comes where they pass away. Anonymity is born of (*il*), which always denotes the name forgotten in
advance" (*PA*, 52–53).

The third genre's resistance to unity reflects the tendency of *il* to
disseminate itself. Dissemination is not the loss of unity but is the
scattering of what has never been gathered and will never be re-
collected. Thus the displacement that *il* effects is infinite, for "it" is a
function of that which has no place. The "non-place [*non-lieu*]" of *il*
opens an other space, which is the space of the Other. In this space, the
"lack [*manque*]" of *il* resounds in the lack of language. Since this lack
cannot be captured in a concept, Blanchot describes *il* with an oxymoron: a "nonconceptualizable 'concept'" (*PA*, 54). That which is
nonconceptualizable has no proper name. The unnameability of *il* is
implied by its irreducible singularity.[24] Since naming presupposes

23. In previous chapters I have noted that Merleau-Ponty, Lacan, and Levinas also
stress the importance of thirdness. In addition to the notion of the third, Merleau-
Ponty uses the terms *entre-deux* and *neutre*.

24. There is an important difference between the singularity of Blanchot's *il* and
Levinas's *illeity*. While Levinas argues that the appeal of *illeity* singles out the subject
in his or her particularity, Blanchot maintains that *il* calls subjectivity into question.
On this point, Levinas's third is closer to that of Kierkegaard, and Blanchot's third is
closer to that of Lacan.

generality, if not universality, a radically singular term cannot name. In not naming, *il* "names something that escapes nomination" (*PA*, 102). That which is nameless is, of course, anonymous. As the impossible name of the nameless, *il* is "the name without name" (*PA*, 162). "Anonymity does not consist of challenging the name while withdrawing from it. Anonymity poses the name, leaves it void, as if the name were there only to let oneself pass through because the name does not name, the non-unity and the nonpresence of the without name [*du sans nom*]. (*il*), which designates nothing but awaits that which is forgotten in it, helps to interrogate this demand for anonymity. Would it suffice nonetheless the say that (*il*), without having value or sense in itself, would permit all that inscribes itself in it to affirm itself in a determination that is always different?" (*PA*, 52).

A determination that is always different would be a determination of difference as such. That which is anonymous has no identity and what has no identity is different—*radically* different. This difference is different from every difference, which, in its difference from its other, constitutes an identity. "*La différence plus essentielle*" is the nonidentical difference that never returns to the same but is perpetually different not only from others but from itself. In Blanchot's terms: "Difference: the nonidentity of the same, the movement of distance, that which carries in carrying away, the becoming of interruption. Difference bears in its prefix the detour where all ability to give sense or direction searches for its origin in the gap that separates it" (*EI*, 254). The fault of difference is "the tear [*la déchirure*], the incisive rupture" that opens the obscure *entretien infini*. The neither/nor of the neuter is an unspeakable and unknowable *Différence* that is an other Other: "the other of the other, the non-known of the other, its refusal to let itself be thought as the other than the one, and its refusal to be only the Other or again the 'other than'" (*PA*, 105). "The non-knowledge [*le non-savoir*]" of such unspeakable altarity "is a menace and a scandal for thought" (*A*, 250). *Das ganz Andere* is a stumbling block for Greek but not for Jew.

In an effort to describe the entertainment that escapes presence and absence, Blanchot uses terms we have already encountered in the writings of Heidegger and Levinas: *proche* (Heidegger's *Nähe*) and *proximité* (Levinas's *proximité*).[25] The proximate approaches, or more precisely is always already approaching "before" the beginning and

25. Whether Blanchot borrows this notion from Levinas or Levinas takes it from Blanchot is both unclear and unimportant. It is clear, though unclear how important, that both Blanchot and Levinas are deeply indebted to Heidegger, as well as to each other.

"after" the end. Ever approaching, *proximité* is never present. Since to be is to be present, the proximate does not exist. The failure of the proximate to stand out (*ex-sistere*) does not mean that it is not. While never present, the near is not absent. *Le proche* cannot simply be identified with nonbeing. "To approach forms the play of the remote [*éloignement*]. The play of the distant and the near is a play of the distant [*lointain*]. To approach from a distance is the formula that tries to burst open [*éclate*] the background [*lointain*] in touch with a present thus described as distant, as in a certain way it always is; thus presence and distance would be hand in glove: presence distant, distance of a presence, the background would be present yonder. The near alone would thus protect against contamination of a presence. To be near is not to be present" (*PA*, 99). As the irresolvable play of presence and absence, the proximate is the *between* of being and nonbeing. If the proximate is, it "is" Not, and if Not "is," is is not.

Always at the edge, always on the verge of being and nonbeing, proximity "is" a "radical exteriority," a "pure exteriority." By stressing the radicality and the purity of this exterior, Blanchot suggests an exteriority that is not the binary opposite of interiority, an outside that is not the antithesis of an inside. "(Pure) exteriority" ([*Pure*] *extériorité*) is "the outside [*le dehors*] 'preceding' every interior" (*EI*, 625). This exterior makes it possible to distinguish interior and exterior; this outside differentiates inside and outside. Such pure exteriority is "inside" everything. The exterior, which is interior, is inside as the outside "hollowing out [*creusant*]" everything as if from within. An exterior that is radical cannot be incorporated, assimilated, or domesticated. *La pure extériorité,* in other words, is not subject to *Er-innerung*—Hegelian or otherwise. The proximate *dedans* of the pure *dehors* subverts the operation of *Aufhebung* and thus suspends both re-collection and re-membering. Such dis-member-ing is "*la coupure,* as strange to identification as to unification" (*A*, 188). This cut severs the member with which the philosopher tries to copula-te. No one, no One, can find himself or itself in this *déchirement.*

"Pure exteriority" marks the eternal return of the "pure interval." The infinitely entertaining interval can be either spatial or temporal—either the emptiness between two objects or subjects, or the delay between two instants or events. "Exteriority thus affirmed is not a tranquil temporal and spatial continuity, continuity for which the logic of logos—discourse without discursus—provides us the key. Exteriority—time and space—is always exterior to itself. It is not correlative, center of correlations, but institutes the connection beginning with an interruption that does not unite. Difference is the restraint from the outside; the outside is the exposition of difference; difference and outside designate the original disjunction—the origin that is the very disjunction and always disjoint from itself. Disjunction, where time and space would rejoin in disjoining, coincides with that which does not coincide, the noncoincident, which in advance turns away from all unity" (*EI*, 241–42).

Altarity: *entretien, entre-deux, neutre, il, coupe, déchirement, différence, dehors, proximité, proche, extériorité, intervalle*—the disjunction where space and time would rejoin in disjoining. The interval marks time . . . marks time by marking space. Rather than a tranquil continuity, the interval is restless discontinuity. The entertainment of the interval allows one, forces One, to space out. The space-time of the interval is the spacing—*l'espacement*—in which space is timed and time is spaced.[26] "Very approximately and provisionally," Blanchot concludes, "the obscurity of this movement is its uncovering, that which is always uncovering without having uncovered itself, and always in advance has reduced to manifestation all movement of hiding or of hiding itself. The present, where all things are present and the 'me,' which is present there, are suspended, still exterior to themselves and the same exteriority of presence; we finally perceive there the point where time and space would rejoin in the original disjunction; 'presence' is as much the intimacy of insistence [*l'instance*] as the dispersion of the Outside; more precisely, it is the intimacy as Outside, the exterior become the intrusion that stifles and the inversion of the one and the other; it is what we have called the vertigo of spacing" (*EI*, 65–66).

The vertigo of spacing opens one/One to the opening of the Open. The Open, as Heidegger explains, is "like the nothing [*Nichts*] we hardly know." This void, which is a non-absent absence, is not only "obscure" and "mysterious;" it is "monstrous" (*ungeheuer:* huge, colossal, frightful, shocking; *geheuer:* uncanny, haunting). When imagined, which *is not* to say understood, in this way, the Open is the doubtful space-time of Thomas the Obscure. Following "the steps" (*les pas*) of Heidegger, Blanchot "sketches" (*reisst-vor*) the "out-line"

26. Compare Derrida's remark about *différance:* "In constituting itself, in dividing itself dynamically, this interval is what might be called *spacing,* the becoming-space of time or the becoming-time of space (*temporization*). And it is this constitution of the present, as an 'originary' and irreducibly nonsimple (and therefore, *stricto sensu* nonoriginary) synthesis of marks, or traces of retentions and protentions . . . that I propose to call archiwriting, archi-trace, or *différance.* Which (is) (simultaneously) spacing (and) temporization" (*M,* 13; 14).

(*Um-riss*) of the Open by considering the poetry of Rilke: "*The open is the poem*"; the poem is the poem of Orpheus—Rilke's *Sonnets to Orpheus* (*SL*, 142; 146).[27]

> Space exceeds us and translates things:
> That the tree's being may succeed for you,
> cast around it the inner space, that space
> which announces itself in you. Surround it with restraint.
> It [*Il*] knows not how to limit itself. Only in taking form
> from your renunciation does it truly become a tree.[28]

The space that exceeds us, the space that announces itself "in" us, the space that is the *il*, is "*Orphic Space*," and Orphic space is "the space of death." In the vertiginous spacing of death, "terror is ravishing" (*l'effroi est ravissement; SL*, 155, 85; 161, 83). The movement toward (but only *vers* and only *vers* through *le vers*) ravishment, ecstasy, r/a/u/-pture "is an infinitely problematic movement, which day condemns as a form of unjustifiable madness, or as the expiation of excess. From day's perspective, the descent into Hell, the movement toward hollow depth, is already excessive. It is inevitable that Orpheus pass beyond the law that forbids him to return, for he has already violated it with his first step [*pas*] toward the shadows. This remark implies that in reality Orpheus has not ceased to be turned toward Eurydice: he saw her invisible, he touched her intact, in her shadowy absence, in that veiled presence that did not hide her absence, which was the presence of her infinite absence. Had he not looked at her, he would not have drawn her toward him; and doubtless she is not there, but in this glance back he himself is absent. He is not less dead than she—dead, not of that tranquil worldly death that is rest, silence, and end, but of

27.   It is worth noting that Blanchot agrees with Heidegger's contention that the nonoriginal origin of art is opening—a *Riss* that is *le déchirement absolu*. In the remainder of the text that begins with the assertion "*The Open is the Poem*," Blanchot writes: "The space where everything returns to deep being, where there is infinite passage between the two domains, where all [*tout*] dies but where death is the knowing companion of life, . . . where celebration laments and lamentation glorifies—the very space toward which 'all worlds hasten as toward their nearest and truest reality,' the space of the greatest circle and of incessant metamorphosis—this is the space of the poem. This is the Orphic space to which the poet doubtless has no access, where he can penetrate only to disappear, which he attains only when he is united with the intimacy of laceration [*déchirure*], which makes him a mouth without understanding, just as it makes him the one who hears and understands the weight of silence. The Open is the work, but the work as origin" (*SL*, 142; 146).

28.   Rilke dates this poem June 1924. Blanchot cites these verses in "Rilke and Death's Demand," *SL*, 143; 147.

that other death that is death without end, the ordeal [*épreuve*] of end's absence" (*SL,* 172; 180–81).

Ever unexpected (even when one awaits *elle*), *la mor-t* (*Mor:* m-other) always involves chance. The *coup* in which Eurydice overtakes Orpheus is *un coup de don* as chancy as *un coup de dés*.[29] Death forever approaches like the throw of a *die*. There is always something "dicey" about Eury-di(c)e. The death—the "little death" she figures in her hymeneal altar is the death that never *comes*. The suffocating "presence" of Eurydice's "infinite absence" cuts off more than the *esprit* of the philosopher.[30] The little death, which never comes, exposes the powerful impotence of death itself. If the other death, the death that is death without end, is the ordeal of death's absence, then death is impossible. Perhaps *elle* (which we now recognize as *il* and vice versa) is the Impossible itself.

Impossibility of Death

At the highest point of contradiction, I was this illegitimate death. Represented in my feelings by a double for whom each feeling was as absurd as for a dead person, at the height of passion I attained the height of estrangement, and I seemed to have been removed [*ravi; ravir:* carry off, ravish] from the human condition because I had truly accomplished it. Since, in each human act, I was the dead person that at once renders it possible and impossible and, if I walked, if I thought, I was the one whose complete absence alone makes the step [*le pas*] or the thought possible. . . . I lost my reason for existing. (*TO,* 93; 134)

How can the timely spacing of a present that is never present be thought? Perhaps by thinking after Nietzsche, or by thinking Nietzsche's "after," which is always already "before" the presence of Hegel.

Nietzsche (if his name serves to name the law of the Eternal Return) and Hegel (if his name invites thought concerning presence as all and the all as presence) permit us to sketch out a mythology: Nietzsche can only come near Hegel, but it is always

29. The other poet Blanchot considers at length in the section of *L'Espace littéraire* entitled "L'œuvre et l'espace de la mort" is Mallarmé. In an essay bearing the title "The *Igitur* Experience," Blanchot considers Mallarmé's poem *Un coup de dés*. See *SL,* 108–19; 108–20. Compare Derrida's discussion of *Un coup de dés* in "The Double Session," *D,* 173–286; 199–318.

30. To dice can also mean to cut up.

before and always after Hegel that he comes and comes again. Before: because, while thought of as absolute, presence has never reassembled within the accomplished totality of knowledge; presence knows itself to be absolute, but its knowledge remains a relative knowledge since it is not carried out in practice, and thus it knows itself only as a present that is not practically satisfied, not reconciled with presence as all: thus Hegel is still only a pseudo-Hegel. And Nietzsche always comes after, because the law that he bears presumes the accomplishment of time as present and, in this accomplishment, presumes its absolute destruction, so that thus the Eternal Return, affirming the future and the past as sole temporal instances and as identical, unrelated instances, freeing the future of all present and the past of all presence, shatters thought until this infinite affirmation will return infinitely in the future to that which under no form and in no time would know how to be present, just as that which, past and never having belonged in any form to the present, reverts infinitely to the past. (PA, 34–35)

Coming *after* Hegel, Nietzsche exposes the immemorial *before* that the System is constructed to recollect. This unrepresentable *anarchie,* which is always (the) outside of thought, is nonetheless thought in the "nonconceptualizable concept" of the Eternal Return. "The 're' of the return inscribes as the 'ex,' opening of all exteriority: as if the return, far from putting an end to it, marks exile, the commencement in its recommencement of exodus. To return, that would be to return again to ex-centering oneself, to erring. Only the *nomadic* affirmation *remains*" (PA, 49). When re-turn is eternal, the ex-teriority, ex-centricity, ex-ile, ex-odus, ex-cess, ex-position, and ex-pense of erring are unavoidable.

Considered in relation to other interpretations of Nietzsche, Blanchot's account of the Eternal Return is undeniably backwards. For most commentators, the horror of the Eternal Return grows out of the prospect of an endless recurrence of what is present here and now. Blanchot, by contrast, does not interpret the future as a re-presentation of the present but reads the future in the past and the past in the future in order to approach the present by way of the detour through past and future.[31] If return is eternal, it not only will never end but it never began in the first place.[32] In the absence of any true origin, nothing is

31. We will see that this intersection of past and future rends rather than closes the circle of time.

32. To deny *arche* and *telos* is to deny the Alpha and Omega, which ontotheology names "God." Anarchy and ateleology meet in an atheology that declares the death of God.

original, which is not to imply that the origin is merely nothing. When nothing is original, (*le*) *tout* is secondary. If, however, all is secondary, something is always missing and everything is always lacking. To think this "lack" (*manque*) is, for Blanchot, to think what Western philosophy leaves unthought.

That which is always already missing is a past that is "infinitely past" because it was never present in the first place. For Blanchot, as for Levinas, what has not been present cannot be re-presented. In Blanchot's rereading of Nietzsche's Eternal Return, the "unrepresentable before" of Levinas's "*an-archie*" recurs as "the terrifyingly ancient [*l'effroyablement ancien*]" that is not subject to *Er-inner-ung*.[33] Since the absolutely "ancient" (*ancien*, from *anteanus*: going before)[34] can be neither re-collect-ed nor re-member-ed, it is irrevocable. "The irrevocable is thus not at all or not only the fact that what has taken place has taken place forever: that is perhaps the means—strange, I admit—for the past to warn us (while sparing us) that it is the void and that the falling due [*echéance*]—the infinite, fragile fall—that it designates, this pit [*puits*], is the depth of that which is without bottom. It is irrevocable, indelible, yes: ineffaceable, but because nothing is inscribed there" (*PA*, 24). *Le vide du puits, la profondeur de ce qui est sans fond:* the void of the pit, the depth of that which is without bottom is *la tombe* marking *le non-lieu* where (the) all falls [*tombe*]. *L'espacement* of this *tombe* is a time without present. The Not of this uncanny space-time is *le pas au-delà*.

> Time, time: the step/not beyond [*le pas au-delà*], which is not accomplished in time, would lead outside of time, without this outside being timeless, but there where time would fall, fragile fall, according to this 'outside of time in time' toward which writing would draw us, if it were permitted of us, vanished from us, from writing the secret of the ancient fear. (*PA*, 8)

Since the "outside of time in time" is never made present, the *tombe* remains—remains empty. *Le reste* of the empty *tombe* is *le puits* surrounded but not contained by the pyramid.

The writing *covering* the pyramid is hieroglyphic. The message returned from the desert of Egypt by the latter-day Moses is that hieroglyphs are images—the images of desire that are the non-stuff of which dreams are made. The terrifyingly ancient never appears; it

33. It would also be possible to interpret this interplay "otherwise" by re-interpreting Levinas's *anarchie* as a repetition of Blanchot's *ancien*.

34. The *ante* of this *anus* might also be understood in terms of Bataille's "solar anus," whose dirt and darkness, we have discovered, blind the philosopher.

only reappears as the dream of the "is" that is not, and the Not that "is." The presence of this dream is the dream of the present in which presence appears but a phantasm. Nietzsche's immemorial law "suspends or makes disappear every present and all presence"—especially the presence of Hegel (*PA, 26*). "The time of time's absence is not dialectical. In this time what appears is the fact that nothing appears. . . . The reversal which, in the absence of time, constantly sends us back to the presence of absence, but to this presence as absence, to absence as affirmation of itself, an affirmation where nothing is affirmed, where nothing never ceases to affirm itself in the torment of the indefinite—this movement is not dialectical. Contradictions do not exclude each other in it, nor are they reconciled" (*SL, 30; 21*). As a result of the irreconcilable contradiction of "an outside of time in time," the past for which we long "is" always future and the future we ardently desire "is" always past. In the absence of a past that was never present, the dream of presence returns eternally to create the nightmare of a future that never arrives. If the encounter with the past has never taken place, the past, paradoxically, is always still to come. *L'avenir*, in other words, is *à venir*. "Under the law of the return, where, between past and future nothing joins [*se conjuge*]— how to jump from one to the other, while the rule [of law] does not permit the passage—how would this jump be possible? Past would be the same as future. Thus there would be but a sole modality, or a double modality functioning in such a way that identity, differed or deferred [*différée*], would regulate difference. But such would be the exigency of the return: it is *under a false appearance of the present* that the past-future ambiguity would invisibly separate the future from the past" (*PA, 21–22*).

Inasmuch as "the law of the Return" is eternal, it exhibits a ceaseless compulsion to repeat itself. As Little Hans's play suggests, the repetition compulsion is tied to death. By repeating the impossibility of presence, the law of Eternal Return implies the inescapability of death. Absolute past and infinite future coincide in the "eternal beginning and eternal end," which is, in Mallarmé's terms, the "Act of Night." The time of this dark act is "Midnight."

> "Certainly a presence of Midnight subsists." But this subsisting presence is not a presence. The substantial present is the negation of the present. It is a vanished present. And Midnight, where first "the absolute present of things" (their unreal essence) gathered itself together, becomes "the dream of a Midnight vanished into itself": it is no longer a present, but the past, symbolized, as is the end of history in Hegel, by a book lying open upon the

table. . . . Night is the book: the silence and inaction of a book when, after everything has been proffered, everything returns into the silence that alone speaks—that speaks from the depth of the past and is at the same time the whole future of the word. For the present Midnight, that hour at which the present is lacking absolutely, is also the hour in which the past touches and, without the intermediary of any present time, immediately attains the extremity of the future. And such, as we have seen, is the very instant of death, which is never present, which is the festival of the absolute future, the instant at which one might say that, in a time without present, what has been will be. (*SL*, 113–14; 114–15)

Death is the absolute future in which the absolute past approaches, but only approaches, for death is never present. The time of death and dying "is the abyss of the present, the reign of a time without a present" (*SL*, 117; 118). In early as well as late writings, Heidegger argues that to think after the end of philosophy, one must rethink being in terms of time. Time appears radical only in relation to death. *Da-sein*, Heidegger maintains, must be understood as "being-toward-death." To think time as death and death as time is to unthink being by uncovering *fort* in *da* and *Nein* in *Sein*.

Echoing Heidegger, Blanchot stresses the unsettling interplay of time and death. Being, which is never present as such, is a tendency toward *l'a-venir*. From this point of view, being is being-toward "the nonarrival of that which comes toward [*advient*]" (*PA*, 132). By interpreting the absolute future, which approaches without arriving, in terms of "death and dying" (*la mort et mourir*),[35] Blanchot is led to an unexpected conclusion. If death only approaches, I (or the I) never die. "One never dies now," Blanchot points out, "one always dies later, in the future [*l'avenir*]—in a future that is never actual, that cannot come except when everything will be over and done. And when everything is accomplished, there will be no more present: the future will again be past" (*SL*, 164–65; 171). Since *la mort* is never present, *elle* (or *il*) never actually occurs.[36] "Midnight is precisely the hour that

35. Blanchot distinguishes *la mort* and *mourir* from *l'être mort*. While being dead (or a dead being) remains an attribute of being, death and dying elude the polarity of being and nonbeing.

36. Elsewhere Blanchot associates death with the anonymity of the neuter. "*One dies:* he who dies is anonymous, and anonymity is the guise in which the ungraspable, the unlimited, the unsituated is most dangerously affirmed near us. Whoever experiences this suffers an anonymous, impersonal force, the force of an event which, being the dissolution of every event, is starting over not only now, but was in its very beginning a beginning again" (*SL*, 241; 253). Since it is never present, death as such

does not toll until after the dice are thrown, the hour that has never come, that never comes, the pure, ungraspable future, the hour eternally past" (*SL*, 116; 117). If Midnight never strikes, death is impossible. The impossibility of death does not mean that life is eternal. To the contrary, the silence of Midnight is the speechless tolling of *le glas* that echoes in and through all things and every one. The impossibility of death is the "non-event" in which the Impossible itself draws near.

The Impossible is a *"nonpower* [non-pouvoir] *that is not simply the negation of power"* (*EI*, 310). As a "nonpower or nonability," the Impossible is inseparable from a certain impotence.[37] This impotence can never be mastered, accomplished, or achieved but can only be suffered patiently. For Blanchot, as for Heidegger, that which is beyond being and nonbeing approaches when one "waits for something that will not have taken place" (*PA*, 88). What does not take place in this waiting is the *es* of *es gibt* or the *il* of *il y a*. As I observed in the analysis of Heidegger and Levinas, the gift of *es* and *il* is *un coup de don* that faults the subject. Blanchot comments on the radical passivity implied in Levinas's notion of *illeity:* "Passivity: we can only evoke it by a language that is reversed or overturned. In the past, I appealed to suffering: suffering such as I could not suffer, so that, in this nonpower [*non-pouvoir*], the 'me,' excluded from mastery and from its status as subject in the first person, destitute, desituated, and even offended, could lose itself as a me capable of suffering: there is suffering [*il y a souffrance*], there would be suffering, there is no longer a suffering 'I,' and suffering is not present, is not born (even less lived) in the present, it is without present, as it is without either beginning or end, time has radically changed its meaning."[38]

Such profound suffering is a "catastrophe" for the centered self. To undergo the impossible approach of death is to be ex-*il*-ed from

---

cannot be thought. Death, in other words, is unthinkable. "Death," for Blanchot, "is only a metaphor that helps us roughly to represent the idea of limit, while the limit excludes all representation, all 'idea' of limit" (*PA*, 75).

37. "Impotent" (*impotens*) and "impossible" (*impossibilis* are both related to the Latin stem *poti:* "Powerful; lord. 1. Latin *potis*, powerful, able: PODESTA. Old Latin *potere*, to be able or powerful (superseded by *posse*, to be able): POTENT, POWER, IMPOTENT, PREPOTENT. 3. Latin compound *posse*, to be able (contracted from *potis*, able + *esse*, to be): POSSESS, POSSIBLE, PUISSANT. 4. Variant of *pet-* in compound *ghost-pet-*, guest-master, host (see *ghosti*)" (*The American Heritage Dictionary of the English Language*, under Indo-European roots, "poti"). In view of this extraordinary range of associations, the Impossible might be understood as the not-so-holy ghost haunting ontotheology.

38. Blanchot, "Discours sur la patience," p. 25.

oneself. The proximity of death is "the beyond" (*l'au-delà*), which "is in us in a manner that forever separates us from ourselves."[39] As the outside that is inside, *le pas au-delà* doubles every one/One. The unmasterable double makes doubting Thomases of us all. The ghostly "twin [Thomas]" is a repetition of the subject that interrupts self-identity.[40] To bear the unavoidable wound of *le coup de don* is to suffer the fate of Ishmael—dispossession. The one who is dispossessed is left to err in the nonplace of a desert wilderness and the nontime of an interminable night. Blanchot describes this night as *Nuit, nuit blanche*.[41] The white of this night is as blinding as the whiteness surrounding the blackness of an Umberg painting, as terrifying as the whiteness of the sea monster or the leviathan in Ishmael's *récit*.

> As Jean Giono writes, 'Man always has a desire for some monstrous object. And his life only has value if he submits entirely to this pursuit.' What gives such grandeur to the hunt for Moby Dick is not the madness of Ahab, his rending [*déchirant*] instinct for vengeance, the fascination that he exerts on his crew; it is the enigmatic character that he lends Moby Dick and that transforms his design into an impossible and fatal dream. Moby Dick became for this half-consumed hero the fundamental obstacle of life, the giant adversary, against which he knew he would shatter but which stood in the way of his existence, the reflection of a dreadful will that haunted him, burned him and which he would only touch in the abyss of his own annihilation.[42]

"The abyss of his own annihilation" obsesses not only Ahab and Melville but also Blanch-ot. The insistence of this obsession is the "murmur" echoing in all Blanchot's writing. While the philosopher writes to silence this lacerating murmur, the writer writes to let it/*il* re-sound.[43] The murmur of writing is the inhuman cry that eternally returns "in" *l'entretien infini*.

39. Blanchot, *Faux pas*, p. 35.

40. At one point, Blanchot observes: "If it is true that there is (in the Chinese language) a written character signifying at once 'man' and 'two,' it is easy to recognize in man that which is always self and other, the fortunate duality of dialogue and the possibility of communication. But it is less easy, more important perhaps, to think that 'man' also means 'two' like the gap that lacks unity, the jump from "O" to duality, the "1" thus giving itself up as forbidden, the between [*l'entre-deux*]" (PA, 57).

41. Blanchot, "Discours sur la patience," p. 22.

42. Blanchot, *Faux pas*, pp. 275–76.

43. Accordingly, Blanchot agrees with Bataille's contention that the aim of philosophy is *l'amortissement*.

Thus we will choose our ideology. This choice will be the only one that can lead us to a nonideological writing: writing outside of language, outside of ideology. Let us call this choice, without shame, humanist. . . . But what is "humanism"?[44] In what terms can we define it without engaging in the logos of a definition? In those terms that will remove it farthest from a language: the cry (that is to say the murmur), cry of need or protest, cry without word, without silence, ignoble cry where, perhaps, the cry writes the graffiti of high walls. It is possible, as one likes to state, that "man passes away." He fades. He even has always already passed, faded, to the extent that he has always been suited for his own disappearance. But, in passing, he cries; he cries in the street, in the desert; he cries while dying; he does not cry, he is the murmur of the cry. (*EI*, 392)

E-cri-ture: le cri écrit et l'écrivain crie.

Art of Erring

Now, in this night, I come forward bearing everything [*le tout*], toward that which infinitely exceeds the all. I progress beyond the totality that I nevertheless tightly embrace. I go on the margins [*marges*] of the universe, boldly walking elsewhere than where I can be, and a little outside my steps. This slight extravagance, this deviation toward that which cannot be, is not only my own movement leading me to a personal madness, but the movement of the reason that I bear within me. With me the laws gravitate outside the laws, the possible outside the possible. O night, now nothing will make me be, nothing will separate me from you. I adhere marvelously to the simplicity to which you invite me. I lean over you, equal to you, offering you a mirror for your perfect nothingness [*néant*], for your shadows that are neither light nor absence of light, for this void that contemplates. . . . I am the origin of that which has no origin. I create that which cannot be created. (*TO*, 107–8; 163–64)

Bearing everything toward that which exceeds the all . . . beyond the totality . . . on the margins of the universe . . . slight extravagance . . . this deviation toward that which cannot be . . . outside

---

44. As will become apparent, this strange humanism is, in a certain sense, inhuman, for it subverts the humanism characteristic of the ontotheological tradition. For Blanchot, as for Levinas, the Western humanism that ends in Hegel's divinization of the human is not human enough.

the laws . . . outside the possible . . . mirror of perfect nothingness . . . the origin of that which has no origin. . . . The "I" of this
text is not only the anonymous voice of Thomas the Obscure; it is also
art. The origin of that which has no origin is the origin of the work
of art. For Blanchot, as for Heidegger and Bataille, the origin of the
work of art is "the intimacy of [the] tear, rent, fissure, cleft [*déchirure*]"
(*SL*, 226; 236). To be open to this tear is to be opened by the work of
the work of art. "This experience is," for Blanchot, "the experience of
art. Art—as images, as words, and as rhythm—indicates the menacing proximity of a vague and empty outside, a neuter existence, null,
without limit, sordid absence, a suffocating condensation where
being ceaselessly perpetuates itself as nothingness" (*SL*, 242–43;
255). The excessive *dehors*, which the work of art neither reveals nor
conceals, is the terrifyingly ancient. "But where [then] has art led us?
To a time before the world, before the beginning. It has cast us out of
our power to begin and to end; it has turned us toward the outside
without intimacy, without place, without rest. It has led us into the
infinite migration of error [*erreur*]. . . . It ruins the origin by returning it to the errant [*errante*] immensity of an eternity gone astray" (*SL*,
244; 257).

By "returning to a time before the world, before the beginning,"
art, in a phrase of Hegel repeated by Blanchot, is "a thing of the past."
The interpretations of the past of art developed by Hegel and Blanchot
differ significantly. Hegel argues that art is past because it has been
surpassed in philosophy. As we have seen, what is imperfectly represented in the artistic image is perfectly presented in the philosophical
concept. Blanchot, by contrast, maintains that the work of art "is very
ancient, terrifyingly ancient, lost in the night of time. It is the origin
that always precedes us and is always given before us, for it is the
approach of what allows us to depart—a thing of the past, in a
different sense from what Hegel said" (*SL*, 229; 239). The past of art
is not a past present that can be represented. Rather, art is bound to
and by the unrepresentable before that is always already past. From
this point of view, all art can be interpreted as *la recherche du temps
perdu*. By persisting in quest-ioning, this "re-search" does not end in
absolute knowledge but repeatedly "relates to the unknown as unknown" (*EI*, 442). Blanchot believes the privileged form of this endless quest is *literature*.

Literature is the work of art when art does not work. For Blanchot,
"the ideal of literature is to say nothing, to speak in order to say
nothing." Literature can approach this ideal only through "a strange
slipping and sliding [*un glissement étrange*] between being and not

being, presence and absence, reality and nonreality."[45] This *glissement* involves the impossible pursuit of that which language always excludes. "Literature, as we discern it, is held apart from every excessively strong determination, hence it is repugnant to masterpieces and even withdraws from the idea of a work [*œuvre*] to the extent that it makes of it a form of nonwork [*désœuvrement*]. Creative, perhaps, but that which it creates is always hollow with respect to what is and this hollowing produces only what is more slippery, less sure of being, and because of that, as though attracted to an other measure, that of its unreality where, in the play of infinite difference, that which nonetheless affirms itself by withdrawing under the veil of the not" (*EI,* 592). Never simply work or a work, literature is (a) play—*le jeu de la différence infinie.* The play of infinite difference, which affirms itself by withdrawing under the veil of the Not, is unspeakable. It/*il* must, therefore, be written.

Writing becomes possible only *after* the work of the author Derrida describes as "the last philosopher of the book" (*OG,* 26; 41). "The cut [*coupure*] required by writing is a break [*coupure*] with thought when thought ascribes to itself immediate proximity, a break with all *empirical* experience of the world. In this sense, writing is also a rupture with all present consciousness, being always already involved in the experience of the nonmanifest or the unknown (understood as the neuter). But let us thus understand why the advent of writing would only have been able to take place after the completion of discourse (for which Hegel at least has shown us a metaphor in absolute knowledge)" (*EI,* 391). Always arriving late, the "after" of writing repeats the "before" that is forever outside the book. This *dehors* is an *Other* that can be neither sublated nor sublimated. "Writing," Blanchot argues, "is the relation to the *other* of every book, to that which would be de-scription or un-writing [*dé-scription*], a writerly [*scripturaire*] exigency outside discourse, outside language. To write [is to write] at the edge, margin, border, rim, hem [*au bord*] of the book, outside the book" (*EI,* 626). That which is other than the book is not a reciprocal or antithetical difference. Instead of a binary opposite, *l'autre* is "alterity itself" (*l'altérité même; EI,* 634). This alterity, which cannot be "taken up into" (*aufgehoben, relevé*) any book, is what we have previously encountered as "pure exteriority." "What summons us to write, when the time of the book determined by the beginning-end relation, and the space of the book determined by deployment from a center, cease to impose themselves? The lure of (pure) exteriority" (*EI,* 625).

45. Blanchot, *La part du feu,* pp. 314; 327.

To heed the summons of the outside, to yield to its lure is to approach the approach of the Impossible. In writing, the proximate draws near by forever withdrawing. "Writing begins only when it is the approach of that point where nothing reveals itself, where, in the bosom [*le sein*] of dissimulation, speaking is still the shadow of speech, a language that is still only its image, an imaginary language and a language of the imaginary, the one no one speaks, the murmur of the incessant and interminable that one has to *silence* if one wants, at last, to be heard or understood" (*SL,* 48; 41). The word, which (impossibly) "reveals" nothing, exposes[46] the "crisis of the word." "The current play of etymology," Blanchot points out, "makes of writing a cutting movement, a tearing or rending, a crisis [*un mouvement coupant, une déchirure, une crise*]" (*EI,* 38–39).[47] The lacerating movement of writing cannot be contained in fixed language or captured by proper words. Either recalling Levinas and anticipating Derrida or recalling Derrida and anticipating Levinas (genealogy, as always, is uncertain), Blanchot describes the improper, excessive, excentric, extravagant, duplicitous word of the writer as "a trace." To write nothing or almost nothing, it is necessary to write and erase *at the same time.* This impossible double gesture, which "is" the restless movement of the Impossible, is staged in the trace.

> To write, that is to go, by the world of traces, toward the efface-
> ment of traces and of all traces, because signs clash with totality
> and always already disperse themselves. . . . Traces do not return
> to the moment of the mark, they are without origin, but not
> without end in the permanence that seems to perpetuate them,
> traces which, even while becoming confounded and replacing
> themselves, are forever there and forever cut off from that whose
> trace they would be, having no other being than their plurality, as
> if there were not *a* trace but traces never the same and always
> repeated. The *mark* [*marque*] of writing. (*PA,* 77)

As the endless repetition of traces, writing is incessant reinscription. Writing, in other words, is never original but always "secondary" or "supplemental" to an origin that is never present.

> To write, in this sense, is always first to rewrite, and to rewrite
> does not refer to any preliminary writing, no more than to an

46. Since writing is never the product of the constructive subject, the writer neither poses nor posits. To the contrary, the writer ex-poses the ex-position of every seemingly secure position.

47. Blanchot continues: "This is simply the reminder of the proper tool for writing, which was also the proper tool for incising: the stylet" (*EI,* 39).

anteriority of language or presence or signification. Rewriting—a doubling that always precedes or suspends unity while demarking it: to rewrite holds itself apart from all productive initiative and pretends to produce *nothing,* not even the past or the future or the present of writing. To rewrite by repeating that which has no place, will have no place, has had no place, inscribes itself in a nonunified system of relations that cross without any point of intersection affirming their coincidence, inscribing themselves under the exigency of the return by which we are torn away from the modes of temporality that are always measured by a unity of presence. (*PA,* 48–49)

By uprooting the unity of presence, writing interrupts the presence of unity. This displacement has both spatial and temporal dimensions. Writing "desituates" presence by differentiating what is not here, and delays the present by "deferring" what is not now. The spacing and timing of *différer* coincide in the polyvalent term *différence.* "*La différence,*" Blanchot contends, "is the play of time and space" (*EI,* 243).[48] The trope of this differential play is *writing:* "writing is difference . . . and difference writes" (*EI,* 247).

As the knot in which space and time are interlaced, *différence,* which is neither present nor absent, is the condition of the possibility of presence and absence. Since it is never present, *différence* is always *hors langage.* The one who tries to write "outside language" in order to evoke that which has no place and has not taken place engages in "the practice of the impossible" (*EI,* 491). Blanchot freely admits that "writing is, perhaps, nonwriting" (*PA,* 67). If writing is nonwriting, then to write is, in effect, to write Not. Not, however, can be written, if at all, only in the absence of writing. To write (in) this absence, the writer must attempt to write the absence of (the) work. "To write [therefore] is to produce the absence of the work (the out-of-work [*le désœuvrement*]). Or again, writing is the absence of the work as it *produces itself* through the work, throughout the work. Writing as unemployment (in the active sense of the word) is the chance [*l'aléa*] between reason and unreason" (*EI,* 623). The unemployment of the writer calls into question the economy of the book. Writing is not "productive," "effective," or "useful." To the contrary, it is "useless to the world where only effectiveness counts, and is useless to itself"

48. At this point it is helpful to recall a passage previously cited in which Blanchot describes *différence:* "Disjunction, where time and space would rejoin in disjoining, coincides with that which does not coincide, the noncoincident that in advance turns away from all unity" (*EI,* 241–42).

(*SL*, 215; 224).[49] Paradoxically, precisely this uselessness makes writing so serious. *Le désœuvrement* marks the trace of a remainder, *un reste pur*, which is *hors tout* (*PA*, 62). This *reste* signals "the absence of the book—the very absence, which, as we have seen, the book is intended to fill.

> Writing is absent from the Book, being the nonabsent absence from which, having absented itself from this absence, the Book makes itself readable . . . and comments on itself by enclosing history: closing of the book, severity of the letter, authority of knowledge. One can say of this writing, absent from the book, yet in a relation of alterity [*altérité*] with it, that it remains strange to readability, unreadable insofar as to read is necessarily to enter by the gaze into a relation of meaning or nonmeaning with a presence. Thus there would be a writing exterior to knowledge that is obtained by reading, and also exterior to the form or the demand of the Law. Writing, (pure) exteriority, strange to every relation of presence, as well as to all legality. (*EI*, 631–32)[50]

The writing that is exterior to reading is irreducibly "fragmentary." "The attraction of (pure) exteriority or the vertigo of space as distance," is, according to Blanchot, the "fragmentation that only sends us back to the fragmentary" (*EI*, 626). Like Kierkegaard's unphilosophical *smuler*, Blanchot's "idle [*désœuvrés*] fragments" can be written only *after* the closure of the book. In contrast to the book, which rolls and unrolls time in the continuity of a present that unites beginning, middle, and end, the fragment is "insufficient, unfinished (because it is strange to the category of accomplishment)" (*EI*, 229). Always secondary, the fragment is an unphilosophical postscript calling for endless supplementary postscripts. Fragmentary writing resists both systems and structures. Its words cannot be unified, assembled, or reduced to "1"; they are irrepressibly equivocal because irreducibly plural. "The plurality of the plural word [*la parole plurielle*]: intermittent, discontinuous word, which, without being insignificant, does not speak because of its power to represent and even to signify. That which speaks in it is not signification, the possibility

49. The excess entailed in this uselessness sometimes leads Blanchot to associate art with the sacred. In a passage recalling the link Bataille establishes between *poésie* and the sacred, Blanchot writes: "The poem names the sacred, and men hear the sacred, not the poem. And yet the poem names the sacred as unnameable; in this silence it speaks the unspeakable" (*SL*, 230; 242).

50. To argue that writing is outside the Law is to imply that the writer is an *outlaw*. I will explore this possibility in chapter 10.

of giving meaning or removing meaning, even a multiple meaning. From which we are led to assert, perhaps too hastily, that the word or speech designates itself beginning with the between—that it is, as it were, on guard around a place of divergence, a space of dis-location that it seeks to encircle . . . separating it from itself, identifying with this gap, an imperceptible interval where the word always returns to itself, identical and nonidentical" (*EI*, 234–35).

By opening *l'espace littéraire,* the writer's fragments expose *l'espace de la dis-location* in which author, reader, and book withdraw. Writing spells "the death of the author." In a section of *The Space of Literature* entitled "The Work and the Errant Word," Blanchot argues that "the work demands of the writer that he lose everything he might construe as his own 'nature,' that he lose all character and that, ceasing to be related to others and to himself by the decision that makes him an 'I,' he becomes the empty place where the impersonal affirmation emerges" (*SL,* 55; 50). Through such kenosis, the writer opens the space of an "anonymous third." Even when apparently speaking for himself, the writer actually writes in the third genre. "I" do not write, the "I" does not write; it writes, *il écrit.* The writer's action is, therefore, a passion, his activity a passivity, his doing an undoing. The third "voice" of the writer does not reiterate the synthetic third of Hegel's *savoir absolu* (which soon will return as *SA*), but re-calls the insistent third of Lacan's discourse of the Other in which, as Blanchot emphasizes, *ça parle; ça désire* (*EI,* 449). Through the "ventriloquistic" ploys of *l'il,* the writer becomes the echo of a silence he cannot silence.[51]

In the effort to make the Impossible readable, the writer makes reading impossible. As I have already noted, the writerly text is unreadable. The writer does not communicate a message that can be comprehended, penetrated, or deciphered by the insightful reader. The death of the author entails the disappearance of the reader. "Writing," Blanchot insists, gives nothing to read, nothing to understand" (*PA,* 89). This *rien* is *le non-savoir* that suspends all certainty "between parentheses."

The only "thesis" of the writer is the nonthesis of a "parenthesis"

---

51. In a manner similar to Bataille's grotesque/grotto-esque *poésie,* the discourse of the ventriloquist [*ventriloquus:* speaking from the belly] is spoken from an outside that is inside. We have already observed that the invagination of the intestine hollows out the body proper. This hole creates the opening for the parasitic voice of the ventriloquist. The intestinal nature of these gh/a/o/stly words leads the philosopher to regard the writer's nonworks as shit.

whose *para* is an indigestible *hors d'œuvre*. In writing, "ambiguity is delivered to its excess."[52] This excess, infinitely exceeding everything . . . beyond the totality . . . on the margins of the universe . . . slight extravagance . . . is *le reste* that the book cannot swallow. Such a remainder makes the author of the book gag until he finally vomits.

For the writer, the book is not present but is always to come. *Le livre est le livre à venir.* In fragmentary writing, the end never arrives but is ever deferred. The infinite deferral of difference inscribed in writing marks and remarks the delay of the *Par-ousia.* In the absence of the Word, exile is eternal, erring endless. "Error signifies wandering, the inability to abide and stay because where the wanderer is, the conditions of a definitive here are lacking. In this absence of here and now what happens does not clearly come to pass as an event based upon which something solid could be achieved. Consequently, what happens does not happen, but does not pass either, into the past; it is never passed. It happens and recurs without cease; it is the horror and confusion and uncertainty of eternal repetition. . . . The wanderer's country is not truth, but exile; he lives outside" (*SL*, 238; 247–48). Erring, wandering, exile: Jew not Greek, Abraham not Ulysses.

If Judaism is destined to take on a meaning for us, it is surely by showing us that it is necessary, at all times, to be ready to start out [*se mettre en route*]. . . . The demand to uproot, the affirmation of nomadic truth. It is in this way that [Judaism] stands out clearly against paganism (all paganism): to be pagan is to settle oneself, to stick to the earth in some manner, to establish oneself through a pact with permanence that authorizes the sojourn and certifies the certitude of the soil. Nomadism responds to a relationship that possession does not satisfy. Each time a Jewish man makes a sign to us in history, it is through a movement. Abraham, happily settled in the Sumerian civilization, broke with this civilization at a certain moment, and renounced the sojourn. Later, the Jewish people made themselves into a people [*peuple*] through the exodus. And where does this night of exodus, which renews itself from year to year, lead them each time? To a place that is not a place and where it is not possible to reside. The desert makes a people of the Egyptian slaves, but a people without land, bound by a word. Later, the exodus becomes exile, accompanied by all the trials of a hunted existence—anxiety, insecurity, unhappiness, hope—settling in each man's heart. But this exile, heavy as it is, is not only recognized as an incomprehensible curse.

52. Blanchot, *La part du feu*, p. 328.

There is a truth in exile, and there is a vocation of exile, and if to be Jewish is to be doomed and devoted [*voué*] to dispersion, that is because dispersion, just as it calls for a sojourn without place, just as it destroys all fixed relationships of power with *one* individual, *one* group, or *one* State, also frees [*dégage*], facing the demand of All, an other demand, and finally prevents the temptation of Unity-Identity (*EI*, 183–84).

A descendant of Abraham, the writer is an Ishmaelite. Always already exiled, his artful erring inscribes the nonabsent absence of the neuter. This entertaining interval in which death is (the) impossible marks the absence of time as the eternity of time rather than the time of eternity. The obsession of the writer is "to make what is ungraspable inescapable." To write obsessively is to write incessantly. Writing is forever rewriting—but always with (a) *différance*.

Overleaf: Anne and Patrick Poirier, *Mimas*. Courtesy of Anne and Patrick Poirier and Galerie Daniel Templon. Photograph © André Morain.

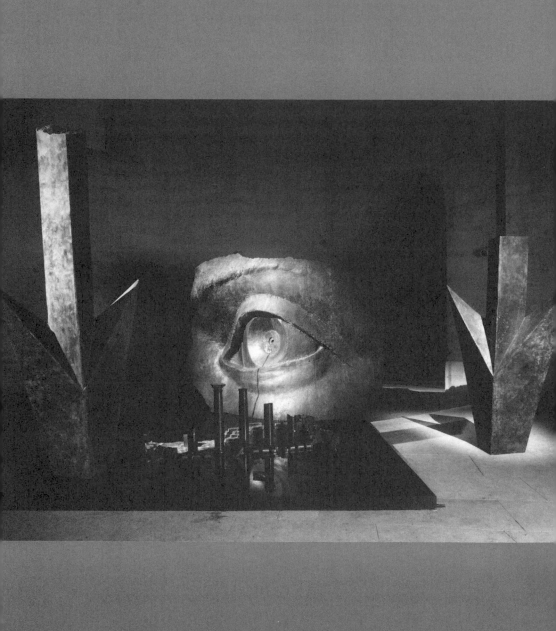

9

Rewriting

JACQUES DERRIDA

Exergue

It is because it touches upon firm structures and physical institutions and not simply upon discourses (speeches, reasonings) or
significant descriptions that deconstruction continually distinguishes itself from an analysis or a critique (*VP*, 25).

Of Grammatology begins with a prefatory supplement entitled
"Exergue." An exergue, in the strict sense of the term, is "a small
space usually on the reverse of a coin or metal, below the central
design, for any minor inscription, the date, engraver's signature, etc."
The basic token of exchange in our economy is no longer metal but is
now paper. We trade (in) papers that are signs whose value is arbitrary.
Since there is no stable referent, no "transcendental signified" securing the signs we swap, our currency floats and flows freely. The sign of
the groundless sign that "grounds" our economy is a barred S: $.
Inasmuch as "grammatology" opens with an "exergue," the best place
to begin the examination of writing might be the backside of $. If, as
Freud suggests, money "is" shit, perhaps grammatology "is" something like scatology—the impossible "science" of "remain(s)."[1] The
questions to be considered in this context are not only economic; they
are psychological, political, social, religious, and literary. When attempting to read the exergue, it is helpful to recall Nietzsche's remark
concerning the currency of truth:

> What, then, is truth? A mobile army of metaphors, metonyms,
> and anthropomorphisms—in short, a sum of human relations,

---

1. The notion of *le reste* plays a very important role in Derrida's rereading of
Hegel. It functions as either a noun or a verb, and the multiple nuances upon which
Derrida plays cannot easily be captured in translation. *Reste* can designate rest,
remainder, residue, trace, vestige, and leavings. *Rester* means to remain, stop, dwell,
continue. In most cases, I will follow John Leavey's imaginative rendering of *reste* as
"remain(s)."

which have been enhanced, transposed, and embellished poetically and rhetorically, and which after long use seem firm, canonical, and obligatory to a people: truths are illusions about which one has forgotten that this is what they are; metaphors that are worn out and without sensuous power; coins that have their obverse effaced and now matter only as metal, no longer as coins.[2]

Capitalism (from *caput,* head) can be understood as an ontotheological political economy. I have argued that the guiding principle of ontotheology is fundamentalist belief—belief in the fundaments named identity and unity. The God in whom ontotheology trusts is ONE. This oneness is the principle that founds the united state(s). The ideal of the capitalist economy is printed on a scroll held in the beak of an eagle: *E Pluribus Unum,* From Many, One. A representation of the eagle, whose imperial name recalls the "strange name" of *the* philosopher par excellence, is on the topside of The Great Seal. In the *Journals of the Continental Congress,* the founding fathers explain the significance of this image.

> ARMS. Paleways of the thirteen pieces, argent {silver; compare, *l'argent,* silver, money, cash}, and gules {the color red indicated on a blazon by engraved vertical lines; from Latin *gula,* throat}; a chief, azure; the escutcheon on the breast of the American eagle displayed proper, holding in his dexter talon an olive branch, and in his sinister a bundle of thirteen arrows, all proper, and in his beak a scroll, inscribed with this motto, *"E pluribus Unum."*
> For the CREST. Over the head of the eagle, which appears above the escutcheon, a glory, or, breaking through a cloud, proper, and surrounding thirteen stars, forming a constellation, argent, on an azure field.[3]

2. Nietzsche, "On Truth and Lie in the Extra-Moral Sense," *The Portable Nietzsche,* ed. W. Kaufmann (New York: Penguin Books, 1980), pp. 46–47.

3. *Journals of the Continental Congress,* 1774–89, vol. 22, January 1–August 9, 1782 (Washington: Government Printing Office, 1914), p. 339.

The exergue of the dollar also includes the exergue of the Great Seal. To the left of the ONE, the backside of the seal appears. The record of the Continental Congress again is instructive.

> REVERSE. A pyramid unfinished. In the zenith, an eye in a triangle surround with a glory proper.[4] Over the eye these words, *"Annuit Coeptis."* On the base of the pyramid the numerical letters MDCCLXXVI. And underneath the following motto, *"Novus Ordo Seclorum."*

In a supplement to this text, the secretary elaborates: "The pyramid signifies strength and duration. The eye over it and the motto allude to the many signal interpositions of providence in favour of the American cause. The date underneath is that of the Declaration of Independence, and the words under it signify the beginning of the new American Era, which commences from that date."[5]

This is a strange exergue: a pyramid which, in the words of Hegel, "has its very tip knocked off" (*PS,* 286; 339).[6] Above the decapitated pyramid there is an eye in a triangle that radiates sunlight. The semicircular legends read: "He has favored our undertakings;" and "A new order of the ages." Pyramid and triangle; an empty *entre-deux;* a circle cut in two; undertaking . . . age. Space and time; spacing and timing. What is this new order or disorder? The die for this exergue within an exergue was never cast. It was a noneventful *coup de dés.* Why?

Whose eye is in the triangle? God's we are told. The image of the eye within a triangle surrounded by rays of the sun is a common symbol for the all-seeing, panoptical, penal, eagle eye of God. God's eye is always the right eye. It is, however, unclear whether the eye in the exergue is the *right* eye. It is possible, perhaps likely, that William Barton, designer of the seal, borrowed the triangulated eye from the apron of the Freemasons. The "father" of the country, whose image adorns the face of the dollar, was, after all, a Mason. Washington, whose monument is an obelisk, is often pictured standing erect with a Masonic apron veiling his generative organ. In a well-known etching ("Washington as a Mason," by George Edward Perine), the first president is wearing an apron embroidered by Madame Lafayette. Although the Freemasons trace their ancestry back to the seventeenth-

---

4. Note the repetition of the word "proper" in these passages.
5. *Journals,* pp. 339–40.
6. Derrida cites these lines from the *Phenomenology* in "The Pit and the Pyramid: Introduction to Hegel's Semiology," *M,* 77n; 89n.

century guilds of English stoneworkers, the practice of wearing elabo-
rately decorated aprons seems to have originated in France. French
and French-influenced aprons usually depict "small temple buildings
reminiscent of the Pantheon in Paris; and columns topped with
pomegranates. Landscape scenes with Egyptian elements such as
sphinxes and obelisks, or with motifs of classical architecture, are
common in the engraved, painted, and embroidered designs."[7] Almost every apron design includes an eye in the midst of a triangle,
which is inserted between two erect columns. Examining these eyes
carefully, one makes a surprising discovery: the Masonic eye is usually
the *left* eye. While the right eye is a traditional symbol of sun, day,
and the future, the left eye is a common symbol of the moon,
night, and the past. In view of the image of the pyramid under the
eye, it is noteworthy that the Egyptian god of the moon is Thoth, the
nocturnal representative of Ra (for whom obelisks are constructed).
The figure of Thoth, Derrida explains,

> is opposed to its other (father, sun, life, speech, origin or orient,
> etc.), but as that which at once supplements and supplants it.
> Thoth extends or opposes by repeating or replacing. By the same
> token, the figure of Thoth takes shape and takes its shape from
> the very thing it resists and for which it substitutes. But it
> thereby opposes *itself,* passes into its other, and this messenger-
> god is truly a god of the absolute passage between opposites. If he
> had any identity—but he is precisely the god of nonidentity—he
> would be that *coincidentia oppositorum* to which we will soon have
> recourse again. In distinguishing himself from his opposite,
> Thoth also imitates it, becomes its sign and representative,
> obeys it and *conforms* to it, replaces it, by violence if need be. He
> is thus the father's other [*l'autre du père*], the father, and the
> subversive movement of replacement. The god of writing is thus
> at once his father, his son, and himself. He cannot be assigned a
> fixed spot in the play of differences. Sly, slippery, and masked, an
> intriguer and a card, like Hermes, he is neither king nor jack
> [*valet*], but rather a sort of *joker,* a floating signifier, a wild card
> [*une carte neutre*], who puts play into play. (D, 92–93; 104)

Une carte neutre: When not simply a valet, "Jack" can be rendered
"Jacques," *Maître Jacques,* Jack-of-all trades.

What eventually was accepted as the Great Seal was not the first
emblem proposed for the nation. Benjamin Franklin and Thomas

---

7. *Bespangled, Painted and Embroidered: Decorated Masonic Aprons in America,
1790—1850* (Lexington, MA: Museum of our National Heritage), p. 25.

Jefferson had earlier suggested different designs. Franklin urged Congress to adopt an image of Moses dividing the Red Sea for the children of Israel, with the waters closing behind them to engulf the Pharaoh. Also drawing on the Old Testament, Jefferson proposed a seal depicting Israel wandering in the wilderness under the guidance of a cloud by day and a column of fire by night. In these alternative suggestions, images proliferate: Israel and Egypt, a red-hot column illuminating the night, the cleaving of/from *la mer;* leaving *la mère* to follow *le père*. *Mer,* the French word for sea, which is almost the word for mother (*mère*), is the Egyptian word for pyramid. In view of the cleavage of *la mer/mère,* might the pyramid be read otherwise?

In some cultures, a pyramid with the tip knocked off serves as a sacrificial altar: like the altar Abraham built, which obsesses Kierkegaard, or the pyramidal altars of sacrifice of the Aztecs and Mayans, which obsess Bataille, or the pyramid atop the obelisk in the Place de la Concorde where the sacrificial scaffold was constructed. When the pyramid serves as such an altar, does it remain a tomb—an empty tomb? Is this tomb merely a sign—a sign of a sign— a letter never raised to spirit? Is the pyramid the empty tomb that marks the inescapability of death rather than the resurrection of life? Is this tomb the crypt of another Abraham, an Abraham named Nicolas? And if we reread the pyramid, must we not also reread the eye in the middle of the triangle? Is this the evil, rather than the providential eye? The eye of Medusa and not God? Is this Bataille's pineal eye at the pinnacle of the obelisk scored with hieroglyphs, which marks the blind spot of philosophy? Or Lacan's fascinating eye in the midst of the Oedipal triangle that petrifies the philosopher? Is this eye, inscribed in the exergue of the exergue of the foundation of the capitalist economy, the eye that signals the decapitation of the whole System? The exergue seems to be a cracked, faulted, fissured, torn, rent seal. Is the origin of this work of art and the origin of the economy that rests upon (which is not to say grounded in) it, the *Riss* of the pyramid? The God in whom we (but who is this "we," this "magisterial *wir*"?) trust, the God named ONE, appears to be suspended between binary opposites: left and right, pyramid and eagle, Jew and Christian, Africa and Europe, Algeria and France (and/or Germany).

With these questions, we do not move beyond the figure of Abraham. To the contrary, we return to the point of departure without having completed a circle. Commenting on the interpretation of Abraham that Hegel presents in his early theological fragments, Derrida writes:

The *Vergleichung* explains the failure [*échec*], the fall, or the precipice. It is found in Deuteronomy 32: "In the regard cast over his political life, he (Moses) compares (*vergleicht*) the way in which his God has led the Jews, through his instrumentality, to the conduct of the eagle (*des Adlers*) that wishes to train its young to fly—it continually beats its wings over the nest, takes the young on its wings, and carries them far and wide."

Thus the eagle set forth in Moses's *Vergleichung*. Hegel begins by reproducing the statement. He transcribes Deuteronomy almost faithfully. Then he completes and corrects in order to return the stone again. In every logic, it is necessary to be stone in order to transform the other into stone. Like the Gorgon, the Jew petrifies the other. Hegel said this; now he marks that the Jew is stone himself. His discourse is not only rhetorical, but of rhetoric, on the subject of rhetoric. "Only the Jews did not finish this beautiful image (*Bild*), these young never became eagles; in relation to their God, they rather afford the image of an eagle, which by mistake, warmed stones, showed them how to fly and carried them on its wings into the clouds, but whose weight could never become flight [*vol*], whose borrowed warmth never broke out [*éclata*] (*aufschlug*) in the flames of life."

The logic of the concept is of the eagle [*de l'aigle*], the remain(s) of stone [*de pierre*].

The Jew falls again [*retombe*]; he signifies that which does not let itself be raised—sublated [*relever*] perhaps but denied from then on as Jew—to the height of the *Begriff*. He holds back, draws the *Aufhebung* toward earth. (*G*, 65–66)

Dissemination begins with an *Hors d'œuvre* that is, in effect, an exergue. The margin marked by this title (if it is *a* title) is a triangle or pyramid—an inverted triangle or pyramid. This overturned pyramid threatens to decapitate the philosopher who attempts to force his reader "to walk on [his] head."[8]

Exergue, derived from *ex:* out of + *ergon:* work, probably was intended to be a quasi-Greek rendering of *hors d'œuvre*, something lying outside the work. When understood as an *hors d'œuvre*, the exergue is *désœuvrement*. The exteriority of this unemployed *hors d'œuvre* is not, however, a simple outside. Though the exergue is *ex ergon*, it is not merely outside the work. The exergue functions as something like a "*frame*" (*cadre*) for the work. As such, it is "*neither*

---

8. In the "Preface" to the *Phenomenology*, Hegel describes his project in the following terms: "When natural consciousness entrusts itself straightway to science, it makes an attempt, induced by it knows not what, to walk on its head too, just this once" (*PS*, 15; 25).

OUTWORK

HORS D'OEUVRE
EXTRATEXT
FOREPLAY
BOOKEND
FACING

inside nor outside, neither over nor under, it foils every opposition but does not remain indeterminate and gives rise to *the work {œuvre}"* (*VP,* 14). If the frame is neither here nor there, then one must ask whether it exists. Does it "stand out" or only "withdraw" (*re-traite*)? The distinguishing "trait" (*trait*) of the frame is that it neither exists nor does not exist. "*There is* framing, but the frame *does not exist* (Il y a *du cadre, mais le cadre* n'existe pas; *VP,* 93). In the *Il y a,* which repeats the *Es gibt,* the frame-works. "The frame works in effect. Place of work, origin structurally bordered with more value, that is to say, overflowing the edge into these two edges through that which it overflows. It works like wood. It crackles, breaks down, falls to pieces even while cooperating in the production with the product extending beyond it and resulting from it. It never simply lets itself be exposed" (*VP,* 87). Though it does not exist and therefore cannot (immodestly) expose itself, the work of the frame is the nonoriginal origin of the work of art.

When the *œuvre* that the *hors d'œuvre* frames is a book, the exergue is a preface. Echoing Blanchot, Derrida asks: What "is" a preface? Does the preface exist any more than the frame? "Prefaces, along with forewords, introductions, preludes, preliminaries, preambles, prologues, and prolegomena, have always been written, it seems, in view of their own self-effacement. Upon reaching the end of the *pre-* (which presents and precedes, or rather forestalls, the presentative production, and, in order to put before the reader's eyes what is not yet visible, is obliged to speak, to predict, and predicate), the route that has been covered must annul itself. But this subtraction leaves a mark of erasure, a *remain(s)*, which is added to the subsequent text and which cannot be completely summed up within it" (*D, 9; 14*). If the book is the encyclopedic book of books, the preface is the *Phenomenology of Spirit.* As I argued when considering Blanchot's account of "the absence of the book," the marginal preface is the condition of the possibility and the impossibility of the book. Hegel must write the preface in order to denounce the preface. This task is, of course, impossible. Faced with this impossibility, the philosopher's writing always undercuts his book. Though intended to be all-inclusive, bookish concepts inevitably leave a *reste* that "falls" [*tombe*] *hors d'œuvre.* For the philosopher, such a remainder is the "shit" (*déchet*) his system is constructed to wipe away (*D, 49; 57*). But the backside of the speculative economy cannot be completely cleaned up, the exergue never totally erased. The eternal return of the exergue is marked by the repeated reinscription of the pyramid.[9] The *tombe* of the *reste* is the crypt of the pyramid. As the spacing of time and timing of space, this crypt is the sign of death—death that can never be overcome since the *Parousia* is always inscribed in *le livre à venir.* "Time is the time of the preface; space—whose time *will have been* the Truth—is the space of the preface. The preface would thus occupy the entire *location* and *duration* of the book" (*D, 13; 18*). As exergue, the preface sounds *le glas* of philosophy.

When rereading the exergue of the speculative economy, the decapitalized pyramid at times appears to be something like an A. Look again. By tracing the pyramid on the backside of the dollar we discover:

9. In his consideration of Genet, Derrida associates toilet, throne, volcano, tipless cone and topless pyramid. This "shithole" (recall the *"Rembrandt déchiré"*) constitutes a gap in the midst of a circle. "The erection in abyss, that is how that [*ça*] signs and how that gets into the saddle, how that reigns, how that is checked, how that signs and that reigns. *Genêts* grow very near volcanoes. 'At the center of the circle, there is the can where one goes to shit. It is a receptacle three meters high, in the form of a truncated cone. It has two ears, one on each side, on which you place your feet after sitting down, and a very low backrest, like that of an Arab saddle, so that

Derrida suggests that the A figured in the pyramid can be read as the A of *différance*.

> Therefore, preliminarily, let me recall that this discreet graphic intervention, which neither primarily nor simply aims to scandalize the reader or the grammarian, came to be formulated in the course of a written investigation of a question about writing. Now it happens, I would say in effect, that this graphic difference (*a* instead of *e*), this marked difference between two apparently vocal notations, between two vowels, remains purely graphic: it is read, or it is written, but it cannot be heard. It cannot be apprehended in speech, and we shall see why it also bypasses the order of understanding [*entendement;* compare *entendre:* to hear] in general. It is offered by a mute mark, by a tacit monument, I would even say by a pyramid [*pyramide*], thinking not only of the form of the letter when it is printed as a capital, but also of the text in Hegel's *Encyclopedia* in which the body of the sign is compared to the Egyptian Pyramid. The *a* of différance, thus, is not heard; it remains silent, secret and discreet as a tomb: *oikesis.* [10] And thereby let us anticipate the delineation of a site, the familial residence of the tomb proper in which is produced, by *différance,* the *economy of death.* This stone—provided that one knows how to decipher its inscription—is not far from announcing the death of the tyrant. (*M,* 4; 4)

In what styles can the stony silence of the pyramid be marked and remarked?

Styles: Flowers and Pillars

FLOWER

water

flows in

time   of water

thought

esteemed for its blossoms

---

when you drop your load you have the majesty of a barbaric king on a metal throne. . . . When I entered the room, what struck me most was the silence of the thirty inmates and, immediately, the solitary, imperial can, center of the moving circle" (*G,* 47).

10. The English translator notes: "'Tomb' in Greek is *oikesis,* which is akin to the Greek *oikos*—house—from which the word 'economy' derives (*oikos*—house— and *nemein*—to manage). Thus Derrida speaks of the 'economy of death' as the 'familial residence and tomb of the proper'" (*M,* 4n). For further comments on *oikos,* see above, chapter 1, note 20.

           blossom
    flow

          v'er-i-ly

                            waves

    moves as a wave

                          words
             vibrate

       between hope and fear   in
                              fact   fluctuating

My process consists of leaving "found words" precisely where they
exist in the columns of Webster's Secondary School Dictionary
© 1913 edition. The "found words" then comprise the statement.
Words as objects, textures, movements, spaces, sounds; words
supporting words, even as a column is built of mortar and stones. [11]

Perhaps one will find that I make quite a bit of use of the dictionary. I try to do this as the signer of the infatuating text (that is
to say, in a genetic style) that does not hesitate to provoke poetics
with Larousse. (*G,* 190)

What comes after "Exergue"? The first chapter in *Of Grammatology*
is entitled "The End of the Book and the Beginning of Writing."
Derrida closes this opening statement by stressing the importance of
Hegel for his grammatological undertaking.

The horizon of absolute knowledge is the effacement of writing in
the logos, the retrieval of the trace in prousia, the reappropriation
of difference, the accomplishment of what I have elsewhere called
the *metaphysics of the proper.*
   Yet all Hegel thought within this horizon, all, that is, except
eschatology, may be reread as a meditation on writing. Hegel
is *also* the thinker of irreducible difference. He rehabilitated
thought as the *memory productive* of signs. And he reintroduced . . .
the essential necessity of the written trace [*trace écrite*] in a philosophical—that is to say Socratic—discourse that had always
believed it possible to do without it: the last philosopher of the
book and the first thinker of writing. (*OG,* 26; 41)

11. Doris Cross, *col.umns* (San Francisco: Trike, 1982). This statement is a preface to the book from which I have borrowed the Cross's "Flower" column.

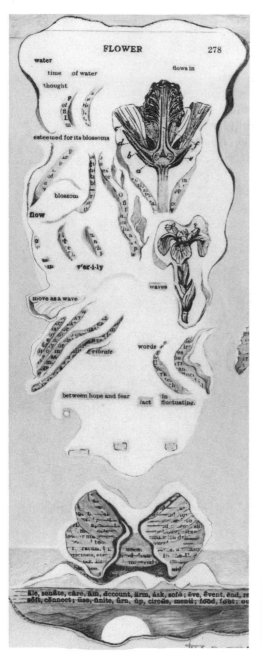

FLOWER 278

water

time of water flows in

thought

esteemed for its blossoms

blossom

flow

v'er-i-ly

waves

move as a wave

words vibrate

between hope and fear fact in fluctuating.

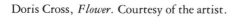

āle, senāte, cãre, ăm, ăccount, ärm, ásk, sofá; ēve, ĕvent, ēnd, re
sŏft, cŏnnect; ūse, ûnite, ûrn, ŭp, circŭs, menū; fōōd, fŏŏt; ou

Doris Cross, *Flower*. Courtesy of the artist.

Gaudimallan Siva Linga. Courtesy of the
Archaeological Survey of India and the
American Institute of Indian Studies.

While philosophy is bookish, thinking is writerly. In the aftermath of Heidegger's interrogation of thinking, the philosopher is not a thinker, *sensu strictissimo,* and the writer is not truly a philosopher. Though Hegel is *the* philosopher in whom the epoch of ontotheology comes to a conclusion, he is, in some sense, already a thinker of writing.[12] This ambiguity is the source of Derrida's endless fascination with Hegel. In a 1971 interview, Derrida goes so far as to insist: "We will never be finished with the reading or rereading of the Hegelian text and, in a certain sense, I do nothing other than attempt to explain myself on this point. I believe, in effect, that the text of Hegel is necessarily fissured [*fissuré*]; that it is something more and other than the circular closure of its representation. It is not reduced to a content of philosophemes, it also necessarily produces a powerful writing operation, a remain(s) of writing [*reste d'écriture*], whose strange relationship to the philosophical content of Hegel's text must be reexamined, that is, the movement by means of which the text exceeds what it intends to say, permits itself to be turned away from, to return to, and to repeat itself outside its self-identity."[13]

To think the fissure, excess, remain(s) of the System, it is not enough to criticize Hegel. As Kierkegaard once observed, when dealing with Hegel, to do the opposite is also a form of imitation.[14] Instead of assuming a stance of direct opposition, Derrida approaches his critical task indirectly by pointing out that "Hegel's own interpretation can be reinterpreted—against him" (*WD,* 260; 382). Developing Bataille's analysis of "the blind spot of Hegelianism," Derrida argues:

12. Two pages before the above description of Hegel, Derrida points out that Hegel "undoubtedly *summed up* the totality of the philosophy of the logos. He determined ontology as absolute logic; he assembled all the delimitations of philosophy as presence; he assigned to presence the eschatology of parousia, of the self-proximity of infinite subjectivity. And for the same reason he had to debase or subordinate writing" (*OG,* 24; 39). Elsewhere Derrida claims: "Hegel is thus at once as close to and as far as possible from a 'modern' conception of the text or of writing: nothing precedes textual generality absolutely" (*D,* 20; 27).

13. Derrida, *Positions,* trans. A. Bass (Chicago: University of Chicago Press, 1981), pp. 77–78. *Positions* (Paris: Les Editions de Minuit, 1972), pp. 103–4. Compare Blanchot's remark: "Is there not another reading of the Book in which the other of the book would cease to be announced in precepts? And, reading thus, would we still read a book? Would we not then be near to reading *the absence of the book?*" (*EI,* 632).

14. In his consideration of Levinas's reading of Hegel, Derrida repeats Kierkegaard's insight: "As soon as *he speaks* against Hegel, Levinas can only confirm Hegel" (*WD,* 120; 176).

In naming the without-reserve [*le sans-réserve*] of absolute expenditure [*dépense absolue*] "abstract negativity," Hegel, through *precipitation,* blinded himself to that which he had laid bare under the rubric of negativity. And did so through precipitation toward the seriousness of meaning and the security of knowledge. This is why "he did not know to what extent he was right." And was wrong for being right, for having triumphed over the negative. To go "to the end" both of "absolute rending" [*déchirement absolu*] and of the negative without "measure," without reserve, is not progressively to pursue *logic* to the point at which, *within discourse,* the *Aufhebung* (discourse itself) makes logic collaborate with the constitution and interiorizing memory of meaning, with *Erinnerung.* On the contrary, it is convulsively to tear apart [*déchirer*] the negative side, that which makes it the reassuring *other* surface of the positive; and it is to exhibit within the negative, in an instant, that which can no longer be called negative. And can no longer be called negative precisely because it has no reserved underside, because it can no longer permit itself to be converted into positivity, because it can no longer *collaborate* with the continuous linking-up/enchaining [*enchaînement*] of meaning, concept, time, and truth in discourse, because it literally can no longer *labor* and let itself be interrogated as the "work of the negative." Hegel saw this without seeing it, showed it while concealing it. Thus, he must be followed to the end without reserve, to the point of agreeing with him against himself and of wresting his discovery from the too *conscientious* interpretation he gave of it. (*WD,* 259–60; 381)

To wrest Hegel's "discovery" from him, it is not sufficient to expose the faults "in" the System by writing *about* the gaps in the Hegelian book. Rather, one must try *to write the fissure itself* by inscribing the remain(s) that Hegel's *œuvre* "shows" while "concealing." Such writing will necessarily be rent and will inevitably rend. The writer who attempts this excessive writing is both slightly cracked and mortally wounded. "Simultaneously, by means of rigorous, philosophically *intransigent* analyses, *and* by means of the inscription of marks that no longer belong to philosophical space, not even to the neighborhood of its other, one would have to displace philosophy's alignment of its own types. To write otherwise [*Ecrire autrement*]. To delimit the space of a closure no longer analogous to what philosophy can represent for itself under this name, according to a straight or circular line enclosing a homogeneous space. To determine, entirely against any philosopheme, the intransigence that prevents it from calculating its margin, by means of a *limitrophic* violence imprinted according to new *types*

(*M,* xxiv–xxv; xx–xxi). What "new *types*" of writing might permit the writer to think what philosophy has left unthought? Is it possible to write *otherwise*—otherwise than being, beyond essence? Or is such writing (the writing of the) impossible?

If the grounding principle of philosophy is One (i.e., identity and unity), then it might be possible to write otherwise by writing duplicitously. To write duplicitously, it is necessary to break the laws and deviate from the methods that implicitly and explicity govern writing in the ontotheological tradition. Strategies have to be devised to *write* what philosophy has not *said* and cannot *say* in language that is nonetheless philosophical. The realization of a writing that is *neither* philosophical *nor* nonphilosophical requires the ceaseless mixing of genres and the constant shifting of styles. To be duplicitous the writer must redouble her [15] efforts by writing with at least two hands at once.

> Two texts, two hands, two visions [*regards*], two ways of listening. Together simultaneously and separately.
>
> The relationship between the two texts, between presence in general (*Anwesenheit*) and that which exceeds it before or beyond Greece—such a relationship can never offer itself in order to be read in the form of presence, supposing that anything else can offer itself in order to be *read* in such a form. And yet, that which gives us to think beyond the closure cannot be simply absent. Absent, either it would give us nothing to think or it still would be a negative mode of presence. Therefore the sign of this excess must be absolutely excessive as concerns all possible presence—absence, all possible production or disappearance of beings in general, and yet, *in some manner,* it must still signify, in a way unthinkable by metaphysics as such. In order to exceed metaphysics it is necessary that a trace be inscribed within the text of metaphysics, a trace that continues to signal not in the direction of another presence, or another form of presence, but in the direction of an entirely other text. Such a trace cannot be thought *more metaphysico.* No philosopheme is prepared to master it. And it (is) that which must elude mastery. Only presence is mastered.
>
> The mode of inscription of such a trace in the text of metaphysics is so unthinkable that it must be described as an erasure of the trace itself. The trace is produced as its own erasure. (*M,* 65; 75–76)

Derrida's most extensive performance of *la double séance* he describes in this passage is his extraordinary nonbook, *Glas.*

15. Like Lacan, Bataille, and Kristeva, Derrida maintains that writing and a certain femininity bear an important relation to each other. The nature of the association between writing and woman will become clearer in what follows.

Columns frame the text. How many columns? Two it seems: one written on Hegel, one written on Genet. But are there *two* columns in *Glas?* The columns in which Derrida deploys his text (which is not an argument proper) fold and refold into each other, repeatedly crossing and crisscrossing, sectioning and intersectioning. Yet they never exactly touch, join, or meet. Appearances to the contrary notwithstanding, it is impossible to know how many columns are graphed in *Glas:* one, two, less than one, more than two?

Perhaps this puzzle can be solved by considering the column itself. What *is* a column? This apparently simple question cannot be answered (though it might permit a *re-pli*). Like the frame whose place it takes, the column does not exist. In an inter-section of "Dissemination," entitled "The Column," which is inserted *between* "The Time before the First" and "The Crossroads of the '*Est*,'" Derrida avers: "The column is nothing, has no meaning in itself. A hollow phallus, cut off from itself, decapitated (i), it guarantees the innumerable passages of dissemination and the playful displacement of the margins. It is never itself, only a writing that endlessly substitutes for itself, doubling it as of its very first surrection" (*D*, 342; 318). In the course of commenting on the implications of Soller's *Nombres*, Derrida underscores the importance of this reading of the column for the critique of ontotheology.

> The "is," which is "Being" as an indication of presence, procures this state of calm, this consciousness of ideal mastery, this power of consciousness in the act of showing, indicating, perceiving, or predicating. . . . Whose discourse tells you: the column *is* this or that, *is there* [est là]; whether it is obvious or hidden behind the multiplicity of apparitions, the column *is*. But the column *has* no Being, nor any being-there [*être-là*], whether here or elsewhere. It belongs to no one. You have no hold over it, you will never absolutely control its extension. You will not take it from somewhere else and put it here. You will not cite it to appear. And from the column's not being (a being), from its not falling under the power of the *is*, all of Western metaphysics, which lives in the certainty of that *is*, has revolved around the column. Not without seeing it but on the contrary in the belief that it sees it. And can be sure, in truth, of the contours of its collapse, as of a center or proper place. (*D*, 352; 391)

To expose the nothingness of the column around which Western philosophy turns, Derrida examines the frame of the encyclopedic book of books—the *Phenomenology of Spirit*. He suspends his reading of Hegel between two columns: a flower (the passing reference to the

religion of flowers in the *Phenomenology*) [16] and a lingam (the consideration of the Indian phallic column in the *Lectures on Aesthetics*). [17]

Why broach the analysis of the culmination/columnation of W-est-
ern philosophy with a consideration of the insignificant detail of a
flower? Opening at the tip of a stem, the flower plays a critical role in
the reproductive process of seed-bearing plants. It includes both male
and female parts. The stamen, which consists of a filament and an
anther, is the pollen-producing organ of the flower. The seed-bearing
organ, the pistil, is made up of the stigma, style, and ovary. The style
is the slender part of the pistil that rises from the ovary, where the
seeds are produced, to the stigma, where fertilization takes place. The
stigma and style extend the connotative range of the "flower."
"Stigma" derives from the Latin *stigma,* which, in turn, comes from
the Greek term for a tattoo mark (*stizein,* to prick, tattoo). In addition
to designating the point on the flower at which fertilization takes
place, "stigma" means: "A mark burned into the skin of a criminal or
slave; a mark or token of infamy, disgrace, or reproach; a mark or spot
on the skin that bleeds as a symptom of hysteria; a mark indicative of a
history of a disease or abnormality; a small mark, spot, or pore, such
as the respiratory spiracle of an insect or an eyespot in certain algae;
marks or sores corresponding to and resembling the crucifixion
wounds of Jesus, sometimes impressed on the bodies of certain persons
in a state of religious ecstasy or hysteria." No temporary mark, the
stigma is a wound that never heals.

The word "style" is no less complex than "stigma." A "style" is not
only the prolongation of the flower's ovary but is also, among other
things: "an instrument made of metal, bone, etc. having one end
sharp-pointed for incising letters on a wax tablet, and the other flat
and broad for smoothing the tablet and erasing what is written; a
weapon of offense, for stabbing, etc.; a hard point for tracing, in
manifold writing; the pin, rod, or triangular plate which forms the
gnomon of a sun-dial; a sponge-spicule pointed at one end; an inscription or legend; the manner of expression characteristic of a particular
writer; a particular mode or form of skilled construction, execution,
or production; the manner in which a work of art is executed; the
definite type of architecture, distinguished by special characteristics
of structure or ornamentation; the attractive quality of a thing." [18]

16. For an account of the place of flower religion in Hegel's overall argument, see
chapter 1, fourth section. I will return to this issue in the third section of this chapter.

17. G. W. F. Hegel, *Lectures on Aesthetics,* trans. T. M. Knox (New York: Oxford
University Press, 1975), 1:641.

18. These definitions of "stigma" and "style" are from *The American Heritage
Dictionary of the English Language.*

As a result of the flower's multiple aspects, it cannot be defined in terms of the binary oppositions that structure thought and language. Derrida insists that the ambiguity of the flower implies aporia that Hegel's System is impotent to resolve.

> The flower is neither an object nor a subject, neither a not-I nor an I, neither a pure alterity without relation to self nor a '*Selbst.*' Innocent to be sure, therefore not culpable, not guilty, but its innocence is declared (what would not be done of the sun or the plant) only insofar as the flower is capable of culpability, culpable [*coupable*] of being able to become culpable or cuttable [*coupable*]. Among all these opposites, the essence of the flower appears in its disappearance, vacillates [*vacille*] like all the representative mediations, but also excludes itself from the oppositional structure. The flower gives the example of every possible representation, but the circular system of the between-representation permits making the flower the trope of every representative middle or saying that every representation is anthomorphous. The flower at once cuts itself (off) by and from itself and abysses itself [*La fleur se coupe d'elle-même et s'abîme à la fois*]. (G, 274)[19]

For Derrida, as for Bataille, "The Language of Flowers,"[20] is always cutting. The cuts by which the flower "cuts itself (off) by and from itself and abysses itself" inscribe a certain "legend" in the column of the text. This incision is the "stigma" [*stizein:* tattoo]" that opens the style of the flower to the other column.

"The legendary representation of gods, the images, the idols, the altars," Derrida explains, "come to be inscribed in tattooing [*tatouage*] on the smooth surface of these rigid columns" (G, 282).

> Second passage [from the *Phenomenology*]: the phallic column of India. The *Aesthetics* describes its form in the chapter on "Independent or Symbolic Architecture." It would spread toward Phrygia, Syria, and Greece, where in the course of Dionysic celebrations (according to Herodotus as cited by Hegel) the women were pulling the thread of a phallus that thus stood in the air, "almost as big as the rest of the body." At the beginning, then, the phallic columns of India, enormous formations, pillars, towers, larger at the base than at the top. Now at the outset—but as a

19. Elsewhere Derrida writes: "The flower is *(de)part(ed)* [*partie*]. It holds, from its being-(de)part(ed), the force of a transcendental excrescence [*excroissance*] that only makes it seem such (transcendental) and that no longer even has to be deflowered [*déflorée*]. Practical deconstruction of the transcendental effect is at work in the structure of the flower, as of every *part*, inasmuch as it *appears* or grows [*pousse*] as such" (*G*, 21–22).

20. See Bataille's essay: "The Language of Flowers," *VE*, 10–16; *OC*, 1: 173–78.

departure that already departed from itself—these columns were intact, unbreached [*inentamées*], smooth. And only later are notches, excavations, openings (*Öffnungen und Aushöhlungen*) made in the columns, in the flank, if such can be said. These hollowings, holes, these lateral marks in depth would be like accidents coming over the phallic columns at first unperforated or apparently unperfortable.[21] Images of the Gods (*Götterbilder*) were set, niched, inserted, embedded, driven in, tattooed on the columns. (*G*, 8–9)

One of the most graphic instances of the phallic column Hegel describes is a South Indian sculpture, dating from the thirteenth century, which depicts the myth of "The Origin of the Lingam [*lingobhava*]." In a well-known Indian tale, Vishnu, the embodiment of the infinite water of life, which contains the seeds of everything in an undifferentiated state, and Brahma, the luminous creator of the universe, who brings form from formlessness, engage in a heated argument over which is the greater god. In the middle of the controversy, a "towering lingam crowned with flame" suddenly bursts out of the fluid expanse surrounding the gods. Vishnu (sometimes a boar) plunges into the depths of the waters, and Brahma (sometimes a gander) soars to the heights of the skies to discover the size of this extraordinary lingam.[22] The column, however, expands beyond the reach of either God. "Presently the side of the prodigious phallus burst open, and in the niche-like aperture the lord of the lingam stood revealed, Shiva, the force supreme of the universe. While Brahma and Vishnu bowed before him in adoration, he solemnly proclaimed himself to be the origin of them both."[23] One of the most elusive of the Indian deities, Shiva cannot be captured in the web of oppositions that structure human thought. In a manner reminiscent of the interplay between Heidegger's earth and sky, Shiva's lingam marks the margin between the principles of undifferentiation (Vishnu) and differentiation (Brahma). When understood in this way, the cuts in the

---

21. As we shall see, Derrida insists that the columns are never uncut but are always scarred by a wound that does not heal.

22. The gander and boar, respectively, figure something like the logic of the eagle (the Christian Hegel) and the stone (the Jewish Abraham). Derrida is fascinated by what lies between these two.

23. Heinrich Zimmer, *Myths and Symbols in Indian Art and Civilization*, ed. J. Campbell (New York: Harper Torchbooks, 1962), p. 129. For further accounts of the interrelation of the lingam and Shiva, see Wendy Doniger O'Flaherty, *Asceticism and Eroticism in the Mythology of Shiva* (New York: Oxford University Press, 1973), and Stella Kramrisch, *The Presence of Siva* (Princeton: Princeton University Press, 1981).

phallic column imply a different difference, an other other—a difference that cannot be reduced to identity, an other that cannot be
returned to same. The "tear" (*Riss*) of the lingam, in other words,
subverts Hegel's book by "rending" (*déchirant*) the speculative identification of identity and difference. The lingam remain(s)—"remains"
(*reste*) an incomprehensible "remain(s)" (*reste*). This incomprehensibility renders the excessive style of the lingam "prodigious."

The cut flower and tattooed phallus are both prodigious. Derrida
unfolds his most extensive account of the inconceivable "notion" of the
prodigious in the context of his analysis of Kant's *Critique of Judgment.*[24] As the point at which the first and second critiques join by
separating and separate by joining, the third (recall, inter alia, the
thirdness of Blanchot's neuter) critique can be understood in *neither*
theoretical *nor* practical terms.[25] That which can be neither theoretically nor practically comprehended is "prodigious." Derrida contends
that the prodigious is "the *Ungeheuer* (the enormous, immense, excessive, astonishing, unheard of—the monstrous). Prodigious things
only become sublime objects if they remain strange to both fear and
seduction—to 'allurement.' The 'prodigious' is an object, which by
its overwhelming, colossal size (*Grosse*), reduces to nothing (*vernichtet*)
the end that constitutes the concept of it. The prodigious exceeds,
putting an end to it—to the final limit. It overflows its end and its
concept" (*VP*, 141, 143). Exceeding every concept, the prodigious
remains suspended "between the presentable and the unpresentable,
the passage as much as the irreducibility of the one to the other"
(*VP*, 164–65). As the un-(re)-present-able that is not absent, the
prodigious is neither here nor there. "*Fort:Da* colossal. That which
comes—there—in front—to erect itself. To erect in front with the
excessive movement of its own disappearance—of its unrepresentable
presentation. The obscenity of its abyss" (*VP*, 166).

The colossal *fort/da* embodied "in" the *between* of the columns is
forever *de trop*. The styles of flowers and pillars mark and remark that
which exceeds language. The "space" of this excess is something like a
silent white space. To enter this opening (in which we always already
"dwell"), it is necessary to return to *la double séance* of *Nombres* and ask
again the question of *le surnombre*: How many columns are in *Glas?*
After opening the Genet column with a reference to *a Rembrandt torn*

24. Derrida suggests that the entire third critique is oriented around the tulip.
See: "Le sans de la coupure pure," *VP*, 95–135.
25. The improper form of Kant's own name is instructive at this point. In
German, *Kante* means edge, corner, lace, brim, margin, or border.

into small, very regular squares and rammed down the shithole," Derrida continues:

> As the rest [*reste*].
>
> Two unequal columns, they say distyle [*disent-ils*], each of which—envelop(e)op(e)(s) or sheath(s) [*gaine*], incalculable reverses, turns inside out, replaces, remarks, overlaps [*recoupe*] the other.
>
> The incalculable *of what remained* calculates itself, elaborates itself, elaborates all the *coups,* twists or scaffolds them in silence, you would wear yourself out even faster by counting them. Each little square is delimited, each column rises with an impassive self-sufficiency, and yet the element of contagion, the infinite circulation of general equivalence relates each sentence, each stump of writing . . . to each other, within each column and from one column to the other of what remained [*ce qui est resté*] infinitely calculable. (*G,* 7)

In the incalculable calculus of the infinitely calculable, $1 + 1 =$ more/less than 1. If there are two, there are always already at least three. The insistence of the third calls into question the integrity of the One. The left and right columns "interlace" (*entrelacent*) "in" an "empty" third that is *neither* one *nor* the other. "There is" (*Il y a, Es gibt*) a white column *between* the two black pillars. Having glimpsed this *espace blanc,* empty columns proliferate. There is not only white space between the two major black columns; there is also an empty margin bordering every page of the book. Furthermore, each seemingly stable pillar of the "book" is itself fissured, cleft, torn, rent, not merely once but many times. When *Glas* is turned on end to form an erection, supplementary columns emerge. As the styles of the text cross and crisscross, *Glas* becomes prodigious, colossal—"Unmasterable in its height, uncontrollable in its extension" (*D,* 365; 405).

A duplicitous text written with (at least) two hands at once cannot be approached single-mindedly. It is necessary to seek different *angles* of entry. In the absence of a unified work, the reader must oscillate back and forth between and among ever-expanding columns. The tattooed columns of Derrida's text recall the tattooed shuttlecock that enacts the rhythmic pulsation of the Lacanian phallus. The interlacing of the columns of *Glas* repeats the shuttling back and forth of Lacan's (as well as Freud's) reel thing. By reading Lacan through Heidegger, and vice versa, we discovered the *fort/da* of the child's play to be inseparably bound to the presence-absence of *le sein* of the m-other. Repeating this complex web of associations, Derrida describes the interval traversed by the shuttling back and forth of textual play as the *cleavage* between two breasts. The white space of the text overflows in the whiteness of intermingling sperm (phallus) and milk (*sein*).

> *Glas* is written neither one way nor the other, the one counting on the other to relieve [*relever*] the double's failure, the colossus the column, the column the colossus. *Glas* strikes between the two [*entre les deux*]. The place that the clapper will, necessarily, have taken up, let us name it *colpos*. In Greek, *colpos* is the breast of the mother [*le sein de la mère*] but also of the nurse, as well as the fold [*pli*] of a garment, the trough of the sea [*repli de la mer*] between two waves, the valley pushing down into the breast [*sein*] of the earth. (*G*, 83)

Always resounding *entre-deux*, the ceaseless altar-ation of the countless columns of *Glas* issues in a tangled fabric that is marked "χ." To the extent that *Glas* "is" anything, it "is" a *chiasmus*. Perhaps Adami's drawings (see, for example, below, under "Death of Literature") capture the rhythms of *Glas* more effectively than any "secondary" text. In the course of responding to Adami's remarkable art works (which themselves are graphic responses to *Glas*), Derrida offers a rare comment on "his" text.

> Crossing privileged by all the texts that I sold under my name and that for good reasons I have noted, I no longer hesitate to bring back to the surface in legendary bulls or bands. We are in an irregular chiasmus [26] . . . according to the χ (the chiasmus) (that we will always be able to consider, hastily, as the thematic design of dissemination), the preface, as *semen* can equally well *remain*, produce and disappear like seminal difference that allows itself to reappropriate in the sublimity of the father. *"Hors livre."* All passes through [There is no way around] this chiasmus, all writing comes from it—practices it. The form of the chiasmus, of the χ, interests me a great deal, not as a symbol of the unknown, but because there is a kind of fork there (that is the series: *crossroad, pronged fulcrum, grill, grid, key,* etc.), which I might add is uneven, one of the points spreading its expanse farther than the other: the figure of the double gesture and of the crossing about which we were just speaking. *Positions.*
>
> χ, the general intersection of *Glas*, of its beginnings or ends, bent from it and pushed away. (*VP*, 189, 192)

26. When placed in the context of the foregoing analysis of Merleau–Ponty's interpretation of the chiasmus, Derrida's comment about the relationship between CHI and ICH is quite instructive: "χ, the letter of chiasmus, is *Chi* in its usual transcription. I thus name this other scene, according, if you like, to the anagrammatical inversion of *Ich* or *Isch* (the Hebraic man)" (*VP*, 189).

.

In the alogical calculus of Derrida's strange text, $\chi = A$, and A is an uncertain χ. So understood, the chiasmus written in *Glas* is the reinscription of the "A" of *différance*.

Derrida maintains that "on the eve and aftermath of philosophy," *différance* provides "the summation of what has been most decisively inscribed in what is conveniently called our epoch."[27] Developing his interpretation of *différance*, Derrida cites its anticipation in the writings of Nietzsche, Husserl, Saussure, Freud, Heidegger, Levinas, and even Hegel.[28] For the reader who is attuned to the "epoch," additional notes reverberate in *différance:* the chiasmus of Merleau–Ponty, the real of Lacan, the excess of Bataille, the abjection of Kristeva, the *différence* of Blanchot . . . perhaps the absolute paradox of Kierkegaard. Any such list is, of course, incomplete.

Différance, "which is neither a word nor a concept," is, according to Derrida, the "nonoriginal origin" of all differences and every identity (*M*, 7; 7). This neologism is intended to underscore two contrasting dimensions of *différer: temporization* and *spacing.* As the irreducible interval in which time and space interweave, *différance* is the "matrix" of all presence and absence.

It is because of *différance* that the movement of signification is possible only if each so-called "present" element, each element appearing on the scene of presence, is related to something other than itself, thereby keeping within itself the mark of the past element, and already letting itself be vitiated by the mark of its relation to the future element, this trace being related no less to what is called the future than to what is called the past, and constituting what is called the present by means of this very relation to what it is not: what it absolutely is not, not even a past or a future as a modified present. An interval [*intervalle*] must separate the present from what it is not in order for the present to be itself, but this interval that constitutes it as present must, by the same token [*du même coup*], divide the present in and of itself, thereby also dividing, along with the present, everything that is thought on the basis of the present, that is, in our metaphysical language, every being, and singular substance or the subject. In constituting itself, in dividing itself dynamically, this interval is what might be called *spacing* [espacement], the becoming-space

27. Derrida, "Différance," *Speech and Phenomena,* p. 130.
28. Though each of these thinkers glimpsed that which escapes every philosophical category, Derrida is persuaded that they all remain caught within an ontotheological framework. In his double readings of their works, Derrida is always careful to underscore both how they extend and how they subvert traditional Western philosophy.

of time or the becoming-time of space (*temporization*). And it is this constitution of the present, as an "originary" and irreducibly nonsimple (and therefore, *stricto sensu*, nonoriginary) synthesis of marks, or traces of retentions and protentions (to reproduce analogically and provisionally a phenomenological and transcendental language that soon will reveal itself to be inadequate), that I propose to call archi-writing [*archi-écriture*] or archi-trace [*archi-trace*]. Which (is) (simultaneously) spacing (and) temporization. (*M*, 13; 13–14)

Though *différance* is the condition of the possibility of presence and absence, as well as being and nonbeing, it is neither present nor absent, neither is nor is not. Like Blanchot's "non-absent absence," the non-presence of *différance* is not a potential present.[29] Never present without being absent, *différance* is an "unrepresentable before." This "terrifyingly ancient" eternally returns as the "monstrous" (*monstrueux*) future that never arrives (*OG*, 5; 14).[30] "'Older' than Being itself, such a *différance* has no name in our language. But we 'already know' that if it is unnameable [*innommable*], it is not provisionally so, not because our language has not yet found or received this *name*, or because we would have to seek it in another language, outside the finite system of our own. It is rather because there is no *name* for it at all, not even the name of essence or of Being, not even that of '*différance*,' which is not a name, which is of a pure nominal unity, and unceasingly dislocates itself in a chain of differing and deferring substitutions" (*M*, 26; 28).

A chain of differing and deferring substitutions: *Cleaving, Carnality, Real, Ecstasy, Woman, Infinity, Nots . . . différance, trace, limen, marge, tympan, hymen, éponge, supplément, abject, mer, mère, greffe, parergon, parasite, paravent, parapluie, éperon, brisure, fourche, fulcrum, faisceau,*

---

29. Derrida's claim that *différance* is always in "the middle voice [*la voix moyenne*]" recalls Blanchot's description of the neuter. "We must consider that in the usage of our language the ending *-ance* remains undecided *between* the active and the passive. And we will see why that which lets itself be designated *différance* is neither simply active nor simply passive, announcing or rather recalling something like a middle voice, saying an operation that is not an operation, an operation that cannot be conceived either as passion or as the action of a subject on an object, or on the basis of the categories of agent or patient, neither on the basis of nor moving toward any of these *terms*" (*M*, 9; 9).

30. Since *différance* is never present, it can never be known properly. Consequently, it is, in a certain sense, "unconscious" (*M*, 21; 21). This unconscious is absolute, for it can never be translated into conscious awareness. Like Lacan and Bataille, Derrida is convinced that the wound inflicted upon the self-conscious subject by such a profound unconscious involves "an absolute loss" from and upon which there is no return (*M*, 21; 21).

blanc, marche, intervalle, écart, carré, carrefour, pharmakon, fissure, voile, pli, repli, angle, chiasme, altérité, préface, hors d'œuvre, hors livre, milieu, entre, entre-deux, entrelacement, lacet, fors, poche, invagination, déhiscence, dehors, brisure, exorbitance, bordure, lemme, cartouche, passe-partout, clé, carte, trait, retrait, taille, détail, col, colonne, énorme, colossal, prodigieux, entame, lait, sperme, semence, graine, limite, rive, sein, tain, charnière, fleur, gaine, gant, gramme, programme, lapsus, coup, cravate, couture, couteau, navette, glissement, reste, écriture, texte, bâtard, gl, glas . . .

Countless "names" of the "unnameable." The unnameable can never be spoken; "it" (*il*) can only be written. To write the unnameable is always to rewrite—to rewrite without beginning or end. Such rewriting generates improper texts, which sometimes are "named" "bastards." The conception or nonconception of the bastard harbors the death of the philosophical tradition that reaches both climax and closure in Hegel's System. "If there were a definition of *différance*," Derrida explains, "it would be precisely the limit, the interruption, the destruction of the Hegelian *relève wherever* it operates. What is at stake here is enormous [*énorme*]. I emphasize the Hegelian *Aufhebung*, such as it is interpreted by a certain Hegelian discourse, for it goes without saying that the double meaning [*le double sens*] of *Aufhebung* could be written otherwise [*autrement*]. Whence its proximity to all the operations conducted *against* Hegel's dialectical speculation."[31] In rewriting *Aufhebung otherwise*, the writer writes the fissure "in" Hegel's System. This fault "is" the tomb in which the "pyramidal silence" that sounds the *glas* of Western philosophy forever echoes. *Ecrire autrement: écrire un texte bâtard . . . récrire gl...gl...gl...Glas.*

Conceiving a Bastard

But if the universal thus easily knocks off the very tip of its pyramid [*die reine Spitze seiner Pyramide*] and, indeed, carries off the victory over the rebellious principle of pure individuality, viz. the family, it has thereby merely entered on a conflict with the divine law, a conflict of self-conscious spirit with what is unconscious. For the latter is the other essential power, and it is therefore not destroyed, but merely wronged by the conscious spirit. (*PS*, 286; 339)

You are beginning to follow the relation between a certain brandished erection and a certain head of speech that is cut off [*coupée*],

31. Derrida, *Positions*, pp. 40–41; 55–56.

Sarah Sussman, untitled. Courtesy of the artist.

the brand or the pole rising up in the manifestation of the cut, incision, split, break, scission [*coupure*], unable to *present* themselves otherwise than in the play, or even the laughter—the display of sharply pointed teeth—of the cut. (*D,* 302; 335)

The question of the bastard circulates through the columns of *Glas.* Why? What is a bastard [*bâtard*]?[32] Can a bastard be conceived? Naturally. We all "know" bastards. But can we *name* them? If so, how—how can a bastard be named? Only improperly, it seems. Bastards appear (and disappear) to enact impropriety. Accordingly, the bastard might be named "impropriety itself"—might, that is, if he/she/it could be named, or if impropriety could be itself. Bastards, however, cannot be named properly and the one thing impropriety cannot be is one thing. But, then, *can* a bastard be conceived?

Hegel thought so—but, then, Hegel was convinced that he could conceive anything and everything.[33] To his credit (or discredit), Hegel once *did* conceive a bastard. The name of his *enfant naturel,* I have noted, was Georg Ludwig (born 1807). In addition to Ludwig, Hegel and his wife, Marie von Tucher, had a daughter, Susanna Maria, who died at birth (1812), and two sons: Karl (born in 1813) and Emmanuel, whose name means "God be with us" (born in 1814). Ludwig, the oldest child, never really fit into the Hegelian family. He was always something of an outsider whom Hegel resisted acknowl-

32. This slippery word carries a surprisingly broad range of meanings. For example, a bastard is a large sail [*voile:* sail or veil] used in the Mediterranean when there is little wind. Though rarely noted, "bastard" is the name of a sweet Spanish wine. "Bastard" can also refer to a cloth or textile of inferior or mixed quality, an unusual make or size (perhaps even an oversized text-ile). The extraordinary texture of this complex word becomes more apparent with the recognition of the relation between *bâtard* and writing. *Ecriture bâtarde* (or simply *bâtard*) is a kind of writing that tends to be aimless scribbling, and thus is not regarded as legitimate. Still within the domain of writing, *bâtard* can be used to describe something that has characteristics of two different and opposite genres. A work, for instance, might be neither an essay nor a novel, neither philosophy nor literature, but *une œuvre bâtarde,* which includes at least two "genres" (*genre:* genre, style, or gender). *Bâtard,* in sum, means, an illegitimate child, *enfant naturel,* degenerate, mongrel, sail/veil, wine, scribbling, mixed *genre,* and improper writing.

33. Derrida satirizes Hegel's self-confidence at the very outset of *Glas* by playing on the association between the speculative philosopher and the eagle, which we have already observed in the writings of several other authors. "His name is so strange. From the eagle [*aigle*] it draws imperial or historic power. Those who still pronounce his name in French (there are some) are ridiculous only up to a certain point; the restitution, semantically infallible for those who have read him a little—but only a little, of the magisterial coldness and imperturbable seriousness, the eagle caught in ice and frost, glass and gel [*le glace et le gel*]" (*G,* 7).

edging. Nonetheless, Ludwig was born at a critical moment in Hegel's life. While Christiana was giving birth to the bastard Ludwig, Hegel was giving birth to his *œuvre bâtarde,* the *Phenomenology of Spirit.* Was this an accident? Perhaps. But there are not supposed to be any accidents in the System. Might the little bastard Ludwig be a thoughtless slip-up that exposes what really goes on between the covers of the Hegelian book? Can we uncover the double meaning of *Aufhebung,* which creates the possibility of writing otherwise, by rereading Hegel's *hors d'œuvre* through the eyes of Ludwig?

If, as Derrida insists, we "begin" as always already having begun, then we cannot "begin" at the beginning but must "begin" in the middle. Accordingly, *Glas* "begins" with a fragment: "what about the remain(s) [*reste*] of a Hegel, for us, today, here, now [*ici, mainte-nant*]?" (*G,* 7). *Le reste, ici, maintenant:* these words raise questions that return throughout *Glas* and anticipate the "end" of "the book." Derrida concludes this text with an unfinished phrase, which both anagrammatizes his name as well as Heidegger's *Riss* and parodies the purported circularity of Hegel's System: "Today, here, now, the debris of [*le débris de*]" (*G,* 291). By beginning with *ici, maintenant,* Derrida begins again with the beginning of the *Phenomenology*—sense certainty. But no sooner has Derrida begun than he becomes entangled in the long excursuses on flowers and phallic columns. The reason for the insertion of these two columns becomes clearer when we recall the overall structure of the *Phenomenology.*

In keeping with his conception of knowledge, Hegel constructs the *Phenomenology* as an intricate series of circles within circles. At the penultimate stage of his analysis of the experience of consciousness (i.e., religion), Hegel returns to his original point of departure. The three moments of natural religion repeat, at a different level, spirit's movement from sense-certainty (the essence of light), through perception (animal religion), to understanding (the artificer). Flower religion, which falls *between* the essence of light and animal religion, occupies a site of passage that is structurally parallel to the margin between sense-certainty and perception. This is the precise point in the unfolding of the experience of consciousness where *writing* first appears in the *Phenomenology.*[34] From this point of view, the stylus of

34. To account for the sublation of sense-certainty and the emergence of perception, Hegel conducts a simple "thought experiment": "In order to test the truth of this sense-certainty, a simple experiment will suffice. We write down this truth; a truth cannot lose anything by being written down, any more than it can lose anything through our preserving it" (*PS,* 60; 81). Compare Blanchot's interpretation of Hegel's account of immediacy in chapter 8, first section.

the flower seems to point to the stylus of the writer and vice versa. No more for Derrida than for Bataille and Blanchot do flowers and writing set in motion the machinery that finally produces absolute knowledge. To the contrary, writing underscores the impossibility of the totalization presupposed in absolute knowledge.

The phallic column is another remain(s) that derails Hegel before he can get started. If there is an undeniable remainder, inassimilable debris, or indigestible crumb, there can be neither System nor absolute knowledge. In *Glas,* Derrida seeks to demonstrate that Hegel leaves unphilosophical fragments that deconstruct what he so carefully constructs. The figures of Bacchus and Dionysus play an important role in Derrida's analysis. Attempting to clarify his account of sense-certainty, Hegel writes: "With this appeal to universal experience we may be permitted to anticipate how the case stands in the practical sphere. In this respect we can tell those who assert the truth and certainty of the reality of sense-objects that they should go back to the most elementary school of wisdom, viz. the ancient Eleusinian Mysteries of Ceres and Bacchus, and that they have still to learn the secret meaning of the eating of bread and the drinking of wine" (*PS,* 65; 87). The mysteries of Ceres and Bacchus, represented in the Eucharist, are supposed to become completely transparent in the course of the *Phenomenology.*[35] In the very effort to reveal the truth concealed in paganism, however, Hegel unwittingly acknowledges vestiges of unbelief at the heart of Christian faith and practice. Bacchus, is, of course, often identified with Dionysus. I have noted that in the passage that Derrida quotes from the *Lectures on Aesthetics,* Hegel stresses the indispensable role of the phallic column in the dionysian festivals staged in ancient Greece. Though Derrida raises this tantalizing point at the outset of his analysis, he leaves it dangling until near the end of *Glas.* Finally picking up the thread he seemed to have lost, Derrida observes that the dionysian festivals and bacchanalian revels were actually "held in honor of Saturn—the Italic god who had been identified with Kronos" (*G,* 258). The errant path that *Glas* cuts through Hegel's dense argument leads from flowers and columns, through Bacchus and Dionysus, to Kronos. As we shall see, *le reste* is inseparable from Kronos or time—time no longer comprehended as the total presence of *ici, maintenant,* which can be known absolutely, but time, which is glimpsed (if at all) in the inescapable vanishing and infinite deferral of remain(s) that render(s) absolute

35. It is important to recall Hegel's often-cited description of the *Phenomenology* as a "bacchanalian revel in which no member is sober."

knowledge forever unattainable. By marking and remarking the non-place of time, phallus and flower open the space of writing, which, in turn and by turns, sounds the death knell for Hegel's System and mourns the passing of the entire philosophical, social, and cultural edifice to which Hegel gave conclusive expression.

But what does all of this have to do with the question of the bastard or, more precisely, with the problem of conceiving a bastard? To respond to this query, it is necessary to listen more carefully to the *Klang* (ringing, clang) of *glas*. In the margin of the Hegel column, Derrida remarks: "without the conception of the concept, it is dead language, writing and deceased word, or resonance without signification (*Klang* and not *Sprache*). An affinity here between *Klang* and writing. Insofar as it resists conception, the *Klingen* of the *Klang* plays for the Hegelian logos the role of mute or mad sound, a kind of mechanical automaton that triggers and operates itself without meaning (to say) anything" (*G,* 16). Through an unexpected twist, Derrida proceeds to relate the senseless "sound" (*son:* English son) of *Klang* to the bastard.

> Illegitimate course [*Démarche bâtarde*].
> Is there a place for the bastard [*le bâtard*] in the ontotheological or in the Hegelian family? Question to leave aside, to hold in the margin or on the leash when one enters into a true family or into the family of truth. Without doubt it is not so exterior to the question of the *Klang;* at least its exteriority presses another exteriority, without correspondence with the Hegelian concept of exteriority, toward the center of the question (*G,* 12).

Through the chain of *Klang*-writing-bastard-exteriority, Derrida attempts to evoke that which resists conception by the Hegelian concept. The curious exteriority of the inconceivable bastard breaks open the domestic economy of Hegel's closed family circle.

Derrida organizes his account of Hegel in *Glas* around the notion of the family. As I stressed in the analysis of speculative philosophy, from the early fragments on love to the mature *Encyclopedia,* Hegel's interpretation of the family serves as the "metaphorical model" for "philosophical exposition" and represents the underlying structure of the entire System (*G,* 28). The most adequate anticipation of speculative knowledge is embodied in the specular relation between father and son. For Hegel, Derrida points out, "the family, according to Christian love, is infinite. It is already what one could call the speculative family. Thus the speculative family follows the infinitely circular trajectory of father/son filiation: the infinity of desire, of marriage and of the interior law remains between the son and the father" (*G,* 44).

The *proper* relation between father and son secures the good name of the father and bestows upon the son the *property* of identity. The name, Derrida maintains, "is the structure of that which returns to the father" (*G*, 92).[36] This return establishes a reflexive relation between father and son in which each relates to *itself* in and through *its own other*. In a marginal aside, Derrida comments "'*in seinem Anderen.*' The 'its other' is the syntagm itself of the Hegelian proper [*propre*], it constitutes negativity in the service of proper sense or literal meaning [*sense propre*]" (*G*, 96).

The negativity that is in the service of the proper, is the reconciling negativity of *Aufhebung*. Drawing on insights initially advanced by Bataille, Derrida argues that, "*Aufhebung*, economic law of absolute reappropriation of absolute loss, is a familial concept" (*G*, 152). By attempting to keep everything in the family, *Aufhebung* struggles to achieve a "harmony" (*con-sonance; Ein-klang*) that is deaf to the tolling of every unsettling *Klang*. When conception is proper, the perfect copulation of subject and object issues in absolute knowledge. "Absolute knowledge" (*savoir absolu*) or *Sa*, as Derrida dubs it, closes the family circle by "binding" (*bandant*) everything together within the "ring" (*bande*) of "absolute reappropriation" (*G*, 248). Insofar as absolute knowledge presupposes absolute reappropriation, it involves total self-possession. To possess *savoir absolu*, in other words, is to have oneself absolutely—*s'avoir absolument*. Complete self-possession is the "*Pure* self-recognition in absolute otherness" (*PS*, 14; 24), which constitutes the *end* of Hegelian philosophy.

But what exactly is the ring or *bande* that is supposed to close the family circle? Is it an ideal band—perhaps a wedding band or ring? Or is it the sound of a band or ringing of a bell—perhaps a soundless sound, a mute ringing that is the *Klang* of *Glas?* And what about Ludwig? Where does he fit into this neat and tidy family romance? Does the illegitimate conception of the bastard exceed the domestic economy? Again echoing Bataille, Derrida contends: "At each instant, the logic of the *Aufhebung* turns itself round into its absolute other [*autre absolu*]. Absolute appropriation is absolute expropriation. Onto-logic can always be reread or rewritten as logic of loss, or the expenditure [*dépense*] without reserve" (*G*, 188).

To rewrite onto-logic in terms of *dépense* is to write *Aufhebung* otherwise by drawing a distinction that Hegel fails to make. Follow-

---

36. The Lacanian overtones of these remarks will become clearer as the analysis unfolds.

ing the lead of psychologists Nicolas Abraham and Maria Torok, Derrida distinguishes introjection and incorporation. Introjection extends autoerotic cathexes through a process of assimilation whose aim is the enlargement of the self. When understood in this way, the activity of introjection repeats the movement of *Aufhebung* in which the subject grasps what opposes it, encircles what is different from itself, and swallows what is other than itself. We have seen that for Hegel, true knowledge leaves no crumbs, permits no debris, tolerates no remain(s). By reversing spirit's "externalization" (*Ent-Äusserung*)" "re-collection" (*Er-Innerung*) attempts to erase the most unsettling remainder of all—time. Having begun with the *ici, maintenant* of sense-certainty, Hegel concludes with the eternal present and presence of absolute knowledge.

In contrast to introjection, incorporation, as Freud argues in "Mourning and Melancholy," is an economic response to the loss of the object. "With the real loss of the object having been rejected and the desire having been maintained but at the same time excluded from introjection (simultaneous conservation and suppression, between which no synthesis is possible), incorporation is a kind of theft [*vol*] to reappropriate the pleasure-object. But that reappropriation is simultaneously rejected: which leads to the paradox of a foreign body preserved as foreign but by the same token [*du même coup*] excluded from a self, which thenceforth deals not with the other but only with itself. The more the safe keeps the foreign as foreign [*l'étranger comme étranger*] in itself, the more it excludes it."[37] This "foreigner" (*l'étranger*) is the strange *ghost* haunting every family and all familial concepts. By preserving the foreign *as foreign,* incorporation guards "the other *as other*" (*l'autre* comme l'autre).[38] The site or, more precisely, the parasite, of this safe-keeping is the *crypt*.

"The crypt is always an interiorization, an inclusion intended as a compromise, but since it is a parasitic inclusion [*inclusion parasitaire*], an inside heterogeneous [*dedans hétérogène*] to the interiority of the self, excluded in the space of general introjection within which it violently

37. Derrida, "Fors," trans. B. Johnson, *Georgia Review* 31 (1977): 72. "Fors," introduction to *Cryptonymie: Le verbier de l'homme au loupes* by Nicolas Abraham and Maria Torok (Paris: Flammarion, 1976), p. 18. In a note to her translation, Johnson explains: "The word *fors* in French, derived from the Latin *foris* ('outside, outdoors'), is an archaic preposition meaning 'except for, barring, save.'" The connotation of barring points to important associations between Derrida's account of *fors* and Lacan's analysis of "$."
38. Ibid., p. 71; 17.

takes place, the cryptic safe [*fors*] can only maintain, in a state of repetition, the mortal conflict it is impotent to resolve."[39] Always suspended *between* the conflicting play of forces, the crypt is utterly paradoxical. It is "the exterior in the interior"—the interiority of the exteriority that turns everything outside in and inside out (*G*, 214). "Crypt," Derrida explains, is what "one would say of the transcendental or of the repressed, the unthought, or the excluded— which organizes the ground to which it does not belong" (*G*, 187).

The guardian of the crypt is (a) woman, and the crypt she guards is the pyramid. This pyramid marks the site of the conflict between self-consciousness and the unconscious. As Lacan points out, the unconscious is the domain of goddesses. For Hegel, the classic account of the contest between self-consciousness and the unconscious is presented in Sophocles' *Antigone*. While Creon represents the law of the human world, which is identified with man or, in Lacan's terms, is the Name-of-the-Father, Antigone speaks another language—the language of the other figured in femininity and divinity. In contrast to Hegel's interpretation of *Antigone* as depicting the first stage of spirit, which carries the seeds of ultimate reconcilation and perfect knowledge, Derrida believes this ancient play involves conflicts that cannot be resolved in Hegel's System. By taking *Antigone* as the point of departure for his consideration of spirit, Hegel inadvertently discloses the impossibility of complete self-consciousness. Commenting on Hegel's interpretation of the conflict between the law of singularity (represented by Antigone) and the law of universality (represented by Creon), Derrida writes:

39. Ibid.; p. 70; 15. In a passage that carries traces of Heidegger's analysis of the cleavage or *Riss,* Betaille's description of "the public square," Mauss's account of *le don* (which both inaugurates and escapes the economic structure of reciprocal exchange), and Lacan's interpretation of the symbolic order, Derrida writes: "Constructing a system of partitions, with their inner and outer surfaces, the cryptic enclave produces a cleavage [*clivage*] in space, in the assembled system of various places, in the architectonics of the open square within space, itself delimited by a generalized closure, in the *forum.* Within this forum, a place where the free circulation and exchange of objects and speeches can occur, the crypt constructs another, more inward, forum like a closed rostrum or speakers box, a *safe:* sealed, and thus internal to itself, a secret interior within the public square but, by the same token, outside it, external to it. Whatever one might write upon them, the crypt's parietal surfaces do not simply separate an inner forum from an outer forum. The inner forum is (a) safe, an outcast outside inside the inside" (67–68; 12–13). We will meet this secret interior again in the consideration of Kierkegaard's account of the notion of "Indesluttet" (*enclosed reserve*).

To this great opposition (the law of singularity/the law of universality) is ordered a whole series of other couples: divine law/ human law, family/city, woman/man, night/day, etc. *Human* law is the law of *day(light)* because it is known, public, visible, *universal;* human law rules, not the family, but the *city,* government, war; and it is made by *man* (*vir*). Human law is the law of man. Divine law is the law of woman; it hides itself, does not offer itself in this opening-manifestation (*Offenbarkeit*) that produces man. Divine law is nocturnal and more natural than the law of universality, just as the family is more natural than the city.[40] . . . Natural, divine, feminine, nocturnal, familial, such is the predicative system, the law of singularity. In this law—this is said more precisely, in this place, of the family—the concept is *"unconscious."* (*G,* 161)

For Hegel, the unconscious is not absolute but is a latent consciousness whose potential is completely realized in speculative philosophy. Absolute knowledge emerges when the unconscious is fully translated into self-consciousness. Though Hegel admits that in Antigone's struggle with Creon, the unconscious "is not destroyed, but merely wounded by the conscious spirit," he is convinced that the self-conscious subject finally masters the unconscious. Analysis, in other words, *is not* interminable.

For Derrida, by contrast, the end of analysis is (the) impossible. The repressed always returns to render hollow the magisterial claims of the self-conscious subject. Following Kierkegaard[41] and implicitly invoking one of Kierkegaard's first French translators, Bataille, Derrida argues that *irony* is the undoing of philosophy. In Derrida's nondomestic *oikonomia,* the ironist is (a) woman.

Human law, the law of the rational community that is instituted against the private law of the family, always suppresses the feminine, stands up against it, girds, squeezes, curbs, compresses it. But the masculine power has a limit—essential and eternal: the arm, the weapon, doubtless impotent, the all-powerful weapon of impotence, the inalienable wound [*coup*] of the woman, is *irony*. Woman, "[the community's] internal enemy," can always burst out laughing [*éclater de rire*] at the last moment; she knows, in tears

40. This understanding of the family obviously reverses Hegel's speculative interpretation of the family circle. The Hegelian family is always founded by and grounded in the name of the father.
41. See especially *The Concept of Irony,* trans. L. Capel (Bloomington: Indiana University Press, 1968).

and in death, how to pervert the power that represses. The power of irony—the ironic position rather—results—syllogistically—from what the master produces and proceeds from what he suppresses, needs, and returns to. Antigone is Cybele, the goddess-Mother who precedes and follows the whole process. She is at all catastrophes, all (down)falls, all carnages, remains invulnerable to them, is killed invulnerable. Her very death does not affect her. (*G,* 209–10)

Cybele, a Phrygian mother-goddess, was the Mother of the Gods. "Zeus once ejaculated on the ground while sleeping on Mount Dindymus. There grew up on this spot a strange creature with both male and female organs. The other gods, alarmed at the thought of what such an offspring of Zeus might do on reaching full size, cut off the male genitals. The castrated creature grew to be the goddess Agdistis, or Cybele. From the severed genitals an almond tree grew. One day Nana,[42] daughter of the river-god Sangarius, placed one of the fruits of this tree in her lap. It vanished and Nana found herself pregnant. In time she gave birth to a boy, whom she exposed. The child, Attis, was somehow suckled by a he-goat and grew up to be a handsome young man. Cybele saw him one day and fell in love with him, but the youth, apparently unaware of this fact, prepared to marry a daughter of the king of Pessinus, a city at the foot of the Dindymus. Madly jealous, Cybele drove both Attis and the king mad. They castrated themselves in their frenzy and Attis died."[43]

The tale of Cybele, with whom Derrida identifies Antigone, is a story of the castration and death that mark the fall of the king and the loss of the son. With this *tombe,* we return to the pyramidal "A" of *différance.* "The *a* of *différance,*" Derrida points out, "is not heard; it remains silent, secret and discreet as a tomb: *oikesis.* And thereby let

42. Derrida refers to the Phrygian legend of Cybele (giving special emphasis to the figure of Nana) in the context of a comment on another sister (i.e., a sister other than Antigone) who upset Hegel's domestic economy: "one would have to name her Christiane, Hegel's sister, or Nanette, 'the young woman who lodged in the family house.' If one is to believe a remark of Bourgeois, she 'had inspired [in Hegel] a feeling perhaps first of love, but which the Frankfurt letters to Nanette Endel reveal as a feeling of sincere friendship.' I do not know of what name Nanette was the diminutive. Nana could always play the sister. In the Phrygian legend of Attis, Nana is a kind of holy virgin" (*G,* 170). At this point the family network becomes hoplessly tangled. Christiane, the name of Hegel's sister, is virtually identical to the name of the woman who mothered Hegel's bastard son—Christiana. Like Nanette, Christiana once lodged in a house where Hegel lived. In the case of Christiana, however, the result was both more and less than (love) letters.

43. Tripp, *Crowell's Handbook of Classical Mythology,* pp. 179–80.

us anticipate the delineation of a site, the familial residence and the tomb of the proper in which is produced, by *différance,* the *economy of death.* This stone [*pierre*]—provided that one knows how to decipher its inscription—is not far from announcing the death of a king" (*M,* 4; 4). The cryptic pyramid holds open the space of time, which is not the space of a presence that is present, not even the space of a time that looks back to a past present or ahead to a future present, but the spacing of a more radical time—a time forever held open at both "ends" by a past that never was present and a future that never will arrive. "Antigone is Cybele, the goddess-Mother who precedes and follows the whole process." "I am (following) [*je suis*] the mother," Derrida explains. "The text. The mother is *behind*[44]—all that I follow, am, do, seem—the mother follows. As she follows absolutely, she always survives [*survit*] a future that will never have been presentable—what she will have engendered, attending, impassive, fascinating and provoking; she survives the interring of the one whose death she has foreseen" (*G,* 134). Always "living on" (*sur-vivant*), woman draws near, without making present, the nonabsent absence of death. Woman's laughter breaks out in the ironic smile of the gri(n)m reaper. Unlike Hegel, Derrida and Kierkegaard never forget the nonspecular eye gazing at them from behind this grin.

In the crypt, the question of the bastard returns. As Hegel's embarrassment about Ludwig and preoccupation with Antigone suggest, the crypt haunts his System. "What the speculative dialectic wants to say is that the crypt can still be incorporated in the System. The transcendental or the repressed, the unthought or the excluded must be assimilated by the corpus, interiorized like moments idealized in the very negativity of their work. The pause [*arrêt*] that only forms a sudden slowing in the introjection of spirit" (*G,* 187). But *can* the philosopher say what he wants to say? Derrida is persuaded that the philosopher actually writes something *other*—writes (by not saying) the very other he does not want to write. This soundless sound resounds throughout all ontotheology. It is the *Klang* echoing in the crypt that marks the passing of the Hegelian System. In one of the most concise formulations of his criticism of Hegel, Derrida writes:

Fascination by a figure irreceivable in the system. Vertiginous insistence on the unclassifiable. And if the absolutely inassimi-

44. The French text makes it clear that Derrida is playing with his own name at this point: "*je suis la mère. Le texte. La mère est* derrière." A free translation might read: "I am the mother. The text. The mother is (the) *behind,* i.e., Derrida."

lable, and indigestible play a fundamental role in the System, rather abyssal, the abyss playing . . . a quasitranscendental role and allowing to be formed above it, as a sort of emanation, a dream of appeasement? Is it not always an element excluded from the system that assures the system possibility of space? The transcendental has always been, strictly, the transcategorical, that which could not be received, formed, terminated in any of the categories interior to the system. The vomit of the system. (G, 171; 183)

Something always remains that resists the powerful thrust of *Aufhebung*. This remain(s) is an exteriority that can never be completely interiorized; it is ungraspable, inassimilable, indigestible. This exteriority is the *other* exteriority, "without correspondence with the Hegelian concept of exteriority." Such an exteriority, we have seen, raises "the question of the *Klang*," which "is not so exterior to" the problem of the bastard.

The exteriority of the bastard is a curious exteriority. The trace of a certain excess, the bastard is not simply an outsider and is never merely outside. He, she, or it is *neither* interior *nor* exterior, *neither* in *nor* out of the family. Paradoxically, this undecidable "exteriority," which is not *properly* exterior, is more radically "exterior" than the outer that opposes the inner. Neither inside nor outside, the bastard hovers along the margin that is the condition of the possibility [*le transcendental*] of every family of oppositions (dialectical as well as binary). As such, the bastard "is" *das ganz Andere*, which can never be conceived. This incomprehensible altarity figures what Bataille labels "the blind spot of Hegelianism." Derrida's approach to Hegel returns again and again to questions Bataille raises. In this return, it often is unclear what or who the Bataille obsessing Derrida really is. Is it Georges or Sylvia, the woman Georges shared with the other Jacques who peeks through the slits in the columns of *Glas*—Jacques Lacan? Or is Bataille, like all purportedly proper names, really improper? Does Bataille imply the struggle of *la bataille* or the ringing of *le batail?*

Toward the end of *Glas,* in the column devoted to the bastard Genet,[45] Derrida explains:

Batail est d'abord un vieux nom pour le battant d'une cloche. Mis en mouvement par le branle, il vient heurter la panse (on dit

45. An observation too long delayed: With the insertion of a bottomless triangle—ˆ—the proper name "Genet" becomes the improper noun *genêt,* the word for a kind of flower.

aussi le pans) comme une sorte de marteau intérieur. Non loin
de la faussure, lieu où la cloche commence à élargir sa courbure,
à s'évaser. On parle aussi de la faussure (ou faulsure) des tours.
(G, 254)

It is impossible to know how to translate this text. Bataille . . .
Batail: an old term for the clapper of a bell. *Le branle:* oscillation,
shaking; an old-fashioned dance;[46] brawl. *Branler:* to oscillate, shake,
stagger, waver, be in jeopardy. *La panse* or *le pans:* the interior part of
the bell where the clapper (*clap*, derives from the Old French *clapoir*,
venereal sore, which derives from *clapier*, brothel, which derives from
clap, a heap of stones [*pierres*]) makes contact or touches. *La panse/le
pans*—the point where *le battant* touches (but does not penetrate) *la
cloche. La/Le, Le/La*—perhaps like the *limen* that is a tympan or
hymen. From the "inside" to the "outside." *La faussure:* the curved
line that traces the *exterior* widening of the bell that leads to its
opening. But *la faussure* also points toward *fissurer.* Is this the fault
line that spoils *"le son pur"* (pure sound, unblemished his, or guiltless
son) of the bell and leaves only clanging? Is this the fissure that
Derrida reads in Hegel's book—the fissure opened by the swinging
to-and-fro of *la faucille* [the *semicircular* sickle]? *La faussure* can also
associated with *fausser:* to bend, twist, warp; to corrupt, falsify, pervert, break, violate. *La faussure* even recalls *faux/fausse,* which at one
time was written *"fauls."* *Faux/fausse,* of course, means false, untrue,
or erroneous. But *la faux* also means scythe (like the one carried by
"Mother" time). *La faussure* was the medieval spelling of *la faulsure.* In
the Middle Ages, *la falusure des tours* referred to the holes in towers,
pillars, or columns through which round stones were hurled at the
attacking enemy. Stones, I have stressed, weigh heavily on the philosopher. While Hegel's speculative logic is the logic of *l'aigle qui vol*
(*l'aigle:* eagle; *vol:* fly, flight; or theft—like *le voleur,* Saint Genet), the
paralogic of *le reste* is the "logic" of *la pierre qui tombe* (*pierre:* rock,
stone; or Peter—like *le Pierre de l'église,* Saint Pierre; *tombe,* fall, sink,
decay; or tomb, grave—like a crypt). Does the cracked bell have
anything to do with "mourning and melancholy"—melancholy,
which Baudelaire, author of *Les Fleurs du Mal,* imaged as/in *La Cloche*

46. Derrida, like Nietzsche, is not unaware of the importance of dancing for the
issues he is considering. "Did Hegel know how to dance? The question is more
obscure than would be thought. Like Rousseau in any case—but does one dance at
them?—he loved balls, and he confided this to Nanette: 'I very much like balls. It is
the happiest thing there is in our sorrowful times.' The *Critique of Judgment* also names
the ball: the example of finality for a lawn surrounded by trees, in a forest" (*G,* 171).

fêlée (The Cracked Bell)? Or with the mother—the mother whose "smutty laugh" left Bataille "impaired like a cracked bell"? This seemingly endless tangle of words and images makes all reading and every translation utterly uncertain.

> *Batail* is first an old term for the clapper of a bell. Put into motion by oscillation,[47] it comes to strike the interior or belly of the bell (one also says *le pans*) like a kind of interior hammer. Not far from the curved exterior, the area where the bell begins to widen its curvature, to flare. One also speaks of *la faussure* (or *falsure*) meaning holes of towers.

Like Nietzsche, Derrida philosophizes (if that is what it is) "with a hammer." Having begun with *ici, maintenant,* he does not end with an eternal present/presence re-collected in absolute knowledge, but feigns concluding with the scattered debris of the repeatedly vanishing *reste.* In order to catch a glimpse (but no more) of this debris, Derrida argues, "it is necessary to introduce the forces of resistance to *Aufhebung,* to the process of truth, to speculative negativity, and it is necessary to make it apparent that these forces of resistance do not constitute, in their turn, sublatable or relevant negativities" (*G,* 53). The most persistent and effective force of resistance to the conception of the concept is the infinite deferral of time resounding in the oscillation of *le batail.*

In a passage to which I have already alluded, Derrida establishes a surprising connection between *Sa* and Saturn.

> One could speak as well—the two words are closely related—of *Sa*'s saturnalia. Festival in honor of Saturn: the Italic god who had been identified with Kronos (an empty play on words and this was the time—that one here would come to celebrate as *Sa*). He would have taken refuge in Italy after his son had dethroned him and thrown him down from the heights of Olympus. With the aid of his mother, Gaia, he himself had cut off the testicles of his father. It is again Gaia who already put the sickle [*la faucille*] between the hands of the son. It is, perhaps, she again who joined forces with Zeus, her grandson, against Kronos, her son, and made him drink a *pharmakon* that forced him to vomit all the children he had eaten. Saturn [i.e., *Sa* or *savoir absolu*] would, then, be a deposed father, whose Latin reign, nevertheless, had permitted the memory of a mythic golden age. He had become the god of agriculture, and more precisely, armed with a sickle

---

47. To prepare the way for what follows, it is helpful to remember that "oscillation" derives from the Latin *oscillare,* by way of *oscillum.* See above p. xxx.

and billhook, he used to preside over the cutting of the vine [*la vigne;* compare, *la vierge:* virgin]. Like Dionysus-Bacchus, he was closely associated with wine.[48] (*G, 258–59*)

In these carefully crafted lines, *Sa* [*savoir absolu*] appears to be the play of the gods: Saturn . . . Kronos . . . Dionysus-Bacchus.

If interpreted in a certain way, this suggestion can be incorporated within the Hegelian System. As we have seen, Hegel is convinced that the dialectic of religion culminates in absolute religion, which is the representation or *Vorstellung* of absolute knowledge. Derrida reformulates Hegel's claim: "The absolute religion is not yet what it is already: *Sa.* The absolute religion (the essence of Christianity, the religion of essence) is already what it is not yet: *Sa,* which itself is already no longer what it still is, the absolute religion" (*G,* 244). The liminal nonplace of *Vorstellung,* i.e., *le déjà du pas-encore ou le déjà-plus de l'encore* is *time.* In Hegel's own terms, time is the *Dasein* of the concept, or "time is the concept itself, which *is there (der* da ist)" [49] (*G,* 255). "The *Da* of the concept (time)," Derrida explains, "at last with the stroke [*du coup*] of time, marks its incompleteness, its interior default, the semantic void that holds it in motion. Time is always of this vacancy with which *Sa* affects itself. Because it affects itself with this, *Sa* empties itself, with a view to determining itself, *it procrastinates, it gives itself time* [*il se donne le temps*]. It imposes upon itself a gap [*écart*] in signing or crossing itself [*se signant*]. The *Da* of *Sa* is nothing other than the movement of signification" (*G,* 255–56). For Hegel, the "vacuous" movement of signification ends in the semantic plenitude of absolute knowledge. In the fullness of time, the unsettling emptiness of temporal representation becomes the reassuring fullness of eternal presentation. This atemporal present/presence marks the arrival of the *Parousia.*

If, however, one follows Derrida's errant rereading of Hegel as the first thinker of writing, the realized eschatology of the System becomes impossible. In an effort to demonstrate this impossibility, Derrida abbreviates *le déjà-là du pas-encore ou l'encore du déjà-plus* with "*pas-là* (the being-there [*da*] of the not [*pas*], which, being there, is not, is not there, [*n'est pas, pas-là*])" (*G,* 245). This abbreviation summarizes Derrida's critique of Hegelianism and all it represents.

Knowledge, truth (of the) phantasm (of) (absolute) philosophy— (absolute) religion, this proposition delineates no limit, is the

48. Perhaps the sweet Spanish wine sometimes called *bâtard.*

49. Derrida again is playing with an anagram of his name in Hegel's phrase *der da ist.*

infinite proposition of hetero-tautological [*hétéro-tautologique*] speculative dialectics. The infinite circle of auto-insemination that entails the *paidea* of every seminar in its phantasm. What can there be outside [*dehors*] of an absolute phantasm? What is one still able to add? Why and how to desire to get out of it?

It is necessary to delay—to give oneself time. The remain(s) of time [*Le reste du temps*]. (*G*, 252)

The *pas-là* is *le reste*, which "is" both "always already" and forever "remain(s)." The restless *reste* repeats the excessive alternation of *fort/da* in which the *da* of the *fort* is the *fort* of the *da*. Debris, which is not and yet is not nothing, cannot be comprehended or re-collected within the System. As the remain(s) that neither is nor is not, *le reste* is the "trace" that always delays the present and endlessly defers presence. The "almost nothing" of time is the swinging "scythe [*faux*]" that castrates the philosopher—the oscillating *batail* that sounds the death knell of philosophy, Hegelian and otherwise. *Glas*, the fragile flower marking the crypt of ontotheology, "is" the empty tomb of the West.

"On the eve of philosophy and beyond it," what remain(s) to be said? Is it any longer possible to write after Hegel? Or does writing only become possible after Hegel? A few lines after explaining that *le batail* is an old name for the clapper of a bell, Derrida returns again to *le reste du temps*. Having begun with a chain of associations leading from *Sa*-to-Saturn-to-Kronos-to-Dionysus-Bacchus, he proceeds to split or cut the column upon which his account of Hegel is tattooed. This opening creates another exergue—this time an *hors d'œuvre* that is a postscript rather than a preface. In this exergue, inserted in the left-hand margin of the left-hand column, there appears the name of another person who faced the dilemma of writing after the advent of *savoir absolu*—Søren Kierkegaard. Long before Derrida, Kierkegaard read *Aufhebung* otherwise.

What would it mean not to comprehend (Hegel) the text of *Sa?* If it is a question of a finite failure, the failure is in advance included, comprehended in the text. If it is a question of an infinite fault [*faute*] or lack [*manque*], one would have to say that *Sa* does not think itself, does not say itself, does not write itself, does not read itself, does not know itself, which no longer means anything by definition. *Sa* always ends by being full, heavy, pregnant with itself. The hypothesis of a bad reading has no place here. It has not even taken place. One must let it fall [*tomber*], in the margin or exergue, as a margin or exergue, as a remain(s) about which one does not *know* if it *works,* in view of or in the service of whom or what. Like such a note at the bottom of the page of *Concluding*

Unscientific Postscript to the Philosophical Fragments, scraps of scraps
[*reliefs de reliefs*] under the last supper scene: . . . "It is presumably the witchery of this ever-continuing process that has inspired
the misunderstanding that one must be a devil of a fellow in
philosophy in order to emancipate himself from Hegel. But this
is by no means the case. All that is needed is sound common-
sense, a fund of humor, and a little Greek ataraxy. Outside the
Logic, and partly also within it, because of a certain ambiguous
light that Hegel has not cared to exclude, Hegel and Hegelianism
constitute an essay in the comic." (*G,* 259)

Why does *le rire déchirant* break out at precisely this point? For
Derrida, as for Kierkegaard, philosophy stages the comic spectacle of
one who *wants* to be finished with time before time has finished with
him. The ironist regards the language of philosophy as the language of
desire. This language is always the discourse of the Other.[50] Indirectly
recalling Freud and Lacan, Derrida insists throughout his interminable
analysis that "*Sa* is *ça.*"[51] Since *ça* can be neither known nor satisfied,
knowledge is always incomplete and thus the System forever faulted.
The tolling of *Glas: débris, le reste, pas-là* "is" the *tombe* of time
inscribed in the pyramidal "A" of *différance.*

Death of Literature

When I speak to you of the unconscious as of that which appears
in the temporal pulsation, you may picture it to yourselves as a
hoop net [*nasse*] that is slightly open, at the bottom of which the
catch of the fish [*la pêche du poisson*] will be realized. . . . So we
must consider the subject, in terms of the hoop net—especially
in relation to its orifice, which constitutes its essential structure—as being interior. What is important is not what goes in
there, conforming to the word of the Gospel, but what comes
out. (*FFC,* 143–44; 131–32)[52]

50. In "*Fors,*" Derrida observes: "The crypt is the sepulchral vault of a desire"
(72; 18).
51. As I have stressed in a previous context, *ça* is the French translation of the
German *es,* which, in English, is rendered "id." This is the *es* of Heidegger *es gibt,* as
well as Freud's *es.* For Lacan's remarks on the relation between *ça* and *es,* see above,
chapter 4, note 25.
52. The fish is, of course, a traditional symbol for the Church, founded by the one
who made of his disciples, all of whom were *men,* "fishers of men." While *pêche* means
fishing or angling, and *pêcher* is to fish for, fish up, drag out and get hold of, *péché*
means sin, trespass, and transgression, and *pécher* is to sin, transgress, offend, and to
be deficient. The *ichtus* harbors the *Ich,* which, we have discovered, can be written as
CHI. The χ of writing dislocates the † of Scripture.

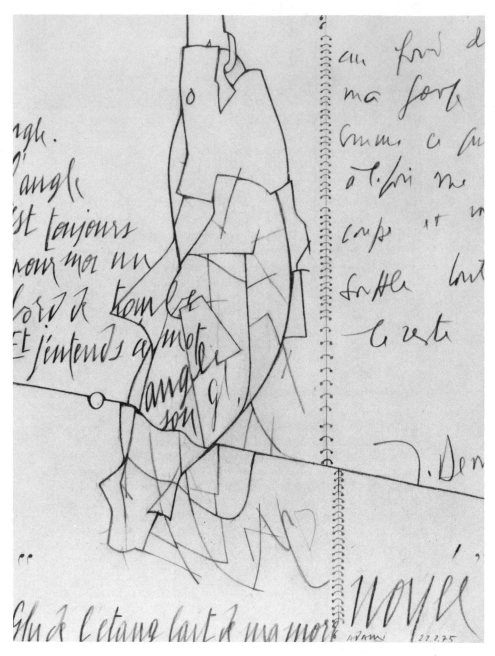

Valerio Adami, untitled. Courtesy of A.D.A.G.P., Paris/V.A.G.A., New York, 1986.

And doubtless each letter, especially *gl,* remarks or draws attention to that which appears as it is pronounced: slippery [*glissante*]
surface, angular character or letter, angular word, edge of the
tomb, bent signature. Each letter, bit, or piece of a word, is
written with two hands, on each page, two times two hands. . . .
Adami breaks it down near the fish tail, not far from the jointed
[*articulée*] binding, in the lower corner [*angle*] of the quarter of a
page, in place of the sinking of the limit, on and under the sea.
Movement of survival, arrest of death [or death sentence: *arrêt de
mort*], final trance, arched jump kept to the bit [*mors*]. Taken in
links or in the angled scales of the *ichtus,* like the signature of
Adami, or rather his initials, because the letters compose a bank
of fish, a band of erections erring toward anguish, while the dominant fish, in contrast, he who bites best and says "I" (I am dead)
or *hoc est corpus meum,* leaves the sea a scaled body of writing, a literal
surface homogeneous with the initials or signature. (*VP,* 182)

In Adami's drawing of *Glas,*[53] the signature of Derrida or Adami's
transcription of Derrida's signature (it is impossible to be certain
whether [this] writing is original or a copy), the last syllable is cut
off.[54] The *da* of Derrida is *fort.* As we have come to suspect, the
repetition of *fort/da* has something to do with death: "*Ça* resounds.
Why call *ça* death? Because *ça* has already [*déjà*] taken place" (*G,* 92).
In a marginal supplement Derrida elaborates:

déjà,[55] already. Death has already taken place, before everything.
How is one to decipher this strange anteriority of a *déjà that is
always already shouldering you with a cadaver? And if, as I have
demonstrated elsewhere . . . I am* and *I am dead* are two statements
indistinguishable in their sense, then the *already* [*déjà*] that I am
[*je suis*] sounds its own proper *glas,* signs itself its own death
sentence [*arrêt de mort*], regards you in advance, sees you advance
without any comprehension of what you will have loved, following, in a column, the funeral march of an erection everyone will
intend to have available from now on.
A more or less argot translation of the *cogito:* 'I am therefore dead.'
This can only be written. (*G,* 92)

53. There something fishy about the supposedly proper names of these artists:
Dorris Cross: dor-Ris(s) Cross and Adami: Adam + I. Suspicions about the propriety
of Hegel's proper names grows when we recall that the maiden name of his mistress,
who mothered Ludwig, was Fischer.

54. Derrida insists that there is "a constant complicity between painting (*zo-
graphia*) and writing" (*D,* 188; 214).

55. Derrida frequently associates his initials, J.D., with the word *déjà.*

To write is always to write: "I am—the 'I' is—dead." Writing, in Blanchot's terms, is *"l'arrêt de mort,* the death sentence."[56] Writing sentences the constructive subject of modern philosophy to death. When the Cartesian "I think, therefore I am" is written it is, in effect, rewritten as "I think, therefore I am not" (*TO,* 99; 146), which, in turn, is rewritten as "I am therefore dead." Derrida credits Blanchot with the recognition that the space-time of death is the spacing-timing of *literature:* "When Maurice Blanchot writes: 'Is man *capable* of a radical interrogation, that is to say, finally, is man *capable* of literature?' one could just as well say, on the basis of a certain conceptualization of life, 'incapable' half the time. Except if one admits that pure literature is nonliterature or death itself" (*WD,* 78; 116). If pure literature is "death itself," then literature is not merely cryptic but is the "absolute crypt." In the margin of another text, Derrida returns to *L'arrêt de mort:*

> The absolute crypt, unreadability itself. And yet the "references" call for an "infinite finite analysis," an infinite-finite reada-translatability. Do not go on about the symbolism of the flower (have done so elsewhere, at length, precisely about the rose). "Symbol" of life (the rosiness of cheeks, imitated by make-up in *L'arrêt de mort*), 'symbol' of death (funeral flower) or of love, the rose is also the paradigm of that which never has to account for itself (*"die Rose ist ohne warum,"* "the rose has no why or where-fore"), the enigmatically arbitrary that signifies the non-significance of the arbitrary, of the thing with no why or where-fore, without origin and without end.[57]

From a writerly point of view, literature, is "the absolute crypt . . . unreadability itself . . . infinite finite analysis . . . infinite-finite reada-translatability . . . non-significance of the arbitrary . . . the thing with no why or wherefore . . . without origin and without end." Speaking at the Sorbonne on the occasion of his thesis defense, Derrida confesses: "my most constant interest, coming even before my philosophical interest I should say, if this is possible, has been directed towards literature, towards that writing which is called literary."[58] The literature that preoccupies Derrida is the literature of death; the death that obsesses Derrida is the death of literature.

---

56. See Maurice Blanchot, *L'arrêt de mort* (Paris: Gallimard, 1948). *Death Sentence,* trans. L. Davis (Barrytown, NY: Station Hill Press, 1978).

57. Derrida, "Living On," pp. 154–55.

58. "The time of a thesis: punctuations," *Philosophy in France Today,* ed. A. Montefiore (New York: Cambridge University Press, 1983), p. 37.

Death, as Blanchot teaches, is not merely an absence and is not simply nonbeing, but is the nonabsent absence that disrupts all presence and interrupts every present. In all his writings, Derrida directly or indirectly returns to Sartre's question: "What is literature?"[59] The space of literary writing is the between—the opening of *l'entre-deux*. This gap forms the fault that is the margin of *différance*. The mark of *différance*, we have discovered, is the mark of death—an empty tomb or a pyramid, inscribed as an almost insignificant silent "A." Derrida struggles to write this deadly silence in *Glas* as "*glas.*" "If gl does not suffice for you, if no enjoyment [*jouissance*] remains for you in it, if you have nothing to fuck in it, if you want to render gl, to myself or to that galley-son surnamed Gallien, one more try. Suppose that what is more properly scaffolded here is still the form of an A, in order to pass the head there and risk the blow [*coup*]. Not to add to it gl (let fall the fallen [*l's tombé*] once more), but to write some italic [*italique*]" (*G*, 141–42).

Which italic? Perhaps the "Italic [*italique*] god, Kronos," whose saturnalia so closely resembles the bacchanalian revel of Dionysus. Derrida breaks off the left column of *Glas* with the following words:

A time to perfect the resemblance between Dionysus and Christ.
Between the two [*Entre les deux*] (already) is elaborated in sum the origin of literature.
But it runs to its ruin [*perte*], for it counted without [*sans*][60]
(*G*, 291)

The Dionysus that Christ resembles is the Dionysus of Nietzsche's eternal return. This Dionysus is also known as "The Anti-Christ."[61] Bataille, writing about the obelisk and pyramid standing on the site once occupied by the scaffold of the guillotine, indirectly clarifies the role of Dionysus in Derrida's analysis. The festival of Dionysus, which releases the delirium of "horror-spreading time," marks "the death of the One whose eternity gave Being an immutable foundation (*VE*,

59. Jean-Paul Sartre, *What is Literature?* (London: Methuen, 1950).
60. To "end" with *sans* (and no period) is not really to end. The "lack" (*manque*) of *sans* signals the insatiability of desire. In *"Pas"* Derrida writes of Blanchot: "This game (without game) of *sans* in his texts: you have just seen that it upsets [*désarticule*] all logic of identity or of contradiction and that it does so from 'the name of death' or the non-identity of the double in the name" (*Gramma* 3/4 [1976]: 139).
61. See: Nietzsche, *On the Genealogy of Morals*, trans. W. Kaufmann (New York: Random House, 1969); and *Beyond Good and Evil*, trans. W. Kaufmann (New York: Random House, 1966).

220; 1 : 510).[62] The death of the ONE and the loss of all of its representatives or, in Nietzsche's terms, "shadows"—philosophical, religious, social, cultural, political, economic, and literary—is the disappearance of the foundation that has been the basis of meaning and
Being throughout the history of the West. In the absence of the One,
what remains (*reste*) is not simply its binary opposite, the Many, but
something far less certain—a *scandalous* absurdity. Derrida rewrites
Bataille's "the deleterious absurdity of TIME" as "*le reste du temps.*" To
write the remain(s) of time, it is necessary to write in a way that eludes
both meaning and nonmeaning. Derrida's remark about Bataille's
writing applies to his own texts.

> This writing . . . folds itself [*se plie*] in order to link up with/
> enchain [*enchaîner*] classical concepts—insofar as they are inevi-
> table . . . —in such a way that these concepts, through a certain
> twist [*tour*], apparently obey their habitual laws; but they do so
> while relating themselves, at a certain point, to the moment of
> sovereignty, to the absolute loss of their meaning, to expenditure
> without reserve, to what can no longer even be called negativity
> or loss of meaning except on its philosophical side; thus they
> relate themselves to a nonmeaning, which is beyond [*au-delà*]
> absolute meaning, beyond the closure or the horizon of absolute
> knowledge. Carried away in this calculated sliding [*glissement*],
> concepts become nonconcepts, they are unthinkable, they become
> *untenable*. (*WD*, 267–68; 393)

In *Glas*, the "calculated *glissement*," slipping and sliding, of words,
terms and concepts is repeated as "*gl . . . gl . . . gl.*" This "*gl*"
(Derrida delights in pointing out that when Hegel signed his letters,
he dropped the vowels and wrote only Hgl) is a guttural stop (Hegel is
reputed to have stuttered), which "arrests [*arrête*]" meaningful
articulation.

> But *gl?* His *gl?* The sound [*le son*] *gl?* The angle of *gl?* His/its *gl?*
> This barely pronounceable writing is not a morpheme, not a word
> if one refrains from going beyond, nothing authorizes going
> beyond, the non-sense, the step of sense [*le pas de sens*]. *gl* does not
> belong to discourse, nor any more closely to space, and nothing
> ensures the past or the future of such a belonging. The suspen-
> sion, however, is no longer an insignificant phenomenon, the

62. These remarks are made in the context of a consideration of Nietzsche. The
section of "The Obelisk" in which Bataille discusses Nietzsche's ecstatic experience is
entitled "The Pyramid of Suleri." For a more detailed account of Bataille's argument,
see above, chapter 5, first section.

noise of the cry [*le cri*] that one naively opposes, like nature or the animal, to language. (*VP*, 182)

Neither quite animal nor quite human, *gl* "breaks out" (*éclate*) somewhere *between* the animal and the human. This liminal cry is *le cri* of *é-cri-ture*.[63] "It" (*Il, Es*) is, Derrida admits, a "mute or a mad sound, a kind of mechanical automaton that triggers and operates itself without meaning (to say) anything (*G*, 16).[64]

Hegel was not always totally deaf to the *Klingen* of *Klang*. Sometimes he heard the cries of the bastard he tried to repress. As death approached, Hegel, no longer able to revel in pure heavenly sound, began to hear a "discordant note—*ein Misston.*" This *Misston* is *le coup de glas* (*G*, 40)—the *coup* that is "the death rattle" (*le râle*).[65] The death that rattles every one and every thing is the tone or mistone created by the oscillating *batail* of *glas*. In "Of an Apocalyptic Tone Recently Adopted in Philosophy," Derrida pauses long enough for a parenthetical aside: "(I think rather of a pure differential vibration [*vibration différentielle pure*], without support, unbearable)."[66] This vibration is "a radical trembling" (*ébranlement radical*), which, Derrida explains, "can only come from the *outside* [*du* dehors]. Therefore, the trembling of which I speak derives no more than any other from some spontaneous decision or philosophical thought after some internal maturation in its history. This trembling is played out in the violent relationship of the *whole* [tout] of the West to its other [*autre*], whether a 'linguistic' relationship (where very quickly the question of the limits of everything [*tout*] leading back to the question of the meaning of Being arises), or ethnological, economic, political, military, relationships, etc." (*M*, 134–35; 162).

63. Recall the association between writing and the cry established by Lacan (*E-cri-ts*) and Blanchot (*é-cri-re*).

64. Elsewhere Derrida explains: "'Undecidability' is not caused by some enigmatic equivocality, some inexhaustible ambivalence of a word in a 'natural' language. . . . What counts here is not the lexical richness, the semantic infiniteness of a word or concept, its depth or breadth, the sedimentation that has produced inside it two contradictory layers of signification (continuity and discontinuity, inside and outside, identity and difference, etc.). What counts here is the formal or syntactical *praxis* that composes and decomposes it" (*D*, 220; 249). This syntactic practice is similar to what I have described as Bataille's "transgressive sintax" and Kristeva's "desemantization."

65. Derrida, "*Pas,*" p. 189.

66. Derrida, "Of an Apocalyptic Tone Recently Adopted in Philosophy," *Semeia* 23 (1982): 84. "D'un ton apocalyptique adopté naguère en philosophie," *Les fins de l'homme: à partir du travail de Jacques Derrida* (Paris: Editions Galilée, 1981), p. 468.

Texts that inscribe the altarity of this outside[67] serve as "a kind of cabal or cabala in which the blanks will never be anything but provisionally filled in, one surface or square always remaining empty, open to the play of permutations, blanks barely glimpsed as blanks (almost) pure spacing, going on forever and not in the expectation of any Messianic fulfillment" (D, 344–45; 383).[68] The infinite delay or interminable deferral of the *Parousia* is the *crisis of the Word* written in the "A" of *différance.* The empty *tombe* does not re-present the presence of renewed life but "is" the sign of the impossibility of presence—an impossibility that "is" the infinite proximity of the nonabsent absence of death. This impossibility is the strange apocalypse of the apocalypse itself. The Impossible draws near with a "Come," which, paradoxically, never comes.

"Come" [*Viens*] cannot come from a voice or at least not from a tone signifying "I" or "self," a so-and-so (male or female) in my "determination." "Come" is *only* derivable [*dérivable*],[69] abso-

67. Precisely such inscription is the function of the text *stricto sensu.* "The thickness of the text thus opens upon the beyond of a whole [*s'œuvre ainsi sur l'au-delà d'un tout*], the nothing or the absolute outside, through which its depth is at once null and infinite—infinite in that each of its layers harbors another layer" (D, 357; 397).

68. The Torah itself is suspended between two "poles." According to this Jewish writer who grew up in Algeria, the interval of the between has something to do with the "origin" of literature. "In Algeria, in the middle of a mosque the colonists would have transformed into a synagogue, the Torah, brought forth from behind the curtains, is promenaded in the arms of a man or a child, and kissed and caressed by the faithful along the way. (The faithful, as you know, are enveloped in a veil. Some wear it all rolled up, like a cord, a sling, or an untied necktie around their neck. Others, more amply spread out on their shoulders and chest and trailing to the floor. Still others—and, at determined moments, everyone—on the head. . . . The dead man is enveloped in his *taleth*—that is the name of the veil—after washing the body and closing all its orifices.) The Torah wears a robe and a crown. Its two rollers are then parted like two legs; the Torah is lifted to arm's length and the rabbi's scepter approximately follows the upright text. The bands in which it was wrapped had been previously undone and entrusted, generally, to a child. The child, comprehending nothing about all these signs full of sense, was to climb up into a gallery where the women, and old women especially, were then to pass them the ragged bands. The old women rolled them up like crepe bands for infants, and then the child brought them back to the Thebah. . . . Maybe the children who watched the pomp of this celebration, even more those who could lend it a hand, dream about it for a long time after, in order to organize there all the pieces and scenes of their lives. What am I doing here? Let's put it that I am working on the origin of literature by miming it. Between the two [*Entre les deux*]" (G, 268–69).

69. *Dérivable* carries a wide range of associations: *dérive:* drift, leeway; *dérivé:* turned or drifted from the shore; *dériver:* to be turned from its proper course, drift, divert, derive. *Rive* designates the bank, shore, margin, border, skirt (of woods, etc.).

lutely derivable, but only from the other [*autre*], from nothing
that may be an origin or a verifiable, decidable, presentable,
appropriable identity, from nothing that may not already be
derivable and arrivable [*arrivable*] without "rive." Perhaps you
will be tempted to call this the disaster, the catastrophe, the
apocalypse. Now here, precisely, is announced—as promise or
threat—an apocalypse without apocalypse, an apocalypse without vision, without truth, without revelation, *of dispatches* [des
envois] (for the "come" is plural in itself, in oneself), of addresses
without message and without destination, without sender or
decidable addressee, without last judgment, without any other
eschatology than the tone of the "Come" itself, its very difference,
an apocalypse beyond good and evil. "Come" does not announce
this or that apocalypse: already it resounds with a certain tone; it
is in itself the apocalypse of the apocalypse; "*Come*" is apocalyptic.[70]

This "Come" is the "*Viens*" of Blanchot—the *Viens* with which
L'arrêt de mort ends. To heed the solicitation of an inconceivable Other
is to leave the comfort of the familial and the security of the familiar in
order to err with neither hope of arriving nor expectation of returning
home. To wander among pyramids is to trace and retrace *les pas* of
Abraham. The space of such erring is the desert. The time of such erring
is the terrifying past that never was, the uncanny present that never is,
and the frightful future that never will be. The space-time of such
erring is the writerly spacing-timing of *Fear and Trembling*.

70. Derrida, "Of An Apocalyptic Tone Recently Adopted in Philosophy,"
p. 89; 468.

Overleaf: Marc Chagall, *Le sacrifice d'Isaac*. Courtesy of the Musées
Nationaux, Paris.

10

Transgression

SØREN KIERKEGAARD

■

Doodling

Everyone shall be remembered, but everyone became great in proportion to his *expectation*. One became great by expecting the possible, another by expecting the eternal; but he who expected the impossible became the greatest of all. Everyone shall be remembered, but everyone was great wholly in proportion to the magnitude of that with which he *struggled*. For he who struggled with the world became great by conquering the world, and he who struggled with himself became great by conquering himself, but he who struggled with God was the greatest of all. Thus did they struggle on earth: there was one who conquered everything by his power, and there was one who conquered God by his powerlessness. . . . Abraham was the greatest of all, great by that power whose strength is powerlessness, great by that wisdom whose secret is foolishness, great by that hope whose form is madness, great by that love that is hatred of oneself. (*FT,* 16; 69)

First and foremost, he does not say anything, and in that form he says what he has to say. (*FT,* 118; 164)

What *can* Abraham say to Sarah—Sarah, the woman who laughs, the woman whose previous name, Sarai, means mockery, the woman who bore a son named "He laughed"? Can he tell her what took place? What did not take place? What *almost* took place? Can he describe "the supernatural hand" that seemed to be placed in his hand? Can he represent the nameless, unimaginable, silent phantom to which that uncanny hand belonged? Can he express the inexpressible? How can he explain that he remains—remains uncertain whether what took place or almost took place was reality or a dream? How can he explain that he is no longer the same, even though nothing actually took place, or perhaps *because* nothing took place—if, that is, nothing can take place, take "its" place, his place, the son's place? How can he explain that his return is not the return of the same? If he tried, Sarah probably would break out laughing.

What *can* Søren—Søren, whose given name eventually comes to mean "Tomfool," and whose surname means "church [*kirke*]" "yard [*gaard*]," or "cemetery"—say to Regina? How can he express his thoughts that tend to "wound from behind"? How can he describe the incurable wound opened by what he obliquely refers to as his "thorn in the flesh"? How can he explain that he has *never* been the same but has *always* been somehow "different"? What can he tell her that she (or, for that matter, he) could understand about this difference? Almost nothing. But how can he say "almost nothing"? Perhaps it is impossible to *say* this difference that is almost nothing. Perhaps it cannot be said directly but only indirectly—"said" by not *saying* but by *writing*, and by always writing "de Silentio." Perhaps Søren's or Johannes's writing is (this) impossibility.

Johannes de Silentio opens and closes *Fear and Trembling* on a commercial note:

Preface
Not only in the business world but also in the world of ideas, our age stages a real sale.

Epilogue
Once when the price of spices in Holland fell, the merchants [*Købmænde*] had a few cargoes sunk in the sea [*Havet*] to jack up the price.

This businesslike approach is well suited to Kierkegaard's audience. His text is directed to merchants whose chief concern is to turn a profit and to speculators whose primary interest is a reasonable return on their investments. *København,* like all cities, is a market town. As its name indicates, Copenhagen is a merchant's harbor.[1] Such a market place is, as Bataille points out, governed by the laws of a restricted economy. The uninterrupted circulation and regular production of this economic system presuppose the mutual recognition of its members and strict adherence to principles of free and fair exchange. Losses and gains, like negatives and positives, have to check and balance each other. In this reciprocal give and take, all expenses must be recovered and every capital out-lay is supposed to return as in-come. To insure adequate compensation, efforts must be made to reduce excess, re-move waste, and eliminate unemployment. Useless expenditures are not allowed; messing up and fooling around are strictly forbidden. Play is permitted only if it makes sense, and it makes sense only when

1. *København—købe:* buy, purchase; *køber:* buyer, purchaser; *købmand:* business-man, merchant; *havn:* harbor, port; *hav:* sea, ocean.

it is in the service of work. In København, everything is taken into account and everyone is expected to be productive.

Kierkegaard was never at home in København. Though he always lived near the center of the city and rarely left town, he could not find his proper place in this closed society of merchants and speculators. Kierkegaard never had a job, never took a position; he was always out of work, perpetually unemployed. He lived off the inheritance (which was not merely monetary) of his father who, after he had been a shepherd and before his early retirement, had been a successful *textile* merchant. Though the reasons for the father's abrupt withdrawal from the world of work are obscure, his retirement seems to be related to a sense of guilt associated with woman and transgression. After the death of his first wife, Michael Pedersen Kierkegaard violated his maid, Anne Sørensdatter Lund. This woman, who, as I have previously observed, never once appears in either Kierkegaard's published books or private journals, married Michael and bore all seven of his children, the youngest of whom was Søren Aabye.

A spoiled child, Søren was always something of a parasite, who was nourished and sustained by the remains of the system he eventually struggled to subvert. Never apologetic about being out of work, he seemed to flaunt his idleness by wandering aimlessly through busy city streets. Such errancy frustrated the capital's productive workers, irritated its serious merchants, and unsettled its speculative investors. When tensions reached the breaking point in January of 1846, the magnitude of the reactive forces that erupted suggests that for many Københavners the integrity of Western society and culture, in their totality, had been called into question by this lonely individual. How could a solitary individual make the entire structure of the West tremble? How could the solicitation of a single unemployed streetwalker cause the delicately balanced restricted economy to totter? How could a useless parasite deconstruct a system it had taken millennia to construct?

Perhaps by writing. Although he was always out of work, Kierkegaard was ever a writer. Like Blanchot, he could be a writer only if he were unemployed. Had his writing become work or his writings works, he no longer would have been a writer. He might have accepted a respectable position as a philosopher, professor, or priest. But he repeatedly resisted assimilation, incorporation, or domestication. Refusing "money, honor, reputation, applause, etc.," Kierkegaard was an unacknowledged outsider who forever remained beyond the law of reciprocal exchange. The writings of such an outlaw might not appear to amount to much. A few scattered fragments, almost nothing—little more than senseless scribbling and idle doodling.

Kierkegaard was an inveterate scribbler and doodler. His handwritten manuscripts are riddled with *Krims-Krams* (scrawl, flourishes)
that sometimes are inscribed in the margins and sometimes in
the midst of the text. The ornate scribbling usually erases what
Kierkegaard had written.[2]

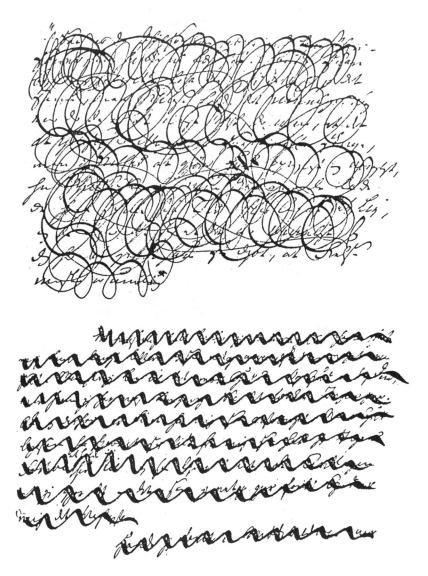

2. The doodles and marginalia included in this chapter can be found in
Kierkegaard's handwritten manuscripts. The following items are reproduced with the

Kierkegaard's doodles, by contrast, are more carefully drawn and differ significantly in their details. In some cases, it is difficult to distinguish scribble and doodle.

An erased *ø,* which, as one of the three "supplementary" letters of the Danish alphabet, is itself an erased *0.*

An effaced *0* and *Z.*

A crossed-out double-cross.

permission of the Søren Kierkegaard Archives, The Royal Library of Copenhagen: I A 324; I C 60; IV B 65, 1; III B 32; I C 27; IV B 6; V A 109; III H 40; II A 339; IV B 207; I C 27; I C 29; IV B 65, 1; D 1, 7 (Letter 17); and the title page of *Fear and Trembling.* With two exceptions, the doodles and marginalia have not, to my knowledge, previously been published.

A chiasmus: X's graphed onto an X that either grows out of or covers an O or a circle.

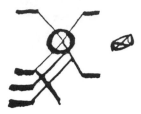

Some are more puzzling.

A grid for the game of X's and O's, tick-tack-toe, modified to form four squares with an empty space in the center and a hyphen on either side.

Seemingly Borgesian stairs that come from and lead nowhere.

Even more menacing, something that looks like either rocking stairs or teeth stripped from the jaw of some leviathan—perhaps a sperm whale.

An ellipse, with two loose ends, which is either raveling or unraveling. In the dangling thread, there appears the hint of a profile of a face.

Others are less obscure and more suggestive.

An erased figure holding a prodigious sword or style in an erect position.

A solitary individual, precariously balanced on a tightrope attached to neither supporting column, who is either looking for help through a spyglass or calling for assistance through a megaphone.

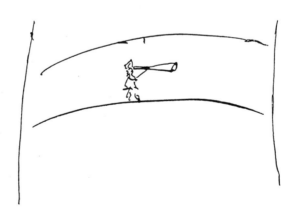

Once Kierkegaard even sketched a flower . . . a single flower . . . a single flower that had been cut.

What is one to make of such scribbles and doodles? Are they significant or insignificant, meaningful or senseless? Can the riddles they pose be solved, the gaps they open be closed? Can scribbling and doodling be deciphered or interpreted? Do such marginalia escape comprehension, resist conception by the concept? Are these scribbles and doodles—*ces griffonnages*—merely the foolish nonwork of an unemployed writer? What does all of this have to do with flowers, with a single flower, a single cut flower?

There is one doodle that Kierkegaard repeats again and again, though always altering it slightly. It is a face—the face of a man. The face is never open to full view but is always diverted, forever looking elsewhere. The direction is always the same: from the right to the left—backward. In all of Kierkegaard's manuscripts, there is not a single profile facing forward, i.e., from left to right. It is as if these men or the many faces of this one man were gazing back toward the past, toward an absolute or impossible past, a past that is always already past, a past that might never have been present. In what is,

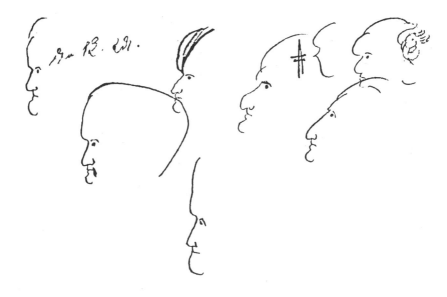

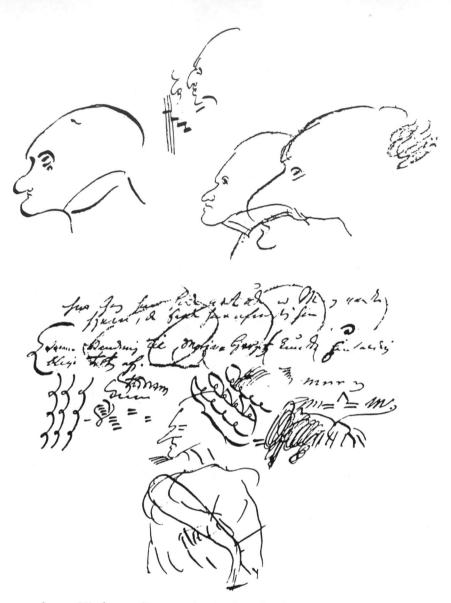

perhaps, Kierkegaard's most intriguing doodle, the figure gazing toward the past arises from or dissolves into a series of faces. The man's heart appears to be haunted by a silhouette with hair long enough to cast doubt on the gender of the figure. The head of the man (directly behind the mouth in the place of the tongue) is filled with Hebrew letters that spill over into the written text.[3]

3. The letters written within the head of the figure are unclear. The Hebrew inserted in the text means "rebuke, rebuke, rebuke."

459. 26.

משפט

הוכיח הוכיח

Index an Chr. nachforschende ἰαρουδίας. 1 Cor. X,11.
1 Thess. 4,15. 1 Cor: 15,51. Gal. 5,7-9. 1 Joh. 2,18. Phil. 4,5.
... indenis reddar mihi.
Vermittelns s. concreditur mihi. Rom 3,2. 1 Thess.
2,4.

I C 10

Who is this man of Hebrew tongue? What does he expect? Whom does he await?

There is but one drawer of faces inscribed in Kierkegaard's published writings. He is a nameless man who appears in a text bearing an undecidable title: "'Guilty?'/'Not Guilty?': A Passion Narrative."

> He had collected a considerable library, but all the books had to do with physiology. Among them were to be found the most costly copper engravings, along with them whole sequences of his own drawings, including faces drawn with the precision of portraits, then a row of faces bound to a single one in a series that showed how the likeness constantly grew less, though a remainder [*en Rest*] of it always returned; there were faces executed according to mathematical propositions, others that illustrated by a few clear lines how a slight alteration in the proportions completely altered the outline; there were faces constructed according to physiological observations, and these, in turn, were checked by other faces sketched in accordance with a hypothetical assumption. (*SLW*, 262; 6:263)[4]

This drawer, however, does not exactly appear *in* Kierkegaard's text. The tracer of faces emerges in one of the apparently "autobiographical" fifth-of-the-month entries. These textual interruptions function as something like marginal asides in "Quidam's Diary." When he was not doodling, the obsessive drawer was employed as a "bookkeeper or an accountant" (*Bogholder*). The bookkeeper's home was not København; he lived across the canal in *Christianhavn*. According to the narrator, who might or might not be Quidam, "one notices immediately that this town [i.e., Christianhavn] is not a capital or royal residence." Rather, it is "remote in an other world" (*afsides i en anden Verden*). People in this other world are different—especially different from Københavners. They "do not seem to be acquainted with the aims and purposes that prompt the inhabitants of the capital." In the town's only square, there stands "a solitary ruin," left by "a conflagration that did not, as pious superstition recounts in other instances, leave the church standing while it consumed everything else, but consumed the church and left only the prison standing." Commerce in this other harbor has come to a halt. Storehouses stand empty and "big warehouses contain nothing and bring in nothing, for though Echo is a very quiet lodger, yet in the way of business and rent, no owner is better for it." Streets, crowded with the idle and un-

---

4. The account developed in the following pages and the quotations cited are from *SLW*, 258–68; 6:259–70.

employed, are haunted by a certain "murmur" (*Larm:* compare the French *larme,* tear). Life in Christianhavn is characterized by "destitution," "wretchedness," "drunkenness," and "madness."

In Christianhavn, the bookkeeper is one of the maddest of the mad. Known by many as a "wanderer" (*Vandrer*) he might be seen (though the reader cannot be certain, for the evasive narrator places his account in the conditional tense) every day between eleven and twelve o'clock, pacing back and forth, lost in thought, with head hung low, "at the southern extremity [*Overgaden; overgaa:* to exceed] of Water Street." This wanderer took an unusual interest in children. "The moment he saw a child, at any time but the hour between eleven and twelve, the monotonous expression on his face became mobile and reflected a great variety of moods, he made up to the child, engaged it in conversation, and all the while regarded it with such close attention that he might have been an artist who painted, scribbled, or scrawled [*malede*] only children's faces." His extraordinary concern for children had its benevolent side. The wanderer was well known throughout Christianhavn for his generosity toward poor children and their hapless mothers. Though he was a successful accountant who was widely respected in the business world for his ability to balance books and settle accounts, the bookkeeper's personal finances appeared to be governed by a different calculus. He freely expended his resources to assist the poor and needy and seemed to expect nothing in return. Unlike the profitable "pawnshops" run by canny København investors, the accountant's "benefactions were in a very strange [*besynderlig*] sense entirely gratuitous." Fascinated by the bookkeeper's errancy and exorbitance, the narrator undertakes an extensive inquiry into the wanderer's background.

Though not immediately evident, the bookkeeper was, in a certain sense, preoccupied with flowers, or with a single flower that *apparently* had been cut—deflowered. As a young man, he was a useful and productive member of a well-run domestic economy. While his responsible labor brought recognition and reward, the bookkeeper, nonetheless, felt his life was missing or lacking something. "He was," the narrator explains, "the son of a subordinate government employee living in modest circumstances. At an early age he got a position with one of the richest merchants. Quiet, retiring, rather shy and embarrassed, he attended to his business with an intelligence and punctuality that soon led the head of the house to discover in him a very useful [*brugbart*] man. He employed his leisure time in reading, in studying foreign languages, in developing his decided talent for drawing and sketching, and in making a daily visit to the house of his parents, where he was the only child. So he lived on without knowledge of the world. He was employed as an accountant, and soon he was the recipient of a considerable salary. If it be true, as the Englishman says, that money makes virtue, it is certain that money makes vice. The young man was not tempted, but as year after year went by he became more and more strange [*fremmed*] to the world. He himself hardly noticed this because his time was always fully occupied. Only once did a presentiment of it dawn upon his soul, he became a stranger to himself, or was like one who suddenly comes to a halt and vaguely recalls something [*Noget*] he must have forgotten, though without being able to comprehend what it was."

After a lengthy investigation, the narrator concludes that what the bookkeeper had "forgotten" was nothing other than his youth. "He had forgotten to be young and to let his heart delight in itself in the manner of youth before the days of youth were past." Although such forgetting is not unusual, it is somewhat strange, for it involves the forgetting of what has never been experienced since it never took place. How can one forget what was never present? How can one remember what is always already past?

In order to appreciate the precise nature of the bookkeeper's dilemma, it is necessary to note a distinction that William Afham, the pseudonymous narrator of the first part of *Stages on Life's Way*, formulates in his *Forerindring* (Prefatory note or recollection; *Erindring:* recollection; *for:* before). "In Vino Veritas: A Recollection" is, among other things, a parody of Plato's *Symposium*. William devotes his Forerindring to an explanation of the difference between "recollection" (*Erindring*) and "memory" (*Huskommelse*). This distinction parallels Hegel's contrast between *Erinnerung* and *Gedächtnis*. For Hegel, as Paul de Man points out,

> memorization [*Gedächtnis*] has to be sharply distinguished from recollection and from imagination. It is entirely devoid of images (*bildlos*), and Hegel speaks derisively of pedagogical attempts to teach children how to read and write by having them associate pictures with specific words. But it is not devoid of materiality altogether. We can learn by heart only when all meaning is forgotten and words read as if they were a mere list of names. "It is well known," says Hegel, "that one knows a text by heart [or by rote] only when one no longer associates any meaning with the words; reciting what one thus knows by heart one necessarily drops all accentuation." . . . Memory, for Hegel, is the learning by rote of *names,* or of words considered as names, and it can therefore be separated from the notation, the inscription, or the

writing down of these names. In order to remember, one is forced to write down what one is likely to forget. The idea, in other words, makes its sensory appearance, in Hegel, as the material inscription of names. Thought is entirely dependent on a mental faculty that is mechanical through and through, as remote as can be from the sounds and the images of the imagination or from the dark mine of recollection, which lies beyond the reach of words and thought.[5]

The final aim of philosophical reflection is to sublate *Gedächtnis* by means of *Erinnerung.* When recollection re-members memory, nothing remains outside speculative comprehension or beyond philosophical mastery.

For William Afham, the difference between recollection and memory seems to be related to the problem of bookkeeping, or to the question of different ways of keeping books and alternative accounting procedures. What, he asks, "if recollection's ledger [*Hovedbog—Hoved:* head, intelligence + *bog:* book] were not other than a scrapbook or a wastebook [*en Kladde*] in which one scribbles [*smører*] whatever comes into one's head?" (*SLW,* 29; 6 : 17). Different ways of keeping books have important economic implications. Recollection is the mode of recalling proper to speculators who are primarily concerned with profit. Furthermore, recollection is the preoccupation of speculative philosophers whose interest is the certainty of useful returns. "For recollection [*Erindringen*] is ideality, but as such it involves effort and responsibility that indifferent memory [*hukommelse*] does not involve. Recollection seeks to assert man's eternal continuity in life and to insure that his earthly existence shall be *uno tenore,* one breath [*Aandedrag: Aand,* spirit; German, *Geist*], and capable of being expressed in one [*i Eet*]. . . . This is the condition for human immortality, that life be *uno tenore"* (*SLW,* 28; 6 : 16). Elsewhere William explains that recollections are one's "profit [*Udbytte:* return, dividend] for eternity. In recollection a man draws a check upon eternity. Eternity is humane enough to honor every draft and to regard everyone as solvent" (*SLW,* 17; 6 : 17). The economy of memory is more difficult, perhaps impossible, to decipher. Eternity, William continues, "is not responsible if a man makes a fool [*Nar*] of himself and remembers [*huske*] instead of recollects [*erindre*], for the remembered [*det huskes*] is also the forgotten [*det glemmes*]. But again memory makes life

5. Paul de Man, "Sign and Symbol in Hegel's *Aesthetics," Critical Inquiry* 8 (1981): 77. Derrida develops a very helpful reading of de Man's argument in *Memories: For Paul de Man,* trans. C. Lindsay, J. Culler, and E. Cadava (New York: Columbia University Press, 1986).

unconstrained [*ugeneret*]. Unconstrained, one passes through the most ludicrous or laughable metamorphoses; even at an advanced age one still plays blindman's bluff [*Blindebuk*], one still plays in life's lottery" (*SLW,* 28–29; 6: 17).

In these brief remarks, William describes two very different economies: one is profitable, the other profitless; one saving, the other expensive; one restrained or restricted, the other unrestrained or unrestricted; in one people are careful, sensible, insightful, intelligent, in the other careless, senseless, blind, foolish; in one accounting results in balanced books, in the other in scrapbooks; one is a comprehensive system, the other leaves the (restricted) economy in ruins. In view of these differences, the distinction between *Erindring* and *Huskommelse* (or between *Errinerung* and *Gedächtnis*) repeats the differences between København and Christianhavn, the employed and the unemployed, the speculator and the idler, and, perhaps, the philosopher and the writer.

The task the bookkeeper set for himself is recollection. He seeks to re-present his past or his youth. This past, however, poses a peculiar problem: the bookkeeper had *never* been young (a complaint Kierkegaard frequently voices about himself). The lost past that is the "object" of his search or research was never present "in the first place." The bookkeeper's task is, therefore, impossible. Recollection, as well as the interiorization it entails, inevitably fails. Paradoxically, this failure of memory is a "forgetting," which is at the same time the "memory" of an exteriority that is never interior, an outside that is never inside, a past that is never present, though it is not simply absent.

In quest of this impossible past, the bookkeeper "became acquainted with a couple of clerks who were men of the world." One night, after an excursion to the forest, which ended with an "extraordinarily splendid" dinner and excessive drinking, the three "visited one of those places where, strangely enough, one gives money for a woman's contemptibility. What happened there even [the bookkeeper] himself did not know." [6] This point bears repeating, for it suggests a strange repetition: the bookkeeper did not know whether or not "his" past transgression actually took place or was only a figment of his heated imagination. Remembering only enough to repress, the bookkeeper withdrew further, until one day he fell desperately ill and "was sick unto death." In the delirium of his fever, "there suddenly awoke in him a recollection, a recollection of that incident, which until then

6. This is a thinly veiled account of one of Kierkegaard's actual experiences. The anxiety attributed to the bookkeeper followed Kierkegaard throughout his entire life.

had not existed for him in any real sense. In his recollection of it, that occurrence assumed a definite form that brought his life to an end along with the loss of his purity. He recovered, but when he left his couch with health restored, he took with him a *possibility,* and this possibility pursued him, and he pursued this possibility in his passionate research and this possibility brooded in his silence, and this possibility it was that set in motion the features of his face when he saw a child—and this possibility was that another being owed his life to him." The bookkeeper, in other words, feared he had unknowingly conceived a bastard. This fear, however, was not founded upon any ordinary recollection. The bookkeeper was not even sure it was based upon a true recollection. Uncertainty about whether a flower had been cut, a hymen ruptured—uncertainty about whether he had lost his purity, smeared his proper name—eventually drove the bookkeeper mad. "What made his madness so dialectical was the fact that he did not so much as know whether his notion was the result of his illness, a fevered imagination, or whether death had actually come to the aid of his memory with a recollection of reality. Behold, it ended therefore with his wandering silently with bowed head along that short path between the hours of eleven and twelve, and with his wandering the rest of the day along the prodigious detour [*uhyre Omvei*] of the desperate twisting of all possibilities to find, if possible, a certainty, and then the thing sought."

Such erring gradually disrupted the bookkeeper's everyday life and work. "In the beginning he was quite capable of attending to the business of the office. He was as precise and punctual as ever. He scanned the ledger and the copybooks, but now and then it came to him in a flash that the whole thing was useless labor, that there was something completely other [*noget ganske Andet*] that he ought to be looking up in books." But how can one look up in a book *noget ganske Andet?* How can one recollect what is wholly Other? The bookkeeper's bind, i.e., to recover a youth that was never present, led to a double bind, i.e., to recollect an event that might never have occurred. This double bind created a "detour" (*Omvei*) that was "monstrous" (*uhyre*) because infinite, infinite because endless, endless because wandering always "ends" in failure. The narrator observes: "whether it was along the specialized historical path of investigation he sought to penetrate [*trænge*] to the origin of that recollection [*Erindrings Udspring*], or whether it was by the prodigious detour of ordinary human observation that he sought wearily, with only the support of deceptive hypotheses, to transform that unknown X into a named dimension—he did not find what he sought."

It is not only the *bookkeeper's* recollection that fails; recollection fails unfailingly. The failure of recollection is the function of a "memory" that is a "forgetting" and a "forgetting" that is a "memory." Such memory is, as Hegel realized but tried to forget, bound to writing or to the impossibility of writing. The impossible "memory" or the "memory" of the impossible subverts all recollection from the beginning (which is not to say at the origin). This impossibility can only be written, for it is, paradoxically, the impossibility *of* writing. Such an impossibility, which can never be spoken, must be written "de Silentio."

Marginalia

Johannes de Silentio has trouble beginning *Fear and Trembling*. In a certain sense, he never truly begins—or ends. Consider the structure of his text: an epigram; a "commercial" Preface; a "Tuning" (*Stemning*) that consists of four fictitious variations of the Old Testament story of Abraham; a eulogy on Abraham; a statement of three problems, interrupted by a lengthy "Preliminaray Expectoration" (*Forel\u00f8big Expectoration*), which can be read as a long clearing of the throat, a disgusting remainder—spit, which is almost as repulsive as vomit, or as a supplementary oration about expectation; and a "commercial" Epilogue. It is difficult to say just where the book begins and impossible to know where it ends. Johannes has no thesis; his writing is interrogative, conditional, hypothetical (without being speculative), and subjunctive. Moreover, Johannes has no conclusions, provides no answers to his own questions, gives no solutions to his problems and offers no results of his research. Perhaps he has not written *a book,* and perhaps *he* has not written a book. Perhaps he has written something "other," and perhaps something or someone "other" has written. "Johannes de Silentio" is, after all, a pseudonym. But for whom or for what? What Other haunts Johannes's text?

Kierkegaard has trouble beginning *Fear and Trembling*. Unlike Johannes, Kierkegaard's problem of beginning begins before the beginning of the text. To begin is inevitably to exclude; writing always involves rewriting. To write, in other words, is to erase and cut. What does Kierkegaard leave outside of (the) work? What remains— remains unemployed? These questions trace the interplay of writing and effacement, scripture and erasure. Along this margin the question of *literary remains* emerges.

Before Johannes begins, Kierkegaard begins by rewriting the title and author, editing the epigram, and erasing important parts of the preface. His effacement, however, leaves traces in the text. These traces mark and remark a certain "Other" that "is" neither Johannes nor Søren.

Titles border or frame works. As such, they are inevitably liminal and unavoidably ambiguous. On the one hand, a title is excessive; it is a supplement that delays the beginning of the work proper. On the other hand, the title opens the work by creating space for its writing. Neither inside nor outside the work, the title is always between, forever marginal. A supplementary excess or excessive supplement, the title might be read as the inscription of a between, or the writing of a margin.

Mellemhverandre [+]
af
Simon Stylita
Solodandser og Privatmand.

udgivet
af
S. Kierkegaard.

[+] *I Marginen:* Bevægelser og Stillinger.

Kierkegaard's handwritten scrapbooks make it clear that in earlier drafts, "Fear and Trembling" is merely a marginal title for the work he is struggling to write. The first suggestion of this title is scribbled along the border of another title. Before settling on "Fear and Trembling," Kierkegaard plays with the idea of coining a word to entitle his work. The word he proposes (for which there is no precise translation) means something like margin: *Mellemhverandere*. To form this improper word, Kierkegaard joins *mellem*, between, and *hverandre*, each other or one another. The title Kierkegaard leaves out of his published work could be translated "Between Each Other." In another marginal aside, Kierkegaard suggests that the two between which this title falls are *"Bevægelser og Stilligner*, movements and positions."[7] Kierkegaard offers no explanation of these richly suggestive terms. However, there seems to be a trace of these erased words in the reference to "Heraclitus the Obscure" (a possible precursor of Blanchot's Thomas) in the last paragaraph of the published version of *Fear and Trembling*. A consideration of the remains that Kierkegaard leaves in his wastebook suggests that the title that eventually becomes marginal by being excluded from the work initially frames his writing, and the title that was once marginal finally opens the work. Through this reversal, the marginal is both included in and excluded from the text. In this way, the title remains *Mellemhverandre*.

Having rewritten his title, Kierkegaard proceeds to change the author of his work. The author of *Mellemhverandre* was to have been Simon Stylita. In Simon, Kierkegaard seems to be searching for something like a Christian analogue to Abraham. The stylites were anchorites who, in response to what they took to be a religious calling, retreated to the solitude of the desert. Their name derives from the practice of sitting atop tall pillars. The column functions as something like a substitute for the sacred mountain (like Mount Moriah) where the encounter with the divine is supposed to occur. Instead of sitting precariously perched on a pillar, some desert monks lived inside hollow columns. Simon Stylites is reported to have fled to the top of a column in 423 to escape crowds of followers. The mountain, pillar, and hollow column mark alternative sites or nonsites for an extraordinary event or nonevent.

Not unlike a title, an epigram is marginal. It always falls betwixt'n between. Lying between the title (itself a boundary that is neither inside nor outside) and the body of the text, the epigram always appears to be something of a supplement that harbors surplus value. It

7. As a noun, *Stille,* which is included in *Stilling,* means calm; as an adjective, still, quiet, tranquil; and as a verb, to satisfy, allay, alleviate.

is less a thesis than a prosthesis. As an addition "before" the beginning, the epigram further delays the commencement of (the) work.
This marginal inscription suggests that the author is almost, but not
quite, ready to begin. Most often, this substitute for a beginning is
not the word of the author himself or herself. The epigram tends to be
the word of an other. The text that follows the epigram is, in an
important sense, a reinscription of what already has been written in
the epigram.

In his epigram, Johannes anticipates the text that follows by citing
a few lines from Hamann about cut flowers.

What Tarquinius Superbus said in the garden by means of the
poppies, the son understood but the messenger did not.

Hamann

The editors of the English edition explain: "When the son of Tarquinius Superbus had craftily gotten Gabii in his power, he sent a messenger to his father asking what he should do with the city. Tarquinius, not trusting the messenger, gave no reply but took him to the garden, where with his cane he cut off the flowers of the tallest poppies. The son understood from this that he should eliminate the leading men of the city" (*FT,* 339). Those who speak through cut flowers and write with pointed style(s) cannot be understood literally or comprehended properly. Indeed, it is not certain whether they can be understood at all.

Johannes's epigram excludes an important part of Hamann's text, which Kierkegaard records in his scrapbook.[8]

> A layman and unbeliever can explain my manner of writing in no other way than as nonsense [*Unsinn*], since I express myself in various tongues and speak the language of sophists, of wordplays [*Wortspiele*], of Cretans and Arabians, of whites and Moors and Creoles, and babble a confusion of criticism, mythology, rebus [*rebus*], and axioms, and argue now in a human way and now in an extraordinary way. (*JP,* 1551; IV B 96 : 4)

This supplement to Johannes's epigram, which is itself a supplement to his work, compounds difficulties and generates further confusion. The reader is cast in the role of a layman or unbeliever for whom writing is "nonsense," "speaking in tongues," "sophistry," "wordplay," "babble," "a confusion of criticism"—a "rebus," not unlike a mad dream. The remainder of the epigram refuses every consolation that would provide an easy way into or out of the text that follows. It is not clear (and it never becomes clear) whether or not the belief that seems to hold a promise of lucid insight and comprehensive certainty is even possible. The reader is left with the unsettling suspicion that the text's curious indirection might finally render it indecipherable. Unlike Tarquinius's message to his father, Johannes's message to his reader might never arrive.

An epigram, as well as everything else, can be read in many ways. As a supplement hovering between title and text, the epigram is an appendage that often appears to be vestigal or useless—like an antecedent appendix. It is, however, possible to read the epigram and hence the text otherwise by reversing the relation between appendix and body. Insofar as the work entails the rewriting of the epigram, the text itself becomes supplementary to the epigram. The text, in other

8. As can be seen in the handwritten manuscript reproduced above, Kierkegaard actually crossed out this part of Hamann's text.

words, is a supplement to a supplement, and writing is nothing other than a play of supplements or supplementary play. When read in this way, all of the nonsense, wordplay, sophistry, babble, and confusion of the supplement come to riddle both the text and writing.

In the movement from title to epigram, to preface, one never leaves the margin or passes beyond the border. As reader and writer, Kierkegaard is fascinated by prefaces. Most of his works are preceded by elaborate prefaces, forewords, and introductions. One of his earliest texts consists of nothing but prefaces. This preoccupation with prefaces is closely related to his criticism of Hegel. Kierkegaard insists that the impossibility of drawing definite conclusions and knowing results absolutely and the impossibility of comprehending first principles or securing an absolute beginning leads to the impossibility of absolute knowledge and the incomprehensibility of Hegel's System. Anticipating the criticism of Hegel that Derrida develops in "*Hors Livre*," Kierkegaard argues that if the System has either a preface or a postscript, it is not really a system. Instead of approaching Hegel directly by attacking his System through an analysis of its preface, i.e., the *Phenomenology*, Kierkegaard develops an indirect critique of Hegel in ironic prefaces, forewords, introductions, fragments, and postscripts that parody systematic philosophy. Of all his prefaces, the most intriguing is Johannes's *Forord* to *Fear and Trembling*. In his "Foreword," Kierkegaard, through a pseudonym, describes his relation to Hegel's System and suggests an unexpected connection between his reading of Hegel and the question of writing.

> The present author is by no means a philosopher. He has not understood the System, whether there is one, whether it is completed; it is already enough for his weak head to ponder what a prodigious [*uhyre*] head everyone must have these days when everyone has such a prodigious thought. Even if someone were able to transpose the whole content of faith into the form of the concept [*Begrebets Form*], it does not follow that he has comprehended faith, comprehended how he entered it or how it entered into him. The present author is by no means a philosopher. He is *poetice et eleganter* [in a poetic and refined way] a supplementary clerk [*en Extra-Skriver*] who neither writes the System nor gives *promises* of the System, who neither exhausts himself on the System nor binds himself to the System. He writes because to him it is a luxury [*Luxus*] that is all the more pleasant and apparent the fewer there are who buy and read what he writes. (*FT,* 7; 3:59)

In this extraordinary passage, Johannes describes himself as a supplementary clerk—*en Extra-Skriver*. *Extra-Skriver* can also be translated "extra writer," or perhaps even "writer of extra." In opposition to the currents circulating in the philosophical mainstream, this *Extra-Skriver* does not write a System. He writes simply because it is a luxury. His writing, therefore, is more like play than work. This playful writing seems to serve no useful purpose and is of little commercial value. The pleasure that writing provokes derives from its resistance to an economy of exchange fueled by speculative buying and selling.

The writer realizes the strength of the forces he resists. Johannes admits that the *Extra-Skriver* "foresees his fate of being totally ignored; he has a terrible foreboding that the zealous critic will call him on the carpet many times. He dreads the even more terrible fate that some enterprising [*driftig*] abstracter, a paragraph-swallower [*Paragraphsluger*] (who, in order to save science, is always willing to do to the writing of others what Trop magnanimously did with [his] work, *The Destruction of the Human Race,* in order to 'save good taste'), will cut him into paragraphs and do so with the same inflexibility as the man who, in order to serve the science of punctuation, divided his discourse by counting out the words, fifty words to a period and thirty-five to a semicolon—I throw myself in deepest submission before every systematic ransacker: 'This is not the System; it has not the least thing to do with the System. I invoke everything good for the System and for the Danish shareholders [*Interessenter*] in the omnibus, for it will hardly become a tower, steeple, or belfry [*Taarn*]'" (*FT,* 8; 3:59–60). Unless, of course, that steeple or belfry is the tower from which there tolls a certain *Glas*—a *glas* that echoes as if within a hollow column. Such a *glas* would be an indigestible "crumb" (*Smule*), an unscientific philosophical "fragment" (*Smule*), an unconcluding p.s. that could not be assimilated by paragraph swallowers. Extra, supplementary, idle, luxurious, pleasurable, nonserious, playful writing—writing that does not work—generates and regenerates an "incessant murmur" that disarticulates the scientific punctuation created by Trop's[9] complementary opposites. The text of the *Extra-Skriver* is also *de trop*—too much, superfluous, excessive. The wound opened by the *de trop* of the writer's playful scripture differs from the symmetrical cut inflicted *de* Trop on the script of his play. By inscribing something excessive or extra, the writer opens a gap that cannot be closed. Writing *always* leaves crumbs or remains—literary remains.

9. Trop is an important character in *Recenscenten og Dyret,* a play by Johan Ludvig Heiberg, who was the leading Danish Hegelian in the nineteenth century. In an effort to save good taste, Trop "tears his manuscript into two *equal* pieces."

In Kierkegaard's literary remains, there are traces of what Johannes left out of his preface.

The present author is by no means a philosopher; he* is a poor supplementary clerk in Danish literature,** who prefers to lock his door and speak cryptically and entirely according to circumstances now dances to honor the deity, now begs at his door, and once in a while does not hesitate to become the modest occasion for the revelation of a more profound wisdom even though he himself may be disgraced.† This does not trouble him; he does not consider himself as one who is condemned from life but condemned for life, and a prisoner for life can certainly easily put up with rasping work—his life is lost anyway.

He acquiesces in the verdict given, because he was not condemned from life but for life.

Respectfully
Joh. d. silentio
formerly a poetic person

In margin: **poetice et eleganter* [in a poetic and refined way] and his whole existence is nothing but poetry.

In margin: **who easily envisions his fate in an age that has crossed out passion in order to serve science,†† and who at most can hope that some anemic abstracter or other, a paragraph-swallower, will reduce it to a few sentences.§ I beseech every systematic snooper: this is not a system, it does not have the least thing to do with the System. I invoke everything good for the System and the shareholders in this omnibus; I wish every participant success and good fortune.

††who foresees the dreadful fate of being totally ignored; I dread the even more dreadful fate

§that in order to save taste he will do to it what Trop is willing to do with the destruction of the human race: cut it down the middle and then cut it up into paragraphs according to a specific norm that uses three pages for every paragraph—just like the man who in order to serve orthography placed a period after every thirty words.

In margin: †which is natural, since he is not writing the System§§ but some scribbles and doodles between each other [*mellem hverandre*].

§§and does not pledge himself to it by promises. (*FT,* 244–45; IV B 80 : 3).

The numerous marginalia in Kierkegaard's draft of the preface make it almost unreadable. Along the border of the text, there are notes to notes, parentheses within parentheses, and supplements to supplements, which ceaselessly interrupt the movement of the text. Several fragments arrest the reader's attention.

In the published version of his text, Johannes fails to note that the *Extra-Skriver* "prefers to lock his door and speak cryptically" (*helst lukke sin Dør og tale i Lødom*). In this erased line Kierkegaard suggests that the place of writing is something like a *crypt* that cannot be penetrated. If the writer always stays behind closed doors, the space of writing is not simply an inside that might become an outside. To the contrary, for the cryptic writer, the interior *cannot* become exterior. Such an interiority actually remains somewhat exterior to all "interiorization" (*Erinnerung, Erindring*) and inaccessible to all "recollection" (*Erinnering, Erindring*). The silence of the writer is not the complement of speech but is a more radical silence. Always excluded from the economy of commercial exchange and reciprocal communication, the *Extra-Skriver* is left (out) to write "de Silentio." Put differently, the writer is too modest to speak openly about cryptic matters. In contrast to the speculative philosopher who attempts "to say it all," the supplementary clerk "does not hesitate to become the modest occasion [*den beskende Anlednig*] for a revelation of deeper, more profound wisdom." His silent "wisdom" is more profound because it comes from depths one cannot sound. Rather than absolute, such wisdom is abyssal—more nonknowledge than knowledge. Abyssal "wisdom" does not come from books; it comes (if at all) from elsewhere, from an other "place" that cannot be spoken but can only be written.

The writer cannot write this nonknowledge (which is not the same as ignorance) by positing theses and antitheses and attempting to "sublate" (*aufheben, ophæve*) both in comprehensive and comprehensible syntheses. In the final inconclusive appendage to this infinitely complex para-graph, Kierkegaard stresses that the *Extra-Skriver* "is not writing the System but some scribbles and doodles between each other [*noget Krims Krams mellem hverandre*]." The shift from System to fragment is the movement from the monumental to the trivial, the significant to the insignificant. "*Mellemhverandre: Krims Krams*— Between Each Other: Scribbles and Doodles." This is the erased title whose traces return throughout Kierkegaard's most important text. Kierkegaard is not a serious philosopher who fills useful books with sensible theses. He is a foolish scribbler and doodler who writes useless, senseless scribblebooks and wastebooks. One would be a fool to take such a writer seriously.

Mistranslation

Though not immediately apparent, Johannes de Silentio is deeply concerned about the issue of translation. More precisely, Johannes is preoccupied with the implications of the inevitability of mistranslation. He devotes most of his work to a consideration of three closely related "Problemata":

I. Is there a Teleological Suspension of the Ethical?
II. Is there an Absolute Duty to God?
III. Was it Ethically Defensible for Abraham to Conceal His Undertaking from Sarah, from Eliezer, and from Isaac?

These questions are, in effect, variations of a single problem: the painful collision between rational reflection and ethical obligation, on the one hand, and, on the other, the absurdity of religious claims and demands. Johannes's poetic meditation on Abraham provides an occasion for Kierkegaard to explore the complex interplay of what he regards as the three principal stages of life: the aesthetic, the ethical, and religious. *Fear and Trembling* is Kierkegaard's most imaginative and effective attack on Hegel's System. While Hegel attempts to synthesize Kant's theoretical and practical reason in order to establish a rationality that is ethical and an ethic that is rational, Kierkegaard's investigation of the tension between the ethical and the religious raises questions about both the integrity of systematic reason and the absoluteness of universal duty.

These remarks imply that, for Kierkegaard, the ethical and the rational cannot be completely separated: the ethical is rational and the rational is ethical. Under the guise of Johannes, Kierkegaard describes the major contours of the rational-ethical, which, in this context, he labels simply "the ethical." [10] In the course of developing, but never answering, the questions posed in the first two problems, it becomes clear that reason and ethics entail a translation process that is always supposed to be lawful. For the rational ethicist and ethical rationalist, "translation" (*trans:* across + *latus:* carried) involves something like a metaphorical process. "Metaphor" (*metapherein:* to transfer; *meta:* involving change + *pherein:* to bear, carry) is "the figure of speech in which a name or descriptive term is transferred to some object different from but analogous to that to which it is 'properly'

10. Kierkegaard takes as his point of departure the form of life that Hegel describes in his account of "The Ethical Order" (*Sittlichkeit*) in the *Phenomenology*.

applicable." In this transference process, something is supposed to appear in and through something else. The vehicle delivers the tenor. The aim of transference is the safe arrival (after a momentary delay) of what is transported. The goal of translation, in other words, is readability. A "good" translation should be lucid, leaving as little ambiguity as possible.[11]

Kierkegaard opens his analysis of the first question ("Is there a Teleological Suspension of the Ethical?") by explaining: "The ethical as such is the universal, and as the universal it applies to everyone, which from another angle means that it applies at all times. It rests immanent in itself, has nothing outside itself that is its *telos* but is itself the *telos* for everything outside itself, and when the ethical has absorbed this into itself, it goes no further" (*FT,* 54; 3 : 104). The rational-ethical is first and foremost *universal,* i.e., all-encompassing and comprehensive. Within any such inclusive totality, there is supposed to be no outside or exterior that is not actually incorporated or potentially assimilable. For the rational and ethical person, Kierkegaard explains, there ought to be "no residual incommensurability [*der intet Incommensurabelt bliver*]." Senseless remains defer rational comprehension and remaining sensuousness frustrates the accomplishment of duty. Everything that differs from the universal must be sublated. For the thinker devoted to reason and the actor dedicated to morality, what "wisdom amounts to is the beautiful proposition that basically everything is the same [*at i Grunden er Alt der Samme*]" (*FT,* 56; 3 : 106). The law of the rational-ethical is "the law of the same." Within the regime of ethics, there is nothing that is finally outside the law and no one who is an irredeemable outlaw. When every outside is inwardized and every exterior recollected, the rational-ethical becomes "a perfect, self-contained sphere."

The realization of this comprehensive and comprehensible sphere presupposes the effective translation of difference to same and the

---

11. Derrida's comment about metaphor illuminates this understanding of translation. "Metaphor, therefore, is determined by philosophy as a provisional loss of meaning, an economy of the proper without irreparable damage, a certainly inevitable detour, but also a history with its sight set on, and within the horizon of circular reappropriation of literal, proper meaning. This is why the philosophical evaluation of metaphor always has been ambiguous: metaphor is dangerous and foreign as concerns *intuition* (vision or contact), *concept* (the grasping of proper presence of the signified), and *consciousness* (proximity of self-presence); but it is in complicity with what it endangers, is necessary to it in the extent to which the detour is a re-turn guided by the function of resemblance (*mimesis* or *homoiosis*), under the law of the same" (*M,* 270; 323).

actual transference of the particular to the universal. "The single individual [*den Enkelte*]," Kierkegaard points out, "sensately and psychically qualified in immediacy, is the individual who has his *telos* in the universal, and it is his ethical task continually to express himself in this, to sublate [*ophæve*] his singularity [*sin Enkelthed*] in order to become the universal" (*FT,* 54; 3 : 104). From a rational and ethical perspective, there is no justifiable exception to the universal law and, therefore, there is never a defensible suspension of the ethical. The universal is, in effect, divine. Kierkegaard acknowledges that "if this train of thought is sound, if there is nothing incommensurable in a human life, and if the incommensurable that is, is near [*ved*] only by an accident from which nothing results insofar as existence is viewed from the idea, then Hegel was right" (*FT,* 68; 3 : 117–18).

It is important to realize that in Hegel's speculative dialectic, translation involves a twofold transference. The particular is carried over into the universal and the universal is carried over into the particular. The synthesis of particularity and universality renders both of them metaphorical. On the one hand, the particular is the vehicle and the universal the tenor, and on the other hand, the universal is the vehicle and the particular the tenor. To decipher the complex play of metaphors, a play that constitutes or is constituted by a tropological process as extensive as the detour of world history as a whole, it is necessary to see through the particular to the universal and to demystify the universal by uncovering the particular. When each becomes transparent to the other, the metaphor is properly comprehended.[12] Successful translation insures the perfect readability that is the goal of reason and ethics. The person who is both reasonable and ethical—ethical because reasonable and reasonable because ethical— "knows that it is beautiful and beneficial to be the single individual who translates himself into the universal [*der oversætte sig selv i det Alt*], the one who, so to speak, personally produces a trim [*ziirlig*], clean [*reen*], and, as far as possible, faultless [*feilfri*] edition of himself, readable for all [*læselig for Alle*]. He knows that it is refreshing to become understandable to himself in the universal in such a way that he understands it, and every individual who understands him in turn understands the universal in him, and both rejoice in the security [*Tryghed*] of the universal. He knows it is beautiful to be born as the single individual who has his home [*har sit Hjem*] in the universal, his friendly abode, which immediately receives him with open arms if he wants to remain in it" (*FT,* 76; 3 : 124).

12. It is obvious that in this case duality does not involve duplicity.

It would, however, be a mistake to think that the individual's completion of a readable translation of himself is a simple undertaking. Translation always encounters difficulties that come, as it were, from below and above. The law of the same places harsh demands on every difference. If the universal is divine and truth is the whole, then everyone must become the same and differences overcome. The universal rules by a totalizing process that includes everything—*without remainder.* "As soon as the single individual asserts himself in his singularity before the universal, he sins, and only by acknowledging this can he be reconciled again with the universal. Every time the single individual, after having entered the universal, feels an impulse to assert himself as the single individual, he is in temptation [*Anfægtelse*], from which he can work himself only by repentantly surrendering [*opgive*] as the single individual in the universal" (*FT,* 54; 3 : 104). Again Kierkegaard admits: "If this is the case, then Hegel is right in 'The Good and Conscience,' where he qualifies man only as the individual and considers this qualification as a 'moral form of evil' . . . that must be sublated in the teleology of the moral in such a way that the single individual who remains in that stage either sins or is immersed in temptation" (*FT,* 54; 3 : 105).

When confronted with the law of the same, there is always a temptation to resist. The reasonable ethicist believes that since the resistance of the single individual grows out of the idiosyncrasy of inclination and partiality of desire, it is irrational and immoral. Accordingly, the rationalist and ethicist maintain that to become an integral subject, desire must be mastered and inclination yield to obligation. Ethical conflict is not, however, always the function of unreasonable force or base sensuality. A person can suffer temptation when faced with irreconcilable ethical claims, each of which, in its own way, is valid. For example, a "higher" moral obligation can force one to forego a "lower" ethical responsibility. Kierkegaard describes this situation as "tragic."

In contrast to Greek tragedy, which is "blind," modern "drama has abandoned destiny, has dramatically emancipated itself, is sighted, gazes inward into itself, absorbs destiny into its dramatic consciousness" (*FT,* 84; 3 : 132). In modern tragedy, blindness gives way to insight. No longer suffering a fate he does not or cannot understand, the actor is totally present to himself in his own self-consciousness. His conflict with the law seems to be a function of the law's conflict with itself. Consider the case of an individual whose civic obligation contradicts his duty as a father. Agamemnon faced precisely such a dilemma. And it is to Agamemnon, especially the Agamemnon of

Euripides's *Iphigenia in Aulis,* that Kierkegaard turns in his examination of the tragic situation.[13] If he is to save the state, Agamemnon must kill his daughter. By so doing, however, Agamemnon does not pass beyond or violate the "perfect self-contained sphere" of ethics. To the contrary, one obligation gives way to another in a movement that preserves the rational structure of ethics. The particular—i.e., the singular individual, Iphigenia, as well as Agamemnon's personal desire expressing a father's attachment to his daughter—is sacrificed to the demands of the universal or the order of the state. Kierkegaard repeatedly stresses that "the tragic hero is still within the ethical. He allows an expression of the ethical to have its *telos* in a higher expression of the ethical; he scales down the ethical relation between father and son, or daughter and father, to a feeling that has its dialectic in its relation to the idea of moral conduct. Here there can be no question of a teleological suspension of the ethical itself" (*FT,* 59; 3 : 109). Since the hero never transgresses the universal, his conduct is perfectly comprehensible. His deed can be read like an open book. Everyone, even Iphigenia, understands Agamemnon's action and recognizes its propriety. Rather than condemning the hero, his compatriots praise his courage and sympathize with his pain. "There but for fortune . . ." Fortune and misfortune, however, are supposed to have disappeared from modern drama. How and why does the conflict endemic to reason and ethics arise? Neither reason nor ethics can reply to this question. To glimpse its answer, or to confront its unanswerability, it is necessary to step beyond the ethical sphere of experience.

Why does Kierkegaard consider Agamemnon in his account of the rational-ethical form of life? Why not Antigone? Is her situation any less tragic? If Antigone's dilemma *is* tragic, then is Agamemnon truly a tragic figure? Is modern tragedy—tragedy that presupposes absolute self-consciousness—really tragic? If there is nothing outside the universal, then is there ever absolute loss? Or does every negative harbor a positive, every loss conceal a gain? Is there a return on every investment? Is every *mort* a-mortized? Why did Kierkegaard delay—infinitely delay—writing the modern version of *Antigone* he repeatedly proposed? Why did he leave Antigone out or speak of her only cryptically? Why did Kierkegaard, unlike Hegel, never attempt to

13. By focusing on Euripides' *Iphigenia in Aulis* rather than Sophocles' *Antigone,* as does Hegel, Kierkegaard concentrates on the conflict between the universal and the particular as it is embodied in a single, inwardly divided individual instead of the clash between two different individuals each of whom is completely devoted to a different law or principle.

unlock the crypt Antigone so faithfully guards? Does the exclusion of Antigone have anything to do with Abraham? Is *he* a tragic hero—or something other?

For a translation to be perfectly readable, it must be absolutely clear and completely transparent. There cannot be anything that remains hidden, concealed, or cryptic. Rational-ethical translation demands not only the carrying over of the particular into the universal and the universal into the particular; it also requires the transference of the inner to the outer. In the third "Problemata" ("Was it Ethically Defensible for Abraham to Conceal his Understanding from Sarah, from Eliezer, and from Isaac?"), Kierkegaard maintains: "The ethical as such is the universal; as the universal it is, in turn, the disclosed, the revealed [*Aabenbar*]. The single individual, qualified as immediate, sensate, and psychical, is hidden, concealed, disguised [*Skjulte*]. Thus his ethical task is to work himself out of his hiddenness and to become disclosed in the universal. Every time he desires to remain in the hidden, he trespasses and is immersed in temptation from which he can only emerge by revealing himself" (*FT*, 82; 3:130). Like the speculative philosopher, the ethicist is supposed to "say it all." "The Hegelian philosophy assumes no justified hiddenness, no justified incommensurability. It is, then, consistent for it to demand disclosure or revelation" (*FT*, 82; 3:130). Kierkegaard explores the intricate relation between concealment and disclosure through a careful consideration of the interplay of silence and speech.

When approached by Johannes de Silentio, silence appears unexpectedly complex. There are numerous, perhaps countless, sounds of silence. In Kierkegaard's rambling elaboration of the final problem, it is possible to identify at least four forms of silence that are of special interest: comic, deceitful, heroic, and demonic.

The simplest form of silence is comic. Kierkegaard does not discuss comic silence in much detail, for he takes it to be commonplace and rather trivial. Intentional secrecy, mistaken identity, and tricky language all contribute to comic situations. Such playful silence is both provocative and enjoyable. In comedy, however, silence is always temporary. In the end, silence is broken; everybody both speaks and sees clearly. When disclosure occurs, comedy issues in a coupling that is a perfect union or satisfying wedding of complementary opposites. Temporary loss is turned to lasting gain and everyone lives happily ever after.

Deceitful silence is more complex. Like the comic, the deceiver intentionally conceals. Unlike comedy, however, deceit renders union impossible—even when coupling is the goal. In order to underscore this point, Kierkegaard rewrites the legend of Agnes and the merman.[14] In Kierkegaard's edition, this tale becomes the story of a deflowering that *almost* takes place.

> The merman is a seducer who rises up from his hidden abyss [*Afgrundens*] and in wild lust seizes and breaks [*bryder*] the innocent flower standing on the beach [*strandbreden*] in all her loveliness and with her head thoughtfully inclined to the whispering of the sea. This has been the poets' interpretation until now. Let us make a change. The merman was a seducer. He has called to Agnes and by his beguiling words has elicited what was hidden in her. In the merman she found what she was seeking, what she was searching for as she stared down to the bottom of the sea. Agnes is willing to follow him. The merman takes her in his arms. Agnes throws her arms around his neck; trusting with all her soul, she gives herself to the stronger one. He is already standing on the beach, crouching to dive out into the sea and plunge down with his prey—then Agnes looks at him once more, not fearfully, not dispairingly, not proud of her good luck, not intoxicated with desire, but in absolute faith and in absolute humility, like the lowly flower [*ringe Blomst*] she thought herself to be, and with this look she entrusts her whole destiny to him in absolute confidence. And look! The sea no longer roars, its wild voice is stilled; nature's passion, which is the merman's strength, forsakes him, and there is deadly calm—and Agnes is still looking at him this way. Then the merman breaks down. He cannot withstand the power of her innocence, his natural element is disloyal to him, and he cannot seduce Agnes. He takes her home again, he explains that he only wanted to show her how beautiful the sea is when it is calm, and Agnes believes him. Then he returns alone, and the sea is wild, but not as wild as the merman's despair. (*FT*, 94; 3:141–42)

There is something monstrous about a merman. Half man, half nonman, with a human "upper" and an inhuman "lower," the *Havmand* is neither, yet somehow both man nor/and beast. The prodigious "middle" man can be met, if at all, only at the edge, along the margin, by the border where land meets sea. A creature of the deep, the merman, like a monstrous sperm whale, surfaces only long enough to disrupt seemingly safe harbors. The *Havmand,* however,

---

14. This tale is recounted in Hans Christian Andersen's *Agnet og Havmand.* Throughout his career, Kierkegaard subjects Andersen to relentless criticism.

can no more live on land than Københavners can live in depth or survive suspended above the deep that measures, if it is not bottomless, at least "70,000 fathoms." [15] Since the merman cannot survive on land, and is unwilling to plunge into the deep with his spoil, he fails to seduce Agnes. A union conceived in deceit can never be consummated. The monstrous, it seems, cannot be domesticated.

Silence, however, need not be comic or deceitful. In certain situations, concealment seems to arise from noble rather than base motives. Agamemnon, for instance, might have chosen to hide his designs from Iphigenia in order to spare her and others sorrow and pain. "When the hero, prey to aesthetic illusion, thinks to save another person by his silence, then [aesthetics] demands silence and rewards it" (FT, 86; 3 : 134). From a certain perspective, this noble silence

15. Kierkegaard often uses the image of a sea "70,000 fathoms deep" to suggest the bottomless abyss over which everyone hangs. In one of his most suggestive uses of water imagery, he brings together the figure of the margin between land and sea, where a "border conflict" takes place, with the notion of the silence involved in cryptic reserve. Kierkegaard prefaces "'Guilty?'/'Not Guilty?'" with a "Notice" (Fremlysning) recounting the unusual circumstances in which the manuscript was discovered in a mysterious lake surrounding Søborg Castle. "It is not easy to get near the lake, for it is surrounded by a rather wide stretch of bog. Here it is that the border conflict [Grændsestridigheden] is carried on day and night between the lake and firm land. There is something sad about this conflict, which is not indicated, however, by any trace [Spor] of destruction. . . . What imparts to the lake a still more inclosed [indesluttet] stamp is the fact that the bog is overgrown luxuriantly with rushes. . . . Only at one place is there still a small open channel, and here is a flat-bottomed boat in which we two . . . poled our way to the lake. . . . Finally we got beyond the reeds, and before us lay the lake, clear as a mirror and still sparkling in the radiance of the afternoon. Everything so still! Silence rested upon the lake. . . . I was almost anxious [angest] at being so infinitely far from men. . . . Now there was a confused voice, a mingled cry of all kinds of fowls, and then stillness prevailed again, almost to the point of making me apprehensive when the sound suddenly ceased and the ear grasped in vain for support in the infinite. My friend the naturalist took out the apparatus with which he drew up submarine plants, cast it down into the water and began his work. . . . With muffled sound it sank into the depths. Perhaps because I did not know well how to use the apparatus, at all events when I wanted to pull it up, I encountered so much resistance that I was almost afraid of proving the weaker of the two. I pulled again, then up rose a bubble from the depths [Dybet], it lasted an instant, then burst—then I succeeded. I had the strangest feeling, and yet I did not have the remotest notion what sort of a find it was I had made. Now when I reflect on it I know all, understand it, I understand that it was a sigh from below, a sigh de profundis, a sigh that I had wrested from the lake its treasure, a sigh from the sky and inclosed lake from which I had wrested its secret. . . . Wrapped in oilskin and provided with many seals was a rosewood box. The box was locked, and when I opened it by force the key lay inside—thus it is that inclosing reserve [Indesluttetheden] is always introverted. In the box was a manuscript written with a very careful and clear hand upon thin paper" (SLW, 181–83; 6 : 177–79).

seems heroic, but from another point of view, it is suspect. The person who has glimpsed the monstrous or encountered an uncanny merman is especially vulnerable to such suspicion, for he realizes that it is not clear whether the "noble" actor knows as much as he thinks he knows.

More interesting than comic silence, more suggestive than deceitful silence, more fascinating than heroic silence is demonic silence. Suppose, Kierkegaard muses, it is not impossible for the merman and Agnes—or for Søren and Regina—to be united. Suppose the union of these apparent opposites is possible on the condition that the merman repent his monstrous desire and reveal his deceit. Suppose the merman recognizes but refuses this possibility for which he, nonetheless, longs. Suppose the *Havmand* conceals both his deceit and his repentance of it. Suppose he guards silence, will not speak, declines to express his inwardness outwardly. This would be nothing less than demonic. "The demonic," according to Kierkegaard, "*is enclosing reserve and the unfreely disclosed*" (det Dæmonisk er det Indeslutte og det ufrivilligt Aabenbate; *CA,* 123;4:391). Since there is nothing inherently incommunicable about the demonic's interiority, this inner remainder or "enclosing reserve" (*Indeslutte*) is freely chosen. Silence can always be broken in a self-revelation that is potentially salvific. "Language [*Sproget*], the word [*Ordet*] is precisely what saves the individual from the empty abstraction of enclosing reserve" (*CA,* 124; 4:392). There is no doubt that the merman can speak, he simply *will* not translate his interiority into exteriority. This resistance constitutes a "residual incommensurability" that *must* be overcome if the ethical is to be truly universal.

Despite the significant differences among comic, deceitful, heroic, and demonic concealment, Kierkegaard insists that they all share an important similarity: each of these forms of silence is a binary opposite of speech. As the complement of speech, silence can, in principle, be broken. Moreover, from the rational-ethical perspective, silence *must* be broken. There is neither justifiable concealment nor defensible silence. The law of the same issues strict orders: where concealment/silence was, disclosure/speech shall be. Every veil must be removed, every curtain lifted, every skirt raised, everything laid bare. Only in this way can the monstrous be mastered, the prodigious controlled, the different assimilated, the heterogeneous homogenized, the irrational rationalized, the excess contained, and the remainder erased.

But what does translation miss? What does transference leave out? What slips between the lines and thus is not said? What remains untranslated because it is untranslatable, not transferred because it is nontransferrable? What remain(s) unsaid because it is unsayable? What if veils "reveal" more veils, curtains more curtains? What if not everything or everyone can be laid—laid bare? If certain secrets *cannot* be told? If certain interiors are irreducibly cryptic? If translation is unavoidably mistranslation? What if, as we have come to suspect, "truth is a woman"?

Crisis of the Word

But what language can arise from such an absence? And above all, who is the philosopher who will now begin to speak? "What of us when, having become sobered, we learn what we are? Lost among idlers in the night, where we can only hate the semblance of light coming from their small talk." In a language stripped of dialectics, at the heart of what it says but also at the root of its possibilities, the philosopher is aware that "we are not everything"; he learns as well that even the philosopher does not inhabit the whole of his language like a secret perfectly fluent god. Next to himself, he discovers the existence of another language that also speaks and that he is unable to dominate, one that strives, fails, and falls silent and that he cannot manipulate, the language he spoke one time and that now has separated itself from him, now gravitating in a space increasingly silent.[16]

In an ironic aside recorded in his wastebook, Kierkegaard comments:

If there is anything to be praised in the marvelous progress of modern philosophy, it certainly is the power of genius with which it seizes and vigorously *holds on to* the phenomenon. Although it is fitting for the phenomenon (which as such is always *fœminini generis*) by reason of its womanly nature [*sin qvindelige Natur*] to surrender to the stronger sex, yet among the knights of the modern age there is frequently a lack of deferential propriety, profound enthusiasm, in place of which one sometimes hears too much the jingle of spurs [*Sporernes Klirren*], etc.—and at times it shrinks before the fellows. (*JP* 3283; III B 12)

Why do "womanly" phenomena shrink before knightly philosophers who approach with swords drawn and spurs jingling? How does the feminine divert masculine advances? The philosopher cannot strip phenomena bare or penetrate the womanly because his language is *impotent*. Language fails, always fails, inevitably fails. The philoso-

16. Foucault, *Language, Counter-Memory, Practice,* pp. 41–42.

pher is forever haunted by this failure. Appearances to the contrary notwithstanding, the philosopher cannot say what he wants to say, and says what he does not want to say. Even the most rudimentary level of experience eludes philosophical comprehension. Philosophy fails (from the beginning) because it cannot translate particularity into universality without destroying the particular as such. The grasp of the philosopher is a stranglehold that eventually becomes suffocating. Another Johannes, Johannes Climacus, explains this important point.

> In immediacy, then, everything is true; but cannot consciousness remain in this immediacy? If this immediacy and that of animals were identical, then the question of consciousness would be annulled, but that would also mean that man is an animal or that man is dumb [*umælende*]. Therefore it is language [*Sproget*] that annuls immediacy; if man could not talk he would remain in the immediate. This could be expressed he [Johannes Climacus] thought, by saying that the immediate is reality [*Realiteten*], language is ideality, since by speaking I produce the contradiction. When I seek to express sense perception in this way, the contradiction is present, for what I say is something wholly Other [*ganske Andet*] from what I want to say. I cannot express reality in language, because I use ideality to characterize it, which is a contradiction, an untruth. (*JP*, 2320; IV B 14:6)

This remark recalls the analysis of sense-certainty that Hegel develops in the *Phenomenology*. Kierkegaard anticipates the questions Merleau–Ponty, Lacan, Bataille, Kristeva, Levinas, Blanchot, and Derrida raise about the possibility of recovering immediacy through the dialectical process of mediation. The immediacy with which Hegel is preoccupied, Kierkegaard insists, is what might be called "immediacy before reflection." If reason is not to be faulted, this sensuous remainder must be transformed into something sensible. Contrary to Hegel, Kierkegaard argues that a sensible translation of the sensuous is impossible. There is always a sensuous excess that cannot be totally mastered. The difficulties become even greater when we recognize that in addition to immediacy before reflection, there is also an "immediacy after reflection," which completely escapes comprehension and control. Kierkegaard points toward this ungraspable remainder with the term "singularity [*Enkelthed*]." [17]

The singular fissures the notion of identity and violates the law of

17. As I noted in the analysis of Levinas, Kierkegaard distinguishes "the individual [*Individet*]" from "the singular [*Enkelthed*]." While the individual is the product of the union of particularity and universality, the singular resists comprehension by and inclusion within every form of universality or generality.

the same. Inescapably heterogeneous, *Enkelthed* is a difference that can never be reduced to identity, a remainder that can never be assimilated, a crypt that cannot be opened. Always beyond the law, singularity is forever excessive. The elusive singular is like an outlaw who leaves traces but is never caught. This outlaw comes (if outlaws come) in the night, like a thief who purloins, dispossesses, expropriates, upsets, and unsettles.[18] Such singularity is the function of a relation, which at the same time is a non-relation, to something wholly Other. *Das ganz Andere* involves radical altarity that is, in Kierkegaard's words, "infinitely and qualitatively different." "Qualitative heterogeneity [*qvalitative Ueensartethed*]" is not the complementary opposite of identity or sameness (*JP,* 3646; X³ A 23). It is a different difference—a difference that is difference itself. Kierkegaard, like those who come after him, asks how difference itself can be articulated without reducing it to the same.

This dilemma and the questions it raises preoccupy Kierkegaard in both his Journals and *Philosophical Fragments* (*Philosophiske Smuler*). In one of the "thought experiments" left out of the book, he writes:

> Let us agree about this difficulty, whether it would be necessary for the understanding that the God [*Guden*] would reveal himself only in order to become discernible through difference [*Forskjelligheden*], for you recall from the foregoing that if the teacher is to be something other than an occasion (under which assumption man would remain the highest), the learner must be untruth, and of this he could not be conscious by himself. It is the same with his knowledge of the God. First he must know the difference, but this he cannot know by himself. The difference which he himself provides is identical with likeness [*Den Forskjellighed han selv tilveiebringer en identisk med Ligheden*], because he cannot get outside himself [*ud af sig selv*]. If, then, he comes to know the difference, he comes to know it absolutely and comes to know the absolute difference. (*JP,* 3081; V B 5 : 10)

If difference is irreducibly and not merely momentarily different (as it is in Hegel's speculative philosophy), then altarity cannot be conceived by reason as such. Awareness of the wholly Other must come from elsewhere; it must be solicited by otherness itself. Kierkegaard names this soliciting Other, which calls every identity out of itself, "God." "God" is an improper "name" for an absolute exteriority that resists all interiorization and recollection. Rather than yielding

---

18. In "Plato's Pharmacy," Derrida associates writing with the outlaw. "Writing, the outlaw [*le hors-la-loi*], the lost son" (*D,* 146; 168).

knowledge, this "name" is a substitute for "the Unknown" (*det Ubekjendte*). As the difference that "precedes" all differences, the Unknown, which is forever unknowable, is the condition of both the possibility and the impossibility of reason. In the course of rewriting the lines left over in his scribblebook, Kierkegaard asks:

> What then is the Unknown? It is the boundary [*Grændsen*] to which reason repeatedly comes, and insofar, substituting a static form of conception for the dynamic, it is the different, the absolutely different. But because it is absolutely different, it has no distinguishing mark. When determined as absolutely different, it seems on the verge of disclosure, but this is not so, for reason cannot even conceive an absolute unlikeness. Reason cannot negate itself absolutely, but uses itself for this purpose, and thus only conceives a difference within itself as it can conceive by means of itself. It absolutely cannot go out of itself, and hence conceives only such a superiority over itself as it can conceive by means of itself. [19]

To "name" the Unknown "God" is, of course, to displace rather than solve the question of qualitative heterogeneity. Kierkegaard stresses that "Reason, in attempting to determine the Unknown as the different, at last goes astray, and confounds the different with likeness. From this there would seem to follow the further consequence, that if man is to receive any true knowledge about the Unknown (the God), he must be made to know that it is different from him, absolutely different from him. This knowledge reason cannot possibly attain of itself; we have already seen that this would be a self-contradiction. It will therefore have to receive this knowledge from God. But even if it receives such knowledge it cannot understand it, and thus is quite unable to possess such knowledge. For how should reason be able to understand the absolutely Different [*absolute Forskjellighed*]?" [20]

Forever inaccessible to reason, the Unknown withdraws in its very approach and approaches by withdrawing. This approaching withdrawal or withdrawing approach is "the *abyss* of distance, the distance of distancing, the *coupe* of spacing, distance itself, if one could still say, which is impossible, distance *itself* [*la distance* elle-même]" (*S*, 49). *Au-delà*—in the *Jenseits* that is the step beyond good and evil (i.e., beyond the ethical)—God appears to be a woman—a woman who can be neither mastered nor possessed, stripped (bare) nor laid (bare), a

19. Kierkegaard, *Philosophical Fragments,* trans. D. F. Swenson and H. V. Hong (Princeton: Princeton University Press, 1971), p. 55; 4:212.

20. Ibid., p. 57; 4:213–14.

woman who de-lays, delays infinitely. The "name" of such a feminine
God is, properly speaking, no name at all. The nameless name is the
feminine name, the name of the mother, which Kierkegaard never
writes, or, perhaps, writes by not writing it. As Blanchot points out
in another context:

> The name God signifies not only that what is named by this name
> does not belong to the language in which this name intervenes,
> but that this name, in a manner difficult to determine, would still
> not be a part of it [i.e., language] even if this were set aside. The
> idolatry of the name or simply the reverence that makes it un-
> pronounceable (sacred) is related to this disappearance of the *name*
> that the name itself makes appear, and which forces language to
> rise up where it conceals [*s'occulte*] itself until forbidding it. Far
> from lifting us to all the lofty significations that theology autho-
> rizes, it gives rise to nothing that would be proper to it: a pure
> name that does not name, but is rather always about to name,
> the name as name, but, in that way, not at all a name, without
> nominative powers, hung on language as if by chance and thus
> passing on to it its (devastating) power of nondesignation that
> relates it to itself. (*PA*, 69–70)

"God" inscribes, without representing, the *lapsus absolu* that repeatedly disrupts the free flow of the restricted speculative economy and
incessantly interrupts the circulation of discourse and the circuit of
communication. The absolutely different or wholly Other cannot be
translated into any language. To the contrary, this altarity inflicts an
incurable wound upon language. Always open, this wound lies between the lines it (impossibly) both supports and undercuts. This loss
of language can never be re-covered. Nor is it a negative that can be
transferred to a positive, an absence that can be carried over into
presence. This difference is not the dialectical contrary of identity;
but is the difference that infinitely defers the eschatological movement of reappropriation. Offering no promise of arrival, this Other
calls: "Come."

How can one hear such a call? How can one "know" the Unknown?
How can one communicate with that which interrupts communication? Perhaps, Kierkegaard replies, through faith—an exorbitant
faith that takes one beyond, albeit while remaining within, the law of
reason. A faith that is neither rational nor irrational, knowledgeable
nor ignorant. Such faith is totally improbable, completely paradoxical, and utterly absurd. "This concept of improbability, the absurd,"
Kierkegaard argues, "ought to be developed, for it is nothing but
superficiality to think that the absurd is not a concept, that all sorts of

absurdities are equally at home in the absurd. No, the concept of the absurd is precisely to grasp the fact that it cannot and must not be grasped [*at begribe at det ikke kan og ikke skal begribes*]. . . . The *absurd,* the *paradox,* is composed in such a way that reason has no power at all to dissolve it in nonsense and prove that it is nonsense; no, it is a symbol, a riddle, a compounded riddle about which reason must say: I cannot solve it, it cannot be understood, but it does not follow thereby that it is nonsense" (*JP, 7*; X² A 354). The Unknown, the absurd, and the paradox are impossible words, which, in their impossibility, create a *crisis of the word.* Kierkegaard explores the dimensions and implications of this crisis in his rereading and rewriting of the story of Abraham.

Abraham is a "knight of faith" who awaits the approach of the unapproachable with neither drawn sword nor jingling spurs. He hears "another language that also speaks and that he is unable to dominate, one that arrives, fails, and falls silent and that he cannot manipulate"²¹ Impotent to understand, Abraham believes—believes "by virtue of the absurd" (*i Kraft nelig af det Absurde*). "The absurd," Kierkegaard explains, "does not belong to the differences [*Differentser*] that lie within the proper [*eget*] domain of understanding" (*FT*, 46; 3:97). The faithful response to the Other that exceeds the differences constitutive of understanding singles out the individual from all other individuals. The relationship to the absolutely different differentiates absolutely. Faith, Kierkegaard maintains, is "this paradox, that the single individual is higher than the universal—yet, please note, in such a way that the movement repeats itself, so that after having been in the universal he, as the single individual, isolates himself as higher than the universal. If this is not faith, then Abraham is lost, then faith has never existed in the world precisely because it has always existed. For if the ethical—that is, social morality—is the highest and if there is in a person no residual incommensurability in some way such that this incommensurability is not evil (i.e., the single individual, who is to be expressed in the universal), then no categories are needed other than what Greek philosophy had or what can be deduced from them by consistent thought. Hegel should not have concealed this, for after all, he had studied Greek philosophy" (*FT*, 55; 3:105). The singularity of the believer constitutes a remainder that *cannot* be comprehended by reason and *cannot* be assimilated by morality. "This proposition [if it is a proposition] cannot be mediated, for all mediation takes place only by virtue of the universal; it is and remains for all

21. Foucault, *Language, Counter-Memory, Practice,* p. 42.

Key to "believe"
"outlaw"

eternity a paradox impervious [*utilgængeligt*] to thought" (*FT,* 56; 3:106). The im-mediacy of faith is an immediacy *after* reflection that breaches all reflexivity. This breach transgresses the law of reason and ethics. The singular individual is, in a certain sense, an outlaw, an unredeemable outlaw. To be an outlaw, however, is not necessarily to be evil. An outlaw might be *beyond* good and evil. If grace is "a gift" (*un don*) outside the restricted economy of the law, then *le coup de grâce* is an excessive expenditure that can be neither comprehended nor controlled by reasonable speculators. In this aberrant economy, the outlaw is graceful.

The crisis of the word is enacted in the transgression of the outlaw. In the examination of Bataille's heterological practice, I stressed that to transgress is to cross the limit of "the Not" (*le Pas*) by taking "a step" (*un pas*) beyond the law. Transgression and law are curiously complicitous; each simultaneously permits and forbids the other. Explaining Bataille's insight, Foucault writes: "The limit and transgression depend on each other for whatever density of being they possess: a limit could not exist if it were absolutely uncrossable and, reciprocally, transgression would be pointless if it merely crossed a limit composed of illusions and shadows."[22] Irreducibly liminal, transgression belongs neither to the realm of darkness nor of light. The margin of transgression is the threshold where the encounter with the wholly Other, the absolutely Different, radical altarity *almost* takes place. Although dangerously near, this Other remains undeniably transcendent. Blanchot underscores the interplay between transgression and transcendence:

> Transcendence, transgression: names too near to each other not to make us suspicious. Might not transgression be a less compromising name for 'transcendence,' seeming, as it does, to remove it from its theological meaning? Whether moral, logical or philosophical, does not transgression continue to allude to what remains of the sacred [*à ce qu'il reste du sacré*], and in the thought of the limit and in its demarcation, impossible to think of, what, in all thinking, would introduce the crossing of the limit that is never and always performed? Even the notion of cutting [*coupure*] in all its strictly epistemological rigor facilitates all the compromises with a certain power of exceeding (or of rupture) [*un pouvoir de dépassement (ou de rupture)*]. (*PA,* 41)

The transgression of transcendence creates a sense of horror—a horror that is not simply repulsive but is at the same time attractive.

22. Ibid., p. 34.

Kierkegaard describes this horror as the *horror religiosus*. Fascinatingly ambiguous, such horror is contagious. It spreads by contact or near contact, generating something like a metonymic displacement that threatens to run wild and drive everyone mad.

Abraham is an outlaw who transgresses the law—the law of reason as well as the moral law. This transgression renders lawful translation impossible. Unlike the rational-ethical person, "who translates himself into the universal, the one who, so to speak, personally produces a trim, clean, and as far as possible faultless edition of himself, readable by all," Abraham's "life is like a book under divine confiscation [*en Bog, der er lagt under guddommeligt Beslag*] and never becomes *publice juris*" (*FT*, 77; 3:125). The text of "Abraham" is finally indecipherable.

When the Other calls, "Come," Abraham follows. He leaves the peace and security of a domestic economy and "wanders [*vandrer*]," yet again in the open space of the desert. "To be a stranger [*Fremmed*], to be in exile [*i Udlædinghed*]," Kierkegaard maintains, "is precisely the characteristic suffering [*Lidelse*] of the religious man" (*JP*, 4650; X³ A 114).[23] The call to approach the altar of sacrifice to which Abraham unknowingly responds is completely private and thus is in no way "public property" (*publice juris*). Abraham's absolute relation to that which is wholly Other is and *must* remain absolutely singular. This singularity cannot be mediated, though it is not simply immediate. "The paradox of faith has lost the intermediary, that is, the universal" (*FT*, 71; 3:120). It is precisely the loss of the universal that makes translation impossible and the impossible untranslatable. Abraham defies understanding and resists comprehension in any language. He cannot even understand what, if anything, is going on. Reality or dream, trial or temptation, sacrifice or murder? Neither Abraham nor the reader can be sure which it is. What later generations tend to exclude from the story of Abraham, Kierkegaard insists, is the offense, fear, agony, dread—the horror . . . *horror religiosus*. Such incomprehensible horror reduces speech to silence. Abraham's silence, however, is different from every other sound of silence. It is the profound silence of difference itself, the difference that is "the absolute Difference." Unlike comic, deceitful, heroic, and demonic

23. Kierkegaard offers this observation in a Journal fragment devoted to Abraham. "Abraham is an eternal prototype [*Forbillede*] of the religious man. Just as he had to leave the land of his fathers for a strange land, so the religious man must be willing to leave, that is, forsake a whole generation of his contemporaries even though he remains among them, but isolated *strange* to them. To be a stranger, to be in exile, is precisely the characteristic suffering of the religious man" (JP, 4650; X³ A 114). These are the terms in which Kierkegaard understands himself.

"faithful silence"

silence, faithful silence is not the complement of speech. Though it be his fondest desire, the knight of faith *cannot* tell it all.

> Abraham remains silent—but he *cannot* speak. Therein lies the distress and anxiety [*Nød og Angesten*]. Even though I go on talking night and day without interruption, if I cannot make myself understood when I speak, then I am not speaking. This is the case with Abraham. He can say it all [*Han kan sige Alt*], but one thing he cannot say, and if he cannot say that—that is, say it in such a way that the other understands it—then he is not speaking. The relief provided by speaking is that it translates me [*oversætter mig*] into the universal. Now, Abraham can describe his love for Isaac in the most beautiful words to be found in any language. But this is not what is on his mind; it is something deeper, that he is going to sacrifice him because it is a trial. No one can understand the latter, and thus everyone can only misunderstand the former. The tragic hero does not know this distress. (*FT,* 113; 3:159)

Even when Abraham tries to speak, language inevitably fails. "First and foremost, he does not say anything, and in that form he says what he has to say." "Speak he cannot; he speaks no human language. And even if he understood all the languages in the world, even if those he loved understood them, he still could not speak—he speaks a divine language, he speaks in tongues" (*FT,* 114; 3:160).

This silence breaches language, thereby deepening the paradox surrounding the singular individual. From the perspective of Hegelianism, the most sophisticated expression of the rational-ethical interpretation of experience, "*das Äussere (die Entäusserung)* is higher than *das Innere*" (*FT,* 68–69; 3:118). The outer that is higher than the inner is the revelation of an outwardness that is, paradoxically, the result of the "interiorizing" (*Er-innerung, Er-indring*) of all exteriority. For Abraham, by contrast, "interiority (*Inderlinghed*) is higher than exteriority [*Yderligheden*]." "The paradox of faith," according to Kierkegaard, "is that there is an interiority that is incommensurable with exteriority, an interiority that is not identical, please note, with the first but is a new interiority" (*FT,* 69; 3:118). This "new interiority" is an extraordinary inwardness. Not simply an inner that is the opposite of an outer, this interiority remains somehow exterior. The interior that is exterior creates an opening that eliminates all closure and faults every identity. The hollowing out of identity through the process of elimination forms an invaginated crypt that cannot be opened. This inaccessible tomb haunts language by leaving it forever open. Since philosophy "assumes no justified hiddenness, no

Key "New interiority"

justified incommensurability," the cryptic silence of faith appears to be a transgression that must be brought to light.

But transgression cannot be mastered. Transgression leads to transgression. *Abraham is an outlaw,* the worst kind of outlaw—a murderer, the worst kind of murderer—a murderer who would kill his own son. Abraham "violates" (*overtræder*) the law. This violation, however, is not simply outside the law. Abraham is an outlaw who freely acknowledges that the law he breaks is, nonetheless, binding. His bind is an irresolvable double bind created by the collision of the demand of the law and the call of the Other. Abraham's betrayal suggests that the outlaw, i.e., that which is outside, beyond, before, or after the law, is "inside" the law as the exterior the law struggles to master, dominate, assimilate, eliminate, or exterminate. The total elimination of all exteriority would not only reduce the outlaw to nothing; it would also mark the end of the law itself. The law, therefore, inevitably fails: the repressed eternally returns and the outlaw always remain(s).

Though Abraham freely acknowledges the stricture of the law, he still oversteps its bounds. While the tragic hero foregoes one duty for the sake of a "higher" ethical demand, "Abraham's situation is different." Johannes de Silentio contends that Abraham "transgressed the ethical altogether and had a higher *telos* outside [*udenfor*] it, in relation to which he suspended it. For I certainly would like to know how Abraham's act can be related to the universal, whether any point of contact between what Abraham did and the universal can be found other than that Abraham transgressed it. It is not to save a nation, not to uphold the idea of the state that Abraham does it; it is also not to appease the angry gods. If it were a matter of the deity's being angry, then he was, after all, angry only with Abraham, and Abraham's act is totally unrelated to the universal, is a purely private undertaking" (*FT,* 59; 3:109). From the rational and ethical perspective, such transgression is "mad," and every transgressor "a criminal."[24] In the k/night of faith, however, transgression harbors the promise of painful pleasure—a pleasure that is "the joy [*den Glæde*] of faith" (*FT,* 34; 3:85).

Since it remains beyond every restricted economy, faith cannot be earned. Faith is not works and does not work. It is a gift, an impossible gift: the gift of the Impossible. Unable to work, the graceful outlaw can only wait, wait without knowing what he is waiting for.

---

24. Søren Kierkegaard, *The Point of View for My Work as An Author: A Report to History,* trans. W. Lowrie (New York: Harper and Row, 1962), p. 95; 13:577.

His greatness is his patience, his *patientia,* his suffering. "Everyone shall be remembered, but everyone became great in proportion to his *expectation.* One became great by expecting the possible, another by expecting the eternal; but he who expected [*forventede; vente:* wait] the Impossible [*det Umulige*] became the greatest of all." To await the Impossible is to wait for what never arrives. In its several variations, Kierkegaard's story of Abraham "remains a story without an event in the traditional sense of the word, the story of language and writing as the inscription of the thing itself as other [*autre*], . . . the paradigm of the thing itself as other thing [*autre chose*], the inaccessible other thing, the impossible subject. The story . . . is indeed a fable [*fable*], a story with the title of fiction, a simulacrum and effect of language (*fabula*), but such that only by means of it can the thing as other and as other thing come to pass with the allure of an inappropriable event (*Ereignis* in abyss). The fable of an allure (I give the name of 'allure' to the action of something that comes without coming [*vient sans venir*], the thing that concerns us in this strange event) where nothing takes place except as it does in this little text." [25]

The transgression does not actually take place. Though Abraham raises the knife, Isaac, the flower of his and Sarah's eye, is not cut. The act is delayed, deferred infinitely. A substitute is sacrificed—a ram instead of a son, a son who himself is a substitute for the exiled son who, wandering over land and sea greets with a demand: "Call me Ishmael," the excluded son who is a bastard (like Ludwig who appears neither in the pages of Hegel's book nor in the leaves of the speculative family tree), the exiled, excluded, bastard son of a woman from Eygpt—the land of cryptic pyramids and hieroglyphs. Entangled in a series of substitutes and supplements, the transgression "takes place" without taking place. It is an event that is a nonevent, an impossible event that might be the eventuality of the Impossible. To await what does not arrive because it *cannot* arrive, what is never present because it *cannot* be present—though it is that from which all arrival and all presence repeatedly are sent—is to await the Impossible. To expect the Impossible is to acknowledge that "everything is possible." [26] If, however, everything is possible, the past is not closed and the future remains open. The ever-open past and the nonstoppable future eternally return to interrupt the reconciling rhythm of *Er-Innerung.* [27] Like

25. Jacques Derrida, *Signéponge/Signsponge,* p. 102.

26. Kierkegaard, *The Sickness Unto Death,* p. 38; 11:151.

27. To discover gaps in the past is to admit the contingency of the future. Commenting on what he regards as Hegel's effort to take chance out of time,

the "re-" of Nietzsche's return, the "re-" of Kierkegaard's repetition inscribes "the 'ex,' opening of all exteriority: as if the [repetition], far from putting an end to it, marks exile, the commencement in its recommencement of exodus. To [repeat] would be to return again to ex-centering oneself, to erring. All that *remains* is *nomadic* affirmation" (*PA*, 49).

The irreducible outside of transgression prevents repetition from becoming the return of the same. Repetition is the return of absolute Difference. In Kierkegaardian repetition/*Repetition*, everything returns, but with a difference. The re-turning of re-petition disrupts philosophy (as if from within). "Recollection [*Erindringen*] is the pagan view of life, repetition [*Gjentagelsen*] the modern; repetition is the *interest* [Interesse] of metaphysics, and also the interest upon which metaphysics founders."[28] As the return of a difference that identity cannot incorporate, and an Other that the same cannot assimilate, repetition subverts the recollection upon which speculative philosophy is based.

> "*Everything returns*" [Tout revient]: this is the logos of totality; in order for "everything" to return, totality has to have received its meaning and the completion of its meaning from discourse and practice. And the present must be the unique moment in time for totality to assert itself in presence and as presence. But "*everything returns*" determines that the infinity of the return would not be able to take the form of the circularity of everything [*du tout*], and determines that no return could affirm itself in the present (whether this present were future or were a past present), that is, it could not assert itself except by excluding all possibility, and all experience of a present, or by asserting a time without present: The thought of *everything returns* thinks time while destroying it, but by this destruction that seems to reduce it to two temporal moments, thinks of it as infinite, the infinity of rupture or interruption substituting an infinite absence for an eternal present. (*PA*, 36)

Kierkegaard writes: "If the past [*Forbigangne*] had become necessary it would not be possible to infer the opposite about the future [*Tilkommende*], but it would rather follow that the future also was necessary. If necessity could gain a foothold at a single point, there would no longer be any distinguishing between the past and the future. To assume to predict the future (prophesy) and to assume to understand the necessity of the past are one and the same thing, and only custom makes the one seem more plausible than the other to a given generation" (*Philosophical Fragments*, p. 96; 4 : 241).

28. Kierkegaard, *Repetition*, p. 149; 3 : 189.

This repetition marks "the end of philosophy" and "the beginning of writing."

"The victim is not killed; the victim is not victim. Faced with murder, the gesture is deferred, as is the decision. The action bifurcates and the tautology starts to predicate; it slips, it jumps to something else. It no longer says *a* is *a;* it substitutes and begins to say *a* is *b* is *c* is *d* . . ."[29] *Glissement*—Slippage: Isaac "is" a ram "is" Regina "is" Søren "is" Johannes de Silentio "is" a text "is" a scribblebook "is" *Fear and Trembling* . . . is the analysis . . . the interminable analysis. . . The Impossible is staged in the text as the text—a text that "is" always something Other, a text that "is" perhaps the discourse of the Other. To write such a discourse is to sacrifice, and to sacrifice is to

29. Michel Serres, *The Parasite,* trans. L. S. Schehr (Baltimore: Johns Hopkins University Press, 1982), p. 160. Serres makes this comment in the context of a consideration of the biblical story of Joseph. The remainder of the passage touches issues that run thoughout my investigation of altarity. "The victim is not fixed in his identity; the victim is anyone: he could be the youngest or the first to arrive. Who is he or she? This one because it is he; that one, because it is she; here and now, Jeptha's daughter, Iphigenia, or Idomeneo's son. . . . The victim is this one, yet this one is an other. May be an other.

"In this circumstance, a sovereign logic emerges that needs explanation. . . . There is no beginning for reason without a link of the following sort: this is not this; this is something else. This chain breaks away from redundance, identity or representation. An object has to be found that can be spoken of in this way. Or a subject, it matters little. It is thus a vital experience that the rejected child never be himself. . . . It is a social experience that the one who is sacrificed is anyone. But it is especially a Judaic invention, an explosive novelty in the Fertile Crescent, that the one who is sacrificed is substituted, that suddenly, the victim is something else: a goat, a kid, but also the beginning of a completely other series.

"I shall call this object the joker. The joker is often a madman, as we know. He is wild, as they say in English. It is not difficult to see the double of the sacrificial king in him, come from the Celebration of Fools, come from the Saturnalia. This white object, like a white domino, has no value so as to have every value. It has no identity, but its identity, its unique character, its difference, as they say, is to be, indifferently, this or that unit of a given set. The joker is king or jack, ace or seven, or deuce. Joseph is a joker; Tamar, queen, just, despised, whore, is also a joker. *A* is *b,c,d,* etc. Fuzzy."

transgress. The writer is a transgressor who is an outlaw. In his posthumously published "Report to History," Kierkegaard writes:

> And then when I acted, which had a bit [*Smule*] of Christian flavor about it, an act that at the same time I was conscious of performing as an act of kindness toward little Denmark—that is to say, when I cast myself as a sacrifice [*Offeret*] before the insurrection of vulgarity—then I was regarded by the public as mad [*gal*] and strange [*sær*], condemned almost as a criminal [*Forbryder*].[30]

The transgressor "invites each person to search behind himself, to find there the source of all alteration [*de toute altération*], a first, individual 'event,' proper to each narrative, a scene, something important and staggering, but one that the person who experiences it can neither master nor determine, and with which he has essential associations of inadequacy. On the one hand, it is a question of going back to a beginning; this begining would be a fact; this fact would be singular, lived as unique, and in this sense ineffable and untranslatable. But, at the same time, this fact is not a fact: it is the center of an unstable and fixed mass of relationships of opposition and identification; it is not a beginning: each scene is always ready to open onto a previous scene, and each conflict is not only itself, but also a more ancient conflict beginning again" (*EI*, 345–46).

Writer calls to reader, "Come." Come on a search that is a research—a research for an impossible event that might be the strange nonevent of the Impossible. Such research is, of course, impossible. It fails, repeatedly fails. And what remains is the writing of this repetition. The only response to the writer's solicitation is to write. The only reply to Kierkegaard is to rewrite his scribbles and doodles . . . endlessly. Altarity . . . Repetition with (a) difference: "We will never be finished with the reading or rereading of the [Kierkegaardian] text and, in a certain way, I have done nothing other than attempt to explain myself on this point."

---

30. Kierkegaard, *The Point of View for My Work as an Author*, pp. 94–95; 13:577.

Index